CLASSICS IN THE HISTORY OF POLITICAL THOUGHT

Classics in the History of Political Thought

An Anthology
Second Edition

VOLUME II

Dome Academic Publishers

Published by Dome Academic Publishers
359 20th Avenue, Suite 304, San Francisco, CA 94121
DomeAcademicPublishers@gmail.com

1st edition published 2007
Printed in the United States of America
Typeface Times 10pt

Classics in the History of Political Thought: An Anthology – 2nd ed.
Volumes I and II
1. Political Science- Political Theory.   2. Political Philosophy
I. Title. II. Title: Anthology, Volumes I and II

ISBN-10: 0-9798174-2-0
ISBN-13: 978-0-9798174-2-7

Front cover illustration: from the 1651 edition of *Leviathan* by Thomas Hobbes

CONTENTS

David Hume

David Hume (b. 1711, Edinburgh, d. 1776, Edinburgh) was a Scottish philosopher and historian. Hume was one of the most influential figures of the Scottish Enlightenment – a tradition of thought, associated with the names of Adam Ferguson, Francis Hutcheson, Thomas Reid, Adam Smith, and others, that prioritized the re-assessment of moral and political philosophy to cohere with the social and economic consequences of the rise of commercial society. A dedicated reader of philosophy since his youth, Hume was largely self-educated, despite a stint at the University of Edinburgh. Hume's first and greatest, philosophical achievement is his magisterial work *A Treatise of Human Nature*. This work, much like his subsequent philosophical work, was influenced by the ideas of empiricists like John Locke and George Berkeley, but also contained a number of Hume's key philosophical innovations, including his account of causation as the constant conjunction of the cause and the effect and his analysis of social norms as conventions.

Published when Hume was only 26, the *Treatise* received little initial notice among critics. Much of Hume's subsequent philosophical output entailed re-writing and expanding the arguments of the *Treatise* into *An Enquiry Concerning Human Understanding*, *An Enquiry Concerning the Principles of Morals*, and a large number of essays on politics, morality, and the arts, from which the essays below are drawn. These post-*Treatise* works brought Hume considerable prominence as a philosopher, and his bestselling multi-volume *History of England* made him a household name among a broad reading public.

Along with those of his contemporary and intellectual rival Immanuel Kant, Hume's ideas are widely considered to be some of the greatest influences on contemporary moral philosophy.

David Hume
OF THE FIRST PRINCIPLES OF GOVERNMENT
(1742)

Nothing appears more surprizing to those, who consider human affairs with a philosophical eye, than the easiness with which the many are governed by the few; and the implicit submission, with which men resign their own sentiments
5 and passions to those of their rulers. When we enquire by what means this wonder is effected, we shall find, that, as Force is always on the side of the governed, the governors have nothing to support them but opinion. It is therefore, on opinion only that government is founded; and this maxim extends to the most despotic and most military governments, as well as to the most free
10 and most popular. The soldan of Egypt, or the emperor of Rome, might drive his harmless subjects, like brute beasts, against their sentiments and inclination: But he must, at least, have led his *mamalukes,* or *prætorian bands,* like men, by their opinion.

Opinion is of two kinds, to wit, opinion of interest, and opinion of right. By
15 opinion of interest, I chiefly understand the sense of the general advantage which is reaped from government; together with the persuasion, that the particular government, which is established, is equally advantageous with any other that could easily be settled. When this opinion prevails among the generality of a state, or among those who have the force in their hands, it gives
20 great security to any government.

Right is of two kinds, right to Power and right to Property. What prevalence opinion of the first kind has over mankind, may easily be understood, by observing the attachment which all nations have to their ancient government, and even to those names, which have had the sanction of antiquity. Antiquity
25 always begets the opinion of right; and whatever disadvantageous sentiments we may entertain of mankind, they are always found to be prodigal both of blood and treasure in the maintenance of public justice. There is, indeed, no particular, in which, at first sight, there may appear a greater contradiction in the frame of the human mind than the present. When men act in a faction, they are apt,
30 without shame or remorse, to neglect all the ties of honour and morality, in order to serve their party; and yet, when a faction is formed upon a point of right or principle, there is no occasion, where men discover a greater obstinacy, and a more determined sense of justice and equity. The same social disposition of mankind is the cause of these contradictory appearances.
35 It is sufficiently understood, that the opinion of right to property is of moment in all matters of government. A noted author has made property the

foundation of all government; and most of our political writers seem inclined to follow him in that particular. This is carrying the matter too far; but still it must be owned, that the opinion of right to property has a great influence in this subject.

5   Upon these three opinions, therefore, of public *interest,* of *right to power,* and of *right to property,* are all governments founded, and all authority of the few over the many. There are indeed other principles, which add force to these, and determine, limit, or alter their operation; such as *self-interest, fear,* and *affection:* But still we may assert, that these other principles can have no

10   influence alone, but suppose the antecedent influence of those opinions above-mentioned. They are, therefore, to be esteemed the secondary, not the original principles of government.

    For, *first,* as to *self-interest,* by which I mean the expectation of particular rewards, distinct from the general protection which we receive from

15   government, it is evident that the magistrate's authority must be antecedently established, at least be hoped for, in order to produce this expectation. The prospect of reward may augment his authority with regard to some particular persons; but can never give birth to it, with regard to the public. Men naturally look for the greatest favours from their friends and acquaintance; and therefore,

20   the hopes of any considerable number of the state would never center in any particular set of men, if these men had no other title to magistracy, and had no separate influence over the opinions of mankind. The same observation may be extended to the other two principles of *fear* and *affection.* No man would have any reason to *fear* the fury of a tyrant, if he had no authority over any but from

25   fear; since, as a single man, his bodily force can reach but a small way, and all the farther power he possesses must be founded either on our own opinion, or on the presumed opinion of others. And though *affection* to wisdom and virtue in a *sovereign* extends very far, and has great influence; yet he must antecedently be supposed invested with a public character, otherwise the public esteem will

30   serve him in no stead, nor will his virtue have any influence beyond a narrow sphere.

    A Government may endure for several ages, though the balance of power, and the balance of property do not coincide. This chiefly happens, where any rank or order of the state has acquired a large share in the property; but from the

35   original constitution of the government, has no share in the power. Under what pretence would any individual of that order assume authority in public affairs? As men are commonly much attached to their ancient government, it is not to be expected, that the public would ever favour such usurpations. But where the original constitution allows any share of power, though small, to an order of

40   men, who possess a large share of the property, it is easy for them gradually to

stretch their authority, and bring the balance of power to coincide with that of property. This has been the case with the house of commons in England.

Most writers, that have treated of the British government, have supposed, that, as the lower house represents all the commons of Great Britain, its weight in the scale is proportioned to the property and power of all whom it represents. But this principle must not be received as absolutely true. For though the people are apt to attach themselves more to the house of commons, than to any other member of the constitution; that house being chosen by them as their representatives, and as the public guardians of their liberty; yet are there instances where the house, even when in opposition to the crown, has not been followed by the people; as we may particularly observe of the *tory* house of commons in the reign of king William. Were the members obliged to receive instructions from their constituents, like the Dutch deputies, this would entirely alter the case; and if such immense power and riches, as those of all the commons of Great Britain, were brought into the scale, it is not easy to conceive, that the crown could either influence that multitude of people, or withstand that overbalance of property. It is true, the crown has great influence over the collective body in the elections of members; but were this influence, which at present is only exerted once in seven years, to be employed in bringing over the people to every vote, it would soon be wasted; and no skill, popularity, or revenue, could support it. I must, therefore, be of opinion, that an alteration in this particular would introduce a total alteration in our government, and would soon reduce it to a pure republic; and, perhaps, to a republic of no inconvenient form. For though the people, collected in a body like the Roman tribes, be quite unfit for government, yet when dispersed in small bodies, they are more susceptible both of reason and order; the force of popular currents and tides is, in a great measure, broken; and the public interest may be pursued with some method and constancy. But it is needless to reason any farther concerning a form of government, which is never likely to have place in Great Britain, and which seems not to be the aim of any party amongst us. Let us cherish and improve our ancient government as much as possible, without encouraging a passion for such dangerous novelties.

David Hume
OF THE ORIGIN OF GOVERNMENT
(1742)

Man, born in a family, is compelled to maintain society, from necessity, from natural inclination, and from habit. The same creature, in his farther progress, is engaged to establish political society, in order to administer justice; without which there can be no peace among them, nor safety, nor mutual
5   intercourse. We are, therefore, to look upon all the vast apparatus of our government, as having ultimately no other object or purpose but the distribution of justice, or, in other words, the support of the twelve judges. Kings and parliaments, fleets and armies, officers of the court and revenue, ambassadors, ministers, and privy-counsellors, are all subordinate in their end to this part of
10 administration. Even the clergy, as their duty leads them to inculcate morality, may justly be thought, so far as regards this world, to have no other useful object of their institution.

All men are sensible of the necessity of justice to maintain peace and order; and all men are sensible of the necessity of peace and order for the maintenance
15 of society. Yet, notwithstanding this strong and obvious necessity, such is the frailty or perverseness of our nature! it is impossible to keep men, faithfully and unerringly, in the paths of justice. Some extraordinary circumstances may happen, in which a man finds his interests to be more promoted by fraud or rapine, than hurt by the breach which his injustice makes in the social union. But
20 much more frequently, he is seduced from his great and important, but distant interests, by the allurement of present, though often very frivolous temptations. This great weakness is incurable in human nature.

Men must, therefore, endeavour to palliate what they cannot cure. They must institute some persons, under the appellation of magistrates, whose
25 peculiar office it is, to point out the decrees of equity, to punish transgressors, to correct fraud and violence, and to oblige men, however reluctant, to consult their own real and permanent interests. In a word, Obedience is a new duty which must be invented to support that of Justice; and the tyes of equity must be corroborated by those of allegiance.

30 But still, viewing matters in an abstract light, it may be thought, that nothing is gained by this alliance, and that the factitious duty of obedience, from its very nature, lays as feeble a hold of the human mind, as the primitive and natural duty of justice. Peculiar interests and present temptations may overcome the one as well as the other. They are equally exposed to the same
35 inconvenience. And the man, who is inclined to be a bad neighbour, must be led

by the same motives, well or ill understood, to be a bad citizen and subject. Not to mention, that the magistrate himself may often be negligent, or partial, or unjust in his administration.

Experience, however, proves, that there is a great difference between the cases. Order in society, we find, is much better maintained by means of government; and our duty to the magistrate is more strictly guarded by the principles of human nature, than our duty to our fellow-citizens. The love of dominion is so strong in the breast of man, that many, not only submit to, but court all the dangers, and fatigues, and cares of government; and men, once raised to that station, though often led astray by private passions, find, in ordinary cases, a visible interest in the impartial administration of justice. The persons, who first attain this distinction by the consent, tacit or express, of the people, must be endowed with superior personal qualities of valour, force, integrity, or prudence, which command respect and confidence: and after government is established, a regard to birth, rank, and station has a mighty influence over men, and enforces the decrees of the magistrate. The prince or leader exclaims against every disorder, which disturbs his society. He summons all his partizans and all men of probity to aid him in correcting and redressing it: and he is readily followed by all indifferent persons in the execution of his office. He soon acquires the power of rewarding these services; and in the progress of society, he establishes subordinate ministers and often a military force, who find an immediate and a visible interest, in supporting his authority. Habit soon consolidates what other principles of human nature had imperfectly founded; and men, once accustomed to obedience, never think of departing from that path, in which they and their ancestors have constantly trod, and to which they are confined by so many urgent and visible motives.

But though this progress of human affairs may appear certain and inevitable, and though the support which allegiance brings to justice, be founded on obvious principles of human nature, it cannot be expected that men should beforehand be able to discover them, or foresee their operation. Government commences more casually and more imperfectly. It is probable, that the first ascendant of one man over multitudes begun during a state of war; where the superiority of courage and of genius discovers itself most visibly, where unanimity and concert are most requisite, and where the pernicious effects of disorder are most sensibly felt. The long continuance of that state, an incident common among savage tribes, enured the people to submission; and if the chieftain possessed as much equity as prudence and valour, he became, even during peace, the arbiter of all differences, and could gradually, by a mixture of force and consent, establish his authority. The benefit sensibly felt from his influence, made it be cherished by the people, at least by the peaceable and well disposed among them; and if his son enjoyed the same good qualities, government advanced the sooner to maturity and perfection; but was still in a feeble state, till the farther progress of improvement procured the magistrate a revenue, and enabled him to bestow rewards on the several instruments of his

5   administration, and to inflict punishments on the refractory and disobedient. Before that period, each exertion of his influence must have been particular, and founded on the peculiar circumstances of the case. After it, submission was no longer a matter of choice in the bulk of the community, but was rigorously exacted by the authority of the supreme magistrate.

10   In all governments, there is a perpetual intestine struggle, open or secret, between Authority and Liberty; and neither of them can ever absolutely prevail in the contest. A great sacrifice of liberty must necessarily be made in every government; yet even the authority, which confines liberty, can never, and perhaps ought never, in any constitution, to become quite entire and

15   uncontroulable. The sultan is master of the life and fortune of any individual; but will not be permitted to impose new taxes on his subjects: a French monarch can impose taxes at pleasure; but would find it dangerous to attempt the lives and fortunes of individuals. Religion also, in most countries, is commonly found to be a very intractable principle; and other principles or prejudices frequently

20   resist all the authority of the civil magistrate; whose power, being founded on opinion, can never subvert other opinions, equally rooted with that of his title to dominion. The government, which, in common appellation, receives the appellation of free, is that which admits of a partition of power among several members, whose united authority is no less, or is commonly greater than that of

25   any monarch; but who, in the usual course of administration, must act by general and equal laws, that are previously known to all the members and to all their subjects. In this sense, it must be owned, that liberty is the perfection of civil society; but still authority must be acknowledged essential to its very existence: and in those contests, which so often take place between the one and the other,

30   the latter may, on that account, challenge the preference. Unless perhaps one may say (and it may be said with some reason) that a circumstance, which is essential to the existence of civil society, must always support itself, and needs be guarded with less jealousy, than one that contributes only to its perfection, which the indolence of men is so apt to neglect, or their ignorance to overlook.

David Hume
OF THE ORIGINAL CONTRACT
(1752)

As no party, in the present age, can well support itself, without a
philosophical or speculative system of principles, annexed to its political or
practical one; we accordingly find, that each of the factions, into which this
nation is divided, has reared up a fabric of the former kind, in order to protect
5   and cover that scheme of actions, which it pursues. The people being commonly
very rude builders, especially in this speculative way, and more especially still,
when actuated by party-zeal; it is natural to imagine, that their workmanship
must be a little unshapely, and discover evident marks of that violence and
hurry, in which it was raised. The one party, by tracing up government to the
10   Deity, endeavour to render it so sacred and inviolate, that it must be little less
than sacrilege, however tyrannical it may become, to touch or invade it, in the
smallest article. The other party, by founding government altogether on the
consent of the People, suppose that there is a kind of *original contract,* by which
the subjects have tacitly reserved the power of resisting their sovereign,
15   whenever they find themselves aggrieved by that authority, with which they
have, for certain purposes, voluntarily entrusted him. These are the speculative
principles of the two parties; and these too are the practical consequences
deduced from them.

I shall venture to affirm, *That both these* systems *of speculative principles*
20   *are just; though not in the sense, intended by the parties:* And, *That both the*
schemes *of practical consequences are prudent; though not in the extremes, to*
which each party, in opposition to the other, has commonly endeavoured to
carry them.

That the Deity is the ultimate author of all government, will never be denied
25   by any, who admit a general providence, and allow, that all events in the
universe are conducted by an uniform plan, and directed to wise purposes. As it
is impossible for the human race to subsist, at least in any comfortable or secure
state, without the protection of government; this institution must certainly have
been intended by that beneficent Being, who means the good of all his creatures:
30   And as it has universally, in fact, taken place, in all countries, and all ages; we
may conclude, with still greater certainty, that it was intended by that omniscient
Being, who can never be deceived by any event or operation. But since he gave
rise to it, not by any particular or miraculous interposition, but by his concealed
and universal efficacy; a sovereign cannot, properly speaking, be called his vice-
35   gerent, in any other sense than every power or force, being derived from him,

may be said to act by his commission. Whatever actually happens is comprehended in the general plan or intention of providence; nor has the greatest and most lawful prince any more reason, upon that account, to plead a peculiar sacredness or inviolable authority, than an inferior magistrate, or even
5 an usurper, or even a robber and a pyrate. The same divine superintendant, who, for wise purposes, invested a Titus or a Trajan with authority, did also, for purposes, no doubt, equally wise, though unknown, bestow power on a Borgia or an Angria. The same causes, which gave rise to the sovereign power in every state, established likewise every petty jurisdiction in it, and every limited
10 authority. A constable, therefore, no less than a king, acts by a divine commission, and possesses an indefeasible right.

    When we consider how nearly equal all men are in their bodily force, and even in their mental powers and faculties, till cultivated by education; we must necessarily allow, that nothing but their own consent could, at first, associate
15 them together, and subject them to any authority. The people, if we trace government to its first origin in the woods and desarts, are the source of all power and jurisdiction, and voluntarily, for the sake of peace and order, abandoned their native liberty, and received laws from their equal and companion. The conditions, upon which they were willing to submit, were either
20 expressed, or were so clear and obvious, that it might well be esteemed superfluous to express them. If this, then, be meant by the *original contract,* it cannot be denied, that all government is, at first, founded on a contract, and that the most ancient rude combinations of mankind were formed chiefly by that principle. In vain, are we asked in what records this charter of our liberties is
25 registered. It was not written on parchment, nor yet on leaves or barks of trees. It preceded the use of writing and all the other civilized arts of life. But we trace it plainly in the nature of man, and in the equality, or something approaching equality, which we find in all the individuals of that species. The force, which now prevails, and which is founded on fleets and armies, is plainly political, and
30 derived from authority, the effect of established government. A man's natural force consists only in the vigour of his limbs, and the firmness of his courage; which could never subject multitudes to the command of one. Nothing but their own consent, and their sense of the advantages resulting from peace and order, could have had that influence.

35   Yet even this consent was long very imperfect, and could not be the basis of a regular administration. The chieftain, who had probably acquired his influence during the continuance of war, ruled more by persuasion than command; and till he could employ force to reduce the refractory and disobedient, the society could scarcely be said to have attained a state of civil government. No compact
40 or agreement, it is evident, was expressly formed for general submission; an idea

far beyond the comprehension of savages: Each exertion of authority in the chieftain must have been particular, and called forth by the present exigencies of the case: The sensible utility, resulting from his interposition, made these exertions become daily more frequent; and their frequency gradually produced an habitual, and, if you please to call it so, a voluntary, and therefore precarious, acquiescence in the people.

But philosophers, who have embraced a party (if that be not a contradiction in terms) are not contented with these concessions. They assert, not only that government in its earliest infancy arose from consent or rather the voluntary acquiescence of the people; but also, that, even at present, when it has attained full maturity, it rests on no other foundation. They affirm, that all men are still born equal, and owe allegiance to no prince or government, unless bound by the obligation and sanction of a *promise*. And as no man, without some equivalent, would forego the advantages of his native liberty, and subject himself to the will of another; this promise is always understood to be conditional, and imposes on him no obligation, unless he meet with justice and protection from his sovereign. These advantages the sovereign promises him in return; and if he fail in the execution, he has broken, on his part, the articles of engagement, and has thereby freed his subject from all obligations to allegiance. Such, according to these philosophers, is the foundation of authority in every government; and such the right of resistance, possessed by every subject.

But would these reasoners look abroad into the world, they would meet with nothing that, in the least, corresponds to their ideas, or can warrant so refined and philosophical a system. On the contrary, we find, every where, princes, who claim their subjects as their property, and assert their independent right of sovereignty, from conquest or succession. We find also, every where, subjects, who acknowledge this right in their prince, and suppose themselves born under obligations of obedience to a certain sovereign, as much as under the ties of reverence and duty to certain parents. These connexions are always conceived to be equally independent of our consent, in Persia and China; in France and Spain; and even in Holland and England, wherever the doctrines above-mentioned have not been carefully inculcated. Obedience or subjection becomes so familiar, that most men never make any enquiry about its origin or cause, more than about the principle of gravity, resistance, or the most universal laws of nature. Or if curiosity ever move them; as soon as they learn, that they themselves and their ancestors have, for several ages, or from time immemorial, been subject to such a form of government or such a family; they immediately acquiesce, and acknowledge their obligation to allegiance. Were you to preach, in most parts of the world, that political connexions are founded altogether on voluntary consent or a mutual promise, the magistrate would soon imprison you, as seditious, for

loosening the ties of obedience; if your friends did not before shut you up as delirious, for advancing such absurdities. It is strange, that an act of the mind, which every individual is supposed to have formed, and after he came to the use of reason too, otherwise it could have no authority; that this act, I say, should be
5   so much unknown to all of them, that, over the face of the whole earth, there scarcely remain any traces or memory of it.

But the contract, on which government is founded, is said to be the *original contract;* and consequently may be supposed too old to fall under the knowledge of the present generation. If the agreement, by which savage men first associated
10 and conjoined their force, be here meant, this is acknowledged to be real; but being so ancient, and being obliterated by a thousand changes of government and princes, it cannot now be supposed to retain any authority. If we would say any thing to the purpose, we must assert, that every particular government, which is lawful, and which imposes any duty of allegiance on the subject, was,
15 at first, founded on consent and a voluntary compact. But besides that this supposes the consent of the fathers to bind the children, even to the most remote generations, (which republican writers will never allow) besides this, I say, it is not justified by history or experience, in any age or country of the world.

Almost all the governments, which exist at present, or of which there
20 remains any record in story, have been founded originally, either on usurpation or conquest, or both, without any pretence of a fair consent, or voluntary subjection of the people. When an artful and bold man is placed at the head of an army or faction, it is often easy for him, by employing, sometimes violence, sometimes false pretences, to establish his dominion over a people a hundred
25 times more numerous than his partizans. He allows no such open communication, that his enemies can know, with certainty, their number or force. He gives them no leisure to assemble together in a body to oppose him. Even all those, who are the instruments of his usurpation, may wish his fall; but their ignorance of each other's intention keeps them in awe, and is the sole cause
30 of his security. By such arts as these, many governments have been established; and this is all the *original contract,* which they have to boast of.

The face of the earth is continually changing, by the encrease of small kingdoms into great empires, by the dissolution of great empires into smaller kingdoms, by the planting of colonies, by the migration of tribes. Is there any
35 thing discoverable in all these events, but force and violence? Where is the mutual agreement or voluntary association so much talked of?

Even the smoothest way, by which a nation may receive a foreign master, by marriage or a will, is not extremely honourable for the people; but supposes them to be disposed of, like a dowry or a legacy, according to the pleasure or
40 interest of their rulers.

11

But where no force interposes, and election takes place; what is this election so highly vaunted? It is either the combination of a few great men, who decide for the whole, and will allow of no opposition: Or it is the fury of a multitude, that follow a seditious ringleader, who is not known, perhaps, to a dozen among 5 them, and who owes his advancement merely to his own impudence, or to the momentary caprice of his fellows.

Are these disorderly elections, which are rare too, of such mighty authority, as to be the only lawful foundation of all government and allegiance?

In reality, there is not a more terrible event, than a total dissolution of 10 government, which gives liberty to the multitude, and makes the determination or choice of a new establishment depend upon a number, which nearly approaches to that of the body of the people: For it never comes entirely to the whole body of them. Every wise man, then, wishes to see, at the head of a powerful and obedient army, a general, who may speedily seize the prize, and 15 give to the people a master, which they are so unfit to chuse for themselves. So little correspondent is fact and reality to those philosophical notions.

Let not the establishment at the *Revolution* deceive us, or make us so much in love with a philosophical origin to government, as to imagine all others monstrous and irregular. Even that event was far from corresponding to these 20 refined ideas. It was only the succession, and that only in the regal part of the government, which was then changed: And it was only the majority of seven hundred, who determined that change for near ten millions. I doubt not, indeed, but the bulk of those ten millions acquiesced willingly in the determination: But was the matter left, in the least, to their choice? Was it not justly supposed to be, 25 from that moment, decided, and every man punished, who refused to submit to the new sovereign? How otherwise could the matter have ever been brought to any issue or conclusion?

The republic of Athens was, I believe, the most extensive democracy, that we read of in history: Yet if we make the requisite allowances for the women, 30 the slaves, and the strangers, we shall find, that that establishment was not, at first, made, nor any law ever voted, by a tenth part of those who were bound to pay obedience to it: Not to mention the islands and foreign dominions, which the Athenians claimed as theirs by right of conquest. And as it is well known, that popular assemblies in that city were always full of licence and disorder, 35 notwithstanding the institutions and laws by which they were checked: How much more disorderly must they prove, where they form not the established constitution, but meet tumultuously on the dissolution of the ancient government, in order to give rise to a new one? How chimerical must it be to talk of a choice in such circumstances?

The Achæans enjoyed the freest and most perfect democracy of all antiquity; yet they employed force to oblige some cities to enter into their league, as we learn from Polybius.[1]

5 Harry the IVth and Harry the VIIth of England, had really no title to the throne but a parliamentary election; yet they never would acknowledge it, lest they should thereby weaken their authority. Strange, if the only real foundation of all authority be consent and promise!

It is in vain to say, that all governments are or should be, at first, founded on popular consent, as much as the necessity of human affairs will admit. This
10 favours entirely my pretension. I maintain, that human affairs will never admit of this consent; seldom of the appearance of it. But that conquest or usurpation, that is, in plain terms, force, by dissolving the ancient governments, is the origin of almost all the new ones, which were ever established in the world. And that in the few cases, where consent may seem to have taken place, it was commonly so
15 irregular, so confined, or so much intermixed either with fraud or violence, that it cannot have any great authority.

My intention here is not to exclude the consent of the people from being one just foundation of government where it has place. It is surely the best and most sacred of any. I only pretend, that it has very seldom had place in any
20 degree, and never almost in its full extent. And that therefore some other foundation of government must also be admitted.

Were all men possessed of so inflexible a regard to justice, that, of themselves, they would totally abstain from the properties of others; they had for ever remained in a state of absolute liberty, without subjection to any magistrate
25 or political society: But this is a state of perfection, of which human nature is justly deemed incapable. Again; were all men possessed of so perfect an understanding, as always to know their own interests, no form of government had ever been submitted to, but what was established on consent, and was fully canvassed by every member of the society: But this state of perfection is
30 likewise much superior to human nature. Reason, history, and experience shew us, that all political societies have had an origin much less accurate and regular; and were one to choose a period of time, when the people's consent was the least regarded in public transactions, it would be precisely on the establishment of a new government. In a settled constitution, their inclinations are often
35 consulted; but during the fury of revolutions, conquests, and public convulsions, military force or political craft usually decides the controversy.

When a new government is established, by whatever means, the people are commonly dissatisfied with it, and pay obedience more from fear and necessity, than from any idea of allegiance or of moral obligation. The prince is watchful
40 and jealous, and must carefully guard against every beginning or appearance of

13

insurrection. Time, by degrees, removes all these difficulties, and accustoms the nation to regard, as their lawful or native princes, that family, which, at first, they considered as usurpers or foreign conquerors. In order to found this opinion, they have no recourse to any notion of voluntary consent or promise, which, they know, never was, in this case, either expected or demanded. The original establishment was formed by violence, and submitted to from necessity. The subsequent administration is also supported by power, and acquiesced in by the people, not as a matter of choice, but of obligation. They imagine not, that their consent gives their prince a title: But they willingly consent, because they think, that, from long possession, he has acquired a title, independent of their choice or inclination.

Should it be said, that, by living under the dominion of a prince, which one might leave, every individual has given a *tacit* consent to his authority, and promised him obedience; it may be answered, that such an implied consent can only have place, where a man imagines, that the matter depends on his choice. But where he thinks (as all mankind do who are born under established governments) that by his birth he owes allegiance to a certain prince or certain form of government; it would be absurd to infer a consent or choice, which he expressly, in this case, renounces and disclaims.

Can we seriously say, that a poor peasant or artizan has a free choice to leave his country, when he knows no foreign language or manners, and lives from day to day, by the small wages which he acquires? We may as well assert, that a man, by remaining in a vessel, freely consents to the dominion of the master; though he was carried on board while asleep, and must leap into the ocean, and perish, the moment he leaves her.

What if the prince forbid his subjects to quit his dominions; as in Tiberius's time, it was regarded as a crime in a Roman knight that he had attempted to fly to the Parthians, in order to escape the tyranny of that emperor?[2] Or as the ancient Muscovites prohibited all travelling under pain of death? And did a prince observe, that many of his subjects were seized with the frenzy of migrating to foreign countries, he would doubtless, with great reason and justice, restrain them, in order to prevent the depopulation of his own kingdom. Would he forfeit the allegiance of all his subjects, by so wise and reasonable a law? Yet the freedom of their choice is surely, in that case, ravished from them.

A company of men, who should leave their native country, in order to people some uninhabited region, might dream of recovering their native freedom; but they would soon find, that their prince still laid claim to them, and called them his subjects, even in their new settlement. And in this he would but act conformably to the common ideas of mankind.

The truest *tacit* consent of this kind, that is ever observed, is when a foreigner settles in any country, and is beforehand acquainted with the prince, and government, and laws, to which he must submit: Yet is his allegiance, though more voluntary, much less expected or depended on, than that of a

5 natural born subject. On the contrary, his native prince still asserts a claim to him. And if he punish not the renegade, when he seizes him in war with his new prince's commission; this clemency is not founded on the municipal law, which in all countries condemns the prisoner; but on the consent of princes, who have agreed to this indulgence, in order to prevent reprisals.

10 Did one generation of men go off the stage at once, and another succeed, as is the case with silk-worms and butterflies, the new race, if they had sense enough to choose their government, which surely is never the case with men, might voluntarily, and by general consent, establish their own form of civil polity, without any regard to the laws or precedents, which prevailed among

15 their ancestors. But as human society is in perpetual flux, one man every hour going out of the world, another coming into it, it is necessary, in order to preserve stability in government, that the new brood should conform themselves to the established constitution, and nearly follow the path which their fathers, treading in the footsteps of theirs, had marked out to them. Some innovations

20 must necessarily have place in every human institution, and it is happy where the enlightened genius of the age give these a direction to the side of reason, liberty, and justice: but violent innovations no individual is entitled to make: they are even dangerous to be attempted by the legislature: more ill than good is ever to be expected from them: and if history affords examples to the contrary,

25 they are not to be drawn into precedent, and are only to be regarded as proofs, that the science of politics affords few rules, which will not admit of some exception, and which may not sometimes be controuled by fortune and accident. The violent innovations in the reign of Henry VIII. proceeded from an imperious monarch, seconded by the appearance of legislative authority: Those in the reign

30 of Charles I. were derived from faction and fanaticism; and both of them have proved happy in the issue: But even the former were long the source of many disorders, and still more dangers; and if the measures of allegiance were to be taken from the latter, a total anarchy must have place in human society, and a final period at once be put to every government.

35 Suppose, that an usurper, after having banished his lawful prince and royal family, should establish his dominion for ten or a dozen years in any country, and should preserve so exact a discipline in his troops, and so regular a disposition in his garrisons, that no insurrection had ever been raised, or even murmur heard, against his administration: Can it be asserted, that the people,

40 who in their hearts abhor his treason, have tacitly consented to his authority, and

15

promised him allegiance, merely because, from necessity, they live under his dominion? Suppose again their native prince restored, by means of an army, which he levies in foreign countries: They receive him with joy and exultation, and shew plainly with what reluctance they had submitted to any other yoke. I

5 may now ask, upon what foundation the prince's title stands? Not on popular consent surely: For though the people willingly acquiesce in his authority, they never imagine, that their consent made him sovereign. They consent; because they apprehend him to be already, by birth, their lawful sovereign. And as to that tacit consent, which may now be inferred from their living under his dominion,

10 this is no more than what they formerly gave to the tyrant and usurper.

When we assert, that all lawful government arises from the consent of the people, we certainly do them a great deal more honour than they deserve, or even expect and desire from us. After the Roman dominions became too unwieldly for the republic to govern them, the people, over the whole known

15 world, were extremely grateful to Augustus for that authority, which, by violence, he had established over them; and they shewed an equal disposition to submit to the successor, whom he left them, by his last will and testament. It was afterwards their misfortune, that there never was, in one family, any long regular succession; but that their line of princes was continually broken, either by

20 private assassinations or public rebellions. The *prætorian* bands, on the failure of every family, set up one emperor; the legions in the East a second; those in Germany, perhaps, a third: And the sword alone could decide the controversy. The condition of the people, in that mighty monarchy, was to be lamented, not because the choice of the emperor was never left to them; for that was

25 impracticable: But because they never fell under any succession of masters, who might regularly follow each other. As to the violence and wars and bloodshed, occasioned by every new settlement; these were not blameable, because they were inevitable.

The house of Lancaster ruled in this island about sixty years; yet the

30 partizans of the white rose seemed daily to multiply in England. The present establishment has taken place during a still longer period. Have all views of right in another family been utterly extinguished; even though scarce any man now alive had arrived at years of discretion, when it was expelled, or could have consented to its dominion, or have promised it allegiance? A sufficient

35 indication surely of the general sentiment of mankind on this head. For we blame not the partizans of the abdicated family, merely on account of the long time, during which they have preserved their imaginary loyalty. We blame them for adhering to a family, which, we affirm, has been justly expelled, and which, from the moment the new settlement took place, had forfeited all title to

40 authority.

16

But would we have a more regular, at least a more philosophical, refutation of this principle of an original contract or popular consent; perhaps, the following observations may suffice.

All *moral* duties may be divided into two kinds. The *first* are those, to
5 which men are impelled by a natural instinct or immediate propensity, which operates on them, independent of all ideas of obligation, and of all views, either to public or private utility. Of this nature are, love of children, gratitude to benefactors, pity to the unfortunate. When we reflect on the advantage, which results to society from such humane instincts, we pay them the just tribute of
10 moral approbation and esteem: But the person, actuated by them, feels their power and influence, antecedent to any such reflection.

The *second* kind of moral duties are such as are not supported by any original instinct of nature, but are performed entirely from a sense of obligation, when we consider the necessities of human society, and the impossibility of
15 supporting it, if these duties were neglected. It is thus *justice* or a regard to the property of others, *fidelity* or the observance of promises, become obligatory, and acquire an authority over mankind. For as it is evident, that every man loves himself better than any other person, he is naturally impelled to extend his acquisitions as much as possible; and nothing can restrain him in this propensity,
20 but reflection and experience, by which he learns the pernicious effects of that licence, and the total dissolution of society which must ensue from it. His original inclination, therefore, or instinct, is here checked and restrained by a subsequent judgment or observation.

The case is precisely the same with the political or civil duty of *allegiance,*
25 as with the natural duties of justice and fidelity. Our primary instincts lead us, either to indulge ourselves in unlimited freedom, or to seek dominion over others: And it is reflection only, which engages us to sacrifice such strong passions to the interests of peace and public order. A small degree of experience and observation suffices to teach us, that society cannot possibly be maintained
30 without the authority of magistrates, and that this authority must soon fall into contempt, where exact obedience is not payed to it. The observation of these general and obvious interests is the source of all allegiance, and of that moral obligation, which we attribute to it.

What necessity, therefore, is there to found the duty of *allegiance* or
35 obedience to magistrates on that of *fidelity* or a regard to promises, and to suppose, that it is the consent of each individual, which subjects him to government; when it appears, that both allegiance and fidelity stand precisely on the same foundation, and are both submitted to by mankind, on account of the apparent interests and necessities of human society? We are bound to obey our
40 sovereign, it is said; because we have given a tacit promise to that purpose. But

why are we bound to observe our promise? It must here be asserted, that the commerce and intercourse of mankind, which are of such mighty advantage, can have no security where men pay no regard to their engagements. In like manner, may it be said, that men could not live at all in society, at least in a civilized
5 society, without laws and magistrates and judges, to prevent the encroachments of the strong upon the weak, of the violent upon the just and equitable. The obligation to allegiance being of like force and authority with the obligation to fidelity, we gain nothing by resolving the one into the other. The general interests or necessities of society are sufficient to establish both.
10 If the reason be asked of that obedience, which we are bound to pay to government, I readily answer, *because society could not otherwise subsist:* And this answer is clear and intelligible to all mankind. Your answer is, *because we should keep our word.* But besides, that no body, till trained in a philosophical system, can either comprehend or relish this answer: Besides this, I say, you find
15 yourself embarrassed, when it is asked, *why we are bound to keep our word?* Nor can you give any answer, but what would, immediately, without any circuit, have accounted for our obligation to allegiance.

But *to whom is allegiance due? And who is our lawful sovereign?* This question is often the most difficult of any, and liable to infinite discussions.
20 When people are so happy, that they can answer, *Our present sovereign, who inherits, in a direct line, from ancestors, that have governed us for many ages;* this answer admits of no reply; even though historians, in tracing up to the remotest antiquity, the origin of that royal family, may find, as commonly happens, that its first authority was derived from usurpation and violence. It is
25 confessed, that private justice, or the abstinence from the properties of others, is a most cardinal virtue: Yet reason tells us, that there is no property in durable objects, such as lands or houses, when carefully examined in passing from hand to hand, but must, in some period, have been founded on fraud and injustice. The necessities of human society, neither in private nor public life, will allow of
30 such an accurate enquiry: And there is no virtue or moral duty, but what may, with facility, be refined away, if we indulge a false philosophy, in sifting and scrutinizing it, by every captious rule of logic, in every light or position, in which it may be placed.

The questions with regard to private property have filled infinite volumes of
35 law and philosophy, if in both we add the commentators to the original text; and in the end, we may safely pronounce, that many of the rules, there established, are uncertain, ambiguous, and arbitrary. The like opinion may be formed with regard to the succession and rights of princes and forms of government. Several cases, no doubt, occur, especially in the infancy of any constitution, which admit
40 of no determination from the laws of justice and equity: And our historian Rapin

pretends, that the controversy between Edward the Third and Philip de Valois was of this nature, and could be decided only by an appeal to heaven, that is, by war and violence.

Who shall tell me, whether Germanicus or Drusus ought to have succeeded
5 to Tiberius, had he died, while they were both alive, without naming any of them for his successor? Ought the right of adoption to be received as equivalent to that of blood, in a nation, where it had the same effect in private families, and had already, in two instances, taken place in the public? Ought Germanicus to be esteemed the elder son because he was born before Drusus; or the younger,
10 because he was adopted after the birth of his brother? Ought the right of the elder to be regarded in a nation, where he had no advantage in the succession of private families? Ought the Roman empire at that time to be deemed hereditary, because of two examples; or ought it, even so early, to be regarded as belonging to the stronger or to the present possessor, as being founded on so recent an
15 usurpation?

Commodus mounted the throne after a pretty long succession of excellent emperors, who had acquired their title, not by birth, or public election, but by the fictitious rite of adoption. That bloody debauchee being murdered by a conspiracy suddenly formed between his wench and her gallant, who happened
20 at that time to be *Prætorian Præfect;* these immediately deliberated about choosing a master to human kind, to speak in the style of those ages; and they cast their eyes on Pertinax. Before the tyrant's death was known, the *Præfect* went secretly to that senator, who, on the appearance of the soldiers, imagined that his execution had been ordered by Commodus. He was immediately saluted
25 emperor by the officer and his attendants; chearfully proclaimed by the populace; unwillingly submitted to by the guards; formally recognized by the senate; and passively received by the provinces and armies of the empire.

The discontent of the *Prætorian* bands broke out in a sudden sedition, which occasioned the murder of that excellent prince: And the world being now
30 without a master and without government, the guards thought proper to set the empire formally to sale. Julian, the purchaser, was proclaimed by the soldiers, recognized by the senate, and submitted to by the people; and must also have been submitted to by the provinces, had not the envy of the legions begotten opposition and resistance. Pescennius Niger in Syria elected himself emperor,
35 gained the tumultuary consent of his army, and was attended with the secret good-will of the senate and people of Rome. Albinus in Britain found an equal right to set up his claim; but Severus, who governed Pannonia, prevailed in the end above both of them. That able politician and warrior, finding his own birth and dignity too much inferior to the imperial crown, professed, at first, an
40 intention only of revenging the death of Pertinax. He marched as general into

Italy; defeated Julian; and without our being able to fix any precise commencement even of the soldiers' consent, he was from necessity acknowledged emperor by the senate and people; and fully established in his violent authority by subduing Niger and Albinus.[3]

5   *Inter hæc Gordianus Cæsar* (says Capitolinus, speaking of another period) *sublatus a militibus.* Imperator *est appellatus, quia non erat alius in præsenti.* It is to be remarked, that Gordian was a boy of fourteen years of age.

Frequent instances of a like nature occur in the history of the emperors; in that of Alexander's successors; and of many other countries: Nor can any thing

10 be more unhappy than a despotic government of this kind; where the succession is disjointed and irregular, and must be determined, on every vacancy, by force or election. In a free government, the matter is often unavoidable, and is also much less dangerous. The interests of liberty may there frequently lead the people, in their own defence, to alter the succession of the crown. And the

15 constitution, being compounded of parts, may still maintain a sufficient stability, by resting on the aristocratical or democratical members, though the monarchical be altered, from time to time, in order to accommodate it to the former.

In an absolute government, when there is no legal prince, who has a title to

20 the throne, it may safely be determined to belong to the first occupant. Instances of this kind are but too frequent, especially in the eastern monarchies. When any race of princes expires, the will or destination of the last sovereign will be regarded as a title. Thus the edict of Lewis the XIVth, who called the bastard princes to the succession in case of the failure of all the legitimate princes,

25 would, in such an event, have some authority.[4] Thus the will of Charles the Second disposed of the whole Spanish monarchy. The cession of the ancient proprietor, especially when joined to conquest, is likewise deemed a good title. The general obligation, which binds us to government, is the interest and necessities of society; and this obligation is very strong. The determination of it

30 to this or that particular prince or form of government is frequently more uncertain and dubious. Present possession has considerable authority in these cases, and greater than in private property; because of the disorders which attend all revolutions and changes of government.

We shall only observe, before we conclude, that, though an appeal to

35 general opinion may justly, in the speculative sciences of metaphysics, natural philosophy, or astronomy, be deemed unfair and inconclusive, yet in all questions with regard to morals, as well as criticism, there is really no other standard, by which any controversy can ever be decided. And nothing is a clearer proof, that a theory of this kind is erroneous, than to find, that it leads to

40 paradoxes, repugnant to the common sentiments of mankind, and to the practice

and opinion of all nations and all ages. The doctrine, which founds all lawful
government on an *original contract,* or consent of the people, is plainly of this
kind; nor has the most noted of its partizans, in prosecution of it, scrupled to
affirm, *that absolute monarchy is inconsistent with civil society, and so can be*
5 *no form of civil government at all;*[5] and *that the supreme power in a state
cannot take from any man, by taxes and impositions, any part of his property,
without his own consent or that of his representatives.*[6] What authority any
moral reasoning can have, which leads into opinions so wide of the general
practice of mankind, in every place but this single kingdom, it is easy to
10 determine.

    The only passage I meet with in antiquity, where the obligation of
obedience to government is ascribed to a promise, is in Plato's *Crito:* where
Socrates refuses to escape from prison, because he had tacitly promised to obey
the laws. Thus he builds a *tory* consequence of passive obedience, on a *whig*
15 foundation of the original contract.

    New discoveries are not to be expected in these matters. If scarce any man,
till very lately, ever imagined that government was founded on compact, it is
certain, that it cannot, in general, have any such foundation.

    The crime of rebellion among the ancients was commonly expressed by the
20 terms νεωτερίζειν, *novas res moliri.*

---

[1] Lib. ii. cap. 38.

[2] Tacit. Ann. vi. cap. 14.

[3] Herodian, lib. ii.

[4] It is remarkable, that, in the remonstrance of the duke of Bourbon and the legitimate
princes, against this destination of Louis the XIVth, the doctrine of the *original contract*
is insisted on, even in that absolute government. The French nation, say they, chusing
Hugh Capet and his posterity to rule over them and their posterity, where the former line
fails, there is a tacit right reserved to choose a new royal family; and this right is invaded
by calling the bastard princes to the throne, without the consent of the nation. But the
Comte de Boulainvilliers, who wrote in defence of the bastard princes, ridicules this
notion of an original contract, especially when applied to Hugh Capet; who mounted the
throne, says he, by the same arts, which have ever been employed by all conquerors and
usurpers. He got his title, indeed, recognized by the states after he had put himself in
possession: But is this a choice or contract? The Comte de Boulainvilliers, we may
observe, was a noted republican; but being a man of learning, and very conversant in
history, he knew that the people were never almost consulted in these revolutions and
new establishments, and that time alone bestowed right and authority on what was
commonly at first founded on force and violence. See *Etat de la France,* Vol. III.

[5] See Locke on Government, chap. vii. § 90.

[6] Id. chap. xi. § 138, 139, 140.

Jean-Jacques Rousseau

Jean-Jacques Rousseau (b. 1712, Geneva, d. 1778, Ermenonville) was a French political theorist and writer. He received an irregular education reading Plutarch and Calvinist sermons as a youth and apprenticing to a notary and an engraver. He continued to read philosophy on his own and taught himself music, becoming a popular composer of his day, and supporting himself with writing and copying music at various points in his life. After moving to Paris from his native Geneva, Rousseau joined the circle of progressive intellectuals headed by Diderot and D'Alambert and contributed a number of influential articles to their *Encyclopedia*. This work and his prize-winning "Discourse on the Arts and Sciences" brought him considerable prominence as a political writer. The governments of Poland and Corsica sought his advce on the writing of their constitutions, and a number of great European sovereigns of his day, including Russian Empress Catherine II and Frederick the Great of Prussia, were influenced by his writings.

Rousseau's key political works are *The Social Contract* and *Discourse of the Origin and Basis of Inequality Among Men*. Rousseau's *Émile, or On Education* is one of the most original, if not the most practical, contributions to the philosophy of education in the modern canon.

Along with those of his contemporary and rival Voltaire, Rousseau's ideas about individual freedom and equality, religion, and popular sovereignty provided the ideological groundwork for the French revolution.

Jean-Jacques Rousseau
DISCOURSE ON THE ORIGIN OF INEQUALITY
(1754)

A DISCOURSE ON A SUBJECT PROPOSED BY THE ACADEMY OF
DIJON: WHAT IS THE ORIGIN OF INEQUALITY AMONG MEN, AND IS
IT AUTHORISED BY NATURAL LAW?

5   We should consider what is natural not in things depraved but in those
which are rightly ordered according to nature. Aristotle, *Politics* I. 5

DEDICATION TO THE REPUBLIC OF GENEVA
MOST HONOURABLE, MAGNIFICENT AND SOVEREIGN LORDS,
convinced that only a virtuous citizen can confer on his country honours which
it can accept, I have been for thirty years past working to make myself worthy to
10   offer you some public homage; and, this fortunate opportunity supplementing in
some degree the insufficiency of my efforts, I have thought myself entitled to
follow in embracing it the dictates of the zeal which inspires me, rather than the
right which should have been my authorisation. Having had the happiness to be
born among you, how could I reflect on the equality which nature has ordained
15   between men, and the inequality which they have introduced, without reflecting
on the profound wisdom by which both are in this State happily combined and
made to coincide, in the manner that is most in conformity with natural law, and
most favourable to society, to the maintenance of public order and to the
happiness of individuals? In my researches after the best rules common sense
20   can lay down for the constitution of a government, I have been so struck at
finding them all in actuality in your own, that even had I not been born within
your walls I should have thought it indispensable for me to offer this picture of
human society to that people, which of all others seems to be possessed of its
greatest advantages, and to have best guarded against its abuses.
25   If I had had to make choice of the place of my birth, I should have preferred
a society which had an extent proportionate to the limits of the human faculties;
that is, to the possibility of being well governed: in which every person being
equal to his occupation, no one should be obliged to commit to others the
functions with which he was entrusted: a State, in which all the individuals
30   being well known to one another, neither the secret machinations of vice, nor the
modesty of virtue should be able to escape the notice and judgment of the
public; and in which the pleasant custom of seeing and knowing one another
should make the love of country rather a love of the citizens than of its soil.

I should have wished to be born in a country in which the interest of the Sovereign and that of the people must be single and identical; to the end that all the movements of the machine might tend always to the general happiness. And as this could not be the case, unless the Sovereign and the people were one and 5 the same person, it follows that I should have wished to be born under a democratic government, wisely tempered.

I should have wished to live and die free: that is, so far subject to the laws that neither I, nor anybody else, should be able to cast off their honourable yoke: the easy and salutary yoke which the haughtiest necks bear with the greater 10 docility, as they are made to bear no other.

I should have wished then that no one within the State should be able to say he was above the law; and that no one without should be able to dictate so that the State should be obliged to recognise his authority. For, be the constitution of a government what it may, if there be within its jurisdiction a single man who is 15 not subject to the law, all the rest are necessarily at his discretion. And if there be a national ruler within, and a foreign ruler without, however they may divide their authority, it is impossible that both should be duly obeyed, or that the State should be well governed.

I should not have chosen to live in a republic of recent institution, however 20 excellent its laws; for fear the government, being perhaps otherwise framed than the circumstances of the moment might require, might disagree with the new citizens, or they with it, and the State run the risk of overthrow and destruction almost as soon as it came into being. For it is with liberty as it is with those solid and succulent foods, or with those generous wines which are well adapted to 25 nourish and fortify robust constitutions that are used to them, but ruin and intoxicate weak and delicate constitutions to which they are not suited. Peoples once accustomed to masters are not in a condition to do without them. If they attempt to shake off the yoke, they still more estrange themselves from freedom, as, by mistaking for it an unbridled license to which it is diametrically opposed, 30 they nearly always manage, by their revolutions, to hand themselves over to seducers, who only make their chains heavier than before. The Roman people itself, a model for all free peoples, was wholly incapable of governing itself when it escaped from the oppression of the Tarquins. Debased by slavery, and the ignominious tasks which had been imposed upon it, it was at first no better 35 than a stupid mob, which it was necessary to control and govern with the greatest wisdom; in order that, being accustomed by degrees to breathe the health-giving air of liberty, minds which had been enervated or rather brutalised under tyranny, might gradually acquire that severity of morals and spirit of fortitude which made it at length the people of all most worthy of respect. I 40 should, then, have sought out for my country some peaceful and happy

Republic, of an antiquity that lost itself, as it were, in the night of time: which had experienced only such shocks as served to manifest and strengthen the courage and patriotism of its subjects; and whose citizens, long accustomed to a wise independence, were not only free, but worthy to be so.

5   I should have wished to choose myself a country, diverted, by a fortunate impotence, from the brutal love of conquest, and secured, by a still more fortunate situation, from the fear of becoming itself the conquest of other States: a free city situated between several nations, none of which should have any interest in attacking it, while each had an interest in preventing it from being
10 attacked by the others; in short, a Republic which should have nothing to tempt the ambition of its neighbours, but might reasonably depend on their assistance in case of need. It follows that a republican State so happily situated could have nothing to fear but from itself; and that, if its members trained themselves to the use of arms, it would be rather to keep alive that military ardour and courageous
15 spirit which are so proper among freemen, and tend to keep up their taste for liberty, than from the necessity of providing for their defence.

    I should have sought a country, in which the right of legislation was vested in all the citizens; for who can judge better than they of the conditions under which they had best dwell together in the same society? Not that I should have
20 approved of Plebiscita, like those among the Romans; in which the rulers in the State, and those most interested in its preservation, were excluded from the deliberations on which in many cases its security depended; and in which, by the most absurd inconsistency, the magistrates were deprived of rights which the meanest citizens enjoyed.

25   On the contrary, I should have desired that, in order to prevent self-interested and ill-conceived projects, and all such dangerous innovations as finally ruined the Athenians, each man should not be at liberty to propose new laws at pleasure; but that this right should belong exclusively to the magistrates; and that even they should use it with so much caution, the people, on its side, be
30 so reserved in giving its consent to such laws, and the promulgation of them be attended with so much solemnity, that before the constitution could be upset by them, there might be time enough for all to be convinced, that it is above all the great antiquity of the laws which makes them sacred and venerable, that men soon learn to despise laws which they see daily altered, and that States, by
35 accustoming themselves to neglect their ancient customs under the pretext of improvement, often introduce greater evils than those they endeavour to remove.

    I should have particularly avoided, as necessarily ill-governed, a Republic in which the people, imagining themselves in a position to do without magistrates, or at least to leave them with only a precarious authority, should
40 imprudently have kept for themselves the administration of civil affairs and the

execution of their own laws. Such must have been the rude constitution of primitive governments, directly emerging from a state of nature; and this was another of the vices that contributed to the downfall of the Republic of Athens.

But I should have chosen a community in which the individuals, content
5   with sanctioning their laws, and deciding the most important public affairs in general assembly and on the motion of the rulers, had established honoured tribunals, carefully distinguished the several departments, and elected year by year some of the most capable and upright of their fellow-citizens to administer justice and govern the State; a community, in short, in which the virtue of the
10   magistrates thus bearing witness to the wisdom of the people, each class reciprocally did the other honour. If in such a case any fatal misunderstandings arose to disturb the public peace, even these intervals of blindness and error would bear the marks of moderation, mutual esteem, and a common respect for the laws; which are sure signs and pledges of a reconciliation as lasting as
15   sincere. Such are the advantages, most honourable, magnificent and sovereign lords, which I should have sought in the country in which I should have chosen to be born. And if providence had added to all these a delightful situation, a temperate climate, a fertile soil, and the most beautiful countryside under Heaven, I should have desired only, to complete my felicity, the peaceful
20   enjoyment of all these blessings, in the bosom of this happy country; to live at peace in the sweet society of my fellow-citizens, and practising towards them, from their own example, the duties of friendship, humanity, and every other virtue, to leave behind me the honourable memory of a good man, and an upright and virtuous patriot.
25   But, if less fortunate or too late grown wise, I had seen myself reduced to end an infirm and languishing life in other climates, vainly regretting that peaceful repose which I had forfeited in the imprudence of youth, I should at least have entertained the same feelings in my heart, though denied the opportunity of making use of them in my native country. Filled with a tender
30   and disinterested love for my distant fellow-citizens, I should have addressed them from my heart, much in the following terms.

"My dear fellow-citizens, or rather my brothers, since the ties of blood, as well as the laws, unite almost all of us, it gives me pleasure that I cannot think of you, without thinking, at the same time, of all the blessings you enjoy, and of
35   which none of you, perhaps, more deeply feels the value than I who have lost them. The more I reflect on your civil and political condition, the less can I conceive that the nature of human affairs could admit of a better. In all other governments, when there is a question of ensuring the greatest good of the State, nothing gets beyond projects and ideas, or at best bare possibilities. But as for
40   you, your happiness is complete, and you have nothing to do but enjoy it; you

require nothing more to be made perfectly happy, than to know how to be satisfied with being so. Your sovereignty, acquired or recovered by the sword, and maintained for two centuries past by your valour and wisdom, is at length fully and universally acknowledged. Your boundaries are fixed, your rights confirmed and your repose secured by honourable treaties. Your constitution is excellent, being not only dictated by the profoundest wisdom, but guaranteed by great and friendly powers. Your State enjoys perfect tranquillity; you have neither wars nor conquerors to fear; you have no other master than the wise laws you have yourselves made; and these are administered by upright magistrates of your own choosing. You are neither so wealthy as to be enervated by effeminacy, and thence to lose, in the pursuit of frivolous pleasures, the taste for real happiness and solid virtue; nor poor enough to require more assistance from abroad than your own industry is sufficient to procure you. In the meantime the precious privilege of liberty, which in great nations is maintained only by submission to the most exorbitant impositions, costs you hardly anything for its preservation.

May a Republic, so wisely and happily constituted, last for ever, for an example to other nations, and for the felicity of its own citizens! This is the only prayer you have left to make, the only precaution that remains to be taken. It depends, for the future, on yourselves alone (not to make you happy, for your ancestors have saved you that trouble), but to render that happiness lasting, by your wisdom in its enjoyment. It is on your constant union, your obedience to the laws, and your respect for their ministers, that your preservation depends. If there remains among you the smallest trace of bitterness or distrust, hasten to destroy it, as an accursed leaven which sooner or later must bring misfortune and ruin on the State. I conjure you all to look into your hearts, and to hearken to the secret voice of conscience. Is there any among you who can find, throughout the universe, a more upright, more enlightened and more honourable body than your magistracy? Do not all its members set you an example of moderation, of simplicity of manners, of respect for the laws, and of the most sincere harmony? Place, therefore, without reserve, in such wise superiors, that salutary confidence which reason ever owes to virtue. Consider that they are your own choice, that they justify that choice, and that the honours due to those whom you have dignified are necessarily yours by reflexion. Not one of you is so ignorant as not to know that, when the laws lose their force and those who defend them their authority, security and liberty are universally impossible. Why, therefore, should you hesitate to do that cheerfully and with just confidence which you would all along have been bound to do by your true interest, your duty and reason itself?

Let not a culpable and pernicious indifference to the maintenance of the constitution ever induce you to neglect, in case of need, the prudent advice of the most enlightened and zealous of your fellow-citizens; but let equity, moderation and firmness of resolution continue to regulate all your proceedings, and to exhibit you to the whole universe as the example of a valiant and modest people, jealous equally of their honour and of their liberty. Beware particularly,

5 as the last piece of advice I shall give you, of sinister constructions and venomous rumours, the secret motives of which are often more dangerous than the actions at which they are levelled. A whole house will be awake and take the first alarm given by a good and trusty watch-dog, who barks only at the approach of thieves; but we hate the importunity of those noisy curs, which are

10 perpetually disturbing the public repose, and whose continual ill-timed warnings prevent our attending to them, when they may perhaps be necessary."

And you, most honourable and magnificent lords, the worthy and revered magistrates of a free people, permit me to offer you in particular my duty and homage. If there is in the world a station capable of conferring honour on those

15 who fill it, it is undoubtedly that which virtue and talents combine to bestow, that of which you have made yourselves worthy, and to which you have been promoted by your fellow-citizens. Their worth adds a new lustre to your own; while, as you have been chosen, by men capable of governing others, to govern themselves, I cannot but hold you as much superior to all other magistrates, as a

20 free people, and particularly that over which you have the honour to preside, is by its wisdom and its reason superior to the populace of other States.

Be it permitted me to cite an example of which there ought to have existed better records, and one which will be ever near to my heart. I cannot recall to mind, without the sweetest emotions, the memory of that virtuous citizen, to

25 whom I owe my being, and by whom I was often instructed, in my infancy, in the respect which is due to you. I see him still, living by the work of his hands, and feeding his soul on the sublimest truths. I see the works of Tacitus, Plutarch, and Grotius lying before him in the midst of the tools of his trade. At his side stands his dear son, receiving, alas with too little profit, the tender instructions of

30 the best of fathers. But, if the follies of youth made me for a while forget his wise lessons, I have at length the happiness to be conscious that, whatever propensity one may have to vice, it is not easy for an education, with which love has mingled, to be entirely thrown away.

Such, my most honourable and magnificent lords, are the citizens, and even

35 the common inhabitants of the State which you govern; such are those intelligent and sensible men, of whom, under the name of workmen and the people, it is usual, in other nations, to have a low and false opinion. My father, I own with pleasure, was in no way distinguished among his fellow-citizens. He was only such as they all are; and yet, such as he was, there is no country, in which his

40 acquaintance would not have been coveted, and cultivated even with advantage

by men of the highest character. It would not become me, nor is it, thank Heaven, at all necessary for me to remind you of the regard which such men have a right to expect of their magistrates, to whom they are equal both by education and by the rights of nature and birth, and inferior only, by their own will, by that preference which they owe to your merit, and, for giving you, can claim some sort of acknowledgment on your side. It is with a lively satisfaction I understand that the greatest candour and condescension attend, in all your behaviour towards them, on that gravity which becomes the ministers of the law; and that you so well repay them, by your esteem and attention, the respect and obedience which they owe to you. This conduct is not only just but prudent; as it happily tends to obliterate the memory of many unhappy events, which ought to be buried in eternal oblivion. It is also so much the more judicious, as it tends to make this generous and equitable people find a pleasure in their duty; to make them naturally love to do you honour, and to cause those who are the most zealous in the maintenance of their own rights to be at the same time the most disposed to respect yours.

It ought not to be thought surprising that the rulers of a civil society should have the welfare and glory of their communities at heart: but it is uncommonly fortunate for the peace of men, when those persons who look upon themselves as the magistrates, or rather the masters of a more holy and sublime country, show some love for the earthly country which maintains them. I am happy in having it in my power to make so singular an exception in our favour, and to be able to rank, among its best citizens, those zealous depositaries of the sacred articles of faith established by the laws, those venerable shepherds of souls whose powerful and captivating eloquence are so much the better calculated to bear to men's hearts the maxims of the gospel, as they are themselves the first to put them into practice. All the world knows of the great success with which the art of the pulpit is cultivated at Geneva; but men are so used to hearing divines preach one thing and practise another, that few have a chance of knowing how far the spirit of Christianity, holiness of manners, severity towards themselves and indulgence towards their neighbours, prevail throughout the whole body of our ministers. It is, perhaps, given to the city of Geneva alone, to produce the edifying example of so perfect a union between its clergy and men of letters. It is in great measure on their wisdom, their known moderation, and their zeal for the prosperity of the State that I build my hopes of its perpetual tranquillity. At the same time, I notice, with a pleasure mingled with surprise and veneration, how much they detest the frightful maxims of those accursed and barbarous men, of whom history furnishes us with more than one example; who, in order to support the pretended rights of God, that is to say their own interests, have been so much the less greedy of human blood, as they were more hopeful their own in particular would be always respected.

I must not forget that precious half of the Republic, which makes the happiness of the other; and whose sweetness and prudence preserve its
5   tranquillity and virtue. Amiable and virtuous daughters of Geneva, it will be always the lot of your sex to govern ours. Happy are we, so long as your chaste influence, solely exercised within the limits of conjugal union, is exerted only for the glory of the State and the happiness of the public. It was thus the female sex commanded at Sparta; and thus you deserve to command at Geneva. What
10 man can be such a barbarian as to resist the voice of honour and reason, coming from the lips of an affectionate wife? Who would not despise the vanities of luxury, on beholding the simple and modest attire which, from the lustre it derives from you, seems the most favourable to beauty? It is your task to perpetuate, by your insinuating influence and your innocent and amiable rule, a
15 respect for the laws of the State, and harmony among the citizens. It is yours to reunite divided families by happy marriages; and, above all things, to correct, by the persuasive sweetness of your lessons and the modest graces of your conversation, those extravagancies which our young people pick up in other countries, whence, instead of many useful things by which they might profit,
20 they bring home hardly anything, besides a puerile air and a ridiculous manner, acquired among loose women, but an admiration for I know not what so-called grandeur, and paltry recompenses for being slaves, which can never come near the real greatness of liberty. Continue, therefore, always to be what you are, the chaste guardians of our morals, and the sweet security for our peace, exerting on
25 every occasion the privileges of the heart and of nature, in the interests of duty and virtue.

I flatter myself that I shall never be proved to have been mistaken, in building on such a foundation my hopes of the general happiness of the citizens and the glory of the Republic. It must be confessed, however, that with all these
30 advantages, it will not shine with that lustre, by which the eyes of most men are dazzled; a puerile and fatal taste for which is the most mortal enemy of happiness and liberty.

Let our dissolute youth seek elsewhere light pleasures and long repentances. Let our pretenders to taste admire elsewhere the grandeur of palaces, the beauty
35 of equipages, sumptuous furniture, the pomp of public entertainments, and all the refinements of luxury and effeminacy. Geneva boasts nothing but men; such a sight has nevertheless a value of its own, and those who have a taste for it are well worth the admirers of all the rest.

Deign, most honourable, magnificent and sovereign lords, to receive, and
40 with equal goodness, this respectful testimony of the interest I take in your

31

common prosperity. And, if I have been so unhappy as to be guilty of any
indiscreet transport in this glowing effusion of my heart, I beseech you to pardon
me, and to attribute it to the tender affection of a true patriot, and to the ardent
and legitimate zeal of a man, who can imagine for himself no greater felicity
5   than to see you happy.

Most honourable, magnificent and sovereign lords, I am, with the most
profound respect,

Your most humble and obedient servant and fellow-citizen.

J. J. ROUSSEAU

10   Chambéry, June 12, 1754

PREFACE

OF all human sciences the most useful and most imperfect appears to me to
be that of mankind: and I will venture to say, the single inscription on the
Temple of Delphi contained a precept more difficult and more important than is
to be found in all the huge volumes that moralists have ever written. I consider
15   the subject of the following discourse as one of the most interesting questions
philosophy can propose, and unhappily for us, one of the most thorny that
philosophers can have to solve. For how shall we know the source of inequality
between men, if we do not begin by knowing mankind? And how shall man
hope to see himself as nature made him, across all the changes which the
20   succession of place and time must have produced in his original constitution?
How can he distinguish what is fundamental in his nature from the changes and
additions which his circumstances and the advances he has made have
introduced to modify his primitive condition? Like the statue of Glaucus, which
was so disfigured by time, seas and tempests, that it looked more like a wild
25   beast than a god, the human soul, altered in society by a thousand causes
perpetually recurring, by the acquisition of a multitude of truths and errors, by
the changes happening to the constitution of the body, and by the continual
jarring of the passions, has, so to speak, changed in appearance, so as to be
hardly recognisable. Instead of a being, acting constantly from fixed and
30   invariable principles, instead of that celestial and majestic simplicity, impressed
on it by its divine Author, we find in it only the frightful contrast of passion
mistaking itself for reason, and of understanding grown delirious.

It is still more cruel that, as every advance made by the human species
removes it still farther from its primitive state, the more discoveries we make,
35   the more we deprive ourselves of the means of making the most important of all.
Thus it is, in one sense, by our very study of man, that the knowledge of him is
put out of our power.

It is easy to perceive that it is in these successive changes in the constitution of man that we must look for the origin of those differences which now distinguish men, who, it is allowed, are as equal among themselves as were the animals of every kind, before physical causes had introduced those varieties

5   which are now observable among some of them.

It is, in fact, not to be conceived that these primary changes, however they may have arisen, could have altered, all at once and in the same manner, every individual of the species. It is natural to think that, while the condition of some of them grew better or worse, and they were acquiring various good or bad

10   qualities not inherent in their nature, there were others who continued a longer time in their original condition. Such was doubtless the first source of the inequality of mankind, which it is much easier to point out thus in general terms, than to assign with precision to its actual causes.

Let not my readers therefore imagine that I flatter myself with having seen

15   what it appears to me so difficult to discover. I have here entered upon certain arguments, and risked some conjectures, less in the hope of solving the difficulty, than with a view to throwing some light upon it, and reducing the question to its proper form. Others may easily proceed farther on the same road, and yet no one find it very easy to get to the end. For it is by no means a light

20   undertaking to distinguish properly between what is original and what is artificial in the actual nature of man, or to form a true idea of a state which no longer exists, perhaps never did exist, and probably never will exist; and of which, it is, nevertheless, necessary to have true ideas, in order to form a proper judgment of our present state. It requires, indeed, more philosophy than can be

25   imagined to enable any one to determine exactly what precautions he ought to take, in order to make solid observations on this subject; and it appears to me that a good solution of the following problem would be not unworthy of the Aristotles and Plinys of the present age. What experiments would have to be made, to discover the natural man? And how are those experiments to be made

30   in a state of society?

So far am I from undertaking to solve this problem, that I think I have sufficiently considered the subject, to venture to declare beforehand that our greatest philosophers would not be too good to direct such experiments, and our most powerful sovereigns to make them. Such a combination we have very little

35   reason to expect, especially attended with the perseverance, or rather succession of intelligence and goodwill necessary on both sides to success.

These investigations, which are so difficult to make, and have been hitherto so little thought of, are, nevertheless, the only means that remain of obviating a multitude of difficulties which deprive us of the knowledge of the real

40   foundations of human society. It is this ignorance of the nature of man, which

casts so much uncertainty and obscurity on the true definition of natural right: for, the idea of right, says Burlamaqui, and more particularly that of natural right, are ideas manifestly relative to the nature of man. It is then from this very nature itself, he goes on, from the constitution and state of man, that we must
5   deduce the first principles of this science.

We cannot see without surprise and disgust how little agreement there is between the different authors who have treated this great subject. Among the more important writers there are scarcely two of the same mind about it. Not to speak of the ancient philosophers, who seem to have done their best purposely to
10   contradict one another on the most fundamental principles, the Roman jurists subjected man and the other animals indiscriminately to the same natural law, because they considered, under that name, rather the law which nature imposes on herself than that which she prescribes to others; or rather because of the particular acceptation of the term law among those jurists; who seem on this
15   occasion to have understood nothing more by it than the general relations established by nature between all animated beings, for their common preservation. The moderns, understanding, by the term law, merely a rule prescribed to a moral being, that is to say intelligent, free and considered in his relations to other beings, consequently confine the jurisdiction of natural law to
20   man, as the only animal endowed with reason. But, defining this law, each after his own fashion, they have established it on such metaphysical principles, that there are very few persons among us capable of comprehending them, much less of discovering them for themselves. So that the definitions of these learned men, all differing in everything else, agree only in this, that it is impossible to
25   comprehend the law of nature, and consequently to obey it, without being a very subtle casuist and a profound metaphysician. All which is as much as to say that mankind must have employed, in the establishment of society, a capacity which is acquired only with great difficulty, and by very few persons, even in a state of society.
30   Knowing so little of nature, and agreeing so ill about the meaning of the word law, it would be difficult for us to fix on a good definition of natural law. Thus all the definitions we meet with in books, setting aside their defect in point of uniformity, have yet another fault, in that they are derived from many kinds of knowledge, which men do not possess naturally, and from advantages of
35   which they can have no idea until they have already departed from that state. Modern writers begin by inquiring what rules it would be expedient for men to agree on for their common interest, and then give the name of natural law to a collection of these rules, without any other proof than the good that would result from their being universally practised. This is undoubtedly a simple way of

making definitions, and of explaining the nature of things by almost arbitrary conveniences.

But as long as we are ignorant of the natural man, it is in vain for us to attempt to determine either the law originally prescribed to him, or that which is
5   best adapted to his constitution. All we can know with any certainty respecting this law is that, if it is to be a law, not only the wills of those it obliges must be sensible of their submission to it; but also, to be natural, it must come directly from the voice of nature.

Throwing aside, therefore, all those scientific books, which teach us only to
10   see men such as they have made themselves, and contemplating the first and most simple operations of the human soul, I think I can perceive in it two principles prior to reason, one of them deeply interesting us in our own welfare and preservation, and the other exciting a natural repugnance at seeing any other sensible being, and particularly any of our own species, suffer pain or death. It is
15   from the agreement and combination which the understanding is in a position to establish between these two principles, without its being necessary to introduce that of sociability, that all the rules of natural right appear to me to be derived – rules which our reason is afterwards obliged to establish on other foundations, when by its successive developments it has been led to suppress nature itself.

20   In proceeding thus, we shall not be obliged to make man a philosopher before he is a man. His duties toward others are not dictated to him only by the later lessons of wisdom; and, so long as he does not resist the internal impulse of compassion, he will never hurt any other man, nor even any sentient being, except on those lawful occasions on which his own preservation is concerned
25   and he is obliged to give himself the preference. By this method also we put an end to the time-honoured disputes concerning the participation of animals in natural law: for it is clear that, being destitute of intelligence and liberty, they cannot recognise that law; as they partake, however, in some measure of our nature, in consequence of the sensibility with which they are endowed, they
30   ought to partake of natural right; so that mankind is subjected to a kind of obligation even toward the brutes. It appears, in fact, that if I am bound to do no injury to my fellow-creatures, this is less because they are rational than because they are sentient beings: and this quality, being common both to men and beasts, ought to entitle the latter at least to the privilege of not being wantonly ill-treated
35   by the former.

The very study of the original man, of his real wants, and the fundamental principles of his duty, is besides the only proper method we can adopt to obviate all the difficulties which the origin of moral inequality presents, on the true foundations of the body politic, on the reciprocal rights of its members, and on
40   many other similar topics equally important and obscure.

If we look at human society with a calm and disinterested eye, it seems, at first, to show us only the violence of the powerful and the oppression of the weak. The mind is shocked at the cruelty of the one, or is induced to lament the blindness of the other; and as nothing is less permanent in life than those external relations, which are more frequently produced by accident than wisdom, and which are called weakness or power, riches or poverty, all human institutions seem at first glance to be founded merely on banks of shifting sand. It is only by taking a closer look, and removing the dust and sand that surround the edifice, that we perceive the immovable basis on which it is raised, and learn to respect its foundations. Now, without a serious study of man, his natural faculties and their successive development, we shall never be able to make these necessary distinctions, or to separate, in the actual constitution of things, that which is the effect of the divine will, from the innovations attempted by human art. The political and moral investigations, therefore, to which the important question before us leads, are in every respect useful; while the hypothetical history of governments affords a lesson equally instructive to mankind.

In considering what we should have become, had we been left to ourselves, we should learn to bless Him, whose gracious hand, correcting our institutions, and giving them an immovable basis, has prevented those disorders which would otherwise have arisen from them, and caused our happiness to come from those very sources which seemed likely to involve us in misery.

A DISSERTATION ON THE ORIGIN AND FOUNDATION OF THE INEQUALITY OF MANKIND

IT is of man that I have to speak; and the question I am investigating shows me that it is to men that I must address myself: for questions of this sort are not asked by those who are afraid to honour truth. I shall then confidently uphold the cause of humanity before the wise men who invite me to do so, and shall not be dissatisfied if I acquit myself in a manner worthy of my subject and of my judges.

I conceive that there are two kinds of inequality among the human species; one, which I call natural or physical, because it is established by nature, and consists in a difference of age, health, bodily strength, and the qualities of the mind or of the soul: and another, which may be called moral or political inequality, because it depends on a kind of convention, and is established, or at least authorised by the consent of men. This latter consists of the different privileges, which some men enjoy to the prejudice of others; such as that of being more rich, more honoured, more powerful or even in a position to exact obedience.

It is useless to ask what is the source of natural inequality, because that question is answered by the simple definition of the word. Again, it is still more useless to inquire whether there is any essential connection between the two inequalities; for this would be only asking, in other words, whether those who
5   command are necessarily better than those who obey, and if strength of body or of mind, wisdom or virtue are always found in particular individuals, in proportion to their power or wealth: a question fit perhaps to be discussed by slaves in the hearing of their masters, but highly unbecoming to reasonable and free men in search of the truth.
10   The subject of the present discourse, therefore, is more precisely this. To mark, in the progress of things, the moment at which right took the place of violence and nature became subject to law, and to explain by what sequence of miracles the strong came to submit to serve the weak, and the people to purchase imaginary repose at the expense of real felicity.
15   The philosophers, who have inquired into the foundations of society, have all felt the necessity of going back to a state of nature; but not one of them has got there. Some of them have not hesitated to ascribe to man, in such a state, the idea of just and unjust, without troubling themselves to show that he must be possessed of such an idea, or that it could be of any use to him. Others have
20   spoken of the natural right of every man to keep what belongs to him, without explaining what they meant by belongs. Others again, beginning by giving the strong authority over the weak, proceeded directly to the birth of government, without regard to the time that must have elapsed before the meaning of the words authority and government could have existed among men. Every one of
25   them, in short, constantly dwelling on wants, avidity, oppression, desires and pride, has transferred to the state of nature ideas which were acquired in society; so that, in speaking of the savage, they described the social man. It has not even entered into the heads of most of our writers to doubt whether the state of nature ever existed; but it is clear from the Holy Scriptures that the first man, having
30   received his understanding and commandments immediately from God, was not himself in such a state; and that, if we give such credit to the writings of Moses as every Christian philosopher ought to give, we must deny that, even before the deluge, men were ever in the pure state of nature; unless, indeed, they fell back into it from some very extraordinary circumstance; a paradox which it would be
35   very embarrassing to defend, and quite impossible to prove.

Let us begin then by laying facts aside, as they do not affect the question. The investigations we may enter into, in treating this subject, must not be considered as historical truths, but only as mere conditional and hypothetical reasonings, rather calculated to explain the nature of things, than to ascertain
40   their actual origin; just like the hypotheses which our physicists daily form

respecting the formation of the world. Religion commands us to believe that, God Himself having taken men out of a state of nature immediately after the creation, they are unequal only because it is His will they should be so: but it does not forbid us to form conjectures based solely on the nature of man, and the
5   beings around him, concerning what might have become of the human race, if it had been left to itself. This then is the question asked me, and that which I propose to discuss in the following discourse. As my subject interests mankind in general, I shall endeavour to make use of a style adapted to all nations, or rather, forgetting time and place, to attend only to men to whom I am speaking. I
10   shall suppose myself in the Lyceum of Athens, repeating the lessons of my masters, with Plato and Xenocrates for judges, and the whole human race for audience.

      O man, of whatever country you are, and whatever your opinions may be, behold your history, such as I have thought to read it, not in books written by
15   your fellow-creatures, who are liars, but in nature, which never lies. All that comes from her will be true; nor will you meet with anything false, unless I have involuntarily put in something of my own. The times of which I am going to speak are very remote: how much are you changed from what you once were! It is, so to speak, the life of your species which I am going to write, after the
20   qualities which you have received, which your education and habits may have depraved, but cannot have entirely destroyed. There is, I feel, an age at which the individual man would wish to stop: you are about to inquire about the age at which you would have liked your whole species to stand still. Discontented with your present state, for reasons which threaten your unfortunate descendants with
25   still greater discontent, you will perhaps wish it were in your power to go back; and this feeling should be a panegyric on your first ancestors, a criticism of your contemporaries, and a terror to the unfortunates who will come after you.

THE FIRST PART

      IMPORTANT as it may be, in order to judge rightly of the natural state of man, to consider him from his origin, and to examine him, as it were, in the
30   embryo of his species; I shall not follow his organisation through its successive developments, nor shall I stay to inquire what his animal system must have been at the beginning, in order to become at length what it actually is. I shall not ask whether his long nails were at first, as Aristotle supposes, only crooked talons; whether his whole body, like that of a bear, was not covered with hair; or
35   whether the fact that he walked upon all fours, with his looks directed toward the earth, confined to a horizon of a few paces, did not at once point out the nature and limits of his ideas. On this subject I could form none but vague and

almost imaginary conjectures. Comparative anatomy has as yet made too little progress, and the observations of naturalists are too uncertain to afford an adequate basis for any solid reasoning. So that, without having recourse to the supernatural information given us on this head, or paying any regard to the

5   changes which must have taken place in the internal, as well as the external, conformation of man, as he applied his limbs to new uses, and fed himself on new kinds of food, I shall suppose his conformation to have been at all times what it appears to us at this day; that he always walked on two legs, made use of his hands as we do, directed his looks over all nature, and measured with his

10 eyes the vast expanse of Heaven.

If we strip this being, thus constituted, of all the supernatural gifts he may have received, and all the artificial faculties he can have acquired only by a long process; if we consider him, in a word, just as he must have come from the hands of nature, we behold in him an animal weaker than some, and less agile

15 than others; but, taking him all round, the most advantageously organised of any. I see him satisfying his hunger at the first oak, and slaking his thirst at the first brook; finding his bed at the foot of the tree which afforded him a repast; and, with that, all his wants supplied.

While the earth was left to its natural fertility and covered with immense

20 forests, whose trees were never mutilated by the axe, it would present on every side both sustenance and shelter for every species of animal. Men, dispersed up and down among the rest, would observe and imitate their industry, and thus attain even to the instinct of the beasts, with the advantage that, whereas every species of brutes was confined to one particular instinct, man, who perhaps has

25 not any one peculiar to himself, would appropriate them all, and live upon most of those different foods which other animals shared among themselves; and thus would find his subsistence much more easily than any of the rest.

Accustomed from their infancy to the inclemencies of the weather and the rigour of the seasons, inured to fatigue, and forced, naked and unarmed, to

30 defend themselves and their prey from other ferocious animals, or to escape them by flight, men would acquire a robust and almost unalterable constitution. The children, bringing with them into the world the excellent constitution of their parents, and fortifying it by the very exercises which first produced it, would thus acquire all the vigour of which the human frame is capable. Nature

35 in this case treats them exactly as Sparta treated the children of her citizens: those who come well formed into the world she renders strong and robust, and all the rest she destroys; differing in this respect from our modern communities, in which the State, by making children a burden to their parents, kills them indiscriminately before they are born.

The body of a savage man being the only instrument he understands, he uses it for various purposes, of which ours, for want of practice, are incapable: for our industry deprives us of that force and agility, which necessity obliges him to acquire. If he had had an axe, would he have been able with his naked
5   arm to break so large a branch from a tree? If he had had a sling, would he have been able to throw a stone with so great velocity? If he had had a ladder, would he have been so nimble in climbing a tree? If he had had a horse, would he have been himself so swift of foot? Give civilised man time to gather all his machines about him, and he will no doubt easily beat the savage; but if you would see a
10   still more unequal contest, set them together naked and unarmed, and you will soon see the advantage of having all our forces constantly at our disposal, of being always prepared for every event, and of carrying one's self, as it were, perpetually whole and entire about one.

      Hobbes contends that man is naturally intrepid, and is intent only upon
15   attacking and fighting. Another illustrious philosopher holds the opposite, and Cumberland and Puffendorf also affirm that nothing is more timid and fearful than man in the state of nature; that he is always in a tremble, and ready to fly at the least noise or the slightest movement. This may be true of things he does not know; and I do not doubt his being terrified by every novelty that presents itself,
20   when he neither knows the physical good or evil he may expect from it, nor can make a comparison between his own strength and the dangers he is about to encounter. Such circumstances, however, rarely occur in a state of nature, in which all things proceed in a uniform manner, and the face of the earth is not subject to those sudden and continual changes which arise from the passions and
25   caprices of bodies of men living together. But savage man, living dispersed among other animals, and finding himself betimes in a situation to measure his strength with theirs, soon comes to compare himself with them; and, perceiving that he surpasses them more in adroitness than they surpass him in strength, learns to be no longer afraid of them. Set a bear, or a wolf, against a robust,
30   agile, and resolute savage, as they all are, armed with stones and a good cudgel, and you will see that the danger will be at least on both sides, and that, after a few trials of this kind, wild beasts, which are not fond of attacking each other, will not be at all ready to attack man, whom they will have found to be as wild and ferocious as themselves. With regard to such animals as have really more
35   strength than man has adroitness, he is in the same situation as all weaker animals, which notwithstanding are still able to subsist; except indeed that he has the advantage that, being equally swift of foot, and finding an almost certain place of refuge in every tree, he is at liberty to take or leave it at every encounter, and thus to fight or fly, as he chooses. Add to this that it does not
40   appear that any animal naturally makes war on man, except in case of self-

defence or excessive hunger, or betrays any of those violent antipathies, which seem to indicate that one species is intended by nature for the food of another.

This is doubtless why negroes and savages are so little afraid of the wild beasts they may meet in the woods. The Caraibs of Venezuela among others live
5 in this respect in absolute security and without the smallest inconvenience. Though they are almost naked, Francis Corréal tells us, they expose themselves freely in the woods, armed only with bows and arrows; but no one has ever heard of one of them being devoured by wild beasts.

But man has other enemies more formidable, against which is is not
10 provided with such means of defence: these are the natural infirmities of infancy, old age, and illness of every kind, melancholy proofs of our weakness, of which the two first are common to all animals, and the last belongs chiefly to man in a state of society. With regard to infancy, it is observable that the mother, carrying her child always with her, can nurse it with much greater ease than the
15 females of many other animals, which are forced to be perpetually going and coming, with great fatigue, one way to find subsistence, and another to suckle or feed their young. It is true that if the woman happens to perish, the infant is in great danger of perishing with her; but this risk is common to many other species of animals, whose young take a long time before they are able to provide
20 for themselves. And if our infancy is longer than theirs, our lives are longer in proportion; so that all things are in this respect fairly equal; though there are other rules to be considered regarding the duration of the first period of life, and the number of young, which do not affect the present subject. In old age, when men are less active and perspire little, the need for food diminishes with the
25 ability to provide it. As the savage state also protects them from gout and rheumatism, and old age is, of all ills, that which human aid can least alleviate, they cease to be, without others perceiving that they are no more, and almost without perceiving it themselves.

With respect to sickness, I shall not repeat the vain and false declamations
30 which most healthy people pronounce against medicine; but I shall ask if any solid observations have been made from which it may be justly concluded that, in the countries where the art of medicine is most neglected, the mean duration of man's life is less than in those where it is most cultivated. How indeed can this be the case, if we bring on ourselves more diseases than medicine can
35 furnish remedies? The great inequality in manner of living, the extreme idleness of some, and the excessive labour of others, the easiness of exciting and gratifying our sensual appetites, the too exquisite foods of the wealthy which overheat and fill them with indigestion, and, on the other hand, the unwholesome food of the poor, often, bad as it is, insufficient for their needs,
40 which induces them, when opportunity offers, to eat voraciously and overcharge

their stomachs; all these, together with sitting up late, and excesses of every kind, immoderate transports of every passion, fatigue, mental exhaustion, the innumerable pains and anxieties inseparable from every condition of life, by which the mind of man is incessantly tormented; these are too fatal proofs that the greater part of our ills are of our own making, and that we might have avoided them nearly all by adhering to that simple, uniform and solitary manner of life which nature prescribed. If she destined man to be healthy, I venture to declare that a state of reflection is a state contrary to nature, and that a thinking man is a depraved animal. When we think of the good constitution of the savages, at least of those whom we have not ruined with our spirituous liquors, and reflect that they are troubled with hardly any disorders, save wounds and old age, we are tempted to believe that, in following the history of civil society, we shall be telling also that of human sickness. Such, at least, was the opinion of Plato, who inferred from certain remedies prescribed, or approved, by Podalirius and Machaon at the siege of Troy, that several sicknesses which these remedies gave rise to in his time, were not then known to mankind: and Celsus tells us that diet, which is now so necessary, was first invented by Hippocrates.

Being subject therefore to so few causes of sickness, man, in the state of nature, can have no need of remedies, and still less of physicians: nor is the human race in this respect worse off than other animals, and it is easy to learn from hunters whether they meet with many infirm animals in the course of the chase. It is certain they frequently meet with such as carry the marks of having been considerably wounded, with many that have had bones or even limbs broken, yet have been healed without any other surgical assistance than that of time, or any other regimen than that of their ordinary life. At the same time their cures seem not to have been less perfect, for their not having been tortured by incisions, poisoned with drugs, or wasted by fasting. In short, however useful medicine, properly administered, may be among us, it is certain that, if the savage, when he is sick and left to himself, has nothing to hope but from nature, he has, on the other hand, nothing to fear but from his disease; which renders his situation often preferable to our own.

We should beware, therefore, of confounding the savage man with the men we have daily before our eyes. Nature treats all the animals left to her care with a predilection that seems to show how jealous she is of that right. The horse, the cat, the bull, and even the ass are generally of greater stature, and always more robust, and have more vigour, strength and courage, when they run wild in the forests than when bred in the stall. By becoming domesticated, they lose half these advantages; and it seems as if all our care to feed and treat them well serves only to deprave them. It is thus with man also: as he becomes sociable and a slave, he grows weak, timid and servile; his effeminate way of life totally

enervates his strength and courage. To this it may be added that there is still a greater difference between savage and civilised man, than between wild and tame beasts: for men and brutes having been treated alike by nature, the several conveniences in which men indulge themselves still more than they do their
5 beasts, are so many additional causes of their deeper degeneracy.

It is not therefore so great a misfortune to these primitive men, nor so great an obstacle to their preservation, that they go naked, have no dwellings and lack all the superfluities which we think so necessary. If their skins are not covered with hair, they have no need of such covering in warm climates; and, in cold
10 countries, they soon learn to appropriate the skins of the beasts they have overcome. If they have but two legs to run with, they have two arms to defend themselves with, and provide for their wants. Their children are slowly and with difficulty taught to walk; but their mothers are able to carry them with ease; an advantage which other animals lack, as the mother, if pursued, is forced either to
15 abandon her young, or to regulate her pace by theirs. Unless, in short, we suppose a singular and fortuitous concurrence of circumstances of which I shall speak later, and which would be unlikely to exist, it is plain in every state of the case, that the man who first made himself clothes or a dwelling was furnishing himself with things not at all necessary; for he had till then done without them,
20 and there is no reason why he should not have been able to put up in manhood with the same kind of life as had been his in infancy.

Solitary, indolent, and perpetually accompanied by danger, the savage cannot but be fond of sleep; his sleep too must be light, like that of the animals, which think but little and may be said to slumber all the time they do not think.
25 Self-preservation being his chief and almost sole concern, he must exercise most those faculties which are most concerned with attack or defence, either for overcoming his prey, or for preventing him from becoming the prey of other animals. On the other hand, those organs which are perfected only by softness and sensuality will remain in a gross and imperfect state, incompatible with any
30 sort of delicacy; so that, his senses being divided on this head, his touch and taste will be extremely coarse, his sight, hearing and smell exceedingly fine and subtle. Such in general is the animal condition, and such, according to the narratives of travellers, is that of most savage nations. It is therefore no matter for surprise that the Hottentots of the Cape of Good Hope distinguish ships at
35 sea, with the naked eye, at as great a distance as the Dutch can do with their telescopes; or that the savages of America should trace the Spaniards, by their smell, as well as the best dogs could have done; or that these barbarous peoples feel no pain in going naked, or that they use large quantities of piemento with their food, and drink the strongest European liquors like water.

Hitherto I have considered merely the physical man; let us now take a view of him on his metaphysical and moral side.

I see nothing in any animal but an ingenious machine, to which nature hath given senses to wind itself up, and to guard itself, to a certain degree, against anything that might tend to disorder or destroy it. I perceive exactly the same things in the human machine, with this difference, that in the operations of the brute, nature is the sole agent, whereas man has some share in his own operations, in his character as a free agent. The one chooses and refuses by instinct, the other from an act of free-will: hence the brute cannot deviate from the rule prescribed to it, even when it would be advantageous for it to do so; and, on the contrary, man frequently deviates from such rules to his own prejudice. Thus a pigeon would be starved to death by the side of a dish of the choicest meats, and a cat on a heap of fruit or grain; though it is certain that either might find nourishment in the foods which it thus rejects with disdain, did it think of trying them. Hence it is that dissolute men run into excesses which bring on fevers and death; because the mind depraves the senses, and the will continues to speak when nature is silent.

Every animal has ideas, since it has senses; it even combines those ideas in a certain degree; and it is only in degree that man differs, in this respect, from the brute. Some philosophers have even maintained that there is a greater difference between one man and another than between some men and some beasts. It is not, therefore, so much the understanding that constitutes the specific difference between the man and the brute, as the human quality of free-agency. Nature lays her commands on every animal, and the brute obeys her voice. Man receives the same impulsion, but at the same time knows himself at liberty to acquiesce or resist: and it is particularly in his consciousness of this liberty that the spirituality of his soul is displayed. For physics may explain, in some measure, the mechanism of the senses and the formation of ideas; but in the power of willing or rather of choosing, and in the feeling of this power, nothing is to be found but acts which are purely spiritual and wholly inexplicable by the laws of mechanism.

However, even if the difficulties attending all these questions should still leave room for difference in this respect between men and brutes, there is another very specific quality which distinguishes them, and which will admit of no dispute. This is the faculty of self-improvement, which, by the help of circumstances, gradually develops all the rest of our faculties, and is inherent in the species as in the individual: whereas a brute is, at the end of a few months, all he will ever be during his whole life, and his species, at the end of a thousand years, exactly what it was the first year of that thousand. Why is man alone liable to grow into a dotard? Is it not because he returns, in this, to his primitive

state; and that, while the brute, which has acquired nothing and has therefore nothing to lose, still retains the force of instinct, man, who loses, by age or accident, all that his perfectibility had enabled him to gain, falls by this means lower than the brutes themselves? It would be melancholy, were we forced to
5   admit that this distinctive and almost unlimited faculty is the source of all human misfortunes; that it is this which, in time, draws man out of his original state, in which he would have spent his days insensibly in peace and innocence; that it is this faculty, which, successively producing in different ages his discoveries and his errors, his vices and his virtues, makes him at length a tyrant
10   both over himself and over nature.[1] It would be shocking to be obliged to regard as a benefactor the man who first suggested to the Oroonoko Indians the use of the boards they apply to the temples of their children, which secure to them some part at least of their imbecility and original happiness.

Savage man, left by nature solely to the direction of instinct, or rather
15   indemnified for what he may lack by faculties capable at first of supplying its place, and afterwards of raising him much above it, must accordingly begin with purely animal functions: thus seeing and feeling must be his first condition, which would be common to him and all other animals. To will, and not to will, to desire and to fear, must be the first, and almost the only operations of his soul,
20   till new circumstances occasion new developments of his faculties.

Whatever moralists may hold, the human understanding is greatly indebted to the passions, which, it is universally allowed, are also much indebted to the understanding. It is by the activity of the passions that our reason is improved; for we desire knowledge only because we wish to enjoy; and it is impossible to
25   conceive any reason why a person who has neither fears nor desires should give himself the trouble of reasoning. The passions, again, originate in our wants, and their progress depends on that of our knowledge; for we cannot desire or fear anything, except from the idea we have of it, or from the simple impulse of nature. Now savage man, being destitute of every species of intelligence, can
30   have no passions save those of the latter kind: his desires never go beyond his physical wants. The only goods he recognises in the universe are food, a female, and sleep: the only evils he fears are pain and hunger. I say pain, and not death: for no animal can know what it is to die; the knowledge of death and its terrors being one of the first acquisitions made by man in departing from an animal
35   state.

It would be easy, were it necessary, to support this opinion by facts, and to show that, in all the nations of the world, the progress of the understanding has been exactly proportionate to the wants which the peoples had received from nature, or been subjected to by circumstances, and in consequence to the
40   passions that induced them to provide for those necessities. I might instance the

arts, rising up in Egypt and expanding with the inundation of the Nile. I might follow their progress into Greece, where they took root afresh, grew up and lowered to the skies, among the rocks and sands of Attica, without being able to germinate on the fertile banks of the Eurotas: I might observe that in general, the people of the North are more industrious than those of the South, because they cannot get on so well without being so: as if nature wanted to equalise matters by giving their understandings the fertility she had refused to their soil.

But who does not see, without recurring to the uncertain testimony of history, that everything seems to remove from savage man both the temptation and the means of changing his condition? His imagination paints no pictures; his heart makes no demands on him. His few wants are so readily supplied, and he is so far from having the knowledge which is needful to make him want more, that he can have neither foresight nor curiosity. The face of nature becomes indifferent to him as it grows familiar. He sees in it always the same order, the same successions: he has not understanding enough to wonder at the greatest miracles; nor is it in his mind that we can expect to find that philosophy man needs, if he is to know how to notice for once what he sees every day. His soul, which nothing disturbs, is wholly wrapped up in the feeling of its present existence, without any idea of the future, however near at hand; while his projects, as limited as his views, hardly extend to the close of day. Such, even at present, is the extent of the native Caribbean's foresight: he will improvidently sell you his cotton-bed in the morning, and come crying in the evening to buy it again, not having foreseen he would want it again the next night.

The more we reflect on this subject, the greater appears the distance between pure sensation and the most simple knowledge: it is impossible indeed to conceive how a man, by his own powers alone, without the aid of communication and the spur of necessity, could have bridged so great a gap. How many ages may have elapsed before mankind were in a position to behold any other fire than that of the heavens. What a multiplicity of chances must have happened to teach them the commonest uses of that element! How often must they have let it out before they acquired the art of reproducing it? and how often may not such a secret have died with him who had discovered it? What shall we say of agriculture, an art which requires so much labour and foresight, which is so dependent on others that it is plain it could only be practised in a society which had at least begun, and which does not serve so much to draw the means of subsistence from the earth – for these it would produce of itself – but to compel it to produce what is most to our taste? But let us suppose that men had so multiplied that the natural produce of the earth was no longer sufficient for their support; a supposition, by the way, which would prove such a life to be very advantageous for the human race; let us suppose that, without forges or

workshops, the instruments of husbandry had dropped from the sky into the hands of savages; that they had overcome their natural aversion to continual labour; that they had learnt so much foresight for their needs; that they had divined how to cultivate the earth, to sow grain and plant trees; that they had
5   discovered the arts of grinding corn, and of setting the grape to ferment – all being things that must have been taught them by the gods, since it is not to be conceived how they could discover them for themselves – yet after all this, what man among them would be so absurd as to take the trouble of cultivating a field, which might be stripped of its crop by the first comer, man or beast, that might
10 take a liking to it; and how should each of them resolve to pass his life in wearisome labour, when, the more necessary to him the reward of his labour might be, the surer he would be of not getting it? In a word, how could such a situation induce men to cultivate the earth, till it was regularly parcelled out among them; that is to say, till the state of nature had been abolished?
15   Were we to suppose savage man as trained in the art of thinking as philosophers make him; were we, like them, to suppose him a very philosopher capable of investigating the sublimest truths, and of forming, by highly abstract chains of reasoning, maxims of reason and justice, deduced from the love of order in general, or the known will of his Creator; in a word, were we to suppose
20 him as intelligent and enlightened, as he must have been, and is in fact found to have been, dull and stupid, what advantage would accrue to the species, from all such metaphysics, which could not be communicated by one to another, but must end with him who made them? What progress could be made by mankind, while dispersed in the woods among other animals? and how far could men
25 improve or mutually enlighten one another, when, having no fixed habitation, and no need of one another's assistance, the same persons hardly met twice in their lives, and perhaps then, without knowing one another or speaking together?

      Let it be considered how many ideas we owe to the use of speech; how far grammar exercises the understanding and facilitates its operations. Let us reflect
30 on the inconceivable pains and the infinite space of time that the first invention of languages must have cost. To these reflections add what preceded, and then judge how many thousand ages must have elapsed in the successive development in the human mind of those operations of which it is capable.

      I shall here take the liberty for a moment, of considering the difficulties of
35 the origin of languages, on which subject I might content myself with a simple repetition of the Abbé Condillac's investigations, as they fully confirm my system, and perhaps even first suggested it. But it is plain, from the manner in which this philosopher solves the difficulties he himself raises, concerning the origin of arbitrary signs, that he assumes what I question, viz., that a kind of
40 society must already have existed among the first inventors of language. While I

refer, therefore, to his observations on this head, I think it right to give my own, in order to exhibit the same difficulties in a light adapted to my subject. The first which presents itself is to conceive how language can have become necessary; for as there was no communication among men and no need for any, we can 5 neither conceive the necessity of this invention, nor the possibility of it, if it was not somehow indispensable. I might affirm, with many others, that languages arose in the domestic intercourse between parents and their children. But this expedient would not obviate the difficulty, and would besides involve the blunder made by those who, in reasoning on the state of nature, always import 10 into it ideas gathered in a state of society. Thus they constantly consider families as living together under one roof, and the individuals of each as observing among themselves a union as intimate and permanent as that which exists among us, where so many common interests unite them: whereas, in this primitive state, men had neither houses, nor huts, nor any kind of property 15 whatever; every one lived where he could, seldom for more than a single night; the sexes united without design, as accident, opportunity or inclination brought them together, nor had they any great need of words to communicate their designs to each other; and they parted with the same indifference. The mother gave suck to her children at first for her own sake; and afterwards, when habit 20 had made them dear, for theirs: but as soon as they were strong enough to go in search of their own food, they forsook her of their own accord; and, as they had hardly any other method of not losing one another than that of remaining continually within sight, they soon became quite incapable of recognising one another when they happened to meet again. It is farther to be observed that the 25 child, having all his wants to explain, and of course more to say to his mother than the mother could have to say to him, must have borne the brunt of the task of invention, and the language he used would be of his own device, so that the number of languages would be equal to that of the individuals speaking them, and the variety would be increased by the vagabond and roving life they led, 30 which would not give time for any idiom to become constant. For to say that the mother dictated to her child the words he was to use in asking her for one thing or another, is an explanation of how languages already formed are taught, but by no means explains how languages were originally formed.

We will suppose, however, that this first difficulty is obviated. Let us for a 35 moment then take ourselves as being on this side of the vast space which must lie between a pure state of nature and that in which languages had become necessary, and, admitting their necessity, let us inquire how they could first be established. Here we have a new and worse difficulty to grapple with; for if men need speech to learn to think, they must have stood in much greater need of the 40 art of thinking, to be able to invent that of speaking. And though we might

48

conceive how the articulate sounds of the voice came to be taken as the conventional interpreters of our ideas, it would still remain for us to inquire what could have been the interpreters of this convention for those ideas, which, answering to no sensible objects, could not be indicated either by gesture or
5   voice; so that we can hardly form any tolerable conjectures about the origin of this art of communicating our thoughts and establishing a correspondence between minds: an art so sublime, that far distant as it is from its origin, philosophers still behold it at such an immeasurable distance from perfection, that there is none rash enough to affirm it will ever reach it, even though the
10   revolutions time necessarily produces were suspended in its favour, though prejudice should be banished from our academies or condemned to silence, and those learned societies should devote themselves uninterruptedly for whole ages to this thorny question.

    The first language of mankind, the most universal and vivid, in a word the
15   only language man needed, before he had occasion to exert his eloquence to persuade assembled multitudes, was the simple cry of nature. But as this was excited only by a sort of instinct on urgent occasions, to implore assistance in case of danger, or relief in case of suffering, it could be of little use in the ordinary course of life, in which more moderate feelings prevail. When the ideas
20   of men began to expand and multiply, and closer communication took place among them, they strove to invent more numerous signs and a more copious language. They multiplied the inflections of the voice, and added gestures, which are in their own nature more expressive, and depend less for their meaning on a prior determination. Visible and movable objects were therefore
25   expressed by gestures, and audible ones by imitative sounds: but, as hardly anything can be indicated by gestures, except objects actually present or easily described, and visible actions; as they are not universally useful – for darkness or the interposition of a material object destroys their efficacy – and as besides they rather request than secure our attention; men at length bethought
30   themselves of substituting for them the articulate sounds of the voice, which, without bearing the same relation to any particular ideas, are better calculated to express them all, as conventional signs. Such an institution could only be made by common consent, and must have been effected in a manner not very easy for men whose gross organs had not been accustomed to any such exercise. It is also
35   in itself still more difficult to conceive, since such a common agreement must have had motives, and speech seems to have been highly necessary to establish the use of it.

    It is reasonable to suppose that the words first made use of by mankind had a much more extensive signification than those used in languages already
40   formed, and that ignorant as they were of the division of discourse into its

constituent parts, they at first gave every single word the sense of a whole proposition. When they began to distinguish subject and attribute, and noun and verb, which was itself no common effort of genius, substantives were first only so many proper names; the present infinitive was the only tense of verbs; and the
5 very idea of adjectives must have been developed with great difficulty; for every adjective is an abstract idea, and abstractions are painful and unnatural operations.

Every object at first received a particular name without regard to genus or species, which these primitive originators were not in a position to distinguish;
10 every individual presented itself to their minds in isolation, as they are in the picture of nature. If one oak was called A, another was called B; for the primitive idea of two things is that they are not the same, and it often takes a long time for what they have in common to be seen: so that, the narrower the limits of their knowledge of things, the more copious their dictionary must have
15 been. The difficulty of using such a vocabulary could not be easily removed; for, to arrange beings under common and generic denominations, it became necessary to know their distinguishing properties: the need arose for observation and definition, that is to say, for natural history and metaphysics of a far more developed kind than men can at that time have possessed.

20 Add to this, that general ideas cannot be introduced into the mind without the assistance of words, nor can the understanding seize them except by means of propositions. This is one of the reasons why animals cannot form such ideas, or ever acquire that capacity for self-improvement which depends on them. When a monkey goes from one nut to another, are we to conceive that he
25 entertains any general idea of that kind of fruit, and compares its archetype with the two individual nuts? Assuredly he does not; but the sight of one of these nuts recalls to his memory the sensations which he received from the other, and his eyes, being modified after a certain manner, give information to the palate of the modification it is about to receive. Every general idea is purely intellectual; if
30 the imagination meddles with it ever so little, the idea immediately becomes particular. If you endeavour to trace in your mind the image of a tree in general, you never attain to your end. In spite of all you can do, you will have to see it as great or little, bare or leafy, light or dark, and were you capable of seeing nothing in it but what is common to all trees, it would no longer be like a tree at
35 all. Purely abstract beings are perceivable in the same manner, or are only conceivable by the help of language. The definition of a triangle alone gives you a true idea of it: the moment you imagine a triangle in your mind, it is some particular triangle and not another, and you cannot avoid giving it sensible lines and a coloured area. We must then make use of propositions and of language in
40 order to form general ideas. For no sooner does the imagination cease to operate

50

than the understanding proceeds only by the help of words. If then the first inventors of speech could give names only to ideas they already had, it follows that the first substantives could be nothing more than proper names.

But when our new grammarians, by means of which I have no conception,
5   began to extend their ideas and generalise their terms, the ignorance of the inventors must have confined this method within very narrow limits; and, as they had at first gone too far in multiplying the names of individuals, from ignorance of their genus and species, they made afterwards too few of these, from not having considered beings in all their specific differences. It would
10 indeed have needed more knowledge and experience than they could have, and more pains and inquiry than they would have bestowed, to carry these distinctions to their proper length. If, even to-day, we are continually discovering new species, which have hitherto escaped observation, let us reflect how many of them must have escaped men who judged things merely from their
15 first appearance! It is superfluous to add that the primitive classes and the most general notions must necessarily have escaped their notice also. How, for instance, could they have understood or thought of the words matter, spirit, substance, mode, figure, motion, when even our philosophers, who have so long been making use of them, have themselves the greatest difficulty in
20 understanding them; and when, the ideas attached to them being purely metaphysical, there are no models of them to be found in nature?

But I stop at this point, and ask my judges to suspend their reading a while, to consider, after the invention of physical substantives, which is the easiest part of language to invent, that there is still a great way to go, before the thoughts of
25 men will have found perfect expression and constant form, such as would answer the purposes of public speaking, and produce their effect on society. I beg of them to consider how much time must have been spent, and how much knowledge needed, to find out numbers, abstract terms, aorists and all the tenses of verbs, particles, syntax, the method of connecting propositions, the forms of
30 reasoning, and all the logic of speech. For myself, I am so aghast at the increasing difficulties which present themselves, and so well convinced of the almost demonstrable impossibility that languages should owe their original institution to merely human means, that I leave, to any one who will undertake it, the discussion of the difficult problem, which was most necessary, the
35 existence of society to the invention of language, or the invention of language to the establishment of society. But be the origin of language and society what they may, it may be at least inferred, from the little care which nature has taken to unite mankind by mutual wants, and to facilitate the use of speech, that she has contributed little to make them sociable, and has put little of her own into all
40 they have done to create such bonds of union. It is in fact impossible to conceive

why, in a state of nature, one man should stand more in need of the assistance of another, than a monkey or a wolf of the assistance of another of its kind: or, granting that he did, what motives could induce that other to assist him; or, even then, by what means they could agree about the conditions. I know it is incessantly repeated that man would in such a state have been the most miserable of creatures; and indeed, if it be true, as I think I have proved, that he must have lived many ages, before he could have either desire or an opportunity of emerging from it, this would only be an accusation against nature, and not against the being which she had thus unhappily constituted. But as I understand the word miserable, it either has no meaning at all, or else signifies only a painful privation of something, or a state of suffering either in body or soul. I should be glad to have explained to me, what kind of misery a free being, whose heart is at ease and whose body is in health, can possibly suffer. I would ask also, whether a social or a natural life is most likely to become insupportable to those who enjoy it. We see around us hardly a creature in civil society, who does not lament his existence: we even see many deprive themselves of as much of it as they can, and laws human and divine together can hardly put a stop to the disorder. I ask, if it was ever known that a savage took it into his head, when at liberty, to complain of life or to make away with himself. Let us therefore judge, with less vanity, on which side the real misery is found. On the other hand, nothing could be more unhappy than savage man, dazzled by science, tormented by his passions, and reasoning about a state different from his own. It appears that Providence most wisely determined that the faculties, which he potentially possessed, should develop themselves only as occasion offered to exercise them, in order that they might not be superfluous or perplexing to him, by appearing before their time, nor slow and useless when the need for them arose. In instinct alone, he had all he required for living in the state of nature; and with a developed understanding he has only just enough to support life in society.

It appears, at first view, that men in a state of nature, having no moral relations or determinate obligations one with another, could not be either good or bad, virtuous or vicious; unless we take these terms in a physical sense, and call, in an individual, those qualities vices which may be injurious to his preservation, and those virtues which contribute to it; in which case, he would have to be accounted most virtuous, who put least check on the pure impulses of nature. But without deviating from the ordinary sense of the words, it will be proper to suspend the judgment we might be led to form on such a state, and be on our guard against our prejudices, till we have weighed the matter in the scales of impartiality, and seen whether virtues or vices preponderate among civilised men; and whether their virtues do them more good than their vices do harm; till we have discovered, whether the progress of the sciences sufficiently

indemnifies them for the mischiefs they do one another, in proportion as they are better informed of the good they ought to do; or whether they would not be, on the whole, in a much happier condition if they had nothing to fear or to hope from any one, than as they are, subjected to universal dependence, and obliged
5   to take everything from those who engage to give them nothing in return.

     Above all, let us not conclude, with Hobbes, that because man has no idea of goodness, he must be naturally wicked; that he is vicious because he does not know virtue; that he always refuses to do his fellow-creatures services which he does not think they have a right to demand; or that by virtue of the right he truly
10 claims to everything he needs, he foolishly imagines himself the sole proprietor of the whole universe. Hobbes had seen clearly the defects of all the modern definitions of natural right: but the consequences which he deduces from his own show that he understands it in an equally false sense. In reasoning on the principles he lays down, he ought to have said that the state of nature, being that
15 in which the care for our own preservation is the least prejudicial to that of others, was consequently the best calculated to promote peace, and the most suitable for mankind. He does say the exact opposite, in consequence of having improperly admitted, as a part of savage man's care for self-preservation, the gratification of a multitude of passions which are the work of society, and have
20 made laws necessary. A bad man, he says, is a robust child. But it remains to be proved whether man in a state of nature is this robust child: and, should we grant that he is, what would he infer? Why truly, that if this man, when robust and strong, were dependent on others as he is when feeble, there is no extravagance he would not be guilty of; that he would beat his mother when she was too slow
25 in giving him her breast; that he would strangle one of his younger brothers, if he should be troublesome to him, or bite the arm of another, if he put him to any inconvenience. But that man in the state of nature is both strong and dependent involves two contrary suppositions. Man is weak when he is dependent, and is his own master before he comes to be strong. Hobbes did not reflect that the
30 same cause, which prevents a savage from making use of his reason, as our jurists hold, prevents him also from abusing his faculties, as Hobbes himself allows: so that it may be justly said that savages are not bad merely because they do not know what it is to be good: for it is neither the development of the understanding nor the restraint of law that hinders them from doing ill; but the
35 peacefulness of their passions, and their ignorance of vice: tanto plus in illis proficit vitiorum ignoratio, quam in his cognitio virtutis.[2]

     There is another principle which has escaped Hobbes; which, having been bestowed on mankind, to moderate, on certain occasions, the impetuosity of egoism, or, before its birth, the desire of self-preservation, tempers the ardour
40 with which he pursues his own welfare, by an innate repugnance at seeing a

fellow-creature suffer.[3] I think I need not fear contradiction in holding man to be possessed of the only natural virtue, which could not be denied him by the most violent detractor of human virtue. I am speaking of compassion, which is a disposition suitable to creatures so weak and subject to so many evils as we
5   certainly are: by so much the more universal and useful to mankind, as it comes before any kind of reflection; and at the same time so natural, that the very brutes themselves sometimes give evident proofs of it. Not to mention the tenderness of mothers for their offspring and the perils they encounter to save them from danger, it is well known that horses show a reluctance to trample on
10 living bodies. One animal never passes by the dead body of another of its species: there are even some which give their fellows a sort of burial; while the mournful lowings of the cattle when they enter the slaughter-house show the impressions made on them by the horrible spectacle which meets them. We find, with pleasure, the author of the Fable of the Bees obliged to own that man is a
15 compassionate and sensible being, and laying aside his cold subtlety of style, in the example he gives, to present us with the pathetic description of a man who, from a place of confinement, is compelled to behold a wild beast tear a child from the arms of its mother, grinding its tender limbs with its murderous teeth, and tearing its palpitating entrails with its claws. What horrid agitation must not
20 the eyewitness of such a scene experience, although he would not be personally concerned! What anxiety would he not suffer at not being able to give any assistance to the fainting mother and the dying infant!

Such is the pure emotion of nature, prior to all kinds of reflection! Such is the force of natural compassion, which the greatest depravity of morals has as
25 yet hardly been able to destroy! for we daily find at our theatres men affected, nay shedding tears at the sufferings of a wretch who, were he in the tyrant's place, would probably even add to the torments of his enemies; like the bloodthirsty Sulla, who was so sensitive to ills he had not caused, or that Alexander of Pheros who did not dare to go and see any tragedy acted, for fear
30 of being seen weeping with Andromache and Priam, though he could listen without emotion to the cries of all the citizens who were daily strangled at his command.

Mollissima corda Humano generi dare se natura fatetur, Quæ lacrimas dedit. Juvenal, Satires, xv. 151.[4]
35 Mandeville well knew that, in spite of all their morality, men would have never been better than monsters, had not nature bestowed on them a sense of compassion, to aid their reason: but he did not see that from this quality alone flow all those social virtues, of which he denied man the possession. But what is generosity, clemency or humanity but compassion applied to the weak, to the
40 guilty, or to mankind in general? Even benevolence and friendship are, if we

judge rightly, only the effects of compassion, constantly set upon a particular object: for how is it different to wish that another person may not suffer pain and uneasiness and to wish him happy? Were it even true that pity is no more than a feeling, which puts us in the place of the sufferer, a feeling, obscure yet lively in
5   a savage, developed yet feeble in civilised man; this truth would have no other consequence than to confirm my argument. Compassion must, in fact, be the stronger, the more the animal beholding any kind of distress identifies himself with the animal that suffers. Now, it is plain that such identification must have been much more perfect in a state of nature than it is in a state of reason. It is
10 reason that engenders self-respect, and reflection that confirms it: it is reason which turns man's mind back upon itself, and divides him from everything that could disturb or afflict him. It is philosophy that isolates him, and bids him say, at sight of the misfortunes of others: "Perish if you will, I am secure." Nothing but such general evils as threaten the whole community can disturb the tranquil
15 sleep of the philosopher, or tear him from his bed. A murder may with impunity be committed under his window; he has only to put his hands to his ears and argue a little with himself, to prevent nature, which is shocked within him, from identifying itself with the unfortunate sufferer. Uncivilised man has not this admirable talent; and for want of reason and wisdom, is always foolishly ready
20 to obey the first promptings of humanity. It is the populace that flocks together at riots and street-brawls, while the wise man prudently makes off. It is the mob and the market-women, who part the combatants, and hinder gentle-folks from cutting one another's throats.

It is then certain that compassion is a natural feeling, which, by moderating
25 the violence of love of self in each individual, contributes to the preservation of the whole species. It is this compassion that hurries us without reflection to the relief of those who are in distress: it is this which in a state of nature supplies the place of laws, morals and virtues, with the advantage that none are tempted to disobey its gentle voice: it is this which will always prevent a sturdy savage
30 from robbing a weak child or a feeble old man of the sustenance they may have with pain and difficulty acquired, if he sees a possibility of providing for himself by other means: it is this which, instead of inculcating that sublime maxim of rational justice. Do to others as you would have them do unto you, inspires all men with that other maxim of natural goodness, much less perfect indeed, but
35 perhaps more useful; Do good to yourself with as little evil as possible to others. In a word, it is rather in this natural feeling than in any subtle arguments that we must look for the cause of that repugnance, which every man would experience in doing evil, even independently of the maxims of education. Although it might belong to Socrates and other minds of the like craft to acquire virtue by reason,

the human race would long since have ceased to be, had its preservation depended only on the reasonings of the individuals composing it.

With passions so little active, and so good a curb, men, being rather wild than wicked, and more intent to guard themselves against the mischief that might be done them, than to do mischief to others, were by no means subject to very perilous dissensions. They maintained no kind of intercourse with one another, and were consequently strangers to vanity, deference, esteem and contempt; they had not the least idea of meum and tuum, and no true conception of justice; they looked upon every violence to which they were subjected, rather as an injury that might easily be repaired than as a crime that ought to be punished; and they never thought of taking revenge, unless perhaps mechanically and on the spot, as a dog will sometimes bite the stone which is thrown at him. Their quarrels therefore would seldom have very bloody consequences; for the subject of them would be merely the question of subsistence. But I am aware of one greater danger, which remains to be noticed.

Of the passions that stir the heart of man, there is one which makes the sexes necessary to each other, and is extremely ardent and impetuous; a terrible passion that braves danger, surmounts all obstacles, and in its transports seems calculated to bring destruction on the human race which it is really destined to preserve. What must become of men who are left to this brutal and boundless rage, without modesty, without shame, and daily upholding their amours at the price of their blood?

It must, in the first place, be allowed that, the more violent the passions are, the more are laws necessary to keep them under restraint. But, setting aside the inadequacy of laws to effect this purpose, which is evident from the crimes and disorders to which these passions daily give rise among us, we should do well to inquire if these evils did not spring up with the laws themselves; for in this case, even if the laws were capable of repressing such evils, it is the least that could be expected from them, that they should check a mischief which would not have arisen without them.

Let us begin by distinguishing between the physical and moral ingredients in the feeling of love. The physical part of love is that general desire which urges the sexes to union with each other. The moral part is that which determines and fixes this desire exclusively upon one particular object; or at least gives it a greater degree of energy toward the object thus preferred. It is easy to see that the moral part of love is a factitious feeling, born of social usage, and enhanced by the women with much care and cleverness, to establish their empire, and put in power the sex which ought to obey. This feeling, being founded on certain ideas of beauty and merit which a savage is not in a position to acquire, and on comparisons which he is incapable of making, must be for

56

him almost non-existent; for, as his mind cannot form abstract ideas of
proportion and regularity, so his heart is not susceptible of the feelings of love
and admiration, which are even insensibly produced by the application of these
ideas. He follows solely the character nature has implanted in him, and not tastes
5   which he could never have acquired; so that every woman equally answers his
purpose.

    Men in a state of nature being confined merely to what is physical in love,
and fortunate enough to be ignorant of those excellences, which whet the
appetite while they increase the difficulty of gratifying it, must be subject to
10   fewer and less violent fits of passion, and consequently fall into fewer and less
violent disputes. The imagination, which causes such ravages among us, never
speaks to the heart of savages, who quietly await the impulses of nature, yield to
them involuntarily, with more pleasure than ardour, and, their wants once
satisfied, lose the desire. It is therefore incontestable that love, as well as all
15   other passions, must have acquired in society that glowing impetuosity, which
makes it so often fatal to mankind. And it is the more absurd to represent
savages as continually cutting one another's throats to indulge their brutality,
because this opinion is directly contrary to experience; the Caribbeans, who
have as yet least of all deviated from the state of nature, being in fact the most
20   peaceable of people in their amours, and the least subject to jealousy, though
they live in a hot climate which seems always to inflame the passions.

    With regard to the inferences that might be drawn, in the case of several
species of animals, the males of which fill our poultry-yards with blood and
slaughter, or in spring make the forests resound with their quarrels over their
25   females; we must begin by excluding all those species, in which nature has
plainly established, in the comparative power of the sexes, relations different
from those which exist among us: thus we can base no conclusion about men on
the habits of fighting cocks. In those species where the proportion is better
observed, these battles must be entirely due to the scarcity of females in
30   comparison with males; or, what amounts to the same thing, to the intervals
during which the female constantly refuses the advances of the male: for if each
female admits the male but during two months in the year, it is the same as if the
number of females were five-sixths less. Now, neither of these two cases is
applicable to the human species, in which the number of females usually
35   exceeds that of males, and among whom it has never been observed, even
among savages, that the females have, like those of other animals, their stated
times of passion and indifference. Moreover, in several of these species, the
individuals all take fire at once, and there comes a fearful moment of universal
passion, tumult and disorder among them; a scene which is never beheld in the
40   human species, whose love is not thus seasonal. We must not then conclude

from the combats of such animals for the enjoyment of the females, that the case would be the same with mankind in a state of nature: and, even if we drew such a conclusion, we see that such contests do not exterminate other kinds of animals, and we have no reason to think they would be more fatal to ours. It is indeed clear that they would do still less mischief than is the case in a state of society; especially in those countries in which, morals being still held in some repute, the jealousy of lovers and the vengeance of husbands are the daily cause of duels, murders, and even worse crimes; where the obligation of eternal fidelity only occasions adultery, and the very laws of honour and continence necessarily increase debauchery and lead to the multiplication of abortions.

Let us conclude then that man in a state of nature, wandering up and down the forests, without industry, without speech, and without home, an equal stranger to war and to all ties, neither standing in need of his fellow-creatures nor having any desire to hurt them, and perhaps even not distinguishing them one from another; let us conclude that, being self-sufficient and subject to so few passions, he could have no feelings or knowledge but such as befitted his situation; that he felt only his actual necessities, and disregarded everything he did not think himself immediately concerned to notice, and that his understanding made no greater progress than his vanity. If by accident he made any discovery, he was the less able to communicate it to others, as he did not know even his own children. Every art would necessarily perish with its inventor, where there was no kind of education among men, and generations succeeded generations without the least advance; when, all setting out from the same point, centuries must have elapsed in the barbarism of the first ages; when the race was already old, and man remained a child.

If I have expatiated at such length on this supposed primitive state, it is because I had so many ancient errors and inveterate prejudices to eradicate, and therefore thought it incumbent on me to dig down to their very root, and show, by means of a true picture of the state of nature, how far even the natural inequalities of mankind are from having that reality and influence which modern writers suppose.

It is in fact easy to see that many of the differences which distinguish men are merely the effect of habit and the different methods of life men adopt in society. Thus a robust or delicate constitution, and the strength or weakness attaching to it, are more frequently the effects of a hardy or effeminate method of education than of the original endowment of the body. It is the same with the powers of the mind; for education not only makes a difference between such as are cultured and such as are not, but even increases the differences which exist among the former, in proportion to their respective degrees of culture: as the distance between a giant and a dwarf on the same road increases with every step

they take. If we compare the prodigious diversity, which obtains in the education and manner of life of the various orders of men in the state of society, with the uniformity and simplicity of animal and savage life, in which every one lives on the same kind of food and in exactly the same manner, and does exactly the
5   same things, it is easy to conceive how much less the difference between man and man must be in a state of nature than in a state of society, and how greatly the natural inequality of mankind must be increased by the inequalities of social institutions.

But even if nature really affected, in the distribution of her gifts, that
10 partiality which is imputed to her, what advantage would the greatest of her favourites derive from it, to the detriment of others, in a state that admits of hardly any kind of relation between them? Where there is no love, of what advantage is beauty? Of what use is wit to those who do not converse, or cunning to those who have no business with others? I hear it constantly repeated
15 that, in such a state, the strong would oppress the weak; but what is here meant by oppression? Some, it is said, would violently domineer over others, who would groan under a servile submission to their caprices. This indeed is exactly what I observe to be the case among us; but I do not see how it can be inferred of men in a state of nature, who could not easily be brought to conceive what we
20 mean by dominion and servitude. One man, it is true, might seize the fruits which another had gathered, the game he had killed, or the cave he had chosen for shelter; but how would he ever be able to exact obedience, and what ties of dependence could there be among men without possessions? If, for instance, I am driven from one tree, I can go to the next; if I am disturbed in one place,
25 what hinders me from going to another? Again, should I happen to meet with a man so much stronger than myself, and at the same time so depraved, so indolent, and so barbarous, as to compel me to provide for his sustenance while he himself remains idle; he must take care not to have his eyes off me for a single moment; he must bind me fast before he goes to sleep, or I shall certainly
30 either knock him on the head or make my escape. That is to say, he must in such a case voluntarily expose himself to much greater trouble than he seeks to avoid, or can give me. After all this, let him be off his guard ever so little; let him but turn his head aside at any sudden noise, and I shall be instantly twenty paces off, lost in the forest, and, my fetters burst asunder, he would never see me again.
35 Without my expatiating thus uselessly on these details, every one must see that as the bonds of servitude are formed merely by the mutual dependence of men on one another and the reciprocal needs that unite them, it is impossible to make any man a slave, unless he be first reduced to a situation in which he cannot do without the help of others: and, since such a situation does not exist in

a state of nature, every one is there his own master, and the law of the strongest is of no effect.

Having proved that the inequality of mankind is hardly felt, and that its influence is next to nothing in a state of nature, I must next show its origin and
5   trace its progress in the successive developments of the human mind. Having shown that human perfectibility, the social virtues, and the other faculties which natural man potentially possessed, could never develop of themselves, but must require the fortuitous concurrence of many foreign causes that might never arise, and without which he would have remained for ever in his primitive condition, I
10 must now collect and consider the different accidents which may have improved the human understanding while depraving the species, and made man wicked while making him sociable; so as to bring him and the world from that distant period to the point at which we now behold them.

I confess that, as the events I am going to describe might have happened in
15 various ways, I have nothing to determine my choice but conjectures: but such conjectures become reasons, when they are the most probable that can be drawn from the nature of things, and the only means of discovering the truth. The consequences, however, which I mean to deduce will not be barely conjectural; as, on the principles just laid down, it would be impossible to form any other
20 theory that would not furnish the same results, and from which I could not draw the same conclusions.

This will be a sufficient apology for my not dwelling on the manner in which the lapse of time compensates for the little probability in the events; on the surprising power of trivial causes, when their action is constant; on the
25 impossibility, on the one hand, of destroying certain hypotheses, though on the other we cannot give them the certainty of known matters of fact; on its being within the province of history, when two facts are given as real, and have to be connected by a series of intermediate facts, which are unknown or supposed to be so, to supply such facts as may connect them; and on its being in the province
30 of philosophy when history is silent, to determine similar facts to serve the same end; and lastly, on the influence of similarity, which, in the case of events, reduces the facts to a much smaller number of different classes than is commonly imagined. It is enough for me to offer these hints to the consideration of my judges, and to have so arranged that the general reader has no need to
35 consider them at all.

THE SECOND PART

THE first man who, having enclosed a piece of ground, bethought himself of saying This is mine, and found people simple enough to believe him, was the

real founder of civil society. From how many crimes, wars and murders, from how many horrors and misfortunes might not any one have saved mankind, by pulling up the stakes, or filling up the ditch, and crying to his fellows, "Beware of listening to this impostor; you are undone if you once forget that the fruits of
5   the earth belong to us all, and the earth itself to nobody." But there is great probability that things had then already come to such a pitch, that they could no longer continue as they were; for the idea of property depends on many prior ideas, which could only be acquired successively, and cannot have been formed all at once in the human mind. Mankind must have made very considerable
10 progress, and acquired considerable knowledge and industry which they must also have transmitted and increased from age to age, before they arrived at this last point of the state of nature. Let us then go farther back, and endeavour to unify under a single point of view that slow succession of events and discoveries in the most natural order.
15   Man's first feeling was that of his own existence, and his first care that of self-preservation. The produce of the earth furnished him with all he needed, and instinct told him how to use it. Hunger and other appetites made him at various times experience various modes of existence; and among these was one which urged him to propagate his species – a blind propensity that, having nothing to
20 do with the heart, produced a merely animal act. The want once gratified, the two sexes knew each other no more; and even the offspring was nothing to its mother, as soon as it could do without her.
        Such was the condition of infant man; the life of an animal limited at first to mere sensations, and hardly profiting by the gifts nature bestowed on him, much
25 less capable of entertaining a thought of forcing anything from her. But difficulties soon presented themselves, and it became necessary to learn how to surmount them: the height of the trees, which prevented him from gathering their fruits, the competition of other animals desirous of the same fruits, and the ferocity of those who needed them for their own preservation, all obliged him to
30 apply himself to bodily exercises. He had to be active, swift of foot, and vigorous in fight. Natural weapons, stones and sticks, were easily found: he learnt to surmount the obstacles of nature, to contend in case of necessity with other animals, and to dispute for the means of subsistence even with other men, or to indemnify himself for what he was forced to give up to a stronger.
35   In proportion as the human race grew more numerous, men's cares increased. The difference of soils, climates and seasons, must have introduced some differences into their manner of living. Barren years, long and sharp winters, scorching summers which parched the fruits of the earth, must have demanded a new industry. On the seashore and the banks of rivers, they
40 invented the hook and line, and became fishermen and eaters of fish. In the

forests they made bows and arrows, and became huntsmen and warriors. In cold countries they clothed themselves with the skins of the beasts they had slain. The lightning, a volcano, or some lucky chance acquainted them with fire, a new resource against the rigours of winter: they next learned how to preserve this element, then how to reproduce it, and finally how to prepare with it the flesh of animals which before they had eaten raw.

This repeated relevance of various beings to himself, and one to another, would naturally give rise in the human mind to the perceptions of certain relations between them. Thus the relations which we denote by the terms, great, small, strong, weak, swift, slow, fearful, bold, and the like, almost insensibly compared at need, must have at length produced in him a kind of reflection, or rather a mechanical prudence, which would indicate to him the precautions most necessary to his security.

The new intelligence which resulted from this development increased his superiority over other animals, by making him sensible of it. He would now endeavour, therefore, to ensnare them, would play them a thousand tricks, and though many of them might surpass him in swiftness or in strength, would in time become the master of some and the scourge of others. Thus, the first time he looked into himself, he felt the first emotion of pride; and, at a time when he scarce knew how to distinguish the different orders of beings, by looking upon his species as of the highest order, he prepared the way for assuming pre-eminence as an individual.

Other men, it is true, were not then to him what they now are to us, and he had no greater intercourse with them than with other animals; yet they were not neglected in his observations. The conformities, which he would in time discover between them, and between himself and his female, led him to judge of others which were not then perceptible; and finding that they all behaved as he himself would have done in like circumstances, he naturally inferred that their manner of thinking and acting was altogether in conformity with his own. This important truth, once deeply impressed on his mind, must have induced him, from an intuitive feeling more certain and much more rapid than any kind of reasoning, to pursue the rules of conduct, which he had best observe towards them, for his own security and advantage.

Taught by experience that the love of well-being is the sole motive of human actions, he found himself in a position to distinguish the few cases, in which mutual interest might justify him in relying upon the assistance of his fellows; and also the still fewer cases in which a conflict of interests might give cause to suspect them. In the former case, he joined in the same herd with them, or at most in some kind of loose association, that laid no restraint on its members, and lasted no longer than the transitory occasion that formed it. In the latter case, every one sought his own private advantage, either by open force, if he thought himself strong enough, or by address and cunning, if he felt himself the weaker.

In this manner, men may have insensibly acquired some gross ideas of
5   mutual undertakings, and of the advantages of fulfilling them: that is, just so far as their present and apparent interest was concerned: for they were perfect strangers to foresight, and were so far from troubling themselves about the distant future, that they hardly thought of the morrow. If a deer was to be taken, every one saw that, in order to succeed, he must abide faithfully by his post: but
10   if a hare happened to come within the reach of any one of them, it is not to be doubted that he pursued it without scruple, and, having seized his prey, cared very little, if by so doing he caused his companions to miss theirs.

It is easy to understand that such intercourse would not require a language much more refined than that of rooks or monkeys, who associate together for
15   much the same purpose. Inarticulate cries, plenty of gestures and some imitative sounds, must have been for a long time the universal language; and by the addition, in every country, of some conventional articulate sounds (of which, as I have already intimated, the first institution is not too easy to explain) particular languages were produced; but these were rude and imperfect, and nearly such as
20   are now to be found among some savage nations.

Hurried on by the rapidity of time, by the abundance of things I have to say, and by the almost insensible progress of things in their beginnings, I pass over in an instant a multitude of ages; for the slower the events were in their succession, the more rapidly may they be described.

25   These first advances enabled men to make others with greater rapidity. In proportion as they grew enlightened, they grew industrious. They ceased to fall asleep under the first tree, or in the first cave that afforded them shelter; they invented several kinds of implements of hard and sharp stones, which they used to dig up the earth, and to cut wood; they then made huts out of branches, and
30   afterwards learnt to plaster them over with mud and clay. This was the epoch of a first revolution, which established and distinguished families, and introduced a kind of property, in itself the source of a thousand quarrels and conflicts. As, however, the strongest were probably the first to build themselves huts which they felt themselves able to defend, it may be concluded that the weak found it
35   much easier and safer to imitate, than to attempt to dislodge them: and of those who were once provided with huts, none could have any inducement to appropriate that of his neighbour; not indeed so much because it did not belong to him, as because it could be of no use, and he could not make himself master of it without exposing himself to a desperate battle with the family which
40   occupied it.

The first expansions of the human heart were the effects of a novel situation, which united husbands and wives, fathers and children, under one roof. The habit of living together soon gave rise to the finest feelings known to humanity, conjugal love and paternal affection. Every family became a little
5 society, the more united because liberty and reciprocal attachment were the only bonds of its union. The sexes, whose manner of life had been hitherto the same, began now to adopt different ways of living. The women became more sedentary, and accustomed themselves to mind the hut and their children, while the men went abroad in search of their common subsistence. From living a softer
10 life, both sexes also began to lose something of their strength and ferocity: but, if individuals became to some extent less able to encounter wild beasts separately, they found it, on the other hand, easier to assemble and resist in common.

    The simplicity and solitude of man's life in this new condition, the paucity
15 of his wants, and the implements he had invented to satisfy them, left him a great deal of leisure, which he employed to furnish himself with many conveniences unknown to his fathers: and this was the first yoke he inadvertently imposed on himself, and the first source of the evils he prepared for his descendants. For, besides continuing thus to enervate both body and
20 mind, these conveniences lost with use almost all their power to please, and even degenerated into real needs, till the want of them became far more disagreeable than the possession of them had been pleasant. Men would have been unhappy at the loss of them, though the possession did not make them happy.

25   We can here see a little better how the use of speech became established, and insensibly improved in each family, and we may form a conjecture also concerning the manner in which various causes may have extended and accelerated the progress of language, by making it more and more necessary. Floods or earthquakes surrounded inhabited districts with precipices or waters:
30 revolutions of the globe tore off portions from the continent, and made them islands. It is readily seen that among men thus collected and compelled to live together, a common idiom must have arisen much more easily than among those who still wandered through the forests of the continent. Thus it is very possible that after their first essays in navigation the islanders brought over the use of
35 speech to the continent: and it is at least very probable that communities and languages were first established in islands, and even came to perfection there before they were known on the mainland.

    Everything now begins to change its aspect. Men, who have up to now been roving in the woods, by taking to a more settled manner of life, come gradually
40 together, form separate bodies, and at length in every country arises a distinct

nation, united in character and manners, not by regulations or laws, but by uniformity of life and food, and the common influence of climate. Permanent neighbourhood could not fail to produce, in time, some connection between different families. Among young people of opposite sexes, living in
5   neighbouring huts, the transient commerce required by nature soon led, through mutual intercourse, to another kind not less agreeable, and more permanent. Men began now to take the difference between objects into account, and to make comparisons; they acquired imperceptibly the ideas of beauty and merit, which soon gave rise to feelings of preference. In consequence of seeing each other
10   often, they could not do without seeing each other constantly. A tender and pleasant feeling insinuated itself into their souls, and the least opposition turned it into an impetuous fury: with love arose jealousy; discord triumphed, and human blood was sacrificed to the gentlest of all passions.

As ideas and feelings succeeded one another, and heart and head were
15   brought into play, men continued to lay aside their original wildness; their private connections became every day more intimate as their limits extended. They accustomed themselves to assemble before their huts round a large tree; singing and dancing, the true offspring of love and leisure, became the amusement, or rather the occupation, of men and women thus assembled
20   together with nothing else to do. Each one began to consider the rest, and to wish to be considered in turn; and thus a value came to be attached to public esteem. Whoever sang or danced best, whoever was the handsomest, the strongest, the most dexterous, or the most eloquent, came to be of most consideration; and this was the first step towards inequality, and at the same
25   time towards vice. From these first distinctions arose on the one side vanity and contempt and on the other shame and envy: and the fermentation caused by these new leavens ended by producing combinations fatal to innocence and happiness.

As soon as men began to value one another, and the idea of consideration
30   had got a footing in the mind, every one put in his claim to it, and it became impossible to refuse it to any with impunity. Hence arose the first obligations of civility even among savages; and every intended injury became an affront; because, besides the hurt which might result from it, the party injured was certain to find in it a contempt for his person, which was often more
35   insupportable than the hurt itself.

Thus, as every man punished the contempt shown him by others, in proportion to his opinion of himself, revenge became terrible, and men bloody and cruel. This is precisely the state reached by most of the savage nations known to us: and it is for want of having made a proper distinction in our ideas,
40   and see how very far they already are from the state of nature, that so many

writers have hastily concluded that man is naturally cruel, and requires civil institutions to make him more mild; whereas nothing is more gentle than man in his primitive state, as he is placed by nature at an equal distance from the stupidity of brutes, and the fatal ingenuity of civilised man. Equally confined by

5   instinct and reason to the sole care of guarding himself against the mischiefs which threaten him, he is restrained by natural compassion from doing any injury to others, and is not led to do such a thing even in return for injuries received. For, according to the axiom of the wise Locke, There can be no injury, where there is no property.

10   But it must be remarked that the society thus formed, and the relations thus established among men, required of them qualities different from those which they possessed from their primitive constitution. Morality began to appear in human actions, and every one, before the institution of law, was the only judge and avenger of the injuries done him, so that the goodness which was suitable in

15   the pure state of nature was no longer proper in the new-born state of society. Punishments had to be made more severe, as opportunities of offending became more frequent, and the dread of vengeance had to take the place of the rigour of the law. Thus, though men had become less patient, and their natural compassion had already suffered some diminution, this period of expansion of

20   the human faculties, keeping a just mean between the indolence of the primitive state and the petulant activity of our egoism, must have been the happiest and most stable of epochs. The more we reflect on it, the more we shall find that this state was the least subject to revolutions, and altogether the very best man could experience; so that he can have departed from it only through some fatal

25   accident, which, for the public good, should never have happened. The example of savages, most of whom have been found in this state, seems to prove that men were meant to remain in it, that it is the real youth of the world, and that all subsequent advances have been apparently so many steps towards the perfection of the individual, but in reality towards the decrepitude of the species.

30   So long as men remained content with their rustic huts, so long as they were satisfied with clothes made of the skins of animals and sewn together with thorns and fish-bones, adorned themselves only with feathers and shells, and continued to paint their bodies different colours, to improve and beautify their bows and arrows and to make with sharp-edged stones fishing boats or clumsy

35   musical instruments; in a word, so long as they undertook only what a single person could accomplish, and confined themselves to such arts as did not require the joint labour of several hands, they lived free, healthy, honest and happy lives, so long as their nature allowed, and as they continued to enjoy the pleasures of mutual and independent intercourse. But from the moment one man

40   began to stand in need of the help of another; from the moment it appeared

advantageous to any one man to have enough provisions for two, equality disappeared, property was introduced, work became indispensable, and vast forests became smiling fields, which man had to water with the sweat of his brow, and where slavery and misery were soon seen to germinate and grow up
5   with the crops.

      Metallurgy and agriculture were the two arts which produced this great revolution. The poets tell us it was gold and silver, but, for the philosophers, it was iron and corn, which first civilised men, and ruined humanity. Thus both were unknown to the savages of America, who for that reason are still savage:
10   the other nations also seem to have continued in a state of barbarism while they practised only one of these arts. One of the best reasons, perhaps, why Europe has been, if not longer, at least more constantly and highly civilised than the rest of the world, is that it is at once the most abundant in iron and the most fertile in corn.

15   It is difficult to conjecture how men first came to know and use iron; for it is impossible to suppose they would of themselves think of digging the ore out of the mine, and preparing it for smelting, before they knew what would be the result. On the other hand, we have the less reason to suppose this discovery the effect of any accidental fire, as mines are only formed in barren places, bare of
20   trees and plants; so that it looks as if nature had taken pains to keep that fatal secret from us. There remains, therefore, only the extraordinary accident of some volcano which, by ejecting metallic substances already in fusion, suggested to the spectators the idea of imitating the natural operation. And we must further conceive them as possessed of uncommon courage and foresight, to
25   undertake so laborious a work, with so distant a prospect of drawing advantage from it; yet these qualities are united only in minds more advanced than we can suppose those of these first discoverers to have been.

      With regard to agriculture, the principles of it were known long before they were put in practice; and it is indeed hardly possible that men, constantly
30   employed in drawing their subsistence from plants and trees, should not readily acquire a knowledge of the means made use of by nature for the propagation of vegetables. It was in all probability very long, however, before their industry took that turn, either because trees, which together with hunting and fishing afforded them food, did not require their attention; or because they were
35   ignorant of the use of corn, or without instruments to cultivate it; or because they lacked foresight to future needs; or lastly, because they were without means of preventing others from robbing them of the fruit of their labour.

      When they grew more industrious, it is natural to believe that they began, with the help of sharp stones and pointed sticks, to cultivate a few vegetables or
40   roots around their huts; though it was long before they knew how to prepare

corn, or were provided with the implements necessary for raising it in any large quantity; not to mention how essential it is, for husbandry, to consent to immediate loss, in order to reap a future gain – a precaution very foreign to the turn of a savage's mind; for, as I have said, he hardly foresees in the morning
5   what he will need at night.

     The invention of the other arts must therefore have been necessary to compel mankind to apply themselves to agriculture. No sooner were artificers wanted to smelt and forge iron, than others were required to maintain them; the more hands that were employed in manufactures, the fewer were left to provide
10 for the common subsistence, though the number of mouths to be furnished with food remained the same: and as some required commodities in exchange for their iron, the rest at length discovered the method of making iron serve for the multiplication of commodities. By this means the arts of husbandry and agriculture were established on the one hand, and the art of working metals and
15 multiplying their uses on the other.

     The cultivation of the earth necessarily brought about its distribution; and property, once recognised, gave rise to the first rules of justice; for, to secure each man his own, it had to be possible for each to have something. Besides, as men began to look forward to the future, and all had something to lose, every
20 one had reason to apprehend that reprisals would follow any injury he might do to another. This origin is so much the more natural, as it is impossible to conceive how property can come from anything but manual labour: for what else can a man add to things which he does not originally create, so as to make them his own property? It is the husbandman's labour alone that, giving him a title to
25 the produce of the ground he has tilled, gives him a claim also to the land itself, at least till harvest, and so, from year to year, a constant possession which is easily transformed into property. When the ancients, says Grotius, gave to Ceres the title of Legislatrix, and to a festival celebrated in her honour the name of Thesmophoria, they meant by that that the distribution of lands had produced a
30 new kind of right: that is to say, the right of property, which is different from the right deducible from the law of nature.

     In this state of affairs, equality might have been sustained, had the talents of individuals been equal, and had, for example, the use of iron and the consumption of commodities always exactly balanced each other; but, as there
35 was nothing to preserve this balance, it was soon disturbed; the strongest did most work; the most skilful turned his labour to best account; the most ingenious devised methods of diminishing his labour: the husbandman wanted more iron, or the smith more corn, and, while both laboured equally, the one gained a great deal by his work, while the other could hardly support himself. Thus natural
40 inequality unfolds itself insensibly with that of combination, and the difference

between men, developed by their different circumstances, becomes more sensible and permanent in its effects, and begins to have an influence, in the same proportion, over the lot of individuals.

Matters once at this pitch, it is easy to imagine the rest. I shall not detain the
5   reader with a description of the successive invention of other arts, the development of language, the trial and utilisation of talents, the inequality of fortunes, the use and abuse of riches, and all the details connected with them which the reader can easily supply for himself. I shall confine myself to a glance at mankind in this new situation.

10 Behold then all human faculties developed, memory and imagination in full play, egoism interested, reason active, and the mind almost at the highest point of its perfection. Behold all the natural qualities in action, the rank and condition of every man assigned him; not merely his share of property and his power to serve or injure others, but also his wit, beauty, strength or skill, merit or talents:
15 and these being the only qualities capable of commanding respect, it soon became necessary to possess or to affect them.

It now became the interest of men to appear what they really were not. To be and to seem became two totally different things; and from this distinction sprang insolent pomp and cheating trickery, with all the numerous vices that go
20 in their train. On the other hand, free and independent as men were before, they were now, in consequence of a multiplicity of new wants, brought into subjection, as it were, to all nature, and particularly to one another; and each became in some degree a slave even in becoming the master of other men: if rich, they stood in need of the services of others; if poor, of their assistance; and
25 even a middle condition did not enable them to do without one another. Man must now, therefore, have been perpetually employed in getting others to interest themselves in his lot, and in making them, apparently at least, if not really, find their advantage in promoting his own. Thus he must have been sly and artful in his behaviour to some, and imperious and cruel to others; being
30 under a kind of necessity to ill-use all the persons of whom he stood in need, when he could not frighten them into compliance, and did not judge it his interest to be useful to them. Insatiable ambition, the thirst of raising their respective fortunes, not so much from real want as from the desire to surpass others, inspired all men with a vile propensity to injure one another, and with a
35 secret jealousy, which is the more dangerous, as it puts on the mask of benevolence, to carry its point with greater security. In a word, there arose rivalry and competition on the one hand, and conflicting interests on the other, together with a secret desire on both of profiting at the expense of others. All these evils were the first effects of property, and the inseparable attendants of
40 growing inequality.

Before the invention of signs to represent riches, wealth could hardly consist in anything but lands and cattle, the only real possessions men can have. But, when inheritances so increased in number and extent as to occupy the whole of the land, and to border on one another, one man could aggrandise
5   himself only at the expense of another; at the same time the supernumeraries, who had been too weak or too indolent to make such acquisitions, and had grown poor without sustaining any loss, because, while they saw everything change around them, they remained still the same, were obliged to receive their subsistence, or steal it, from the rich; and this soon bred, according to their
10   different characters, dominion and slavery, or violence and rapine. The wealthy, on their part, had no sooner begun to taste the pleasure of command, than they disdained all others, and, using their old slaves to acquire new, thought of nothing but subduing and enslaving their neighbours; like ravenous wolves, which, having once tasted human flesh, despise every other food and thenceforth
15   seek only men to devour.

Thus, as the most powerful or the most miserable considered their might or misery as a kind of right to the possessions of others, equivalent, in their opinion, to that of property, the destruction of equality was attended by the most terrible disorders. Usurpations by the rich, robbery by the poor, and the
20   unbridled passions of both, suppressed the cries of natural compassion and the still feeble voice of justice, and filled men with avarice, ambition and vice. Between the title of the strongest and that of the first occupier, there arose perpetual conflicts, which never ended but in battles and bloodshed. The new-born state of society thus gave rise to a horrible state of war; men thus harassed
25   and depraved were no longer capable of retracing their steps or renouncing the fatal acquisitions they had made, but, labouring by the abuse of the faculties which do them honour, merely to their own confusion, brought themselves to the brink of ruin.

Attonitus novitate mali, divesque miserque,
30   Effugere optat opes; et quæ modo voverat odit.[5]

It is impossible that men should not at length have reflected on so wretched a situation, and on the calamities that overwhelmed them. The rich, in particular, must have felt how much they suffered by a constant state of war, of which they bore all the expense; and in which, though all risked their lives, they alone
35   risked their property. Besides, however speciously they might disguise their usurpations, they knew that they were founded on precarious and false titles; so that, if others took from them by force what they themselves had gained by force, they would have no reason to complain. Even those who had been enriched by their own industry, could hardly base their proprietorship on better
40   claims. It was in vain to repeat, "I built this well; I gained this spot by my

70

industry." Who gave you your standing, it might be answered, and what right have you to demand payment of us for doing what we never asked you to do? Do you not know that numbers of your fellow-creatures are starving, for want of what you have too much of? You ought to have had the express and universal
5 consent of mankind, before appropriating more of the common subsistence than you needed for your own maintenance. Destitute of valid reasons to justify and sufficient strength to defend himself, able to crush individuals with ease, but easily crushed himself by a troop of bandits, one against all, and incapable, on account of mutual jealousy, of joining with his equals against numerous enemies
10 united by the common hope of plunder, the rich man, thus urged by necessity, conceived at length the profoundest plan that ever entered the mind of man: this was to employ in his favour the forces of those who attacked him, to make allies of his adversaries, to inspire them with different maxims, and to give them other institutions as favourable to himself as the law of nature was unfavourable.
15 With this view, after having represented to his neighbours the horror of a situation which armed every man against the rest, and made their possessions as burdensome to them as their wants, and in which no safety could be expected either in riches or in poverty, he readily devised plausible arguments to make them close with his design. "Let us join," said he, "to guard the weak from
20 oppression, to restrain the ambitious, and secure to every man the possession of what belongs to him: let us institute rules of justice and peace, to which all without exception may be obliged to conform; rules that may in some measure make amends for the caprices of fortune, by subjecting equally the powerful and the weak to the observance of reciprocal obligations. Let us, in a word, instead
25 of turning our forces against ourselves, collect them in a supreme power which may govern us by wise laws, protect and defend all the members of the association, repulse their common enemies, and maintain eternal harmony among us."
Far fewer words to this purpose would have been enough to impose on men
30 so barbarous and easily seduced; especially as they had too many disputes among themselves to do without arbitrators, and too much ambition and avarice to go long without masters. All ran headlong to their chains, in hopes of securing their liberty; for they had just wit enough to perceive the advantages of political institutions, without experience enough to enable them to foresee the dangers.
35 The most capable of foreseeing the dangers were the very persons who expected to benefit by them; and even the most prudent judged it not inexpedient to sacrifice one part of their freedom to ensure the rest; as a wounded man has his arm cut off to save the rest of his body.
Such was, or may well have been, the origin of society and law, which
40 bound new fetters on the poor, and gave new powers to the rich; which

irretrievably destroyed natural liberty, eternally fixed the law of property and inequality, converted clever usurpation into unalterable right, and, for the advantage of a few ambitious individuals, subjected all mankind to perpetual labour, slavery and wretchedness. It is easy to see how the establishment of one
5   community made that of all the rest necessary, and how, in order to make head against united forces, the rest of mankind had to unite in turn. Societies soon multiplied and spread over the face of the earth, till hardly a corner of the world was left in which a man could escape the yoke, and withdraw his head from beneath the sword which he saw perpetually hanging over him by a thread. Civil
10 right having thus become the common rule among the members of each community, the law of nature maintained its place only between different communities, where, under the name of the right of nations, it was qualified by certain tacit conventions, in order to make commerce practicable, and serve as a substitute for natural compassion, which lost, when applied to societies, almost
15 all the influence it had over individuals, and survived no longer except in some great cosmopolitan spirits, who, breaking down the imaginary barriers that separate different peoples, follow the example of our Sovereign Creator, and include the whole human race in their benevolence.

But bodies politic, remaining thus in a state of nature among themselves,
20 presently experienced the inconveniences which had obliged individuals to forsake it; for this state became still more fatal to these great bodies than it had been to the individuals of whom they were composed. Hence arose national wars, battles, murders, and reprisals, which shock nature and outrage reason; together with all those horrible prejudices which class among the virtues the
25 honour of shedding human blood. The most distinguished men hence learned to consider cutting each other's throats a duty; at length men massacred their fellow-creatures by thousands without so much as knowing why, and committed more murders in a single day's fighting, and more violent outrages in the sack of a single town, than were committed in the state of nature during whole ages over
30 the whole earth. Such were the first effects which we can see to have followed the division of mankind into different communities. But let us return to their institutions.

I know that some writers have given other explanations of the origin of political societies, such as the conquest of the powerful, or the association of the
35 weak. It is, indeed, indifferent to my argument which of these causes we choose. That which I have just laid down, however, appears to me the most natural for the following reasons. First: because, in the first case, the right of conquest, being no right in itself, could not serve as a foundation on which to build any other; the victor and the vanquished people still remained with respect to each
40 other in the state of war, unless the vanquished, restored to the full possession of

their liberty, voluntarily made choice of the victor for their chief. For till then, whatever capitulation may have been made being founded on violence, and therefore ipso facto void, there could not have been on this hypothesis either a real society or body politic, or any law other than that of the strongest. Secondly:
5   because the words strong and weak are, in the second case, ambiguous; for during the interval between the establishment of a right of property, or prior occupancy, and that of political government, the meaning of these words is better expressed by the terms rich and poor: because, in fact, before the institution of laws, men had no other way of reducing their equals to submission,
10   than by attacking their goods, or making some of their own over to them. Thirdly: because, as the poor had nothing but their freedom to lose, it would have been in the highest degree absurd for them to resign voluntarily the only good they still enjoyed, without getting anything in exchange: whereas the rich having feelings, if I may so express myself, in every part of their possessions, it
15   was much easier to harm them, and therefore more necessary for them to take precautions against it; and, in short, because it is more reasonable to suppose a thing to have been invented by those to whom it would be of service, than by those whom it must have harmed.
      Government had, in its infancy, no regular and constant form. The want of
20   experience and philosophy prevented men from seeing any but present inconveniences, and they thought of providing against others only as they presented themselves. In spite of the endeavours of the wisest legislators, the political state remained imperfect, because it was little more than the work of chance; and, as it had begun ill, though time revealed its defects and suggested
25   remedies, the original faults were never repaired. It was continually being patched up, when the first task should have been to get the site cleared and all the old materials removed, as was done by Lycurgus at Sparta, if a stable and lasting edifice was to be erected. Society consisted at first merely of a few general conventions, which every member bound himself to observe; and for the
30   performance of covenants the whole body went security to each individual. Experience only could show the weakness of such a constitution, and how easily it might be infringed with impunity, from the difficulty of convicting men of faults, where the public alone was to be witness and judge: the laws could not but be eluded in many ways; disorders and inconveniences could not but
35   multiply continually, till it became necessary to commit the dangerous trust of public authority to private persons, and the care of enforcing obedience to the deliberations of the people to the magistrate. For to say that chiefs were chosen before the confederacy was formed, and that the administrators of the laws were there before the laws themselves, is too absurd a supposition to consider
40   seriously.

It would be as unreasonable to suppose that men at first threw themselves irretrievably and unconditionally into the arms of an absolute master, and that the first expedient which proud and unsubdued men hit upon for their common security was to run headlong into slavery. For what reason, in fact, did they take
5   to themselves superiors, if it was not in order that they might be defended from oppression, and have protection for their lives, liberties and properties, which are, so to speak, the constituent elements of their being? Now, in the relations between man and man, the worst that can happen is for one to find himself at the mercy of another, and it would have been inconsistent with common-sense to
10   begin by bestowing on a chief the only things they wanted his help to preserve. What equivalent could he offer them for so great a right? And if he had presumed to exact it under pretext of defending them, would he not have received the answer recorded in the fable: "What more can the enemy do to us?" It is therefore beyond dispute, and indeed the fundamental maxim of all political
15   right, that people have set up chiefs to protect their liberty, and not to enslave them. If we have a prince, said Pliny to Trajan, it is to save ourselves from having a master.

      Politicians indulge in the same sophistry about the love of liberty as philosophers about the state of nature. They judge, by what they see, of very
20   different things, which they have not seen; and attribute to man a natural propensity to servitude, because the slaves within their observation are seen to bear the yoke with patience; they fail to reflect that it is with liberty as with innocence and virtue; the value is known only to those who possess them, and the taste for them is forfeited when they are forfeited themselves. "I know the
25   charms of your country," said Brasidas to a satrap, who was comparing the life at Sparta with that at Persepolis, "but you cannot know the pleasures of mine."

      An unbroken horse erects his mane, paws the ground and starts back impetuously at the sight of the bridle; while one which is properly trained suffers patiently even whip and spur: so savage man will not bend his neck to
30   the yoke to which civilised man submits without a murmur, but prefers the most turbulent state of liberty to the most peaceful slavery. We cannot therefore, from the servility of nations already enslaved, judge of the natural disposition of mankind for or against slavery; we should go by the prodigious efforts of every free people to save itself from oppression. I know that the former are for ever
35   holding forth in praise of the tranquillity they enjoy in their chains, and that they call a state of wretched servitude a state of peace: miserrimam servitutem pacem appellant.[6] But when I observe the latter sacrificing pleasure, peace, wealth, power and life itself to the preservation of that one treasure, which is so disdained by those who have lost it; when I see free-born animals dash their
40   brains out against the bars of their cage, from an innate impatience of captivity;

when I behold numbers of naked savages, that despise European pleasures, braving hunger, fire, the sword and death, to preserve nothing but their independence, I feel that it is not for slaves to argue about liberty.

5   With regard to paternal authority, from which some writers have derived absolute government and all society, it is enough, without going back to the contrary arguments of Locke and Sidney, to remark that nothing on earth can be further from the ferocious spirit of despotism than the mildness of that authority which looks more to the advantage of him who obeys than to that of him who commands; that, by the law of nature, the father is the child's master no longer

10   than his help is necessary; that from that time they are both equal, the son being perfectly independent of the father, and owing him only respect and not obedience. For gratitude is a duty which ought to be paid, but not a right to be exacted: instead of saying that civil society is derived from paternal authority, we ought to say rather that the latter derives its principal force from the former.

15   No individual was ever acknowledged as the father of many, till his sons and daughters remained settled around him. The goods of the father, of which he is really the master, are the ties which keep his children in dependence, and he may bestow on them, if he pleases, no share of his property, unless they merit it by constant deference to his will. But the subjects of an arbitrary despot are so far

20   from having the like favour to expect from their chief, that they themselves and everything they possess are his property, or at least are considered by him as such; so that they are forced to receive, as a favour, the little of their own he is pleased to leave them. When he despoils them, he does but justice, and mercy in that he permits them to live.

25   By proceeding thus to test fact by right, we should discover as little reason as truth in the voluntary establishment of tyranny. It would also be no easy matter to prove the validity of a contract binding on only one of the parties, where all the risk is on one side, and none on the other; so that no one could suffer but he who bound himself. This hateful system is indeed, even in modern

30   times, very far from being that of wise and good monarchs, and especially of the kings of France; as may be seen from several passages in their edicts; particularly from the following passage in a celebrated edict published in 1667 in the name and by order of Louis XIV.

    "Let it not, therefore, be said that the Sovereign is not subject to the laws of

35   his State; since the contrary is a true proposition of the right of nations, which flattery has sometimes attacked but good princes have always defended as the tutelary divinity of their dominions. How much more legitimate is it to say with the wise Plato, that the perfect felicity of a kingdom consists in the obedience of subjects to their prince, and of the prince to the laws, and in the laws being just

40   and constantly directed to the public good!"[7]

I shall not stay here to inquire whether, as liberty is the noblest faculty of man, it is not degrading our very nature, reducing ourselves to the level of the brutes, which are mere slaves of instinct, and even an affront to the Author of our being, to renounce without reserve the most precious of all His gifts, and to bow to the necessity of committing all the crimes He has forbidden, merely to gratify a mad or a cruel master; or if this sublime craftsman ought not to be less angered at seeing His workmanship entirely destroyed than thus dishonoured. I will waive (if my opponents please) the authority of Barbeyrac, who, following Locke, roundly declares that no man can so far sell his liberty as to submit to an arbitrary power which may use him as it likes. For, he adds, this would be to sell his own life, of which he is not master. I shall ask only what right those who were not afraid thus to debase themselves could have to subject their posterity to the same ignominy, and to renounce for them those blessings which they do not owe to the liberality of their progenitors, and without which life itself must be a burden to all who are worthy of it.

Puffendorf says that we may divest ourselves of our liberty in favour of other men, just as we transfer our property from one to another by contracts and agreements. But this seems a very weak argument. For in the first place, the property I alienate becomes quite foreign to me, nor can I suffer from the abuse of it; but it very nearly concerns me that my liberty should not be abused, and I cannot without incurring the guilt of the crimes I may be compelled to commit, expose myself to become an instrument of crime. Besides, the right of property being only a convention of human institution, men may dispose of what they possess as they please: but this is not the case with the essential gifts of nature, such as life and liberty, which every man is permitted to enjoy, and of which it is at least doubtful whether any have a right to divest themselves. By giving up the one, we degrade our being; by giving up the other, we do our best to annul it; and, as no temporal good can indemnify us for the loss of either, it would be an offence against both reason and nature to renounce them at any price whatsoever. But, even if we could transfer our liberty, as we do our property, there would be a great difference with regard to the children, who enjoy the father's substance only by the transmission of his right; whereas, liberty being a gift which they hold from nature as being men, their parents have no right whatever to deprive them of it. As then, to establish slavery, it was necessary to do violence to nature, so, in order to perpetuate such a right, nature would have to be changed. Jurists, who have gravely determined that the child of a slave comes into the world a slave, have decided, in other words, that a man shall come into the world not a man.

I regard it then as certain, that government did not begin with arbitrary power, but that this is the depravation, the extreme term, of government, and brings it back, finally, to just the law of the strongest, which it was originally designed to remedy. Supposing, however, it had begun in this manner, such power, being in itself illegitimate, could not have served as a basis for the laws of society, nor, consequently, for the inequality they instituted.

5   Without entering at present upon the investigations which still remain to be made into the nature of the fundamental compact underlying all government, I content myself with adopting the common opinion concerning it, and regard the establishment of the political body as a real contract between the people and the chiefs chosen by them: a contract by which both parties bind themselves to

10 observe the laws therein expressed, which form the ties of their union. The people having in respect of their social relations concentrated all their wills in one, the several articles, concerning which this will is explained, become so many fundamental laws, obligatory on all the members of the State without exception, and one of these articles regulates the choice and power of the

15 magistrates appointed to watch over the execution of the rest. This power extends to everything which may maintain the constitution, without going so far as to alter it. It is accompanied by honours, in order to bring the laws and their administrators into respect. The ministers are also distinguished by personal prerogatives, in order to recompense them for the cares and labour which good

20 administration involves. The magistrate, on his side, binds himself to use the power he is entrusted with only in conformity with the intention of his constituents, to maintain them all in the peaceable possession of what belongs to them, and to prefer on every occasion the public interest to his own.

Before experience had shown, or knowledge of the human heart enabled

25 men to foresee, the unavoidable abuses of such a constitution, it must have appeared so much the more excellent, as those who were charged with the care of its preservation had themselves most interest in it; for magistracy and the rights attaching to it being based solely on the fundamental laws, the magistrates would cease to be legitimate as soon as these ceased to exist; the people would

30 no longer owe them obedience; and as not the magistrates, but the laws, are essential to the being of a State, the members of it would regain the right to their natural liberty.

If we reflect with ever so little attention on this subject, we shall find new arguments to confirm this truth, and be convinced from the very nature of the

35 contract that it cannot be irrevocable: for, if there were no superior power capable of ensuring the fidelity of the contracting parties, or compelling them to perform their reciprocal engagements, the parties would be sole judges in their own cause, and each would always have a right to renounce the contract, as soon as he found that the other had violated its terms, or that they no longer suited his

40 convenience. It is upon this principle that the right of abdication may possibly be

founded. Now, if, as here, we consider only what is human in this institution, it is certain that, if the magistrate, who has all the power in his own hands, and appropriates to himself all the advantages of the contract, has none the less a right to renounce his authority, the people, who suffer for all the faults of their chief, must have a much better right to renounce their dependence. But the terrible and innumerable quarrels and disorders that would necessarily arise from so dangerous a privilege, show, more than anything else, how much human government stood in need of a more solid basis than mere reason, and how expedient it was for the public tranquillity that the divine will should interpose to invest the sovereign authority with a sacred and inviolable character, which might deprive subjects of the fatal right of disposing of it. If the world had received no other advantages from religion, this would be enough to impose on men the duty of adopting and cultivating it, abuses and all, since it has been the means of saving more blood than fanaticism has ever spilt. But let us follow the thread of our hypothesis.

The different forms of government owe their origin to the differing degrees of inequality which existed between individuals at the time of their institution. If there happened to be any one man among them pre-eminent in power, virtue, riches or personal influence, he became sole magistrate, and the State assumed the form of monarchy. If several, nearly equal in point of eminence, stood above the rest, they were elected jointly, and formed an aristocracy. Again, among a people who had deviated less from a state of nature, and between whose fortune or talents there was less disproportion, the supreme administration was retained in common, and a democracy was formed. It was discovered in process of time which of these forms suited men the best. Some peoples remained altogether subject to the laws; others soon came to obey their magistrates. The citizens laboured to preserve their liberty; the subjects, irritated at seeing others enjoying a blessing they had lost, thought only of making slaves of their neighbours. In a word, on the one side arose riches and conquests, and on the other happiness and virtue.

In these different governments, all the offices were at first elective; and when the influence of wealth was out of the question, the preference was given to merit, which gives a natural ascendancy, and to age, which is experienced in business and deliberate in council. The Elders of the Hebrews, the Gerontes at Sparta, the Senate at Rome, and the very etymology of our word Seigneur, show how old age was once held in veneration. But the more often the choice fell upon old men, the more often elections had to be repeated, and the more they became a nuisance; intrigues set in, factions were formed, party feeling grew bitter, civil wars broke out; the lives of individuals were sacrificed to the pretended happiness of the State; and at length men were on the point of relapsing into their primitive anarchy. Ambitious chiefs profited by these circumstances to perpetuate their offices in their own families: at the same time the people, already used to dependence, ease, and the conveniences of life, and already incapable of breaking its fetters, agreed to an increase of its slavery, in order to secure its tranquillity. Thus magistrates, having become hereditary, contracted the habit of considering their offices as a family estate, and themselves as proprietors of the communities of which they were at first only the officers, of regarding their fellow-citizens as their slaves, and numbering them, like cattle, among their belongings, and of calling themselves the equals of the gods and kings of kings.

    If we follow the progress of inequality in these various revolutions, we shall find that the establishment of laws and of the right of property was its first term, the institution of magistracy the second, and the conversion of legitimate into arbitrary power the third and last; so that the condition of rich and poor was authorised by the first period; that of powerful and weak by the second; and only by the third that of master and slave, which is the last degree of inequality, and the term at which all the rest remain, when they have got so far, till the government is either entirely dissolved by new revolutions, or brought back again to legitimacy.

    To understand this progress as necessary we must consider not so much the motives for the establishment of the body politic, as the forms it assumes in actuality, and the faults that necessarily attend it: for the flaws which make social institutions necessary are the same as make the abuse of them unavoidable. If we except Sparta, where the laws were mainly concerned with the education of children, and where Lycurgus established such morality as practically made laws needles – for laws as a rule, being weaker than the passions, restrain men without altering them – it would not be difficult to prove that every government, which scrupulously complied with the ends for which it was instituted, and guarded carefully against change and corruption, was set up unnecessarily. For a country, in which no one either evaded the laws or made a bad use of magisterial power, could require neither laws nor magistrates.

    Political distinctions necessarily produce civil distinctions. The growing equality between the chiefs and the people is soon felt by individuals, and modified in a thousand ways according to passions, talents and circumstances. The magistrate could not usurp any illegitimate power, without giving distinction to the creatures with whom he must share it. Besides, individuals only allow themselves to be oppressed so far as they are hurried on by blind ambition, and, looking rather below than above them, come to love authority more than independence, and submit to slavery, that they may in turn enslave others. It is no easy matter to reduce to obedience a man who has no ambition to

command; nor would the most adroit politician find it possible to enslave a people whose only desire was to be independent. But inequality easily makes its way among cowardly and ambitious minds, which are ever ready to run the risks of fortune, and almost indifferent whether they command or obey, as it is
5 favourable or adverse. Thus, there must have been a time, when the eyes of the people were so fascinated, that their rules had only to say to the least of men, "Be great, you and all your posterity," to make him immediately appear great in the eyes of every one as well as in his own. His descendants took still more upon them, in proportion to their distance from him; the more obscure and uncertain
10 the cause, the greater the effect: the greater the number of idlers one could count in a family, the more illustrious it was held to be.

   If this were the place to go into details, I could readily explain how, even without the intervention of government, inequality of credit and authority became unavoidable among private persons, as soon as their union in a single
15 society made them compare themselves one with another, and take into account the differences which they found out from the continual intercourse every man had to have with his neighbours.[8] These differences are of several kinds; but riches, nobility or rank, power and personal merit being the principal distinctions by which men form an estimate of each other in society, I could
20 prove that the harmony or conflict of these different forces is the surest indication of the good or bad constitution of a State. I could show that among these four kinds of inequality, personal qualities being the origin of all the others, wealth is the one to which they are all reduced in the end; for, as riches tend most immediately to the prosperity of individuals, and are easiest to
25 communicate, they are used to purchase every other distinction. By this observation we are enabled to judge pretty exactly how far a people has departed from its primitive constitution, and of its progress towards the extreme term of corruption. I could explain how much this universal desire for reputation, honours and advancement, which inflames us all, exercises and holds up to
30 comparison our faculties and powers; how it excites and multiplies our passions, and, by creating universal competition and rivalry, or rather enmity, among men, occasions numberless failures, successes and disturbances of all kinds by making so many aspirants run the same course. I could show that it is to this desire of being talked about, and this unremitting rage of distinguishing
35 ourselves, that we owe the best and the worst things we possess, both our virtues and our vices, our science and our errors, our conquerors and our philosophers; that is to say, a great many bad things, and a very few good ones. In a word, I could prove that, if we have a few rich and powerful men on the pinnacle of fortune and grandeur, while the crowd grovels in want and obscurity, it is
40 because the former prize what they enjoy only in so far as others are destitute of

it; and because, without changing their condition, they would cease to be happy the moment the people ceased to be wretched.

These details alone, however, would furnish matter for a considerable work, in which the advantages and disadvantages of every kind of government might
5 be weighed, as they are related to man in the state of nature, and at the same time all the different aspects, under which inequality has up to the present appeared, or may appear in ages yet to come, according to the nature of the several governments, and the alterations which time must unavoidably occasion in them, might be demonstrated. We should then see the multitude oppressed
10 from within, in consequence of the very precautions it had taken to guard against foreign tyranny. We should see oppression continually gain ground without it being possible for the oppressed to know where it would stop, or what legitimate means was left them of checking its progress. We should see the rights of citizens, and the freedom of nations slowly extinguished, and the complaints,
15 protests and appeals of the weak treated as seditious murmurings. We should see the honour of defending the common cause confined by statecraft to a mercenary part of the people. We should see taxes made necessary by such means, and the disheartened husbandman deserting his fields even in the midst of peace, and leaving the plough to gird on the sword. We should see fatal and
20 capricious codes of honour established; and the champions of their country sooner or later becoming its enemies, and for ever holding their daggers to the breasts of their fellow-citizens. The time would come when they would be heard saying to the oppressor of their country –

Pectore si fratris gladium juguloque parentis
25 Condere me jubeas, gravidæque in viscera partu
Conjugis, invita peragam tamen omnia dextrâ.
Lucan, i. 376

From great inequality of fortunes and conditions, from the vast variety of passions and of talents, of useless and pernicious arts, of vain sciences, would
30 arise a multitude of prejudices equally contrary to reason, happiness and virtue. We should see the magistrates fomenting everything that might weaken men united in society, by promoting dissension among them; everything that might sow in it the seeds of actual division, while it gave society the air of harmony; everything that might inspire the different ranks of people with mutual hatred
35 and distrust, by setting the rights and interests of one against those of another, and so strengthen the power which comprehended them all.

It is from the midst of this disorder and these revolutions, that despotism, gradually raising up its hideous head and devouring everything that remained sound and untainted in any part of the State, would at length trample on both the
40 laws and the people, and establish itself on the ruins of the republic. The times

which immediately preceded this last change would be times of trouble and calamity; but at length the monster would swallow up everything, and the people would no longer have either chiefs or laws, but only tyrants. From this moment there would be no question of virtue or morality; for despotism *cui ex honesto nulla est spes*, wherever it prevails, admits no other master; it no sooner speaks than probity and duty lose their weight and blind obedience is the only virtue which slaves can still practise.

This is the last term of inequality, the extreme point that closes the circle, and meets that from which we set out. Here all private persons return to their first equality, because they are nothing; and, subjects having no law but the will of their master, and their master no restraint but his passions, all notions of good and all principles of equity again vanish. There is here a complete return to the law of the strongest, and so to a new state of nature, differing from that we set out from; for the one was a state of nature in its first purity, while this is the consequence of excessive corruption. There is so little difference between the two states in other respects, and the contract of government is so completely dissolved by despotism, that the despot is master only so long as he remains the strongest; as soon as he can be expelled, he has no right to complain of violence. The popular insurrection that ends in the death or deposition of a Sultan is as lawful an act as those by which he disposed, the day before, of the lives and fortunes of his subjects. As he was maintained by force alone, it is force alone that overthrows him. Thus everything takes place according to the natural order; and, whatever may be the result of such frequent and precipitate revolutions, no one man has reason to complain of the injustice of another, but only of his own ill-fortune or indiscretion.

If the reader thus discovers and retraces the lost and forgotten road, by which man must have passed from the state of nature to the state of society; if he carefully restores, along with the intermediate situations which I have just described, those which want of time has compelled me to suppress, or my imagination has failed to suggest, he cannot fail to be struck by the vast distance which separates the two states. It is in tracing this slow succession that he will find the solution of a number of problems of politics and morals, which philosophers cannot settle. He will feel that, men being different in different ages, the reason why Diogenes could not find a man was that he sought among his contemporaries a man of an earlier period. He will see that Cato died with Rome and liberty, because he did not fit the age in which he lived; the greatest of men served only to astonish a world which he would certainly have ruled, had he lived five hundred years sooner. In a word, he will explain how the soul and the passions of men insensibly change their very nature; why our wants and pleasures in the end seek new objects; and why, the original man having

vanished by degrees, society offers to us only an assembly of artificial men and factitious passions, which are the work of all these new relations, and without any real foundation in nature. We are taught nothing on this subject, by reflection, that is not entirely confirmed by observation. The savage and the
5   civilised man differ so much in the bottom of their hearts and in their inclinations, that what constitutes the supreme happiness of one would reduce the other to despair. The former breathes only peace and liberty; he desires only to live and be free from labour; even the ataraxia of the Stoic falls far short of his profound indifference to every other object. Civilised man, on the other
10   hand, is always moving, sweating, toiling and racking his brains to find still more laborious occupations: he goes on in drudgery to his last moment, and even seeks death to put himself in a position to live, or renounces life to acquire immortality. He pays his court to men in power, whom he hates, and to the wealthy, whom he despises; he stops at nothing to have the honour of serving
15   them; he is not ashamed to value himself on his own meanness and their protection; and, proud of his slavery, he speaks with disdain of those, who have not the honour of sharing it. What a sight would the perplexing and envied labours of a European minister of State present to the eyes of a Caribbean! How many cruel deaths would not this indolent savage prefer to the horrors of such a
20   life, which is seldom even sweetened by the pleasure of doing good! But, for him to see into the motives of all this solicitude, the words power and reputation, would have to bear some meaning in his mind; he would have to know that there are men who set a value on the opinion of the rest of the world; who can be made happy and satisfied with themselves rather on the testimony of other
25   people than on their own. In reality, the source of all these differences is, that the savage lives within himself, while social man lives constantly outside himself, and only knows how to live in the opinion of others, so that he seems to receive the consciousness of his own existence merely from the judgment of others concerning him. It is not to my present purpose to insist on the indifference to
30   good and evil which arises from this disposition, in spite of our many fine works on morality, or to show how, everything being reduced to appearances, there is but art and mummery in even honour, friendship, virtue, and often vice itself, of which we at length learn the secret of boasting; to show, in short, how, always asking others what we are, and never daring to ask ourselves, in the midst of so
35   much philosophy, humanity and civilisation, and of such sublime codes of morality, we have nothing to show for ourselves but a frivolous and deceitful appearance, honour without virtue, reason without wisdom, and pleasure without happiness. It is sufficient that I have proved that this is not by any means the original state of man, but that it is merely the spirit of society, and the inequality
40   which society produces, that thus transform and alter all our natural inclinations.

I have endeavoured to trace the origin and progress of inequality, and the institution and abuse of political societies, as far as these are capable of being deduced from the nature of man merely by the light of reason, and independently of those sacred dogmas which give the sanction of divine right to sovereign authority. It follows from this survey that, as there is hardly any inequality in the state of nature, all the inequality which now prevails owes its strength and growth to the development of our faculties and the advance of the human mind, and becomes at last permanent and legitimate by the establishment of property and laws. Secondly, it follows that moral inequality, authorised by positive right alone, clashes with natural right, whenever it is not proportionate to physical inequality; a distinction which sufficiently determines what we ought to think of that species of inequality which prevails in all civilised, countries; since it is plainly contrary to the law of nature, however defined, that children should command old men, fools wise men, and that the privileged few should gorge themselves with superfluities, while the starving multitude are in want of the bare necessities of life.

APPENDIX[9]

A FAMOUS author, reckoning up the good and evil of human life, and comparing the aggregates, finds that our pains greatly exceed our pleasures: so that, all things considered, human life is not at all a valuable gift. This conclusion does not surprise me; for the writer drew all his arguments from man in civilisation. Had he gone back to the state of nature, his inquiries would clearly have had a different result, and man would have been seen to be subject to very few evils not of his own creation. It has indeed cost us not a little trouble to make ourselves as wretched as we are. When we consider, on the one hand, the immense labours of mankind, the many sciences brought to perfection, the arts invented, the powers employed, the deeps filled up, the mountains levelled, the rocks shattered, the rivers made navigable, the tracts of land cleared, the lakes emptied, the marshes drained, the enormous structures erected on land, and the teeming vessels that cover the sea; and, on the other hand, estimate with ever so little thought, the real advantages that have accrued from all these works to mankind, we cannot help being amazed at the vast disproportion there is between these things, and deploring the infatuation of man, which, to gratify his silly pride and vain self-admiration, induces him eagerly to pursue all the miseries he is capable of feeling, though beneficent nature had kindly placed them out of his way.

That men are actually wicked, a sad and continual experience of them proves beyond doubt: but, all the same, I think I have shown that man is

naturally good. What then can have depraved him to such an extent, except the changes that have happened in his constitution, the advances he has made, and the knowledge he has acquired? We may admire human society as much as we please; it will be none the less true that it necessarily leads men to hate each
5   other in proportion as their interests clash, and to do one another apparent services, while they are really doing every imaginable mischief. What can be thought of a relation, in which the interest of every individual dictates rules directly opposite to those the public reason dictates to the community in general – in which every man finds his profit in the misfortunes of his neighbour? There
10   is not perhaps any man in a comfortable position who has not greedy heirs, and perhaps even children, secretly wishing for his death; not a ship at sea, of which the loss would not be good news to some merchant or other; not a house, which some debtor of bad faith would not be glad to see reduced to ashes with all the papers it contains; not a nation which does not rejoice at the disasters that befall
15   its neighbours. Thus it is that we find our advantage in the misfortunes of our fellow-creatures, and that the loss of one man almost always constitutes the prosperity of another. But it is still more pernicious that public calamities are the objects of the hopes and expectations of innumerable individuals. Some desire sickness, some mortality, some war, and some famine. I have seen men wicked
20   enough to weep for sorrow at the prospect of a plentiful season; and the great and fatal fire of London, which cost so many unhappy persons their lives or their fortunes, made the fortunes of perhaps ten thousand others. I know that Montaigne censures Demades the Athenian for having caused to be punished a workman who, by selling his coffins very dear, was a great gainer by the deaths
25   of his fellow-citizens; but, the reason alleged by Montaigne being that everybody ought to be punished, my point is clearly confirmed by it. Let us penetrate, therefore, the superficial appearances of benevolence, and survey what passes in the inmost recesses of the heart. Let us reflect what must be the state of things, when men are forced to caress and destroy one another at the
30   same time; when they are born enemies by duty, and knaves by interest. It will perhaps be said that society is so formed that every man gains by serving the rest. That would be all very well, if he did not gain still more by injuring them. There is no legitimate profit so great, that it cannot be greatly exceeded by what may be made illegitimately; we always gain more by hurting our neighbours
35   than by doing them good. Nothing is required but to know how to act with impunity; and to this end the powerful employ all their strength, and the weak all their cunning.

     Savage man, when he has dined, is at peace with all nature, and the friend of all his fellow-creatures. If a dispute arises about a meal, he rarely comes to
40   blows, without having first compared the difficulty of conquering his antagonist

with the trouble of finding subsistence elsewhere: and, as pride does not come in, it all ends in a few blows; the victor eats, and the vanquished seeks provision somewhere else, and all is at peace. The case is quite different with man in the state of society, for whom first necessaries have to be provided, and then

5   superfluities; delicacies follow next, then immense wealth, then subjects, and then slaves. He enjoys not a moment's relaxation; and what is yet stranger, the less natural and pressing his wants, the more headstrong are his passions, and, still worse, the more he has it in his power to gratify them; so that after a long course of prosperity, after having swallowed up treasures and ruined multitudes,

10   the hero ends up by cutting every throat till he finds himself, at last, sole master of the world. Such is in miniature the moral picture, if not of human life, at least of the secret pretensions of the heart of civilised man.

      Compare without partiality the state of the citizen with that of the savage, and trace out, if you can, how many inlets the former has opened to pain and

15   death, besides those of his vices, his wants and his misfortunes. If you reflect on the mental afflictions that prey on us, the violent passions that waste and exhaust us, the excessive labour with which the poor are burdened, the still more dangerous indolence to which the wealthy give themselves up, so that the poor perish of want, and the rich of surfeit; if you reflect but a moment on the

20   heterogeneous mixtures and pernicious seasonings of foods; the corrupt state in which they are frequently eaten; on the adulteration of medicines, the wiles of those who sell them, the mistakes of those who administer them, and the poisonous vessels in which they are prepared; on the epidemics bred by foul air in consequence of great numbers of men being crowded together, or those which

25   are caused by our delicate way of living, by our passing from our houses into the open air and back again, by the putting on or throwing off our clothes with too little care, and by all the precautions which sensuality has converted into necessary habits, and the neglect of which sometimes costs us our life or health; if you take into account the conflagrations and earthquakes, which, devouring or

30   overwhelming whole cities, destroy the inhabitants by thousands; in a word, if you add together all the dangers with which these causes are always threatening us, you will see how dearly nature makes us pay for the contempt with which we have treated her lessons.

      I shall not here repeat, what I have elsewhere said of the calamities of war;

35   but wish that those, who have sufficient knowledge, were willing or bold enough to make public the details of the villainies committed in armies by the contractors for commissariat and hospitals: we should see plainly that their monstrous frauds, already none too well concealed, which cripple the finest armies in less than no time, occasion greater destruction among the soldiers than

40   the swords of the enemy.

The number of people who perish annually at sea, by famine, the scurvy, pirates, fire and shipwrecks, affords matter for another shocking calculation. We must also place to the credit of the establishment of property, and consequently to the institution of society, assassinations, poisonings, highway robberies, and
5   even the punishments inflicted on the wretches guilty of these crimes; which, though expedient to prevent greater evils, yet by making the murder of one man cost the lives of two or more, double the loss to the human race.

What shameful methods are sometimes practised to prevent the birth of men, and cheat nature; either by brutal and depraved appetites which insult her
10   most beautiful work-appetites unknown to savages or mere animals, which can spring only from the corrupt imagination of mankind in civilised countries; or by secret abortions, the fitting effects of debauchery and vitiated notions of honour; or by the exposure or murder of multitudes of infants, who fall victims to the poverty of their parents, or the cruel shame of their mothers; or, finally, by the
15   mutilation of unhappy wretches, part of whose life, with their hope of posterity, is given up to vain singing, or, still worse, the brutal jealousy of other men: a mutilation which, in the last case, becomes a double outrage against nature from the treatment of those who suffer it, and from the use to which they are destined. But is it not a thousand times more common and more dangerous for paternal
20   rights openly to offend against humanity? How many talents have not been thrown away, and inclinations forced, by the unwise constraint of fathers? How many men, who would have distinguished themselves in a fitting estate, have died dishonoured and wretched in another for which they had no taste! How many happy, but unequal, marriages have been broken or disturbed, and how
25   many chaste wives have been dishonoured, by an order of things continually in contradiction with that of nature! How many good and virtuous husbands and wives are reciprocally punished for having been ill-assorted! How many young and unhappy victims of their parents' avarice plunge into vice, or pass their melancholy days in tears, groaning in the indissoluble bonds which their hearts
30   repudiate and gold alone has formed! Fortunate sometimes are those whose courage and virtue remove them from life before inhuman violence makes them spend it in crime or in despair. Forgive me, father and mother, whom I shall ever regret: my complaint embitters your griefs; but would they might be an eternal and terrible example to every one who dares, in the name of nature, to violate
35   her most sacred right.

If I have spoken only of those ill-starred unions which are the result of our system, is it to be thought that those over which love and sympathy preside are free from disadvantages? What if I should undertake to show humanity attacked in its very source, and even in the most sacred of all ties, in which fortune is
40   consulted before nature, and, the disorders of society confounding all virtue and

vice, continence becomes a criminal precaution, and a refusal to give life to a fellow-creature, an act of humanity? But, without drawing aside the veil which hides all these horrors, let us content ourselves with pointing out the evil which others will have to remedy.

5   To all this add the multiplicity of unhealthy trades, which shorten men's lives or destroy their bodies, such as working in the mines, and the preparing of metals and minerals, particularly lead, copper, mercury, cobalt, and arsenic: add those other dangerous trades which are daily fatal to many tilers, carpenters, masons and miners: put all these together and we can see, in the establishment
10 and perfection of societies, the reasons for that diminution of our species, which has been noticed by many philosophers.

     Luxury, which cannot be prevented among men who are tenacious of their own convenience and of the respect paid them by others, soon completes the evil society had begun, and, under the pretence of giving bread to the poor, whom it
15 should never have made such, impoverishes all the rest, and sooner or later depopulates the State. Luxury is a remedy much worse than the disease it sets up to cure; or rather it is in itself the greatest of all evils, for every State, great or small: for, in order to maintain all the servants and vagabonds it creates, it brings oppression and ruin on the citizen and the labourer; it is like those scorching
20 winds, which, covering the trees and plants with devouring insects, deprive useful animals of their subsistence and spread famine and death wherever they blow.

     From society and the luxury to which it gives birth arise the liberal and mechanical arts, commerce, letters, and all those superfluities which make
25 industry flourish, and enrich and ruin nations. The reason for such destruction is plain. It is easy to see, from the very nature of agriculture, that it must be the least lucrative of all the arts; for, its produce being the most universally necessary, the price must be proportionate to the abilities of the very poorest of mankind.
30   From the same principle may be deduced this rule, that the arts in general are more lucrative in proportion as they are less useful; and that, in the end, the most useful becomes the most neglected. From this we may learn what to think of the real advantages of industry and the actual effects of its progress.

     Such are the sensible causes of all the miseries, into which opulence at
35 length plunges the most celebrated nations. In proportion as arts and industry flourish, the despised husbandman, burdened with the taxes necessary for the support of luxury, and condemned to pass his days between labour and hunger, forsakes his native field, to seek in towns the bread he ought to carry thither. The more our capital cities strike the vulgar eye with admiration, the greater
40 reason is there to lament the sight of the abandoned countryside, the large tracts

of land that lie uncultivated, the roads crowded with unfortunate citizens turned beggars or highwaymen, and doomed to end their wretched lives either on a dunghill or on the gallows. Thus the State grows rich on the one hand, and feeble and depopulated on the other; the mightiest monarchies, after having
5   taken immense pains to enrich and depopulate themselves, fall at last a prey to some poor nation, which has yielded to the fatal temptation of invading them, and then, growing opulent and weak in its turn, is itself invaded and ruined by some other.

      Let any one inform us what produced the swarms of barbarians, who
10   overran Europe, Asia and Africa for so many ages. Was their prodigious increase due to their industry and arts, to the wisdom of their laws, or to the excellence of their political system? Let the learned tell us why, instead of multiplying to such a degree, these fierce and brutal men, without sense or science, without education, without restraint, did not destroy each other hourly
15   in quarrelling over the productions of their fields and woods. Let them tell us how these wretches could have the presumption to oppose such clever people as we were, so well trained in military discipline, and possessed of such excellent laws and institutions: and why, since society has been brought to perfection in northern countries, and so much pains taken to instruct their inhabitants in their
20   social duties and in the art of living happily and peaceably together, we see them no longer produce such numberless hosts as they used once to send forth to be the plague and terror of other nations. I fear some one may at last answer me by saying, that all these fine things, arts, sciences and laws, were wisely invented by men, as a salutary plague, to prevent the too great multiplication of mankind,
25   lest the world, which was given us for a habitation, should in time be too small for its inhabitants.

      What, then, is to be done? Must societies be totally abolished? Must meum and tuum be annihilated, and must we return again to the forests to live among bears? This is a deduction in the manner of my adversaries, which I would as
30   soon anticipate as let them have the shame of drawing. O you, who have never heard the voice of heaven, who think man destined only to live this little life and die in peace; you, who can resign in the midst of populous cities your fatal acquisitions, your restless spirits, your corrupt hearts and endless desires; resume, since it depends entirely on ourselves, your ancient and primitive
35   innocence: retire to the woods, there to lose the sight and remembrance of the crimes of your contemporaries; and be not apprehensive of degrading your species, by renouncing its advances in order to renounce its vices. As for men like me, whose passions have destroyed their original simplicity, who can no longer subsist on plants or acorns, or live without laws and magistrates; those
40   who were honoured in their first father with supernatural instructions; those who

discover, in the design of giving human actions at the start a morality which they must otherwise have been so long in acquiring, the reason for a precept in itself indifferent and inexplicable on every other system; those, in short, who are persuaded that the Divine Being has called all mankind to be partakers in the happiness and perfection of celestial intelligences, all these will endeavour to merit the eternal prize they are to expect from the practice of those virtues, which they make themselves follow in learning to know them. They will respect the sacred bonds of their respective communities; they will love their fellow-citizens, and serve them with all their might: they will scrupulously obey the laws, and all those who make or administer them; they will particularly honour those wise and good princes, who find means of preventing, curing or even palliating all these evils and abuses, by which we are constantly threatened; they will animate the zeal of their deserving rulers, by showing them, without flattery or fear, the importance of their office and the severity of their duty. But they will not therefore have less contempt for a constitution that cannot support itself without the aid of so many splendid characters, much oftener wished for than found; and from which, notwithstanding all their pains and solicitude, there always arise more real calamities than even apparent advantages.

---

[1] See Appendix.

[2] Justin, Hist. ii. 2. So much more does the ignorance of vice profit the one sort than the knowledge of virtue the other.

[3] Egoism must not be confused with self-respect: for they differ both in themselves and in their effects. Self-respect is a natural feeling which leads every animal to look to its own preservation, and which, guided in man by reason and modified by compassion, creates humanity and virtue. Egoism is a purely relative and factitious feeling, which arises in the state of society, leads each individual to make more of himself than of any other, causes all the mutual damage men inflict one on another, and is the real source of the "sense of honour." This being understood, I maintain that, in our primitive condition, in the true state of nature, egoism did not exist; for as each man regarded himself as the only observer of his actions, the only being in the universe who took any interest in him, and the sole judge of his deserts, no feeling arising from comparisons he could not be led to make could take root in his soul; and for the same reason, he could know neither hatred nor the desire for revenge, since these passions can spring only from a sense of injury: and as it is the contempt or the intention to hurt, and not the harm done, which constitutes the injury, men who neither valued nor compared themselves could do one another much violence, when it suited them, without feeling any sense of injury. In a word, each man, regarding his fellows almost as he regarded animals of different species, might seize the prey of a weaker or yield up his own to a stronger, and yet consider these acts of violence as mere natural occurrences, without the slightest emotion of insolence or despite, or any other feeling than the joy or grief of success or failure.

[4] Nature avows she gave the human race the softest hearts, who gave them tears.

[5] Ovid, Metamorphoses, xi. 127.
Both rich and poor, shocked at their new-found ills,
Would fly from wealth, and lose what they had sought.

---

[6] Tacitus, Hist. iv. 17. The most wretched slavery they call peace.

[7] Of the Rights of the Most Christian Queen over Various States of the Monarchy of Spain, 1667.

[8] Distributive justice would oppose this rigorous equality of the state of nature, even were it practicable in civil society; as all the members of the State owe it their services in proportion to their talents and abilities, they ought, on their side, to be distinguished and favoured in proportion to the services they have actually rendered. It is in this sense we must understand that passage of Isocrates, in which he extols the primitive Athenians, for having determined which of the two kinds of equality was the most useful, viz., that which consists in dividing the same advantages indiscriminately among all the citizens, or that which consists in distributing them to each according to his deserts. These able politicians, adds the orator, banishing that unjust inequality which makes no distinction between good and bad men, adhered inviolably to that which rewards and punishes every man according to his deserts.

But in the first place, there never existed a society, however corrupt some may have become, where no difference was made between the good and the bad; and with regard to morality, where no measures can be prescribed by law exact enough to serve as a practical rule for a magistrate, it is with great prudence that, in order not to leave the fortune or quality of the citizens to his discretion, it prohibits him from passing judgment on persons and confines his judgment to actions. Only morals such as those of the ancient Romans can bear censors, and such a tribunal among us would throw everything into confusion. The difference between good and bad men is determined by public esteem; the magistrate being strictly a judge of right alone; whereas the public is the truest judge of morals, and is of such integrity and penetration on this head, that although it may be sometimes deceived, it can never be corrupted. The rank of citizens ought, therefore, to be regulated, not according to their personal merit – for this would put it in the power of the magistrate to apply the law almost arbitrarily – but according to the actual services done to the State, which are capable of being more exactly estimated.

[9] Part I, para. 17.

Jean-Jacques Rousseau
THE SOCIAL CONTRACT OR PRINCIPLES OF POLITICAL RIGHT
(1762)

> Foederis æquas Dicamus leges.
> Virgil, *Æneid* xi.

FOREWARD

This little treatise is part of a longer work which I began years ago without realising my limitations, and long since abandoned. Of the various fragments that might have been extracted from what I wrote, this is the most considerable, and, I think, the least unworthy of being offered to the public. The rest no longer
5 exists.

BOOK I

I MEAN to inquire if, in the civil order, there can be any sure and legitimate rule of administration, men being taken as they are and laws as they might be. In this inquiry I shall endeavour always to unite what right sanctions with what is prescribed by interest, in order that justice and utility may in no case be divided.
10 I enter upon my task without proving the importance of the subject. I shall be asked if I am a prince or a legislator, to write on politics. I answer that I am neither, and that is why I do so. If I were a prince or a legislator, I should not waste time in saying what wants doing; I should do it, or hold my peace.

As I was born a citizen of a free State, and a member of the Sovereign, I
15 feel that, however feeble the influence my voice can have on public affairs, the right of voting on them makes it my duty to study them: and I am happy, when I reflect upon governments, to find my inquiries always furnish me with new reasons for loving that of my own country.

1. SUBJECT OF THE FIRST BOOK

MAN is born free; and everywhere he is in chains. One thinks himself the
20 master of others, and still remains a greater slave than they. How did this change come about? I do not know. What can make it legitimate? That question I think I can answer.

If I took into account only force, and the effects derived from it, I should say: "As long as a people is compelled to obey, and obeys, it does well; as soon
25 as it can shake off the yoke, and shakes it off, it does still better; for, regaining

92

its liberty by the same right as took it away, either it is justified in resuming it, or there was no justification for those who took it away." But the social order is a sacred right which is the basis of all other rights. Nevertheless, this right does not come from nature, and must therefore be founded on conventions. Before
5 coming to that, I have to prove what I have just asserted.

2. THE FIRST SOCIETIES

THE most ancient of all societies, and the only one that is natural, is the family: and even so the children remain attached to the father only so long as they need him for their preservation. As soon as this need ceases, the natural bond is dissolved. The children, released from the obedience they owed to the
10 father, and the father, released from the care he owed his children, return equally to independence. If they remain united, they continue so no longer naturally, but voluntarily; and the family itself is then maintained only by convention.

This common liberty results from the nature of man. His first law is to provide for his own preservation, his first cares are those which he owes to
15 himself; and, as soon as he reaches years of discretion, he is the sole judge of the proper means of preserving himself, and consequently becomes his own master.

The family then may be called the first model of political societies: the ruler corresponds to the father, and the people to the children; and all, being born free and equal, alienate their liberty only for their own advantage. The whole
20 difference is that, in the family, the love of the father for his children repays him for the care he takes of them, while, in the State, the pleasure of commanding takes the place of the love which the chief cannot have for the peoples under him.

Grotius denies that all human power is established in favour of the
25 governed, and quotes slavery as an example. His usual method of reasoning is constantly to establish right by fact.[1] It would be possible to employ a more logical method, but none could be more favourable to tyrants.

It is then, according to Grotius, doubtful whether the human race belongs to a hundred men, or that hundred men to the human race: and, throughout his
30 book, he seems to incline to the former alternative, which is also the view of Hobbes. On this showing, the human species is divided into so many herds of cattle, each with its ruler, who keeps guard over them for the purpose of devouring them.

As a shepherd is of a nature superior to that of his flock, the shepherds of
35 men, i.e., their rulers, are of a nature superior to that of the peoples under them. Thus, Philo tells us, the Emperor Caligula reasoned, concluding equally well either that kings were gods, or that men were beasts.

The reasoning of Caligula agrees with that of Hobbes and Grotius. Aristotle, before any of them, had said that men are by no means equal naturally, but that some are born for slavery, and others for dominion.

Aristotle was right; but he took the effect for the cause. Nothing can be
5 more certain than that every man born in slavery is born for slavery. Slaves lose everything in their chains, even the desire of escaping from them: they love their servitude, as the comrades of Ulysses loved their brutish condition.[2] If then there are slaves by nature, it is because there have been slaves against nature. Force made the first slaves, and their cowardice perpetuated the condition.
10 I have said nothing of King Adam, or Emperor Noah, father of the three great monarchs who shared out the universe, like the children of Saturn, whom some scholars have recognised in them. I trust to getting due thanks for my moderation; for, being a direct descendant of one of these princes, perhaps of the eldest branch, how do I know that a verification of titles might not leave me the
15 legitimate king of the human race? In any case, there can be no doubt that Adam was sovereign of the world, as Robinson Crusoe was of his island, as long as he was its only inhabitant; and this empire had the advantage that the monarch, safe on his throne, had no rebellions, wars, or conspirators to fear.

3. THE RIGHT OF THE STRONGEST

THE strongest is never strong enough to be always the master, unless he
20 transforms strength into right, and obedience into duty. Hence the right of the strongest, which, though to all seeming meant ironically, is really laid down as a fundamental principle. But are we never to have an explanation of this phrase? Force is a physical power, and I fail to see what moral effect it can have. To yield to force is an act of necessity, not of will – at the most, an act of prudence.
25 In what sense can it be a duty?

Suppose for a moment that this so-called "right" exists. I maintain that the sole result is a mass of inexplicable nonsense. For, if force creates right, the effect changes with the cause: every force that is greater than the first succeeds to its right. As soon as it is possible to disobey with impunity, disobedience is
30 legitimate; and, the strongest being always in the right, the only thing that matters is to act so as to become the strongest. But what kind of right is that which perishes when force fails? If we must obey perforce, there is no need to obey because we ought; and if we are not forced to obey, we are under no obligation to do so. Clearly, the word "right" adds nothing to force: in this
35 connection, it means absolutely nothing.

Obey the powers that be. If this means yield to force, it is a good precept, but superfluous: I can answer for its never being violated. All power comes from God, I admit; but so does all sickness: does that mean that we are forbidden to call in the doctor? A brigand surprises me at the edge of a wood: must I not merely surrender my purse on compulsion; but, even if I could withhold it, am I in conscience bound to give it up? For certainly the pistol he holds is also a power.

5   Let us then admit that force does not create right, and that we are obliged to obey only legitimate powers. In that case, my original question recurs.

4. SLAVERY

SINCE no man has a natural authority over his fellow, and force creates no right, we must conclude that conventions form the basis of all legitimate authority among men.

10   If an individual, says Grotius, can alienate his liberty and make himself the slave of a master, why could not a whole people do the same and make itself subject to a king? There are in this passage plenty of ambiguous words which would need explaining; but let us confine ourselves to the word alienate. To alienate is to give or to sell. Now, a man who becomes the slave of another does
15   not give himself; he sells himself, at the least for his subsistence: but for what does a people sell itself? A king is so far from furnishing his subjects with their subsistence that he gets his own only from them; and, according to Rabelais, kings do not live on nothing. Do subjects then give their persons on condition that the king takes their goods also? I fail to see what they have left to preserve.
20   It will be said that the despot assures his subjects civil tranquillity. Granted; but what do they gain, if the wars his ambition brings down upon them, his insatiable avidity, and the vexations conduct of his ministers press harder on them than their own dissensions would have done? What do they gain, if the very tranquillity they enjoy is one of their miseries? Tranquillity is found also in
25   dungeons; but is that enough to make them desirable places to live in? The Greeks imprisoned in the cave of the Cyclops lived there very tranquilly, while they were awaiting their turn to be devoured.

To say that a man gives himself gratuitously, is to say what is absurd and inconceivable; such an act is null and illegitimate, from the mere fact that he
30   who does it is out of his mind. To say the same of a whole people is to suppose a people of madmen; and madness creates no right.

Even if each man could alienate himself, he could not alienate his children: they are born men and free; their liberty belongs to them, and no one but they has the right to dispose of it. Before they come to years of discretion, the father
35   can, in their name, lay down conditions for their preservation and well-being, but he cannot give them irrevocably and without conditions: such a gift is contrary to the ends of nature, and exceeds the rights of paternity. It would therefore be necessary, in order to legitimise an arbitrary government, that in

every generation the people should be in a position to accept or reject it; but, were this so, the government would be no longer arbitrary.

To renounce liberty is to renounce being a man, to surrender the rights of humanity and even its duties. For him who renounces everything no indemnity
5 is possible. Such a renunciation is incompatible with man's nature; to remove all liberty from his will is to remove all morality from his acts. Finally, it is an empty and contradictory convention that sets up, on the one side, absolute authority, and, on the other, unlimited obedience. Is it not clear that we can be under no obligation to a person from whom we have the right to exact
10 everything? Does not this condition alone, in the absence of equivalence or exchange, in itself involve the nullity of the act? For what right can my slave have against me, when all that he has belongs to me, and, his right being mine, this right of mine against myself is a phrase devoid of meaning?

Grotius and the rest find in war another origin for the so-called right of
15 slavery. The victor having, as they hold, the right of killing the vanquished, the latter can buy back his life at the price of his liberty; and this convention is the more legitimate because it is to the advantage of both parties.

But it is clear that this supposed right to kill the conquered is by no means deducible from the state of war. Men, from the mere fact that, while they are
20 living in their primitive independence, they have no mutual relations stable enough to constitute either the state of peace or the state of war, cannot be naturally enemies. War is constituted by a relation between things, and not between persons; and, as the state of war cannot arise out of simple personal relations, but only out of real relations, private war, or war of man with man, can
25 exist neither in the state of nature, where there is no constant property, nor in the social state, where everything is under the authority of the laws.

Individual combats, duels and encounters, are acts which cannot constitute a state; while the private wars, authorised by the Establishments of Louis IX, King of France, and suspended by the Peace of God, are abuses of feudalism, in itself
30 an absurd system if ever there was one, and contrary to the principles of natural right and to all good polity.

War then is a relation, not between man and man, but between State and State, and individuals are enemies only accidentally, not as men, nor even as citizens,[3] but as soldiers; not as members of their country, but as its defenders.
35 Finally, each State can have for enemies only other States, and not men; for between things disparate in nature there can be no real relation.

Furthermore, this principle is in conformity with the established rules of all times and the constant practice of all civilised peoples. Declarations of war are intimations less to powers than to their subjects. The foreigner, whether king,
40 individual, or people, who robs, kills or detains the subjects, without declaring

war on the prince, is not an enemy, but a brigand. Even in real war, a just prince, while laying hands, in the enemy's country, on all that belongs to the public, respects the lives and goods of individuals: he respects rights on which his own are founded. The object of the war being the destruction of the hostile State, the
5   other side has a right to kill its defenders, while they are bearing arms; but as soon as they lay them down and surrender, they cease to be enemies or instruments of the enemy, and become once more merely men, whose life no one has any right to take. Sometimes it is possible to kill the State without killing a single one of its members; and war gives no right which is not
10   necessary to the gaining of its object. These principles are not those of Grotius: they are not based on the authority of poets, but derived from the nature of reality and based on reason.

      The right of conquest has no foundation other than the right of the strongest. If war does not give the conqueror the right to massacre the conquered peoples,
15   the right to enslave them cannot be based upon a right which does not exist. No one has a right to kill an enemy except when he cannot make him a slave, and the right to enslave him cannot therefore be derived from the right to kill him. It is accordingly an unfair exchange to make him buy at the price of his liberty his life, over which the victor holds no right. Is it not clear that there is a vicious
20   circle in founding the right of life and death on the right of slavery, and the right of slavery on the right of life and death?

      Even if we assume this terrible right to kill everybody, I maintain that a slave made in war, or a conquered people, is under no obligation to a master, except to obey him as far as he is compelled to do so. By taking an equivalent
25   for his life, the victor has not done him a favour; instead of killing him without profit, he has killed him usefully. So far then is he from acquiring over him any authority in addition to that of force, that the state of war continues to subsist between them: their mutual relation is the effect of it, and the usage of the right of war does not imply a treaty of peace. A convention has indeed been made; but
30   this convention, so far from destroying the state of war, presupposes its continuance.

      So, from whatever aspect we regard the question, the right of slavery is null and void, not only as being illegitimate, but also because it is absurd and meaningless. The words slave and right contradict each other, and are mutually
35   exclusive. It will always be equally foolish for a man to say to a man or to a people: "I make with you a convention wholly at your expense and wholly to my advantage; I shall keep it as long as I like, and you will keep it as long as I like."

5. THAT WE MUST ALWAYS GO BACK TO A FIRST CONVENTION

EVEN if I granted all that I have been refuting, the friends of despotism
would be no better off. There will always be a great difference between
subduing a multitude and ruling a society. Even if scattered individuals were
successively enslaved by one man, however numerous they might be, I still see
5   no more than a master and his slaves, and certainly not a people and its ruler; I
see what may be termed an aggregation, but not an association; there is as yet
neither public good nor body politic. The man in question, even if he has
enslaved half the world, is still only an individual; his interest, apart from that of
others, is still a purely private interest. If this same man comes to die, his
10   empire, after him, remains scattered and without unity, as an oak falls and
dissolves into a heap of ashes when the fire has consumed it.

A people, says Grotius, can give itself to a king. Then, according to Grotius,
a people is a people before it gives itself. The gift is itself a civil act, and implies
public deliberation. It would be better, before examining the act by which a
15   people gives itself to a king, to examine that by which it has become a people;
for this act, being necessarily prior to the other, is the true foundation of society.

Indeed, if there were no prior convention, where, unless the election were
unanimous, would be the obligation on the minority to submit to the choice of
the majority? How have a hundred men who wish for a master the right to vote
20   on behalf of ten who do not? The law of majority voting is itself something
established by convention, and presupposes unanimity, on one occasion at least.

6. THE SOCIAL COMPACT

I SUPPOSE men to have reached the point at which the obstacles in the
way of their preservation in the state of nature show their power of resistance to
be greater than the resources at the disposal of each individual for his
25   maintenance in that state. That primitive condition can then subsist no longer;
and the human race would perish unless it changed its manner of existence.

But, as men cannot engender new forces, but only unite and direct existing
ones, they have no other means of preserving themselves than the formation, by
aggregation, of a sum of forces great enough to overcome the resistance. These
30   they have to bring into play by means of a single motive power, and cause to act
in concert.

This sum of forces can arise only where several persons come together: but,
as the force and liberty of each man are the chief instruments of his self-
preservation, how can he pledge them without harming his own interests, and
35   neglecting the care he owes to himself? This difficulty, in its bearing on my
present subject, may be stated in the following terms:

"The problem is to find a form of association which will defend and protect with the whole common force the person and goods of each associate, and in which each, while uniting himself with all, may still obey himself alone, and remain as free as before." This is the fundamental problem of which the Social

5   Contract provides the solution.

The clauses of this contract are so determined by the nature of the act that the slightest modification would make them vain and ineffective; so that, although they have perhaps never been formally set forth, they are everywhere the same and everywhere tacitly admitted and recognised, until, on the violation

10 of the social compact, each regains his original rights and resumes his natural liberty, while losing the conventional liberty in favour of which he renounced it.

These clauses, properly understood, may be reduced to one – the total alienation of each associate, together with all his rights, to the whole community; for, in the first place, as each gives himself absolutely, the

15 conditions are the same for all; and, this being so, no one has any interest in making them burdensome to others.

Moreover, the alienation being without reserve, the union is as perfect as it can be, and no associate has anything more to demand: for, if the individuals retained certain rights, as there would be no common superior to decide between

20 them and the public, each, being on one point his own judge, would ask to be so on all; the state of nature would thus continue, and the association would necessarily become inoperative or tyrannical.

Finally, each man, in giving himself to all, gives himself to nobody; and as there is no associate over whom he does not acquire the same right as he yields

25 others over himself, he gains an equivalent for everything he loses, and an increase of force for the preservation of what he has.

If then we discard from the social compact what is not of its essence, we shall find that it reduces itself to the following terms:

"Each of us puts his person and all his power in common under the supreme

30 direction of the general will, and, in our corporate capacity, we receive each member as an indivisible part of the whole."

At once, in place of the individual personality of each contracting party, this act of association creates a moral and collective body, composed of as many members as the assembly contains votes, and receiving from this act its unity, its

35 common identity, its life and its will. This public person, so formed by the union of all other persons formerly took the name of city,[4] and now takes that of Republic or body politic; it is called by its members State when passive. Sovereign when active, and Power when compared with others like itself. Those who are associated in it take collectively the name of people, and severally are

40 called citizens, as sharing in the sovereign power, and subjects, as being under

the laws of the State. But these terms are often confused and taken one for another: it is enough to know how to distinguish them when they are being used with precision.

7. THE SOVEREIGN

THIS formula shows us that the act of association comprises a mutual
5   undertaking between the public and the individuals, and that each individual, in making a contract, as we may say, with himself, is bound in a double capacity; as a member of the Sovereign he is bound to the individuals, and as a member of the State to the Sovereign. But the maxim of civil right, that no one is bound by undertakings made to himself, does not apply in this case; for there is a great
10   difference between incurring an obligation to yourself and incurring one to a whole of which you form a part.

Attention must further be called to the fact that public deliberation, while competent to bind all the subjects to the Sovereign, because of the two different capacities in which each of them may be regarded, cannot, for the opposite
15   reason, bind the Sovereign to itself; and that it is consequently against the nature of the body politic for the Sovereign to impose on itself a law which it cannot infringe. Being able to regard itself in only one capacity, it is in the position of an individual who makes a contract with himself; and this makes it clear that there neither is nor can be any kind of fundamental law binding on the body of
20   the people – not even the social contract itself. This does not mean that the body politic cannot enter into undertakings with others, provided the contract is not infringed by them; for in relation to what is external to it, it becomes a simple being, an individual.

But the body politic or the Sovereign, drawing its being wholly from the
25   sanctity of the contract, can never bind itself, even to an outsider, to do anything derogatory to the original act, for instance, to alienate any part of itself, or to submit to another Sovereign. Violation of the act by which it exists would be self-annihilation; and that which is itself nothing can create nothing.

As soon as this multitude is so united in one body, it is impossible to offend
30   against one of the members without attacking the body, and still more to offend against the body without the members resenting it. Duty and interest therefore equally oblige the two contracting parties to give each other help; and the same men should seek to combine, in their double capacity, all the advantages dependent upon that capacity.

35   Again, the Sovereign, being formed wholly of the individuals who compose it, neither has nor can have any interest contrary to theirs; and consequently the sovereign power need give no guarantee to its subjects, because it is impossible for the body to wish to hurt all its members. We shall also see later on that it

cannot hurt any in particular. The Sovereign, merely by virtue of what it is, is always what it should be.

This, however, is not the case with the relation of the subjects to the Sovereign, which, despite the common interest, would have no security that they 5 would fulfil their undertakings, unless it found means to assure itself of their fidelity.

In fact, each individual, as a man, may have a particular will contrary or dissimilar to the general will which he has as a citizen. His particular interest may speak to him quite differently from the common interest: his absolute and 10 naturally independent existence may make him look upon what he owes to the common cause as a gratuitous contribution, the loss of which will do less harm to others than the payment of it is burdensome to himself; and, regarding the moral person which constitutes the State as a persona ficta, because not a man, he may wish to enjoy the rights of citizenship without being ready to fulfil the 15 duties of a subject. The continuance of such an injustice could not but prove the undoing of the body politic.

In order then that the social compact may not be an empty formula, it tacitly includes the undertaking, which alone can give force to the rest, that whoever refuses to obey the general will shall be compelled to do so by the whole body. 20 This means nothing less than that he will be forced to be free; for this is the condition which, by giving each citizen to his country, secures him against all personal dependence. In this lies the key to the working of the political machine; this alone legitimises civil undertakings, which, without it, would be absurd, tyrannical, and liable to the most frightful abuses.

8. THE CIVIL STATE

25 THE passage from the state of nature to the civil state produces a very remarkable change in man, by substituting justice for instinct in his conduct, and giving his actions the morality they had formerly lacked. Then only, when the voice of duty takes the place of physical impulses and right of appetite, does man, who so far had considered only himself, find that he is forced to act on 30 different principles, and to consult his reason before listening to his inclinations. Although, in this state, he deprives himself of some advantages which he got from nature, he gains in return others so great, his faculties are so stimulated and developed, his ideas so extended, his feelings so ennobled, and his whole soul so uplifted, that, did not the abuses of this new condition often degrade him below 35 that which he left, he would be bound to bless continually the happy moment which took him from it for ever, and, instead of a stupid and unimaginative animal, made him an intelligent being and a man.

Let us draw up the whole account in terms easily commensurable. What man loses by the social contract is his natural liberty and an unlimited right to everything he tries to get and succeeds in getting; what he gains is civil liberty and the proprietorship of all he possesses. If we are to avoid mistake in weighing one against the other, we must clearly distinguish natural liberty, which is bounded only by the strength of the individual, from civil liberty, which is limited by the general will; and possession, which is merely the effect of force or the right of the first occupier, from property, which can be founded only on a positive title.

We might, over and above all this, add, to what man acquires in the civil state, moral liberty, which alone makes him truly master of himself; for the mere impulse of appetite is slavery, while obedience to a law which we prescribe to ourselves is liberty. But I have already said too much on this head, and the philosophical meaning of the word liberty does not now concern us.

9. REAL PROPERTY

EACH member of the community gives himself to it, at the moment of its foundation, just as he is, with all the resources at his command, including the goods he possesses. This act does not make possession, in changing hands, change its nature, and become property in the hands of the Sovereign; but, as the forces of the city are incomparably greater than those of an individual, public possession is also, in fact, stronger and more irrevocable, without being any more legitimate, at any rate from the point of view of foreigners. For the State, in relation to its members, is master of all their goods by the social contract, which, within the State, is the basis of all rights; but, in relation to other powers, it is so only by the right of the first occupier, which it holds from its members.

The right of the first occupier, though more real than the right of the strongest, becomes a real right only when the right of property has already been established. Every man has naturally a right to everything he needs; but the positive act which makes him proprietor of one thing excludes him from everything else. Having his share, he ought to keep to it, and can have no further right against the community. This is why the right of the first occupier, which in the state of nature is so weak, claims the respect of every man in civil society. In this right we are respecting not so much what belongs to another as what does not belong to ourselves.

In general, to establish the right of the first occupier over a plot of ground, the following conditions are necessary: first, the land must not yet be inhabited; secondly, a man must occupy only the amount he needs for his subsistence; and, in the third place, possession must be taken, not by an empty ceremony, but by labour and cultivation, the only sign of proprietorship that should be respected by others, in default of a legal title.

In granting the right of first occupancy to necessity and labour, are we not really stretching it as far as it can go? Is it possible to leave such a right
5   unlimited? Is it to be enough to set foot on a plot of common ground, in order to be able to call yourself at once the master of it? Is it to be enough that a man has the strength to expel others for a moment, in order to establish his right to prevent them from ever returning? How can a man or a people seize an immense territory and keep it from the rest of the world except by a punishable
10 usurpation, since all others are being robbed, by such an act, of the place of habitation and the means of subsistence which nature gave them in common? When Nunez Balboa, standing on the sea-shore, took possession of the South Seas and the whole of South America in the name of the crown of Castile, was that enough to dispossess all their actual inhabitants, and to shut out from them
15 all the princes of the world? On such a showing, these ceremonies are idly multiplied, and the Catholic King need only take possession all at once, from his apartment, of the whole universe, merely making a subsequent reservation about what was already in the possession of other princes.

We can imagine how the lands of individuals, where they were contiguous
20 and came to be united, became the public territory, and how the right of Sovereignty, extending from the subjects over the lands they held, became at once real and personal. The possessors were thus made more dependent, and the forces at their command used to guarantee their fidelity. The advantage of this does not seem to have been felt by ancient monarchs, who called themselves
25 Kings of the Persians, Scythians, or Macedonians, and seemed to regard themselves more as rulers of men than as masters of a country. Those of the present day more cleverly call themselves Kings of France, Spain, England, etc.: thus holding the land, they are quite confident of holding the inhabitants.

The peculiar fact about this alienation is that, in taking over the goods of
30 individuals, the community, so far from despoiling them, only assures them legitimate possession, and changes usurpation into a true right and enjoyment into proprietorship. Thus the possessors, being regarded as depositaries of the public good, and having their rights respected by all the members of the State and maintained against foreign aggression by all its forces, have, by a cession
35 which benefits both the public and still more themselves, acquired, so to speak, all that they gave up. This paradox may easily be explained by the distinction between the rights which the Sovereign and the proprietor have over the same estate, as we shall see later on.

It may also happen that men begin to unite one with another before they
40 possess anything, and that, subsequently occupying a tract of country which is

enough for all, they enjoy it in common, or share it out among themselves, either equally or according to a scale fixed by the Sovereign. However the acquisition be made, the right which each individual has to his own estate is always subordinate to the right which the community has over all: without this, there
5   would be neither stability in the social tie, nor real force in the exercise of Sovereignty.

I shall end this chapter and this book by remarking on a fact on which the whole social system should rest: i.e., that, instead of destroying natural inequality, the fundamental compact substitutes, for such physical inequality as
10 nature may have set up between men, an equality that is moral and legitimate, and that men, who may be unequal in strength or intelligence, become every one equal by convention and legal right.[5]

BOOK II

1. THAT SOVEREIGNTY IS INALIENABLE

THE first and most important deduction from the principles we have so far laid down is that the general will alone can direct the State according to the
15 object for which it was instituted, i.e., the common good: for if the clashing of particular interests made the establishment of societies necessary, the agreement of these very interests made it possible. The common element in these different interests is what forms the social tie; and, were there no point of agreement between them all, no society could exist. It is solely on the basis of this common
20 interest that every society should be governed.

I hold then that Sovereignty, being nothing less than the exercise of the general will, can never be alienated, and that the Sovereign, who is no less than a collective being, cannot be represented except by himself: the power indeed may be transmitted, but not the will.
25 In reality, if it is not impossible for a particular will to agree on some point with the general will, it is at least impossible for the agreement to be lasting and constant; for the particular will tends, by its very nature, to partiality, while the general will tends to equality. It is even more impossible to have any guarantee of this agreement; for even if it should always exist, it would be the effect not of
30 art, but of chance. The Sovereign may indeed say: "I now will actually what this man wills, or at least what he says he wills"; but it cannot say: "What he wills tomorrow, I too shall will" because it is absurd for the will to bind itself for the future, nor is it incumbent on any will to consent to anything that is not for the good of the being who wills. If then the people promises simply to obey, by that
35 very act it dissolves itself and loses what makes it a people; the moment a

master exists, there is no longer a Sovereign, and from that moment the body politic has ceased to exist.

This does not mean that the commands of the rulers cannot pass for general wills, so long as the Sovereign, being free to oppose them, offers no opposition. In such a case, universal silence is taken to imply the consent of the people. This will be explained later on.

2. THAT SOVEREIGNTY IS INDIVISIBLE

SOVEREIGNTY, for the same reason as makes it inalienable, is indivisible; for will either is, or is not, general;[6] it is the will either of the body of the people, or only of a part of it. In the first case, the will, when declared, is an act of Sovereignty and constitutes law: in the second, it is merely a particular will, or act of magistracy – at the most a decree.

But our political theorists, unable to divide Sovereignty in principle, divide it according to its object: into force and will; into legislative power and executive power; into rights of taxation, justice and war; into internal administration and power of foreign treaty. Sometimes they confuse all these sections, and sometimes they distinguish them; they turn the Sovereign into a fantastic being composed of several connected pieces: it is as if they were making man of several bodies, one with eyes, one with arms, another with feet, and each with nothing besides. We are told that the jugglers of Japan dismember a child before the eyes of the spectators; then they throw all the members into the air one after another, and the child falls down alive and whole. The conjuring tricks of our political theorists are very like that; they first dismember the Body politic by an illusion worthy of a fair, and then join it together again we know not how.

This error is due to a lack of exact notions concerning the Sovereign authority, and to taking for parts of it what are only emanations from it. Thus, for example, the acts of declaring war and making peace have been regarded as acts of Sovereignty; but this is not the case, as these acts do not constitute law, but merely the application of a law, a particular act which decides how the law applies, as we shall see clearly when the idea attached to the word law has been defined.

If we examined the other divisions in the same manner, we should find that, whenever Sovereignty seems to be divided, there is an illusion: the rights which are taken as being part of Sovereignty are really all subordinate, and always imply supreme wills of which they only sanction the execution.

It would be impossible to estimate the obscurity this lack of exactness has thrown over the decisions of writers who have dealt with political right, when they have used the principles laid down by them to pass judgment on the respective rights of kings and peoples. Every one can see, in Chapters III and IV of the First Book of Grotius, how the learned man and his translator, Barbeyrac, entangle and tie themselves up in their own sophistries, for fear of saying too little or too much of what they think, and so offending the interests they have to conciliate. Grotius, a refugee in France, ill-content with his own country, and desirous of paying his court to Louis XIII, to whom his book is dedicated, spares no pains to rob the peoples of all their rights and invest kings with them by every conceivable artifice. This would also have been much to the taste of Barbeyrac, who dedicated his translation to George I of England. But unfortunately the expulsion of James II, which he called his "abdication," compelled him to use all reserve, to shuffle and to tergiversate, in order to avoid making William out a usurper. If these two writers had adopted the true principles, all difficulties would have been removed, and they would have been always consistent; but it would have been a sad truth for them to tell, and would have paid court for them to no one save the people. Moreover, truth is no road to fortune, and the people dispenses neither ambassadorships, nor professorships, nor pensions.

3. WHETHER THE GENERAL WILL IS FALLIBLE

IT follows from what has gone before that the general will is always right and tends to the public advantage; but it does not follow that the deliberations of the people are always equally correct. Our will is always for our own good, but we do not always see what that is; the people is never corrupted, but it is often deceived, and on such occasions only does it seem to will what is bad.

There is often a great deal of difference between the will of all and the general will; the latter considers only the common interest, while the former takes private interest into account, and is no more than a sum of particular wills: but take away from these same wills the pluses and minuses that cancel one another,[7] and the general will remains as the sum of the differences.

If, when the people, being furnished with adequate information, held its deliberations, the citizens had no communication one with another, the grand total of the small differences would always give the general will, and the decision would always be good. But when factions arise, and partial associations are formed at the expense of the great association, the will of each of these associations becomes general in relation to its members, while it remains particular in relation to the State: it may then be said that there are no longer as many votes as there are men, but only as many as there are associations. The differences become less numerous and give a less general result. Lastly, when one of these associations is so great as to prevail over all the rest, the result is no longer a sum of small differences, but a single difference; in this case there is no longer a general will, and the opinion which prevails is purely particular.

It is therefore essential, if the general will is to be able to express itself, that there should be no partial society within the State, and that each citizen should
5 think only his own thoughts:[8] which was indeed the sublime and unique system established by the great Lycurgus. But if there are partial societies, it is best to have as many as possible and to prevent them from being unequal, as was done by Solon, Numa and Servius. These precautions are the only ones that can guarantee that the general will shall be always enlightened, and that the people
10 shall in no way deceive itself.

4. THE LIMITS OF THE SOVEREIGN POWER

IF the State is a moral person whose life is in the union of its members, and if the most important of its cares is the care for its own preservation, it must have a universal and compelling force, in order to move and dispose each part as may be most advantageous to the whole. As nature gives each man absolute
15 power over all his members, the social compact gives the body politic absolute power over all its members also; and it is this power which, under the direction of the general will, bears, as I have said, the name of Sovereignty.

But, besides the public person, we have to consider the private persons composing it, whose life and liberty are naturally independent of it. We are
20 bound then to distinguish clearly between the respective rights of the citizens and the Sovereign,[9] and between the duties the former have to fulfil as subjects, and the natural rights they should enjoy as men.

Each man alienates, I admit, by the social compact, only such part of his powers, goods and liberty as it is important for the community to control; but it
25 must also be granted that the Sovereign is sole judge of what is important.

Every service a citizen can render the State he ought to render as soon as the Sovereign demands it; but the Sovereign, for its part, cannot impose upon its subjects any fetters that are useless to the community, nor can it even wish to do so; for no more by the law of reason than by the law of nature can anything
30 occur without a cause.

The undertakings which bind us to the social body are obligatory only because they are mutual; and their nature is such that in fulfilling them we cannot work for others without working for ourselves. Why is it that the general will is always in the right, and that all continually will the happiness of each
35 one, unless it is because there is not a man who does not think of "each" as meaning him, and consider himself in voting for all? This proves that equality of rights and the idea of justice which such equality creates originate in the preference each man gives to himself, and accordingly in the very nature of

man. It proves that the general will, to be really such, must be general in its object as well as its essence; that it must both come from all and apply to all; and that it loses its natural rectitude when it is directed to some particular and determinate object, because in such a case we are judging of something foreign to us, and have no true principle of equity to guide us.

Indeed, as soon as a question of particular fact or right arises on a point not previously regulated by a general convention, the matter becomes contentious. It is a case in which the individuals concerned are one party, and the public the other, but in which I can see neither the law that ought to be followed nor the judge who ought to give the decision. In such a case, it would be absurd to propose to refer the question to an express decision of the general will, which can be only the conclusion reached by one of the parties and in consequence will be, for the other party, merely an external and particular will, inclined on this occasion to injustice and subject to error. Thus, just as a particular will cannot stand for the general will, the general will, in turn, changes its nature, when its object is particular, and, as general, cannot pronounce on a man or a fact. When, for instance, the people of Athens nominated or displaced its rulers, decreed honours to one, and imposed penalties on another, and, by a multitude of particular decrees, exercised all the functions of government indiscriminately, it had in such cases no longer a general will in the strict sense; it was acting no longer as Sovereign, but as magistrate. This will seem contrary to current views; but I must be given time to expound my own.

It should be seen from the foregoing that what makes the will general is less the number of voters than the common interest uniting them; for, under this system, each necessarily submits to the conditions he imposes on others: and this admirable agreement between interest and justice gives to the common deliberations an equitable character which at once vanishes when any particular question is discussed, in the absence of a common interest to unite and identify the ruling of the judge with that of the party.

From whatever side we approach our principle, we reach the same conclusion, that the social compact sets up among the citizens an equality of such a kind, that they all bind themselves to observe the same conditions and should therefore all enjoy the same rights. Thus, from the very nature of the compact, every act of Sovereignty, i.e., every authentic act of the general will, binds or favours all the citizens equally; so that the Sovereign recognises only the body of the nation, and draws no distinctions between those of whom it is made up. What, then, strictly speaking, is an act of Sovereignty? It is not a convention between a superior and an inferior, but a convention between the body and each of its members. It is legitimate, because based on the social contract, and equitable, because common to all; useful, because it can have no

other object than the general good, and stable, because guaranteed by the public force and the supreme power. So long as the subjects have to submit only to conventions of this sort, they obey no-one but their own will; and to ask how far the respective rights of the Sovereign and the citizens extend, is to ask up to
5   what point the latter can enter into undertakings with themselves, each with all, and all with each.

We can see from this that the sovereign power, absolute, sacred and inviolable as it is, does not and cannot exceed the limits of general conventions, and that every man may dispose at will of such goods and liberty as these
10   conventions leave him; so that the Sovereign never has a right to lay more charges on one subject than on another, because, in that case, the question becomes particular, and ceases to be within its competency.

When these distinctions have once been admitted, it is seen to be so untrue that there is, in the social contract, any real renunciation on the part of the
15   individuals, that the position in which they find themselves as a result of the contract is really preferable to that in which they were before. Instead of a renunciation, they have made an advantageous exchange: instead of an uncertain and precarious way of living they have got one that is better and more secure; instead of natural independence they have got liberty, instead of the power to
20   harm others security for themselves, and instead of their strength, which others might overcome, a right which social union makes invincible. Their very life, which they have devoted to the State, is by it constantly protected; and when they risk it in the State's defence, what more are they doing than giving back what they have received from it? What are they doing that they would not do
25   more often and with greater danger in the state of nature, in which they would inevitably have to fight battles at the peril of their lives in defence of that which is the means of their preservation? All have indeed to fight when their country needs them; but then no one has ever to fight for himself. Do we not gain something by running, on behalf of what gives us our security, only some of the
30   risks we should have to run for ourselves, as soon as we lost it?

5. THE RIGHT OF LIFE AND DEATH

THE question is often asked how individuals, having no right to dispose of their own lives, can transfer to the Sovereign a right which they do not possess. The difficulty of answering this question seems to me to lie in its being wrongly stated. Every man has a right to risk his own life in order to preserve it. Has it
35   ever been said that a man who throws himself out of the window to escape from a fire is guilty of suicide? Has such a crime ever been laid to the charge of him who perishes in a storm because, when he went on board, he knew of the danger?

The social treaty has for its end the preservation of the contracting parties. He who wills the end wills the means also, and the means must involve some risks, and even some losses. He who wishes to preserve his life at others' expense should also, when it is necessary, be ready to give it up for their sake.

5 Furthermore, the citizen is no longer the judge of the dangers to which the law-desires him to expose himself; and when the prince says to him: "It is expedient for the State that you should die," he ought to die, because it is only on that condition that he has been living in security up to the present, and because his life is no longer a mere bounty of nature, but a gift made conditionally by the

10 State.

The death-penalty inflicted upon criminals may be looked on in much the same light: it is in order that we may not fall victims to an assassin that we consent to die if we ourselves turn assassins. In this treaty, so far from disposing of our own lives, we think only of securing them, and it is not to be assumed that

15 any of the parties then expects to get hanged.

Again, every malefactor, by attacking social rights, becomes on forfeit a rebel and a traitor to his country; by violating its laws be ceases to be a member of it; he even makes war upon it. In such a case the preservation of the State is inconsistent with his own, and one or the other must perish; in putting the guilty

20 to death, we slay not so much the citizen as an enemy. The trial and the judgment are the proofs that he has broken the social treaty, and is in consequence no longer a member of the State. Since, then, he has recognised himself to be such by living there, he must be removed by exile as a violator of the compact, or by death as a public enemy; for such an enemy is not a moral

25 person, but merely a man; and in such a case the right of war is to kill the vanquished.

But, it will be said, the condemnation of a criminal is a particular act. I admit it: but such condemnation is not a function of the Sovereign; it is a right the Sovereign can confer without being able itself to exert it. All my ideas are

30 consistent, but I cannot expound them all at once.

We may add that frequent punishments are always a sign of weakness or remissness on the part of the government. There is not a single ill-doer who could not be turned to some good. The State has no right to put to death, even for the sake of making an example, any one whom it can leave alive without

35 danger.

The right of pardoning or exempting the guilty from a penalty imposed by the law and pronounced by the judge belongs only to the authority which is superior to both judge and law, i.e., the Sovereign; each its right in this matter is far from clear, and the cases for exercising it are extremely rare. In a well-

40 governed State, there are few punishments, not because there are many pardons,

but because criminals are rare; it is when a State is in decay that the multitude of crimes is a guarantee of impunity. Under the Roman Republic, neither the Senate nor the Consuls ever attempted to pardon; even the people never did so, though it sometimes revoked its own decision. Frequent pardons mean that
5   crime will soon need them no longer, and no one can help seeing whither that leads. But I feel my heart protesting and restraining my pen; let us leave these questions to the just man who has never offended, and would himself stand in no need of pardon.

6. LAW

BY the social compact we have given the body politic existence and life; we
10   have now by legislation to give it movement and will. For the original act by which the body is formed and united still in no respect determines what it ought to do for its preservation.

What is well and in conformity with order is so by the nature of things and independently of human conventions. All justice comes from God, who is its
15   sole source; but if we knew how to receive so high an inspiration, we should need neither government nor laws. Doubtless, there is a universal justice emanating from reason alone; but this justice, to be admitted among us, must be mutual. Humanly speaking, in default of natural sanctions, the laws of justice are ineffective among men: they merely make for the good of the wicked and the
20   undoing of the just, when the just man observes them towards everybody and nobody observes them towards him. Conventions and laws are therefore needed to join rights to duties and refer justice to its object. In the state of nature, where everything is common, I owe nothing to him whom I have promised nothing; I recognise as belonging to others only what is of no use to me. In the state of
25   society all rights are fixed by law, and the case becomes different.

But what, after all, is a law? As long as we remain satisfied with attaching purely metaphysical ideas to the word, we shall go on arguing without arriving at an understanding; and when we have defined a law of nature, we shall be no nearer the definition of a law of the State.
30   I have already said that there can be no general will directed to a particular object. Such an object must be either within or outside the State. If outside, a will which is alien to it cannot be, in relation to it, general; if within, it is part of the State, and in that case there arises a relation between whole and part which makes them two separate beings, of which the part is one, and the whole minus
35   the part the other. But the whole minus a part cannot be the whole; and while this relation persists, there can be no whole, but only two unequal parts; and it follows that the will of one is no longer in any respect general in relation to the other.

But when the whole people decrees for the whole people, it is considering only itself; and if a relation is then formed, it is between two aspects of the entire object, without there being any division of the whole. In that case the matter about which the decree is made is, like the decreeing will, general. This act is what I call a law.

When I say that the object of laws is always general, I mean that law considers subjects en masse and actions in the abstract, and never a particular person or action. Thus the law may indeed decree that there shall be privileges, but cannot confer them on anybody by name. It may set up several classes of citizens, and even lay down the qualifications for membership of these classes, but it cannot nominate such and such persons as belonging to them; it may establish a monarchical government and hereditary succession, but it cannot choose a king, or nominate a royal family. In a word, no function which has a particular object belongs to the legislative power.

On this view, we at once see that it can no longer be asked whose business it is to make laws, since they are acts of the general will; nor whether the prince is above the law, since he is a member of the State; nor whether the law can be unjust, since no one is unjust to himself; nor how we can be both free and subject to the laws, since they are but registers of our wills.

We see further that, as the law unites universality of will with universality of object, what a man, whoever he be, commands of his own motion cannot be a law; and even what the Sovereign commands with regard to a particular matter is no nearer being a law, but is a decree, an act, not of sovereignty, but of magistracy.

I therefore give the name "Republic" to every State that is governed by laws, no matter what the form of its administration may be: for only in such a case does the public interest govern, and the res publica rank as a reality. Every legitimate government is republican;[10] what government is I will explain later on.

Laws are, properly speaking, only the conditions of civil association. The people, being subject to the laws, ought to be their author: the conditions of the society ought to be regulated solely by those who come together to form it. But how are they to regulate them? Is it to be by common agreement, by a sudden inspiration? Has the body politic an organ to declare its will? Who can give it the foresight to formulate and announce its acts in advance? Or how is it to announce them in the hour of need? How can a blind multitude, which often does not know what it wills, because it rarely knows what is good for it, carry out for itself so great and difficult an enterprise as a system of legislation? Of itself the people wills always the good, but of itself it by no means always sees it. The general will is always in the right, but the judgment which guides it is not always enlightened. It must be got to see objects as they are, and sometimes as they ought to appear to it; it must be shown the good road it is in search of, secured from the seductive influences of individual wills, taught to see times and spaces as a series, and made to weigh the attractions of present and sensible

5   advantages against the danger of distant and hidden evils. The individuals see the good they reject; the public wills the good it does not see. All stand equally in need of guidance. The former must be compelled to bring their wills into conformity with their reason; the latter must be taught to know what it wills. If that is done, public enlightenment leads to the union of understanding and will

10   in the social body: the parts are made to work exactly together, and the whole is raised to its highest power. This makes a legislator necessary.

7. THE LEGISLATOR

  IN order to discover the rules of society best suited to nations, a superior intelligence beholding all the passions of men without experiencing any of them would be needed. This intelligence would have to be wholly unrelated to our

15   nature, while knowing it through and through; its happiness would have to be independent of us, and yet ready to occupy itself with ours; and lastly, it would have, in the march of time, to look forward to a distant glory, and, working in one century, to be able to enjoy in the next.[11] It would take gods to give men laws.

20   What Caligula argued from the facts, Plato, in the dialogue called the Politicus, argued in defining the civil or kingly man, on the basis of right. But if great princes are rare, how much more so are great legislators? The former have only to follow the pattern which the latter have to lay down. The legislator is the engineer who invents the machine, the prince merely the mechanic who sets it

25   up and makes it go. "At the birth of societies," says Montesquieu, "the rulers of Republics establish institutions, and afterwards the institutions mould the rulers."[12]

  He who dares to undertake the making of a people's institutions ought to feel himself capable, so to speak, of changing human nature, of transforming

30   each individual, who is by himself a complete and solitary whole, into part of a greater whole from which he in a manner receives his life and being; of altering man's constitution for the purpose of strengthening it; and of substituting a partial and moral existence for the physical and independent existence nature has conferred on us all. He must, in a word, take away from man his own

35   resources and give him instead new ones alien to him, and incapable of being made use of without the help of other men. The more completely these natural resources are annihilated, the greater and the more lasting are those which he acquires, and the more stable and perfect the new institutions; so that if each

citizen is nothing and can do nothing without the rest, and the resources acquired by the whole are equal or superior to the aggregate of the resources of all the individuals, it may be said that legislation is at the highest possible point of perfection.

5   The legislator occupies in every respect an extraordinary position in the State. If he should do so by reason of his genius, he does so no less by reason of his office, which is neither magistracy, nor Sovereignty. This office, which sets up the Republic, nowhere enters into its constitution; it is an individual and superior function, which has nothing in common with human empire; for if he

10   who holds command over men ought not to have command over the laws, he who has command over the laws ought not any more to have it over men; or else his laws would be the ministers of his passions and would often merely serve to perpetuate his injustices: his private aims would inevitably mar the sanctity of his work.

15   When Lycurgus gave laws to his country, he began by resigning the throne. It was the custom of most Greek towns to entrust the establishment of their laws to foreigners. The Republics of modern Italy in many cases followed this example; Geneva did the same and profited by it.[13] Rome, when it was most prosperous, suffered a revival of all the crimes of tyranny, and was brought to

20   the verge of destruction, because it put the legislative authority and the sovereign power into the same hands.

    Nevertheless, the decemvirs themselves never claimed the right to pass any law merely on their own authority. "Nothing we propose to you," they said to the people, "can pass into law without your consent. Romans, be yourselves the

25   authors of the laws which are to make you happy."

    He, therefore, who draws up the laws has, or should have, no right of legislation, and the people cannot, even if it wishes, deprive itself of this incommunicable right, because, according to the fundamental compact, only the general will can bind the individuals, and there can be no assurance that a

30   particular will is in conformity with the general will, until it has been put to the free vote of the people. This I have said already; but it is worth while to repeat it.

    Thus in the task of legislation we find together two things which appear to be incompatible: an enterprise too difficult for human powers, and, for its

35   execution, an authority that is no authority.

    There is a further difficulty that deserves attention. Wise men, if they try to speak their language to the common herd instead of its own, cannot possibly make themselves understood. There are a thousand kinds of ideas which it is impossible to translate into popular language. Conceptions that are too general

40   and objects that are too remote are equally out of its range: each individual,

having no taste for any other plan of government than that which suits his particular interest, finds it difficult to realise the advantages he might hope to draw from the continual privations good laws impose. For a young people to be able to relish sound principles of political theory and follow the fundamental rules of statecraft, the effect would have to become the cause; the social spirit, which should be created by these institutions, would have to preside over their very foundation; and men would have to be before law what they should become by means of law. The legislator therefore, being unable to appeal to either force or reason, must have recourse to an authority of a different order, capable of constraining without violence and persuading without convincing.

This is what has, in all ages, compelled the fathers of nations to have recourse to divine intervention and credit the gods with their own wisdom, in order that the peoples, submitting to the laws of the State as to those of nature, and recognising the same power in the formation of the city as in that of man, might obey freely, and bear with docility the yoke of the public happiness.

This sublime reason, far above the range of the common herd, is that whose decisions the legislator puts into the mouth of the immortals, in order to constrain by divine authority those whom human prudence could not move.[14] But it is not anybody who can make the gods speak, or get himself believed when he proclaims himself their interpreter. The great soul of the legislator is the only miracle that can prove his mission. Any man may grave tablets of stone, or buy an oracle, or feign secret intercourse with some divinity, or train a bird to whisper in his ear, or find other vulgar ways of imposing on the people. He whose knowledge goes no further may perhaps gather round him a band of fools; but he will never found an empire, and his extravagances will quickly perish with him. Idle tricks form a passing tie; only wisdom can make it lasting. The Judaic law, which still subsists, and that of the child of Ishmael, which, for ten centuries, has ruled half the world, still proclaim the great men who laid them down; and, while the pride of philosophy or the blind spirit of faction sees in them no more than lucky impostures, the true political theorist admires, in the institutions they set up, the great and powerful genius which presides over things made to endure.

We should not, with Warburton, conclude from this that politics and religion have among us a common object, but that, in the first periods of nations, the one is used as an instrument for the other.

8. THE PEOPLE

AS, before putting up a large building, the architect surveys and sounds the site to see if it will bear the weight, the wise legislator does not begin by laying down laws good in themselves, but by investigating the fitness of the people, for which they are destined, to receive them. Plato refused to legislate for the Arcadians and the Cyrenæans, because he knew that both peoples were rich and could not put up with equality; and good laws and bad men were found together in Crete, because Minos had inflicted discipline on a people already burdened with vice.

5

A thousand nations have achieved earthly greatness, that could never have endured good laws; even such as could have endured them could have done so only for a very brief period of their long history. Most peoples, like most men, are docile only in youth; as they grow old they become incorrigible. When once customs have become established and prejudices inveterate, it is dangerous and useless to attempt their reformation; the people, like the foolish and cowardly patients who rave at sight of the doctor, can no longer bear that any one should lay hands on its faults to remedy them.

10

There are indeed times in the history of States when, just as some kinds of illness turn men's heads and make them forget the past, periods of violence and revolutions do to peoples what these crises do to individuals: horror of the past takes the place of forgetfulness, and the State, set on fire by civil wars, is born again, so to speak, from its ashes, and takes on anew, fresh from the jaws of death, the vigour of youth. Such were Sparta at the time of Lycurgus, Rome after the Tarquins, and, in modern times, Holland and Switzerland after the expulsion of the tyrants.

15

20

But such events are rare; they are exceptions, the cause of which is always to be found in the particular constitution of the State concerned. They cannot even happen twice to the same people, for it can make itself free as long as it remains barbarous, but not when the civic impulse has lost its vigour. Then disturbances may destroy it, but revolutions cannot mend it: it needs a master, and not a liberator. Free peoples, be mindful of this maxim: "Liberty may be gained, but can never be recovered."

25

Youth is not infancy. There is for nations, as for men, a period of youth, or, shall we say, maturity, before which they should not be made subject to laws; but the maturity of a people is not always easily recognisable, and, if it is anticipated, the work is spoilt. One people is amenable to discipline from the beginning; another, not after ten centuries. Russia will never be really civilised, because it was civilised too soon. Peter had a genius for imitation; but he lacked true genius, which is creative and makes all from nothing. He did some good things, but most of what he did was out of place. He saw that his people was barbarous, but did not see that it was not ripe for civilisation: he wanted to civilise it when it needed only hardening. His first wish was to make Germans or Englishmen, when he ought to have been making Russians; and he prevented his subjects from ever becoming what they might have been by persuading them

30

35

40

that they were what they are not. In this fashion too a French teacher turns out his pupil to be an infant prodigy, and for the rest of his life to be nothing whatsoever. The empire of Russia will aspire to conquer Europe, and will itself be conquered. The Tartars, its subjects or neighbours, will become its masters

5   and ours, by a revolution which I regard as inevitable. Indeed, all the kings of Europe are working in concert to hasten its coming.

9. THE PEOPLE (continued)

As nature has set bounds to the stature of a well-made man, and, outside those limits, makes nothing but giants or dwarfs, similarly, for the constitution of a State to be at its best, it is possible to fix limits that will make it neither too

10   large for good government, nor too small for self-maintenance. In every body politic there is a maximum strength which it cannot exceed and which it only loses by increasing in size. Every extension of the social tie means its relaxation; and, generally speaking, a small State is stronger in proportion than a great one.

A thousand arguments could be advanced in favour of this principle. First,

15   long distances make administration more difficult, just as a weight becomes heavier at the end of a longer lever. Administration therefore becomes more and more burdensome as the distance grows greater; for, in the first place, each city has its own, which is paid for by the people: each district its own, still paid for by the people: then comes each province, and then the great governments,

20   satrapies, and vice-royalties, always costing more the higher you go, and always at the expense of the unfortunate people. Last of all comes the supreme administration, which eclipses all the rest. All these over charges are a continual drain upon the subjects; so far from being better governed by all these different orders, they are worse governed than if there were only a single authority over

25   them. In the meantime, there scarce remain resources enough to meet emergencies; and, when recourse must be had to these, the State is always on the eve of destruction.

This is not all; not only has the government less vigour and promptitude for securing the observance of the laws, preventing nuisances, correcting abuses,

30   and guarding against seditious undertakings begun in distant places; the people has less affection for its rulers, whom it never sees, for its country, which, to its eyes, seems like the world, and for its fellow-citizens, most of whom are unknown to it. The same laws cannot suit so many diverse provinces with different customs, situated in the most various climates, and incapable of

35   enduring a uniform government. Different laws lead only to trouble and confusion among peoples which, living under the same rulers and in constant communication one with another, intermingle and intermarry, and, coming under the sway of new customs, never know if they can call their very

117

patrimony their own. Talent is buried, virtue unknown and vice unpunished, among such a multitude of men who do not know one another, gathered together in one place at the seat of the central administration. The leaders, overwhelmed with business, see nothing for themselves; the State is governed by clerks.
5 Finally, the measures which have to be taken to maintain the general authority, which all these distant officials wish to escape or to impose upon, absorb all the energy of the public, so that there is none left for the happiness of the people. There is hardly enough to defend it when need arises, and thus a body which is too big for its constitution gives way and falls crushed under its own weight.
10 Again, the State must assure itself a safe foundation, if it is to have stability, and to be able to resist the shocks it cannot help experiencing, as well as the efforts it will be forced to make for its maintenance; for all peoples have a kind of centrifugal force that makes them continually act one against another, and tend to aggrandise themselves at their neighbours' expense, like the vortices of
15 Descartes. Thus the weak run the risk of being soon swallowed up; and it is almost impossible for any one to preserve itself except by putting itself in a state of equilibrium with all, so that the pressure is on all sides practically equal.

It may therefore be seen that there are reasons for expansion and reasons for contraction; and it is no small part of the statesman's skill to hit between them
20 the mean that is most favourable to the preservation of the State. It may be said that the reason for expansion, being merely external and relative, ought to be subordinate to the reasons for contraction, which are internal and absolute. A strong and healthy constitution is the first thing to look for; and it is better to count on the vigour which comes of good government than on the resources a
25 great territory furnishes.

It may be added that there have been known States so constituted that the necessity of making conquests entered into their very constitution, and that, in order to maintain themselves, they were forced to expand ceaselessly. It may be that they congratulated themselves greatly on this fortunate necessity, which
30 none the less indicated to them, along with the limits of their greatness, the inevitable moment of their fall.

10. THE PEOPLE (continued)

A BODY politic may be measured in two ways – either by the extent of its territory, or by the number of its people; and there is, between these two measurements, a right relation which makes the State really great. The men
35 make the State, and the territory sustains the men; the right relation therefore is that the land should suffice for the maintenance of the inhabitants, and that there should be as many inhabitants as the land can maintain. In this proportion lies the maximum strength of a given number of people; for, if there is too much

land, it is troublesome to guard and inadequately cultivated, produces more than is needed, and soon gives rise to wars of defence; if there is not enough, the State depends on its neighbours for what it needs over and above, and this soon gives rise to wars of offence. Every people, to which its situation gives no

5 choice save that between commerce and war, is weak in itself: it depends on its neighbours, and on circumstances; its existence can never be more than short and uncertain. It either conquers others, and changes its situation, or it is conquered and becomes nothing. Only insignificance or greatness can keep it free.

10 No fixed relation can be stated between the extent of territory and the population that are adequate one to the other, both because of the differences in the quality of land, in its fertility, in the nature of its products, and in the influence of climate, and because of the different tempers of those who inhabit it; for some in a fertile country consume little, and others on an ungrateful soil

15 much. The greater or less fecundity of women, the conditions that are more or less favourable in each country to the growth of population, and the influence the legislator can hope to exercise by his institutions, must also be taken into account. The legislator therefore should not go by what he sees, but by what he foresees; he should stop not so much at the state in which he actually finds the

20 population, as at that to which it ought naturally to attain. Lastly, there are countless cases in which the particular local circumstances demand or allow the acquisition of a greater territory than seems necessary. Thus, expansion will be great in a mountainous country, where the natural products, i.e., woods and pastures, need less labour, where we know from experience that women are

25 more fertile than in the plains, and where a great expanse of slope affords only a small level tract that can be counted on for vegetation. On the other hand, contraction is possible on the coast, even in lands of rocks and nearly barren sands, because there fishing makes up to a great extent for the lack of land-produce, because the inhabitants have to congregate together more in order to

30 repel pirates, and further because it is easier to unburden the country of its superfluous inhabitants by means of colonies.

To these conditions of law-giving must be added one other which, though it cannot take the place of the rest, renders them all useless when it is absent. This is the enjoyment of peace and plenty; for the moment at which a State sets its

35 house in order is, like the moment when a battalion is forming up, that when its body is least capable of offering resistance and easiest to destroy. A better resistance could be made at a time of absolute disorganisation than at a moment of fermentation, when each is occupied with his own position and not with the danger. If war, famine, or sedition arises at this time of crisis, the State will

40 inevitably be overthrown.

Not that many governments have not been set up during such storms; but in such cases these governments are themselves the State's destroyers. Usurpers always bring about or select troublous times to get passed, under cover of the public terror, destructive laws, which the people would never adopt in cold
5 blood. The moment chosen is one of the surest means of distinguishing the work of the legislator from that of the tyrant.

What people, then, is a fit subject for legislation? One which, already bound by some unity of origin, interest, or convention, has never yet felt the real yoke of law; one that has neither customs nor superstitions deeply ingrained, one
10 which stands in no fear of being overwhelmed by sudden invasion; one which, without entering into its neighbours' quarrels, can resist each of them single-handed, or get the help of one to repel another; one in which every member may be known by every other, and there is no need to lay on any man burdens too heavy for a man to bear; one which can do without other peoples, and without
15 which all others can do;[15] one which is neither rich nor poor, but self-sufficient; and, lastly, one which unites the consistency of an ancient people with the docility of a new one. Legislation is made difficult less by what it is necessary to build up than by what has to be destroyed; and what makes success so rare is the impossibility of finding natural simplicity together with social requirements. All
20 these conditions are indeed rarely found united, and therefore few States have good constitutions.

There is still in Europe one country capable of being given laws – Corsica. The valour and persistency with which that brave people has regained and defended its liberty well deserves that some wise man should teach it how to
25 preserve what it has won. I have a feeling that some day that little island will astonish Europe.

11. THE VARIOUS SYSTEMS OF LEGISLATION

IF we ask in what precisely consists the greatest good of all, which should be the end of every system of legislation, we shall find it reduce itself to two main objects, liberty and equality – liberty, because all particular dependence
30 means so much force taken from the body of the State and equality, because liberty cannot exist without it.

I have already defined civil liberty; by equality, we should understand, not that the degrees of power and riches are to be absolutely identical for everybody; but that power shall never be great enough for violence, and shall always be
35 exercised by virtue of rank and law; and that, in respect of riches, no citizen shall ever be wealthy enough to buy another, and none poor enough to be forced to sell himself:[16] which implies, on the part of the great, moderation in goods

and position, and, on the side of the common sort, moderation in avarice and covetousness.

Such equality, we are told, is an unpractical ideal that cannot actually exist. But if its abuse is inevitable, does it follow that we should not at least make
5 regulations concerning it? It is precisely because the force of circumstances tends continually to destroy equality that the force of legislation should always tend to its maintenance.

But these general objects of every good legislative system need modifying in every country in accordance with the local situation and the temper of the
10 inhabitants; and these circumstances should determine, in each case, the particular system of institutions which is best, not perhaps in itself, but for the State for which it is destined. If, for instance, the soil is barren and unproductive, or the land too crowded for its inhabitants, the people should turn to industry and the crafts, and exchange what they produce for the commodities they lack.
15 If, on the other hand, a people dwells in rich plains and fertile slopes, or, in a good land, lacks inhabitants, it should give all its attention to agriculture, which causes men to multiply, and should drive out the crafts, which would only result in depopulation, by grouping in a few localities the few inhabitants there are.[17] If a nation dwells on an extensive and convenient coast-line, let it cover the sea
20 with ships and foster commerce and navigation. It will have a life that will be short and glorious. If, on its coasts, the sea washes nothing but almost inaccessible rocks, let it remain barbarous and ichthyophagous: it will have a quieter, perhaps a better, and certainly a happier life. In a word, besides the principles that are common to all, every nation has in itself something that gives
25 them a particular application, and makes its legislation peculiarly its own. Thus, among the Jews long ago and more recently among the Arabs, the chief object was religion, among the Athenians letters, at Carthage and Tyre commerce, at Rhodes shipping, at Sparta war, at Rome virtue. The author of The Spirit of the Laws has shown with many examples by what art the legislator directs the
30 constitution towards each of these objects. What makes the constitution of a State really solid and lasting is the due observance of what is proper, so that the natural relations are always in agreement with the laws on every point, and law only serves, so to speak, to assure, accompany and rectify them. But if the legislator mistakes his object and adopts a principle other than circumstances
35 naturally direct; if his principle makes for servitude while they make for liberty, or if it makes for riches, while they make for populousness, or if it makes for peace, while they make for conquest – the laws will insensibly lose their influence, the constitution will alter, and the State will have no rest from trouble till it is either destroyed or changed, and nature has resumed her invincible
40 sway.

12. THE DIVISION OF THE LAWS

IF the whole is to be set in order, and the commonwealth put into the best possible shape, there are various relations to be considered. First, there is the action of the complete body upon itself, the relation of the whole to the whole, of the Sovereign to the State; and this relation, as we shall see, is made up of the relations of the intermediate terms.

The laws which regulate this relation bear the name of political laws, and are also called fundamental laws, not without reason if they are wise. For, if there is, in each State, only one good system, the people that is in possession of it should hold fast to this; but if the established order is bad, why should laws that prevent men from being good be regarded as fundamental? Besides, in any case, a people is always in a position to change its laws, however good; for, if it choose to do itself harm, who can have a right to stop it?

The second relation is that of the members one to another, or to the body as a whole; and this relation should be in the first respect as unimportant, and in the second as important, as possible. Each citizen would then be perfectly independent of all the rest, and at the same time very dependent on the city; which is brought about always by the same means, as the strength of the State can alone secure the liberty of its members. From this second relation arise civil laws.

We may consider also a third kind of relation between the individual and the law, a relation of disobedience to its penalty. This gives rise to the setting up of criminal laws, which, at bottom, are less a particular class of law than the sanction behind all the rest.

Along with these three kinds of law goes a fourth, most important of all, which is not graven on tablets of marble or brass, but on the hearts of the citizens. This forms the real constitution of the State, takes on every day new powers, when other laws decay or die out, restores them or takes their place, keeps a people in the ways in which it was meant to go, and insensibly replaces authority by the force of habit. I am speaking of morality, of custom, above all of public opinion; a power unknown to political thinkers, on which none the less success in everything else depends. With this the great legislator concerns himself in secret, though he seems to confine himself to particular regulations; for these are only the arc of the arch, while manners and morals, slower to arise, form in the end its immovable keystone.

Among the different classes of laws, the political, which determine the forms of the government, are alone relevant to my subject.

BOOK III

BEFORE speaking of the different forms of government, let us try to fix the exact sense of the word, which has not yet been very clearly explained.

1. GOVERNMENT IN GENERAL

I WARN the reader that this chapter requires careful reading, and that I am unable to make myself clear to those who refuse to be attentive. Every free
5   action is produced by the concurrence of two causes; one moral, i.e., the will which determines the act; the other physical, i.e., the power which executes it. When I walk towards an object, it is necessary first that I should will to go there, and, in the second place, that my feet should carry me. If a paralytic wills to run and an active man wills not to, they will both stay where they are. The body
10   politic has the same motive powers; here too force and will are distinguished, will under the name of legislative power and force under that of executive power. Without their concurrence, nothing is, or should be, done.

We have seen that the legislative power belongs to the people, and can belong to it alone. It may, on the other hand, readily be seen, from the principles
15   laid down above, that the executive power cannot belong to the generality as legislature or Sovereign, because it consists wholly of particular acts which fall outside the competency of the law, and consequently of the Sovereign, whose acts must always be laws.

The public force therefore needs an agent of its own to bind it together and
20   set it to work under the direction of the general will, to serve as a means of communication between the State and the Sovereign, and to do for the collective person more or less what the union of soul and body does for man. Here we have what is, in the State, the basis of government, often wrongly confused with the Sovereign, whose minister it is.

25   What then is government? An intermediate body set up between the subjects and the Sovereign, to secure their mutual correspondence, charged with the execution of the laws and the maintenance of liberty, both civil and political.

The members of this body are called magistrates or kings, that is to say governors, and the whole body bears the name prince.[18] Thus those who hold
30   that the act, by which a people puts itself under a prince, is not a contract, are certainly right. It is simply and solely a commission, an employment, in which the rulers, mere officials of the Sovereign, exercise in their own name the power of which it makes them depositaries. This power it can limit, modify or recover at pleasure; for the alienation of such a right is incompatible with the nature of
35   the social body, and contrary to the end of association.

I call then government, or supreme administration, the legitimate exercise of the executive power, and prince or magistrate the man or the body entrusted with that administration.

In government reside the intermediate forces whose relations make up that of the whole to the whole, or of the Sovereign to the State. This last relation may be represented as that between the extreme terms of a continuous proportion, which has government as its mean proportional. The government gets from the Sovereign the orders it gives the people, and, for the State to be properly balanced, there must, when everything is reckoned in, be equality between the product or power of the government taken in itself, and the product or power of the citizens, who are on the one hand sovereign and on the other subject.

Furthermore, none of these three terms can be altered without the equality being instantly destroyed. If the Sovereign desires to govern, or the magistrate to give laws, or if the subjects refuse to obey, disorder takes the place of regularity, force and will no longer act together, and the State is dissolved and falls into despotism or anarchy. Lastly, as there is only one mean proportional between each relation, there is also only one good government possible for a State. But, as countless events may change the relations of a people, not only may different governments be good for different peoples, but also for the same people at different times.

In attempting to give some idea of the various relations that may hold between these two extreme terms, I shall take as an example the number of a people, which is the most easily expressible.

Suppose the State is composed of ten thousand citizens. The Sovereign can only be considered collectively and as a body; but each member, as being a subject, is regarded as an individual: thus the Sovereign is to the subject as ten thousand to one, i.e., each member of the State has as his share only a ten-thousandth part of the sovereign authority, although he is wholly under its control. If the people numbers a hundred thousand, the condition of the subject undergoes no change, and each equally is under the whole authority of the laws, while his vote, being reduced to a hundred-thousandth part, has ten times less influence in drawing them up. The subject therefore remaining always a unit, the relation between him and the Sovereign increases with the number of the citizens. From this it follows that, the larger the State, the less the liberty.

When I say the relation increases, I mean that it grows more unequal. Thus the greater it is in the geometrical sense, the less relation there is in the ordinary sense of the word. In the former sense, the relation, considered according to quantity, is expressed by the quotient; in the latter, considered according to identity, it is reckoned by similarity.

Now, the less relation the particular wills have to the general will, that is, morals and manners to laws, the more should the repressive force be increased. The government, then, to be good, should be proportionately stronger as the people is more numerous.

5 On the other hand, as the growth of the State gives the depositaries of the public authority more temptations and chances of abusing their power, the greater the force with which the government ought to be endowed for keeping the people in hand, the greater too should be the force at the disposal of the Sovereign for keeping the government in hand. I am speaking, not of absolute
10 force, but of the relative force of the different parts of the State.

It follows from this double relation that the continuous proportion between the Sovereign, the prince and the people, is by no means an arbitrary idea, but a necessary consequence of the nature of the body politic. It follows further that, one of the extreme terms, viz., the people, as subject, being fixed and
15 represented by unity, whenever the duplicate ratio increases or diminishes, the simple ratio does the same, and is changed accordingly. From this we see that there is not a single unique and absolute form of government, but as many governments differing in nature as there are States differing in size.

If, ridiculing this system, any one were to say that, in order to find the mean
20 proportional and give form to the body of the government, it is only necessary, according to me, to find the square root of the number of the people, I should answer that I am here taking this number only as an instance; that the relations of which I am speaking are not measured by the number of men alone, but generally by the amount of action, which is a combination of a multitude of
25 causes; and that, further, if, to save words, I borrow for a moment the terms of geometry, I am none the less well aware that moral quantities do not allow of geometrical accuracy.

The government is on a small scale what the body politic which includes it is on a great one. It is a moral person endowed with certain faculties, active like
30 the Sovereign and passive like the State, and capable of being resolved into other similar relations. This accordingly gives rise to a new proportion, within which there is yet another, according to the arrangement of the magistracies, till an indivisible middle term is reached, i.e., a single ruler or supreme magistrate, who may be represented, in the midst of this progression, as the unity between
35 the fractional and the ordinal series.

Without encumbering ourselves with this multiplication of terms, let us rest content with regarding government as a new body within the State, distinct from the people and the Sovereign, and intermediate between them.

There is between these two bodies this essential difference, that the State
40 exists by itself, and the government only through the Sovereign. Thus the

dominant will of the prince is, or should be, nothing but the general will or the law; his force is only the public force concentrated in his hands, and, as soon as he tries to base any absolute and independent act on his own authority, the tie that binds the whole together begins to be loosened. If finally the prince should
5 come to have a particular will more active than the will of the Sovereign, and should employ the public force in his hands in obedience to this particular will, there would be, so to speak, two Sovereigns, one rightful and the other actual, the social union would evaporate instantly, and the body politic would be dissolved.
10 However, in order that the government may have a true existence and a real life distinguishing it from the body of the State, and in order that all its members may be able to act in concert and fulfill the end for which it was set up, it must have a particular personality, a sensibility common to its members, and a force and will of its own making for its preservation. This particular existence implies
15 assemblies, councils, power and deliberation and decision, rights, titles, and privileges belonging exclusively to the prince and making the office of magistrate more honourable in proportion as it is more troublesome. The difficulties lie in the manner of so ordering this subordinate whole within the whole, that it in no way alters the general constitution by affirmation of its own,
20 and always distinguishes the particular force it possesses, which is destined to aid in its preservation, from the public force, which is destined to the preservation of the State; and, in a word, is always ready to sacrifice the government to the people, and never to sacrifice the people to the government.
Furthermore, although the artificial body of the government is the work of
25 another artificial body, and has, we may say, only a borrowed and subordinate life, this does not prevent it from being able to act with more or less vigour or promptitude, or from being, so to speak, in more or less robust health. Finally, without departing directly from the end for which it was instituted, it may deviate more or less from it, according to the manner of its constitution.
30 From all these differences arise the various relations which the government ought to bear to the body of the State, according to the accidental and particular relations by which the State itself is modified, for often the government that is best in itself will become the most pernicious, if the relations in which it stands have altered according to the defects of the body politic to which it belongs.

2. THE CONSTITUENT PRINCIPLE IN THE VARIOUS FORMS OF GOVERNMENT

35 TO set forth the general cause of the above differences, we must here distinguish between government and its principle, as we did before between the State and the Sovereign.

The body of the magistrate may be composed of a greater or a less number of members. We said that the relation of the Sovereign to the subjects was greater in proportion as the people was more numerous, and, by a clear analogy, we may say the same of the relation of the government to the magistrates.

5 But the total force of the government, being always that of the State, is invariable; so that, the more of this force it expends on its own members, the less it has left to employ on the whole people.

The more numerous the magistrates, therefore, the weaker the government. This principle being fundamental, we must do our best to make it clear.

10 In the person of the magistrate we can distinguish three essentially different wills: first, the private will of the individual, tending only to his personal advantage; secondly, the common will of the magistrates, which is relative solely to the advantage of the prince, and may be called corporate will, being general in relation to the government, and particular in relation to the State, of

15 which the government forms part; and, in the third place, the will of the people or the sovereign will, which is general both in relation to the State regarded as the whole, and to the government regarded as a part of the whole.

In a perfect act of legislation, the individual or particular will should be at zero; the corporate will belonging to the government should occupy a very

20 subordinate position; and, consequently, the general or sovereign will should always predominate and should be the sole guide of all the rest.

According to the natural order, on the other hand, these different wills become more active in proportion as they are concentrated. Thus, the general will is always the weakest, the corporate will second, and the individual will

25 strongest of all: so that, in the government, each member is first of all himself, then a magistrate, and then a citizen – in an order exactly the reverse of what the social system requires.

This granted, if the whole government is in the hands of one man, the particular and the corporate will are wholly united, and consequently the latter is

30 at its highest possible degree of intensity. But, as the use to which the force is put depends on the degree reached by the will, and as the absolute force of the government is invariable, it follows that the most active government is that of one man.

Suppose, on the other hand, we unite the government with the legislative

35 authority, and make the Sovereign prince also, and all the citizens so many magistrates: then the corporate will, being confounded with the general will, can possess no greater activity than that will, and must leave the particular will as strong as it can possibly be. Thus, the government, having always the same absolute force, will be at the lowest point of its relative force or activity.

These relations are incontestable, and there are other considerations which still further confirm them. We can see, for instance, that each magistrate is more active in the body to which he belongs than each citizen in that to which he belongs, and that consequently the particular will has much more influence on the acts of the government than on those of the Sovereign; for each magistrate is almost always charged with some governmental function, while each citizen, taken singly, exercises no function of Sovereignty. Furthermore, the bigger the State grows, the more its real force increases, though not in direct proportion to its growth; but, the State remaining the same, the number of magistrates may increase to any extent, without the government gaining any greater real force; for its force is that of the State, the dimension of which remains equal. Thus the relative force or activity of the government decreases, while its absolute or real force cannot increase.

Moreover, it is a certainty that promptitude in execution diminishes as more people are put in charge of it: where prudence is made too much of, not enough is made of fortune; opportunity is let slip, and deliberation results in the loss of its object.

I have just proved that the government grows remiss in proportion as the number of the magistrates increases; and I previously proved that, the more numerous the people, the greater should be the repressive force. From this it follows that the relation of the magistrates to the government should vary inversely to the relation of the subjects to the Sovereign; that is to say, the larger the State, the more should the government be tightened, so that the number of the rulers diminish in proportion to the increase of that of the people.

It should be added that I am here speaking of the relative strength of the government, and not of its rectitude: for, on the other hand, the more numerous the magistracy, the nearer the corporate will comes to the general will; while, under a single magistrate, the corporate will is, as I said, merely a particular will. Thus, what may be gained on one side is lost on the other, and the art of the legislator is to know how to fix the point at which the force and the will of the government, which are always in inverse proportion, meet in the relation that is most to the advantage of the State.

3. THE DIVISION OF GOVERNMENTS

WE saw in the last chapter what causes the various kinds or forms of government to be distinguished according to the number of the members composing them: it remains in this to discover how the division is made.

In the first place, the Sovereign may commit the charge of the government to the whole people or to the majority of the people, so that more citizens are magistrates than are mere private individuals. This form of government is called democracy.

Or it may restrict the government to a small number, so that there are more private citizens than magistrates; and this is named aristocracy.

5   Lastly, it may concentrate the whole government in the hands of a single magistrate from whom all others hold their power. This third form is the most usual, and is called monarchy, or royal government.

It should be remarked that all these forms, or at least the first two, admit of degree, and even of very wide differences; for democracy may include the
10   whole people, or may be restricted to half. Aristocracy, in its turn, may be restricted indefinitely from half the people down to the smallest possible number. Even royalty is susceptible of a measure of distribution. Sparta always had two kings, as its constitution provided; and the Roman Empire saw as many as eight emperors at once, without it being possible to say that the Empire was
15   split up. Thus there is a point at which each form of government passes into the next, and it becomes clear that, under three comprehensive denominations, government is really susceptible of as many diverse forms as the State has citizens.

There are even more: for, as the government may also, in certain aspects, be
20   subdivided into other parts, one administered in one fashion and one in another, the combination of the three forms may result in a multitude of mixed forms, each of which admits of multiplication by all the simple forms.

There has been at all times much dispute concerning the best form of government, without consideration of the fact that each is in some cases the best,
25   and in others the worst.

If, in the different States, the number of supreme magistrates should be in inverse ratio to the number of citizens, it follows that, generally, democratic government suits small States, aristocratic government those of middle size, and monarchy great ones. This rule is immediately deducible from the principle laid
30   down. But it is impossible to count the innumerable circumstances which may furnish exceptions.

4. DEMOCRACY

HE who makes the law knows better than any one else how it should be executed and interpreted. It seems then impossible to have a better constitution than that in which the executive and legislative powers are united; but this very
35   fact renders the government in certain respects inadequate, because things which should be distinguished are confounded, and the prince and the Sovereign, being the same person, form, so to speak, no more than a government without government.

129

It is not good for him who makes the laws to execute them, or for the body of the people to turn its attention away from a general standpoint and devote it to particular objects. Nothing is more dangerous than the influence of private interests in public affairs, and the abuse of the laws by the government is a less
5 evil than the corruption of the legislator, which is the inevitable sequel to a particular standpoint. In such a case, the State being altered in substance, all reformation becomes impossible, A people that would never misuse governmental powers would never misuse independence; a people that would always govern well would not need to be governed.
10 If we take the term in the strict sense, there never has been a real democracy, and there never will be. It is against the natural order for the many to govern and the few to be governed. It is unimaginable that the people should remain continually assembled to devote their time to public affairs, and it is clear that they cannot set up commissions for that purpose without the form of
15 administration being changed.

In fact, I can confidently lay down as a principle that, when the functions of government are shared by several tribunals, the less numerous sooner or later acquire the greatest authority, if only because they are in a position to expedite affairs, and power thus naturally comes into their hands.
20 Besides, how many conditions that are difficult to unite does such a government presuppose! First, a very small State, where the people can readily be got together and where each citizen can with ease know all the rest; secondly, great simplicity of manners, to prevent business from multiplying and raising thorny problems; next, a large measure of equality in rank and fortune, without
25 which equality of rights and authority cannot long subsist; lastly, little or no luxury – for luxury either comes of riches or makes them necessary; it corrupts at once rich and poor, the rich by possession and the poor by covetousness; it sells the country to softness and vanity, and takes away from the State all its citizens, to make them slaves one to another, and one and all to public opinion.
30 This is why a famous writer has made virtue the fundamental principle of Republics;[19] for all these conditions could not exist without virtue. But, for want of the necessary distinctions, that great thinker was often inexact, and sometimes obscure, and did not see that, the sovereign authority being everywhere the same, the same principle should be found in every well-constituted State, in a
35 greater or less degree, it is true, according to the form of the government.

It may be added that there is no government so subject to civil wars and intestine agitations as democratic or popular government, because there is none which has so strong and continual a tendency to change to another form, or which demands more vigilance and courage for its maintenance as it is. Under
40 such a constitution above all, the citizen should arm himself with strength and

constancy, and say, every day of his life, what a virtuous Count Palatine[20] said in the Diet of Poland: Malo periculosam libertatem quam quietum servitium.[21]

Were there a people of gods, their government would be democratic. So perfect a government is not for men.

5. ARISTOCRACY

5   WE have here two quite distinct moral persons, the government and the Sovereign, and in consequence two general wills, one general in relation to all the citizens, the other only for the members of the administration. Thus, although the government may regulate its internal policy as it pleases, it can never speak to the people save in the name of the Sovereign, that is, of the

10   people itself, a fact which must not be forgotten.

The first societies governed themselves aristocratically. The heads of families took counsel together on public affairs. The young bowed without question to the authority of experience. Hence such names as priests, elders, senate, and gerontes. The savages of North America govern themselves in this

15   way even now, and their government is admirable.

But, in proportion as artificial inequality produced by institutions became predominant over natural inequality, riches or power[22] were put before age, and aristocracy became elective. Finally, the transmission of the father's power along with his goods to his children, by creating patrician families, made

20   government hereditary, and there came to be senators of twenty.

There are then three sorts of aristocracy – natural, elective and hereditary. The first is only for simple peoples; the third is the worst of all governments; the second is the best, and is aristocracy properly so called.

Besides the advantage that lies in the distinction between the two powers, it

25   presents that of its members being chosen; for, in popular government, all the citizens are born magistrates; but here magistracy is confined to a few, who become such only by election.[23] By this means uprightness, understanding, experience and all other claims to pre-eminence and public esteem become so many further guarantees of wise government.

30   Moreover, assemblies are more easily held, affairs better discussed and carried out with more order and diligence, and the credit of the State is better sustained abroad by venerable senators than by a multitude that is unknown or despised.

In a word, it is the best and most natural arrangement that the wisest should

35   govern the many, when it is assured that they will govern for its profit, and not for their own. There is no need to multiply instruments, or get twenty thousand men to do what a hundred picked men can do even better. But it must not be forgotten that corporate interest here begins to direct the public power less under

the regulation of the general will, and that a further inevitable propensity takes away from the laws part of the executive power.

If we are to speak of what is individually desirable, neither should the State be so small, nor a people so simple and upright, that the execution of the laws
5   follows immediately from the public will, as it does in a good democracy. Nor should the nation be so great that the rulers have to scatter in order to govern it and are able to play the Sovereign each in his own department, and, beginning by making themselves independent, end by becoming masters.

But if aristocracy does not demand all the virtues needed by popular
10 government, it demands others which are peculiar to itself; for instance, moderation on the side of the rich and contentment on that of the poor; for it seems that thorough-going equality would be out of place, as it was not found even at Sparta.

Furthermore, if this form of government carries with it a certain inequality
15 of fortune, this is justifiable in order that as a rule the administration of public affairs may be entrusted to those who are most able to give them their whole time, but not, as Aristotle maintains, in order that the rich may always be put first. On the contrary, it is of importance that an opposite choice should occasionally teach the people that the deserts of men offer claims to pre-
20 eminence more important than those of riches.

6. MONARCHY

So far, we have considered the prince as a moral and collective person, unified by the force of the laws, and the depositary in the State of the executive power. We have now to consider this power when it is gathered together into the hands of a natural person, a real man, who alone has the right to dispose of it in
25 accordance with the laws. Such a person is called a monarch or king.

In contrast with other forms of administration, in which a collective being stands for an individual, in this form an individual stands for a collective being; so that the moral unity that constitutes the prince is at the same time a physical unity, and all the qualities, which in the other case are only with difficulty
30 brought together by the law, are found naturally united.

Thus the will of the people, the will of the prince, the public force of the State, and the particular force of the government, all answer to a single motive power; all the springs of the machine are in the same hands, the whole moves towards the same end; there are no conflicting movements to cancel one another,
35 and no kind of constitution can be imagined in which a less amount of effort produces a more considerable amount of action. Archimedes, seated quietly on the bank and easily drawing a great vessel afloat, stands to my mind for a skilful

monarch, governing vast states from his study, and moving everything while he seems himself unmoved.

But if no government is more vigorous than this, there is also none in which the particular will holds more sway and rules the rest more easily. Everything
5   moves towards the same end indeed, but this end is by no means that of the public happiness, and even the force of the administration constantly shows itself prejudicial to the State.

Kings desire to be absolute, and men are always crying out to them from afar that the best means of being so is to get themselves loved by their people.
10   This precept is all very well, and even in some respects very true. Unfortunately, it will always be derided at court. The power which comes of a people's love is no doubt the greatest; but it is precarious and conditional, and princes will never rest content with it. The best kings desire to be in a position to be wicked, if they please, without forfeiting their mastery: political sermonisers may tell them to
15   their hearts' content that, the people's strength being their own, their first interest is that the people should be prosperous, numerous and formidable; they are well aware that this is untrue. Their first personal interest is that the people should be weak, wretched, and unable to resist them. I admit that, provided the subjects remained always in submission, the prince's interest would indeed be
20   that it should be powerful, in order that its power, being his own, might make him formidable to his neighbours; but, this interest being merely secondary and subordinate, and strength being incompatible with submission, princes naturally give the preference always to the principle that is more to their immediate advantage. This is what Samuel put strongly before the Hebrews, and what
25   Machiavelli has clearly shown. He professed to teach kings; but it was the people he really taught. His Prince is the book of Republicans.[24]

We found, on general grounds, that monarchy is suitable only for great States, and this is confirmed when we examine it in itself. The more numerous the public administration, the smaller becomes the relation between the prince
30   and the subjects, and the nearer it comes to equality, so that in democracy the ratio is unity, or absolute equality. Again, as the government is restricted in numbers the ratio increases and reaches its maximum when the government is in the hands of a single person. There is then too great a distance between prince and people, and the State lacks a bond of union. To form such a bond, there
35   must be intermediate orders, and princes, personages and nobility to compose them. But no such things suit a small State, to which all class differences mean ruin.

If, however, it is hard for a great State to be well governed, it is much harder for it to be so by a single man; and every one knows what happens when
40   kings substitute others for themselves.

An essential and inevitable defect, which will always rank monarchical below the republican government, is that in a republic the public voice hardly ever raises to the highest positions men who are not enlightened and capable, and such as to fill them with honour; while in monarchies those who rise to the top are most often merely petty blunderers, petty swindlers, and petty intriguers, whose petty talents cause them to get into the highest positions at Court, but, as soon as they have got there, serve only to make their ineptitude clear to the public. The people is far less often mistaken in its choice than the prince; and a man of real worth among the king's ministers is almost as rare as a fool at the head of a republican government. Thus, when, by some fortunate chance, one of these born governors takes the helm of State in some monarchy that has been nearly overwhelmed by swarms of "gentlemanly" administrators, there is nothing but amazement at the resources he discovers, and his coming marks an era in his country's history.

For a monarchical State to have a chance of being well governed, its population and extent must be proportionate to the abilities of its governor. It is easier to conquer than to rule. With a long enough lever, the world could be moved with a single finger; to sustain it needs the shoulders of Hercules. However small a State may be, the prince is hardly ever big enough for it. When, on the other hand, it happens that the State is too small for its ruler, in these rare cases too it is ill governed, because the ruler, constantly pursuing his great designs, forgets the interests of the people, and makes it no less wretched by misusing the talents he has, than a ruler of less capacity would make it for want of those he had not. A kingdom should, so to speak, expand or contract with each reign, according to the prince's capabilities; but, the abilities of a senate being more constant in quantity, the State can then have permanent frontiers without the administration suffering.

The disadvantage that is most felt in monarchical government is the want of the continuous succession which, in both the other forms, provides an unbroken bond of union. When one king dies, another is needed; elections leave dangerous intervals and are full of storms; and unless the citizens are disinterested and upright to a degree which very seldom goes with this kind of government, intrigue and corruption abound. He to whom the State has sold itself can hardly help selling it in his turn and repaying himself, at the expense of the weak, the money the powerful have wrung from him. Under such an administration, venality sooner or later spreads through every part, and peace so enjoyed under a king is worse than the disorders of an interregnum.

What has been done to prevent these evils? Crowns have been made hereditary in certain families, and an order of succession has been set up, to prevent disputes from arising on the death of kings. That is to say, the

disadvantages of regency have been put in place of those of election, apparent tranquillity has been preferred to wise administration, and men have chosen rather to risk having children, monstrosities, or imbeciles as rulers to having disputes over the choice of good kings. It has not been taken into account that, in
5 so exposing ourselves to the risks this possibility entails, we are setting almost all the chances against us. There was sound sense in what the younger Dionysius said to his father, who reproached him for doing some shameful deed by asking, "Did I set you the example?" "No," answered his son, "but your father was not king."
10   Everything conspires to take away from a man who is set in authority over others the sense of justice and reason. Much trouble, we are told, is taken to teach young princes the art of reigning; but their education seems to do them no good. It would be better to begin by teaching them the art of obeying. The greatest kings whose praises history tells were not brought up to reign: reigning
15 is a science we are never so far from possessing as when we have learnt too much of it, and one we acquire better by obeying than by commanding. "Nam utilissimus idem ac brevissimus bonarum malarumque rerum delectus cogitare quid aut nolueris sub alio principe, aut volueris."[25]
       One result of this lack of coherence is the inconstancy of royal government,
20 which, regulated now on one scheme and now on another, according to the character of the reigning prince or those who reign for him, cannot for long have a fixed object or a consistent policy – and this variability, not found in the other forms of government, where the prince is always the same, causes the State to be always shifting from principle to principle and from project to project. Thus we
25 may say that generally, if a court is more subtle in intrigue, there is more wisdom in a senate, and Republics advance towards their ends by more consistent and better considered policies; while every revolution in a royal ministry creates a revolution in the State; for the principle common to all ministers and nearly all kings is to do in every respect the reverse of what was
30 done by their predecessors.
       This incoherence further clears up a sophism that is very familiar to royalist political writers; not only is civil government likened to domestic government, and the prince to the father of a family – this error has already been refuted – but the prince is also freely credited with all the virtues he ought to possess, and is
35 supposed to be always what he should be. This supposition once made, royal government is clearly preferable to all others, because it is incontestably the strongest, and, to be the best also, wants only a corporate will more in conformity with the general will.
       But if, according to Plato,[26] the "king by nature" is such a rarity, how often
40 will nature and fortune conspire to give him a crown? And, if royal education

necessarily corrupts those who receive it, what is to be hoped from a series of men brought up to reign? It is, then, wanton self-deception to confuse royal government with government by a good king. To see such government as it is in itself, we must consider it as it is under princes who are incompetent or wicked: for either they will come to the throne wicked or incompetent, or the throne will make them so.

These difficulties have not escaped our writers, who, all the same, are not troubled by them. The remedy, they say, is to obey without a murmur: God sends bad kings in His wrath, and they must be borne as the scourges of Heaven. Such talk is doubtless edifying; but it would be more in place in a pulpit than in a political book. What are we to think of a doctor who promises miracles, and whose whole art is to exhort the sufferer to patience? We know for ourselves that we must put up with a bad government when it is there; the question is how to find a good one.

7. MIXED GOVERNMENTS

STRICTLY speaking, there is no such thing as a simple government. An isolated ruler must have subordinate magistrates; a popular government must have a head. There is therefore, in the distribution of the executive power, always a gradation from the greater to the lesser number, with the difference that sometimes the greater number is dependent on the smaller, and sometimes the smaller on the greater.

Sometimes the distribution is equal, when either the constituent parts are in mutual dependence, as in the government of England, or the authority of each section is independent, but imperfect, as in Poland. This last form is bad; for it secures no unity in the government, and the State is left without a bond of union.

Is a simple or a mixed government the better? Political writers are always debating the question, which must be answered as we have already answered a question about all forms of government.

Simple government is better in itself, just because it is simple. But when the executive power is not sufficiently dependent upon the legislative power, i.e., when the prince is more closely related to the Sovereign than the people to the prince, this lack of proportion must be cured by the division of the government; for all the parts have then no less authority over the subjects, while their division makes them all together less strong against the Sovereign.

The same disadvantage is also prevented by the appointment of intermediate magistrates, who leave the government entire, and have the effect only of balancing the two powers and maintaining their respective rights. Government is then not mixed, but moderated.

The opposite disadvantages may be similarly cured, and, when the government is too lax, tribunals may be set up to concentrate it. This is done in all democracies. In the first case, the government is divided to make it weak; in the second, to make it strong: for the maxima of both strength and weakness are
5   found in simple governments, while the mixed forms result in a mean strength.

8. THAT ALL FORMS OF GOVERNMENT DO NOT SUIT ALL COUNTRIES

LIBERTY, not being a fruit of all climates, is not within the reach of all peoples. The more this principle, laid down by Montesquieu,[27] is considered, the more its truth is felt; the more it is combated, the more chance is given to confirm it by new proofs.

10   In all the governments that there are, the public person consumes without producing. Whence then does it get what it consumes? From the labour of its members. The necessities of the public are supplied out of the superfluities of individuals. It follows that the civil State can subsist only so long as men's labour brings them a return greater than their needs.

15   The amount of this excess is not the same in all countries. In some it is considerable, in others middling, in yet others nil, in some even negative. The relation of product to subsistence depends on the fertility of the climate, on the sort of labour the land demands, on the nature of its products, on the strength of its inhabitants, on the greater or less consumption they find necessary, and on
20   several further considerations of which the whole relation is made up.

On the other side, all governments are not of the same nature: some are less voracious than others, and the differences between them are based on this second principle, that the further from their source the public contributions are removed, the more burdensome they become. The charge should be measured
25   not by the amount of the impositions, but by the path they have to travel in order to get back to those from whom they came. When the circulation is prompt and well-established, it does not matter whether much or little is paid; the people is always rich and, financially speaking, all is well. On the contrary, however little the people gives, if that little does not return to it, it is soon exhausted by giving
30   continually: the State is then never rich, and the people is always a people of beggars.

It follows that, the more the distance between people and government increases, the more burdensome tribute becomes: thus, in a democracy, the people bears the least charge; in an aristocracy, a greater charge; and, in
35   monarchy, the weight becomes heaviest. Monarchy therefore suits only wealthy nations; aristocracy, States of middling size and wealth; and democracy, States that are small and poor.

In fact, the more we reflect, the more we find the difference between free and monarchical States to be this: in the former, everything is used for the public advantage; in the latter, the public forces and those of individuals are affected by each other, and either increases as the other grows weak; finally, instead of governing subjects to make them happy, despotism makes them wretched in order to govern them.

We find then, in every climate, natural causes according to which the form of government which it requires can be assigned, and we can even say what sort of inhabitants it should have.

Unfriendly and barren lands, where the product does not repay the labour, should remain desert and uncultivated, or peopled only by savages; lands where men's labour brings in no more than the exact minimum necessary to subsistence should be inhabited by barbarous peoples: in such places all polity is impossible. Lands where the surplus of product over labour is only middling are suitable for free peoples; those in which the soil is abundant and fertile and gives a great product for a little labour call for monarchical government, in order that the surplus of superfluities among the subjects may be consumed by the luxury of the prince: for it is better for this excess to be absorbed by the government than dissipated among the individuals. I am aware that there are exceptions; but these exceptions themselves confirm the rule, in that sooner or later they produce revolutions which restore things to the natural order.

General laws should always be distinguished from individual causes that may modify their effects. If all the South were covered with Republics and all the North with despotic States, it would be none the less true that, in point of climate, despotism is suitable to hot countries, barbarism to cold countries, and good polity to temperate regions. I see also that, the principle being granted, there may be disputes on its application; it may be said that there are cold countries that are very fertile, and tropical countries that are very unproductive. But this difficulty exists only for those who do not consider the question in all its aspects. We must, as I have already said, take labour, strength, consumption, etc., into account.

Take two tracts of equal extent, one of which brings in five and the other ten. If the inhabitants of the first consume four and those of the second nine, the surplus of the first product will be a fifth and that of the second a tenth. The ratio of these two surpluses will then be inverse to that of the products, and the tract which produces only five will give a surplus double that of the tract which produces ten.

But there is no question of a double product, and I think no one would put the fertility of cold countries, as a general rule, on an equality with that of hot ones. Let us, however, suppose this equality to exist: let us, if you will, regard

England as on the same level as Sicily, and Poland as Egypt – further south, we shall have Africa and the Indies; further north, nothing at all. To get this equality of product, what a difference there must be in tillage: in Sicily, there is only need to scratch the ground; in England, how men must toil! But, where more
5 hands are needed to get the same product, the superfluity must necessarily be less.

Consider, besides, that the same number of men consume much less in hot countries. The climate requires sobriety for the sake of health; and Europeans who try to live there as they would at home all perish of dysentery and
10 indigestion. "We are," says Chardin, "carnivorous animals, wolves, in comparison with the Asiatics. Some attribute the sobriety of the Persians to the fact that their country is less cultivated; but it is my belief that their country abounds less in commodities because the inhabitants need less. If their frugality," he goes on, "were the effect of the nakedness of the land, only the
15 poor would eat little; but everybody does so. Again, less or more would be eaten in various provinces, according to the land's fertility; but the same sobriety is found throughout the kingdom. They are very proud of their manner of life, saying that you have only to look at their hue to recognise how far it excels that of the Christians. In fact, the Persians are of an even hue; their skins are fair,
20 fine and smooth; while the hue of their subjects, the Armenians, who live after the European fashion, is rough and blotchy, and their bodies are gross and unwieldy."

The nearer you get to the equator, the less people live on. Meat they hardly touch; rice, maize, curcur, millet and cassava are their ordinary food. There are
25 in the Indies millions of men whose subsistence does not cost a halfpenny a day. Even in Europe we find considerable differences of appetite between Northern and Southern peoples. A Spaniard will live for a week on a German's dinner. In the countries in which men are more voracious, luxury therefore turns in the direction of consumption. In England, luxury appears in a well-filled table; in
30 Italy, you feast on sugar and flowers.

Luxury in clothes shows similar differences. In climates in which the changes of season are prompt and violent, men have better and simpler clothes; where they clothe themselves only for adornment, what is striking is more thought of than what is useful; clothes themselves are then a luxury. At Naples,
35 you may see daily walking in the Pausilippeum men in gold-embroidered upper garments and nothing else. It is the same with buildings; magnificence is the sole consideration where there is nothing to fear from the air. In Paris and London, you desire to be lodged warmly and comfortably; in Madrid, you have superb salons, but not a window that closes, and you go to bed in a mere hole.

In hot countries foods are much more substantial and succulent; and the third difference cannot but have an influence on the second. Why are so many vegetables eaten in Italy? Because there they are good, nutritious and excellent in taste. In France, where they are nourished only on water, they are far from
5 nutritious and are thought nothing of at table. They take up all the same no less ground, and cost at least as much pains to cultivate. It is a proved fact that the wheat of Barbary, in other respects inferior to that of France, yields much more flour, and that the wheat of France in turn yields more than that of northern countries; from which it may be inferred that a like gradation in the same
10 direction, from equator to pole, is found generally. But is it not an obvious disadvantage for an equal product to contain less nourishment?

To all these points may be added another, which at once depends on and strengthens them. Hot countries need inhabitants less than cold countries, and can support more of them. There is thus a double surplus, which is all to the
15 advantage of despotism. The greater the territory occupied by a fixed number of inhabitants, the more difficult revolt becomes, because rapid or secret concerted action is impossible, and the government can easily unmask projects and cut communications; but the more a numerous people is gathered together, the less can the government usurp the Sovereign's place: the people's leaders can
20 deliberate as safely in their houses as the prince in council, and the crowd gathers as rapidly in the squares as the prince's troops in their quarters. The advantage of tyrannical government therefore lies in acting at great distances. With the help of the rallying-points it establishes, its strength, like that of the lever,[28] grows with distance. The strength of the people, on the other hand, acts
25 only when concentrated: when spread abroad, it evaporates and is lost, like powder scattered on the ground, which catches fire only grain by grain. The least populous countries are thus the fittest for tyranny: fierce animals reign only in deserts.

9. THE MARKS OF A GOOD GOVERNMENT

THE question "What absolutely is the best government?" is unanswerable
30 as well as indeterminate; or rather, there are as many good answers as there are possible combinations in the absolute and relative situations of all nations.

But if it is asked by what sign we may know that a given people is well or ill governed, that is another matter, and the question, being one of fact, admits of an answer.
35 It is not, however, answered, because everyone wants to answer it in his own way. Subjects extol public tranquillity, citizens individual liberty; the one class prefers security of possessions, the other that of person; the one regards as the best government that which is most severe, the other maintains that the

mildest is the best; the one wants crimes punished, the other wants them prevented; the one wants the State to be feared by its neighbours, the other prefers that it should be ignored; the one is content if money circulates, the other demands that the people shall have bread. Even if an agreement were come to on
5   these and similar points, should we have got any further? As moral qualities do not admit of exact measurement, agreement about the mark does not mean agreement about the valuation.

For my part, I am continually astonished that a mark so simple is not recognised, or that men are of so bad faith as not to admit it. What is the end of
10   political association? The preservation and prosperity of its members. And what is the surest mark of their preservation and prosperity? Their numbers and population. Seek then nowhere else this mark that is in dispute. The rest being equal, the government under which, without external aids, without naturalisation or colonies, the citizens increase and multiply most, is beyond question the best.
15   The government under which a people wanes and diminishes is the worst. Calculators, it is left for you to count, to measure, to compare.[29]

10. THE ABUSE OF GOVERNMENT AND ITS TENDENCY TO DEGENERATE

AS the particular will acts constantly in opposition to the general will, the government continually exerts itself against the Sovereignty. The greater this exertion becomes, the more the constitution changes; and, as there is in this case
20   no other corporate will to create an equilibrium by resisting the will of the prince, sooner or later the prince must inevitably suppress the Sovereign and break the social treaty. This is the unavoidable and inherent defect which, from the very birth of the body politic, tends ceaselessly to destroy it, as age and death end by destroying the human body.
25   There are two general courses by which government degenerates: i.e., when it undergoes contraction, or when the State is dissolved.

Government undergoes contraction when it passes from the many to the few, that is, from democracy to aristocracy, and from aristocracy to royalty. To do so is its natural propensity.[30] If it took the backward course from the few to
30   the many, it could be said that it was relaxed; but this inverse sequence is impossible.

Indeed, governments never change their form except when their energy is exhausted and leaves them too weak to keep what they have. If a government at once extended its sphere and relaxed its stringency, its force would become
35   absolutely nil, and it would persist still less. It is therefore necessary to wind up the spring and tighten the hold as it gives way: or else the State it sustains will come to grief.

The dissolution of the State may come about in either of two ways.

First, when the prince ceases to administer the State in accordance with the laws, and usurps the Sovereign power. A remarkable change then occurs: not the government, but the State, undergoes contraction; I mean that the great State is dissolved, and another is formed within it, composed solely of the members of the government, which becomes for the rest of the people merely master and tyrant. So that the moment the government usurps the Sovereignty, the social compact is broken, and all private citizens recover by right their natural liberty, and are forced, but not bound, to obey.

The same thing happens when the members of the government severally usurp the power they should exercise only as a body; this is as great an infraction of the laws, and results in even greater disorders. There are then, so to speak, as many princes as there are magistrates, and the State, no less divided than the government, either perishes or changes its form.

When the State is dissolved, the abuse of government, whatever it is, bears the common name of anarchy. To distinguish, democracy degenerates into ochlocracy, and aristocracy into oligarchy; and I would add that royalty degenerates into tyranny; but this last word is ambiguous and needs explanation.

In vulgar usage, a tyrant is a king who governs violently and without regard for justice and law. In the exact sense, a tyrant is an individual who arrogates to himself the royal authority without having a right to it. This is how the Greeks understood the word "tyrant": they applied it indifferently to good and bad princes whose authority was not legitimate.[31] Tyrant and usurper are thus perfectly synonymous terms.

In order that I may give different things different names, I call him who usurps the royal authority a tyrant, and him who usurps the sovereign power a despot. The tyrant is he who thrusts himself in contrary to the laws to govern in accordance with the laws; the despot is he who sets himself above the laws themselves. Thus the tyrant cannot be a despot, but the despot is always a tyrant.

11. THE DEATH OF THE BODY POLITIC

SUCH is the natural and inevitable tendency of the best constituted governments. If Sparta and Rome perished, what State can hope to endure for ever? If we would set up a long-lived form of government, let us not even dream of making it eternal. If we are to succeed, we must not attempt the impossible, or flatter ourselves that we are endowing the work of man with a stability of which human conditions do not permit.

The body politic, as well as the human body, begins to die as soon as it is born, and carries in itself the causes of its destruction. But both may have a constitution that is more or less robust and suited to preserve them a longer or a

142

shorter time. The constitution of man is the work of nature; that of the State the work of art. It is not in men's power to prolong their own lives; but it is for them to prolong as much as possible the life of the State, by giving it the best possible constitution. The best constituted State will have an end; but it will end later
5   than any other, unless some unforeseen accident brings about its untimely destruction.

The life-principle of the body politic lies in the sovereign authority. The legislative power is the heart of the State; the executive power is its brain, which causes the movement of all the parts. The brain may become paralysed and the
10 individual still live. A man may remain an imbecile and live; but as soon as the heart ceases to perform its functions, the animal is dead.

The State subsists by means not of the laws, but of the legislative power. Yesterday's law is not binding to-day; but silence is taken for tacit consent, and the Sovereign is held to confirm incessantly the laws it does not abrogate as it
15 might. All that it has once declared itself to will it wills always, unless it revokes its declaration.

Why then is so much respect paid to old laws? For this very reason. We must believe that nothing but the excellence of old acts of will can have preserved them so long: if the Sovereign had not recognised them as throughout
20 salutary, it would have revoked them a thousand times. This is why, so far from growing weak, the laws continually gain new strength in any well constituted State; the precedent of antiquity makes them daily more venerable: while wherever the laws grow weak as they become old, this proves that there is no longer a legislative power, and that the State is dead.

12. HOW THE SOVEREIGN AUTHORITY MAINTAINS ITSELF

25 THE Sovereign, having no force other than the legislative power, acts only by means of the laws; and the laws being solely the authentic acts of the general will, the Sovereign cannot act save when the people is assembled. The people in assembly, I shall be told, is a mere chimera. It is so to-day, but two thousand years ago it was not so. Has man's nature changed?
30 The bounds of possibility, in moral matters, are less narrow than we imagine: it is our weaknesses, our vices and our prejudices that confine them. Base souls have no belief in great men; vile slaves smile in mockery at the name of liberty.

Let us judge of what can be done by what has been done. I shall say nothing
35 of the Republics of ancient Greece; but the Roman Republic was, to my mind, a great State, and the town of Rome a great town. The last census showed that there were in Rome four hundred thousand citizens capable of bearing arms, and

the last computation of the population of the Empire showed over four million citizens, excluding subjects, foreigners, women, children and slaves.

What difficulties might not be supposed to stand in the way of the frequent assemblage of the vast population of this capital and its neighbourhood. Yet few
5 weeks passed without the Roman people being in assembly, and even being so several times. It exercised not only the rights of Sovereignty, but also a part of those of government. It dealt with certain matters, and judged certain cases, and this whole people was found in the public meeting-place hardly less often as magistrates than as citizens.
10 If we went back to the earliest history of nations, we should find that most ancient governments, even those of monarchical form, such as the Macedonian and the Frankish, had similar councils. In any case, the one incontestable fact I have given is an answer to all difficulties; it is good logic to reason from the actual to the possible.

13. THE SAME (continued)
15 IT is not enough for the assembled people to have once fixed the constitution of the State by giving its sanction to a body of law; it is not enough for it to have set up a perpetual government, or provided once for all for the election of magistrates. Besides the extraordinary assemblies unforeseen circumstances may demand, there must be fixed periodical assemblies which
20 cannot be abrogated or prorogued, so that on the proper day the people is legitimately called together by law, without need of any formal summoning.

But, apart from these assemblies authorised by their date alone, every assembly of the people not summoned by the magistrates appointed for that purpose, and in accordance with the prescribed forms, should be regarded as
25 unlawful, and all its acts as null and void, because the command to assemble should itself proceed from the law.

The greater or less frequency with which lawful assemblies should occur depends on so many considerations that no exact rules about them can be given. It can only be said generally that the stronger the government the more often
30 should the Sovereign show itself.

This, I shall be told, may do for a single town; but what is to be done when the State includes several? Is the sovereign authority to be divided? Or is it to be concentrated in a single town to which all the rest are made subject?

Neither the one nor the other, I reply. First, the sovereign authority is one
35 and simple, and cannot be divided without being destroyed. In the second place, one town cannot, any more than one nation, legitimately be made subject to another, because the essence of the body politic lies in the reconciliation of

obedience and liberty, and the words subject and Sovereign are identical correlatives the idea of which meets in the single word "citizen."

I answer further that the union of several towns in a single city is always bad, and that, if we wish to make such a union, we should not expect to avoid its
5 natural disadvantages. It is useless to bring up abuses that belong to great States against one who desires to see only small ones; but how can small States be given the strength to resist great ones, as formerly the Greek towns resisted the Great King, and more recently Holland and Switzerland have resisted the House of Austria?
10 Nevertheless, if the State cannot be reduced to the right limits, there remains still one resource; this is, to allow no capital, to make the seat of government move from town to town, and to assemble by turn in each the Provincial Estates of the country.

People the territory evenly, extend everywhere the same rights, bear to
15 every place in it abundance and life: by these means will the State become at once as strong and as well governed as possible. Remember that the walls of towns are built of the ruins of the houses of the countryside. For every palace I see raised in the capital, my mind's eye sees a whole country made desolate.

14. THE SAME (continued)

THE moment the people is legitimately assembled as a sovereign body, the
20 jurisdiction of the government wholly lapses, the executive power is suspended, and the person of the meanest citizen is as sacred and inviolable as that of the first magistrate; for in the presence of the person represented, representatives no longer exist. Most of the tumults that arose in the comitia at Rome were due to ignorance or neglect of this rule. The consuls were in them merely the presidents
25 of the people; the tribunes were mere speakers;[32] the senate was nothing at all.

These intervals of suspension, during which the prince recognises or ought to recognise an actual superior, have always been viewed by him with alarm; and these assemblies of the people, which are the aegis of the body politic and the curb on the government, have at all times been the horror of rulers: who
30 therefore never spare pains, objections, difficulties, and promises, to stop the citizens from having them. When the citizens are greedy, cowardly, and pusillanimous, and love ease more than liberty, they do not long hold out against the redoubled efforts of the government; and thus, as the resisting force incessantly grows, the sovereign authority ends by disappearing, and most cities
35 fall and perish before their time.

But between the sovereign authority and arbitrary government there sometimes intervenes a mean power of which something must be said.

15. DEPUTIES OR REPRESENTATIVES

AS soon as public service ceases to be the chief business of the citizens, and they would rather serve with their money than with their persons, the State is not far from its fall. When it is necessary to march out to war, they pay troops and stay at home: when it is necessary to meet in council, they name deputies and
5   stay at home. By reason of idleness and money, they end by having soldiers to enslave their country and representatives to sell it.

It is through the hustle of commerce and the arts, through the greedy self-interest of profit, and through softness and love of amenities that personal services are replaced by money payments. Men surrender a part of their profits
10 in order to have time to increase them at leisure. Make gifts of money, and you will not be long without chains. The word finance is a slavish word, unknown in the city-state. In a country that is truly free, the citizens do everything with their own arms and nothing by means of money; so far from paying to be exempted from their duties, they would even pay for the privilege of fulfilling them
15 themselves. I am far from taking the common view: I hold enforced labour to be less opposed to liberty than taxes.

The better the constitution of a State is, the more do public affairs encroach on private in the minds of the citizens. Private affairs are even of much less importance, because the aggregate of the common happiness furnishes a greater
20 proportion of that of each individual, so that there is less for him to seek in particular cares. In a well-ordered city every man flies to the assemblies: under a bad government no one cares to stir a step to get to them, because no one is interested in what happens there, because it is foreseen that the general will will not prevail, and lastly because domestic cares are all-absorbing. Good laws lead
25 to the making of better ones; bad ones bring about worse. As soon as any man says of the affairs of the State What does it matter to me? the State may be given up for lost.

The lukewarmness of patriotism, the activity of private interest, the vastness of States, conquest and the abuse of government suggested the method of having
30 deputies or representatives of the people in the national assemblies. These are what, in some countries, men have presumed to call the Third Estate. Thus the individual interest of two orders is put first and second; the public interest occupies only the third place.

Sovereignty, for the same reason as makes it inalienable, cannot be
35 represented; it lies essentially in the general will, and will does not admit of representation: it is either the same, or other; there is no intermediate possibility. The deputies of the people, therefore, are not and cannot be its representatives: they are merely its stewards, and can carry through no definitive acts. Every law the people has not ratified in person is null and void – is, in fact, not a law. The

146

people of England regards itself as free; but it is grossly mistaken; it is free only during the election of members of parliament. As soon as they are elected, slavery overtakes it, and it is nothing. The use it makes of the short moments of liberty it enjoys shows indeed that it deserves to lose them.

5   The idea of representation is modern; it comes to us from feudal government, from that iniquitous and absurd system which degrades humanity and dishonours the name of man. In ancient republics and even in monarchies, the people never had representatives; the word itself was unknown. It is very singular that in Rome, where the tribunes were so sacrosanct, it was never even

10   imagined that they could usurp the functions of the people, and that in the midst of so great a multitude they never attempted to pass on their own authority a single plebiscitum. We can, however, form an idea of the difficulties caused sometimes by the people being so numerous, from what happened in the time of the Gracchi, when some of the citizens had to cast their votes from the roofs of

15   buildings.

     Where right and liberty are everything, disadvantages count for nothing. Among this wise people everything was given its just value, its lictors were allowed to do what its tribunes would never have dared to attempt; for it had no fear that its lictors would try to represent it.

20   To explain, however, in what way the tribunes did sometimes represent it, it is enough to conceive how the government represents the Sovereign. Law being purely the declaration of the general will, it is clear that, in the exercise of the legislative power, the people cannot be represented; but in that of the executive power, which is only the force that is applied to give the law effect, it both can

25   and should be represented. We thus see that if we looked closely into the matter we should find that very few nations have any laws. However that may be, it is certain that the tribunes, possessing no executive power, could never represent the Roman people by right of the powers entrusted to them, but only by usurping those of the senate.

30   In Greece, all that the people had to do, it did for itself; it was constantly assembled in the public square. The Greeks lived in a mild climate; they had no natural greed; slaves did their work for them; their great concern was with liberty. Lacking the same advantages, how can you preserve the same rights? Your severer climates add to your needs;[33] for half the year your public squares

35   are uninhabitable; the flatness of your languages unfits them for being heard in the open air; you sacrifice more for profit than for liberty, and fear slavery less than poverty.

     What then? Is liberty maintained only by the help of slavery? It may be so. Extremes meet. Everything that is not in the course of nature has its

40   disadvantages, civil society most of all. There are some unhappy circumstances

in which we can only keep our liberty at others' expense, and where the citizen can be perfectly free only when the slave is most a slave. Such was the case with Sparta. As for you, modern peoples, you have no slaves, but you are slaves yourselves; you pay for their liberty with your own. It is in vain that you boast
5 of this preference; I find in it more cowardice than humanity.

I do not mean by all this that it is necessary to have slaves, or that the right of slavery is legitimate: I am merely giving the reasons why modern peoples, believing themselves to be free, have representatives, while ancient peoples had none. In any case, the moment a people allows itself to be represented, it is no
10 long free: it no longer exists.

All things considered, I do not see that it is possible henceforth for the Sovereign to preserve among us the exercise of its rights, unless the city is very small. But if it is very small, it will be conquered? No. I will show later on how the external strength of a great people[34] may be combined with the convenient
15 polity and good order of a small State.

16. THAT THE INSTITUTION OF GOVERNMENT IS NOT A CONTRACT

THE legislative power once well established, the next thing is to establish similarly the executive power; for this latter, which operates only by particular acts, not being of the essence of the former, is naturally separate from it. Were it possible for the Sovereign, as such, to possess the executive power, right and
20 fact would be so confounded that no one could tell what was law and what was not; and the body politic, thus disfigured, would soon fall a prey to the violence it was instituted to prevent.

As the citizens, by the social contract, are all equal, all can prescribe what all should do, but no one has a right to demand that another shall do what he
25 does not do himself. It is strictly this right, which is indispensable for giving the body politic life and movement, that the Sovereign, in instituting the government, confers upon the prince.

It has been held that this act of establishment was a contract between the people and the rulers it sets over itself, – a contract in which conditions were
30 laid down between the two parties binding the one to command and the other to obey. It will be admitted, I am sure, that this is an odd kind of contract to enter into. But let us see if this view can be upheld.

First, the supreme authority can no more be modified than it can be alienated; to limit it is to destroy it. It is absurd and contradictory for the
35 Sovereign to set a superior over itself; to bind itself to obey a master would be to return to absolute liberty.

148

Moreover, it is clear that this contract between the people and such and such persons would be a particular act; and from this is follows that it can be neither a law nor an act of Sovereignty, and that consequently it would be illegitimate.

It is plain too that the contracting parties in relation to each other would be
5   under the law of nature alone and wholly without guarantees of their mutual undertakings, a position wholly at variance with the civil state. He who has force at his command being always in a position to control execution, it would come to the same thing if the name "contract" were given to the act of one man who said to another: "I give you all my goods, on condition that you give me back as
10 much of them as you please."

There is only one contract in the State, and that is the act of association, which in itself excludes the existence of a second. It is impossible to conceive of any public contract that would not be a violation of the first.

17. THE INSTITUTION OF GOVERNMENT

UNDER what general idea then should the act by which government is
15 instituted be conceived as falling? I will begin by stating that the act is complex, as being composed of two others – the establishment of the law and its execution.

By the former, the Sovereign decrees that there shall be a governing body established in this or that form; this act is clearly a law.

20 By the latter, the people nominates the rulers who are to be entrusted with the government that has been established. This nomination, being a particular act, is clearly not a second law, but merely a consequence of the first and a function of government.

The difficulty is to understand how there can be a governmental act before
25 government exists, and how the people, which is only Sovereign or subject, can, under certain circumstances, become a prince or magistrate.

It is at this point that there is revealed one of the astonishing properties of the body politic, by means of which it reconciles apparently contradictory operations; for this is accomplished by a sudden conversion of Sovereignty into
30 democracy, so that, without sensible change, and merely by virtue of a new relation of all to all, the citizens become magistrates and pass from general to particular acts, from legislation to the execution of the law.

This changed relation is no speculative subtlety without instances in practice: it happens every day in the English Parliament, where, on certain
35 occasions, the Lower House resolves itself into Grand Committee, for the better discussion of affairs, and thus, from being at one moment a sovereign court, becomes at the next a mere commission; so that subsequently it reports to itself,

as House of Commons, the result of its proceedings in Grand Committee, and debates over again under one name what it has already settled under another.

It is, indeed, the peculiar advantage of democratic government that it can be established in actuality by a simple act of the general will. Subsequently, this
5 provisional government remains in power, if this form is adopted, or else establishes in the name of the Sovereign the government that is prescribed by law; and thus the whole proceeding is regular. It is impossible to set up government in any other manner legitimately and in accordance with the principles so far laid down.

18. HOW TO CHECK THE USURPATIONS OF GOVERNMENT

10 WHAT we have just said confirms Chapter 16, and makes it clear that the institution of government is not a contract, but a law; that the depositaries of the executive power are not the people's masters, but its officers; that it can set them up and pull them down when it likes; that for them there is no question of contract, but of obedience and that in taking charge of the functions the State
15 imposes on them they are doing no more than fulfilling their duty as citizens, without having the remotest right to argue about the conditions.

When therefore the people sets up an hereditary government, whether it be monarchical and confined to one family, or aristocratic and confined to a class, what it enters into is not an undertaking; the administration is given a
20 provisional form, until the people chooses to order it otherwise.

It is true that such changes are always dangerous, and that the established government should never be touched except when it comes to be incompatible with the public good; but the circumspection this involves is a maxim of policy and not a rule of right, and the State is no more bound to leave civil authority in
25 the hands of its rulers than military authority in the hands of its generals.

It is also true that it is impossible to be too careful to observe, in such cases, all the formalities necessary to distinguish a regular and legitimate act from a seditious tumult, and the will of a whole people from the clamour of a faction. Here above all no further concession should be made to the untoward possibility
30 than cannot, in the strictest logic, be refused it. From this obligation the prince derives a great advantage in preserving his power despite the people, without it being possible to say he has usurped it; for, seeming to avail himself only of his rights, he finds it very easy to extend them, and to prevent, under the pretext of keeping the peace, assemblies that are destined to the re-establishment of order;
35 with the result that he takes advantage of a silence he does not allow to be broken, or of irregularities he causes to be committed, to assume that he has the support of those whom fear prevents from speaking, and to punish those who dare to speak. Thus it was that the decemvirs, first elected for one year and then

kept on in office for a second, tried to perpetuate their power by forbidding the comitia to assemble; and by this easy method every government in the world, once clothed with the public power, sooner or later usurps the sovereign authority.

5 The periodical assemblies of which I have already spoken are designed to prevent or postpone this calamity, above all when they need no formal summoning; for in that case, the prince cannot stop them without openly declaring himself a law-breaker and an enemy of the State.

The opening of these assemblies, whose sole object is the maintenance of 10 the social treaty, should always take the form of putting two propositions that may not be suppressed, which should be voted on separately.

The first is: "Does it please the Sovereign to preserve the present form of government?"

The second is: "Does it please the people to leave its administration in the 15 hands of those who are actually in charge of it?"

I am here assuming what I think I have shown; that there is in the State no fundamental law that cannot be revoked, not excluding the social compact itself; for if all the citizens assembled of one accord to break the compact, it is impossible to doubt that it would be very legitimately broken. Grotius even 20 thinks that each man can renounce his membership of his own State, and recover his natural liberty and his goods on leaving the country.[35] It would be indeed absurd if all the citizens in assembly could not do what each can do by himself.

BOOK IV

1. THAT THE GENERAL WILL IS INDESTRUCTIBLE

AS long as several men in assembly regard themselves as a single body, they have only a single will which is concerned with their common preservation 25 and general well-being. In this case, all the springs of the State are vigorous and simple and its rules clear and luminous; there are no embroilments or conflicts of interests; the common good is everywhere clearly apparent, and only good sense is needed to perceive it. Peace, unity and equality are the enemies of political subtleties. Men who are upright and simple are difficult to deceive 30 because of their simplicity; lures and ingenious pretexts fail to impose upon them, and they are not even subtle enough to be dupes. When, among the happiest people in the world, bands of peasants are seen regulating affairs of State under an oak, and always acting wisely, can we help scorning the ingenious methods of other nations, which make themselves illustrious and 35 wretched with so much art and mystery?

A State so governed needs very few laws; and, as it becomes necessary to issue new ones, the necessity is universally seen. The first man to propose them merely says what all have already felt, and there is no question of factions or intrigues or eloquence in order to secure the passage into law of what every one
5 has already decided to do, as soon as he is sure that the rest will act with him.

Theorists are led into error because, seeing only States that have been from the beginning wrongly constituted, they are struck by the impossibility of applying such a policy to them. They make great game of all the absurdities a clever rascal or an insinuating speaker might get the people of Paris or London
10 to believe. They do not know that Cromwell would have been put to "the bells" by the people of Berne, and the Duc de Beaufort on the treadmill by the Genevese.

But when the social bond begins to be relaxed and the State to grow weak, when particular interests begin to make themselves felt and the smaller societies
15 to exercise an influence over the larger, the common interest changes and finds opponents: opinion is no longer unanimous; the general will ceases to be the will of all; contradictory views and debates arise; and the best advice is not taken without question.

Finally, when the State, on the eve of ruin, maintains only a vain, illusory
20 and formal existence, when in every heart the social bond is broken, and the meanest interest brazenly lays hold of the sacred name of "public good," the general will becomes mute: all men, guided by secret motives, no more give their views as citizens than if the State had never been; and iniquitous decrees directed solely to private interest get passed under the name of laws.

25 Does it follow from this that the general will is exterminated or corrupted? Not at all: it is always constant, unalterable and pure; but it is subordinated to other wills which encroach upon its sphere. Each man, in detaching his interest from the common interest, sees clearly that he cannot entirely separate them; but his share in the public mishaps seems to him negligible beside the exclusive
30 good he aims at making his own. Apart from this particular good, he wills the general good in his own interest, as strongly as any one else. Even in selling his vote for money, he does not extinguish in himself the general will, but only eludes it. The fault he commits is that of changing the state of the question, and answering something different from what he is asked. Instead of saying, by his
35 vote, "It is to the advantage of the State," he says, "It is of advantage to this or that man or party that this or that view should prevail." Thus the law of public order in assemblies is not so much to maintain in them the general will as to secure that the question be always put to it, and the answer always given by it.

I could here set down many reflections on the simple right of voting in
40 every act of Sovereignty – a right which no one can take from the citizens – and

also on the right of stating views, making proposals, dividing and discussing, which the government is always most careful to leave solely to its members, but this important subject would need a treatise to itself, and it is impossible to say everything in a single work.

2. VOTING

5   IT may be seen, from the last chapter, that the way in which general business is managed may give a clear enough indication of the actual state of morals and the health of the body politic. The more concert reigns in the assemblies, that is, the nearer opinion approaches unanimity, the greater is the dominance of the general will. On the other hand, long debates, dissensions and 10 tumult proclaim the ascendancy of particular interests and the decline of the State.

     This seems less clear when two or more orders enter into the constitution, as patricians and plebeians did at Rome; for quarrels between these two orders often disturbed the comitia, even in the best days of the Republic. But the 15 exception is rather apparent than real; for then, through the defect that is inherent in the body politic, there were, so to speak, two States in one, and what is not true of the two together is true of either separately. Indeed, even in the most stormy times, the plebiscita of the people, when the Senate did not interfere with them, always went through quietly and by large majorities. The 20 citizens having but one interest, the people had but a single will.

     At the other extremity of the circle, unanimity recurs; this is the case when the citizens, having fallen into servitude, have lost both liberty and will. Fear and flattery then change votes into acclamation; deliberation ceases, and only worship or malediction is left. Such was the vile manner in which the senate 25 expressed its views under the Emperors. It did so sometimes with absurd precautions. Tacitus observes that, under Otho, the senators, while they heaped curses on Vitellius, contrived at the same time to make a deafening noise, in order that, should he ever become their master, he might not know what each of them had said.

30   On these various considerations depend the rules by which the methods of counting votes and comparing opinions should be regulated, according as the general will is more or less easy to discover, and the State more or less in its decline.

     There is but one law which, from its nature, needs unanimous consent. This 35 is the social compact; for civil association is the most voluntary of all acts. Every man being born free and his own master, no one, under any pretext whatsoever, can make any man subject without his consent. To decide that the son of a slave is born a slave is to decide that he is not born a man.

If then there are opponents when the social compact is made, their opposition does not invalidate the contract, but merely prevents them from being included in it. They are foreigners among citizens. When the State is instituted, residence constitutes consent; to dwell within its territory is to submit to the
5   Sovereign.[36]

Apart from this primitive contract, the vote of the majority always binds all the rest. This follows from the contract itself. But it is asked how a man can be both free and forced to conform to wills that are not his own. How are the opponents at once free and subject to laws they have not agreed to?
10   I retort that the question is wrongly put. The citizen gives his consent to all the laws, including those which are passed in spite of his opposition, and even those which punish him when he dares to break any of them. The constant will of all the members of the State is the general will; by virtue of it they are citizens and free.[37] When in the popular assembly a law is proposed, what the
15   people is asked is not exactly whether it approves or rejects the proposal, but whether it is in conformity with the general will, which is their will. Each man, in giving his vote, states his opinion on that point; and the general will is found by counting votes. When therefore the opinion that is contrary to my own prevails, this proves neither more nor less than that I was mistaken, and that
20   what I thought to be the general will was not so. If my particular opinion had carried the day I should have achieved the opposite of what was my will; and it is in that case that I should not have been free.

This presupposes, indeed, that all the qualities of the general will still reside in the majority: when they cease to do so, whatever side a man may take, liberty
25   is no longer possible.

In my earlier demonstration of how particular wills are substituted for the general will in public deliberation, I have adequately pointed out the practicable methods of avoiding this abuse; and I shall have more to say of them later on. I have also given the principles for determining the proportional number of votes
30   for declaring that will. A difference of one vote destroys equality; a single opponent destroys unanimity; but between equality and unanimity, there are several grades of unequal division, at each of which this proportion may be fixed in accordance with the condition and the needs of the body politic.

There are two general rules that may serve to regulate this relation. First, the
35   more grave and important the questions discussed, the nearer should the opinion that is to prevail approach unanimity. Secondly, the more the matter in hand calls for speed, the smaller the prescribed difference in the numbers of votes may be allowed to become: where an instant decision has to be reached, a majority of one vote should be enough. The first of these two rules seems more
40   in harmony with the laws, and the second with practical affairs. In any case, it is

the combination of them that gives the best proportions for determining the majority necessary.

3. ELECTIONS

IN the elections of the prince and the magistrates, which are, as I have said, complex acts, there are two possible methods of procedure, choice and lot. Both
5   have been employed in various republics, and a highly complicated mixture of the two still survives in the election of the Doge at Venice.

"Election by lot," says Montesquieu, "is democratic in nature."[38] I agree that it is so; but in what sense? "The lot," he goes on, "is a way of making choice that is unfair to nobody; it leaves each citizen a reasonable hope of
10   serving his country." These are not reasons.

If we bear in mind that the election of rulers is a function of government, and not of Sovereignty, we shall see why the lot is the method more natural to democracy, in which the administration is better in proportion as the number of its acts is small.

15   In every real democracy, magistracy is not an advantage, but a burdensome charge which cannot justly be imposed on one individual rather than another. The law alone can lay the charge on him on whom the lot falls. For, the conditions being then the same for all, and the choice not depending on any human will, there is no particular application to alter the universality of the law.

20   In an aristocracy, the prince chooses the prince, the government is preserved by itself, and voting is rightly ordered.

The instance of the election of the Doge of Venice confirms, instead of destroying, this distinction; the mixed form suits a mixed government. For it is an error to take the government of Venice for a real aristocracy. If the people has
25   no share in the government, the nobility is itself the people. A host of poor Barnabotes never gets near any magistracy, and its nobility consists merely in the empty title of Excellency, and in the right to sit in the Great Council. As this Great Council is as numerous as our General Council at Geneva, its illustrious members have no more privileges than our plain citizens. It is indisputable that,
30   apart from the extreme disparity between the two republics, the bourgeoisie of Geneva is exactly equivalent to the patriciate of Venice; our natives and inhabitants correspond to the townsmen and the people of Venice; our peasants correspond to the subjects on the mainland; and, however that republic be regarded, if its size be left out of account, its government is no more aristocratic
35   than our own. The whole difference is that, having no life-ruler, we do not, like Venice, need to use the lot.

Election by lot would have few disadvantages in a real democracy, in which, as equality would everywhere exist in morals and talents as well as in

principles and fortunes, it would become almost a matter of indifference who
was chosen. But I have already said that a real democracy is only an ideal.

When choice and lot are combined, positions that require special talents,
such as military posts, should be filled by the former; the latter does for cases,
5 such as judicial offices, in which good sense, justice, and integrity are enough,
because in a State that is well constituted, these qualities are common to all the
citizens.

Neither lot nor vote has any place in monarchical government. The monarch
being by right sole prince and only magistrate, the choice of his lieutenants
10 belongs to none but him. When the Abbé de Saint-Pierre proposed that the
Councils of the King of France should be multiplied, and their members elected
by ballot, he did not see that he was proposing to change the form of
government.

I should now speak of the methods of giving and counting opinions in the
15 assembly of the people; but perhaps an account of this aspect of the Roman
constitution will more forcibly illustrate all the rules I could lay down. It is
worth the while of a judicious reader to follow in some detail the working of
public and private affairs in a Council consisting of two hundred thousand men.

4. THE ROMAN COMITIA
WE are without well-certified records of the first period of Rome's
20 existence; it even appears very probable that most of the stories told about it are
fables; indeed, generally speaking, the most instructive part of the history of
peoples, that which deals with their foundation, is what we have least of.
Experience teaches us every day what causes lead to the revolutions of empires;
but, as no new peoples are now formed, we have almost nothing beyond
25 conjecture to go upon in explaining how they were created.

The customs we find established show at least that these customs had an
origin. The traditions that go back to those origins, that have the greatest
authorities behind them, and that are confirmed by the strongest proofs, should
pass for the most certain. These are the rules I have tried to follow in inquiring
30 how the freest and most powerful people on earth exercised its supreme power.

After the foundation of Rome, the new-born republic, that is, the army of its
founder, composed of Albans, Sabines and foreigners, was divided into three
classes, which, from this division, took the name of tribes. Each of these tribes
was subdivided into ten curiæ, and each curia into decuriæ, headed by leaders
35 called curiones and decuriones.

Besides this, out of each tribe was taken a body of one hundred Equites or
Knights, called a century, which shows that these divisions, being unnecessary
in a town, were at first merely military. But an instinct for greatness seems to

have led the little township of Rome to provide itself in advance with a political system suitable for the capital of the world.

Out of this original division an awkward situation soon arose. The tribes of the Albans (Ramnenses) and the Sabines (Tatienses) remained always in the
5 same condition, while that of the foreigners (Luceres) continually grew as more and more foreigners came to live at Rome, so that it soon surpassed the others in strength. Servius remedied this dangerous fault by changing the principle of cleavage, and substituting for the racial division, which he abolished, a new one based on the quarter of the town inhabited by each tribe. Instead of three tribes
10 he created four, each occupying and named after one of the hills of Rome. Thus, while redressing the inequality of the moment, he also provided for the future; and in order that the division might be one of persons as well as localities, he forbade the inhabitants of one quarter to migrate to another, and so prevented the mingling of the races.
15 He also doubled the three old centuries of Knights and added twelve more, still keeping the old names, and by this simple and prudent method, succeeded in making a distinction between the body of Knights, and the people, without a murmur from the latter.

To the four urban tribes Servius added fifteen others called rural tribes,
20 because they consisted of those who lived in the country, divided into fifteen cantons. Subsequently, fifteen more were created, and the Roman people finally found itself divided into thirty-five tribes, as it remained down to the end of the Republic.

The distinction between urban and rural tribes had one effect which is worth
25 mention, both because it is without parallel elsewhere, and because to it Rome owed the preservation of her morality and the enlargement of her empire. We should have expected that the urban tribes would soon monopolise power and honours, and lose no time in bringing the rural tribes into disrepute; but what happened was exactly the reverse. The taste of the early Romans for country life
30 is well known. This taste they owed to their wise founder, who made rural and military labours go along with liberty, and, so to speak, relegated to the town arts, crafts, intrigue, fortune and slavery.

Since therefore all Rome's most illustrious citizens lived in the fields and tilled the earth, men grew used to seeking there alone the mainstays of the
35 republic. This condition, being that of the best patricians, was honoured by all men; the simple and laborious life of the villager was preferred to the slothful and idle life of the bourgeoisie of Rome; and he who, in the town, would have been but a wretched proletarian, became, as a labourer in the fields, a respected citizen. Not without reason, says Varro, did our great-souled ancestors establish
40 in the village the nursery of the sturdy and valiant men who defended them in

time of war and provided for their sustenance in time of peace. Pliny states positively that the country tribes were honoured because of the men of whom they were composed; while cowards men wished to dishonour were transferred, as a public disgrace, to the town tribes. The Sabine Appius Claudius, when he

5 had come to settle in Rome, was loaded with honours and enrolled in a rural tribe, which subsequently took his family name. Lastly, freedmen always entered the urban, arid never the rural, tribes: nor is there a single example, throughout the Republic, of a freedman, though he had become a citizen, reaching any magistracy.

10 This was an excellent rule; but it was carried so far that in the end it led to a change and certainly to an abuse in the political system.

First the censors, after having for a long time claimed the right of transferring citizens arbitrarily from one tribe to another, allowed most persons to enrol themselves in whatever tribe they pleased. This permission certainly did

15 no good, and further robbed the censorship of one of its greatest resources. Moreover, as the great and powerful all got themselves enrolled in the country tribes, while the freedmen who had become citizens remained with the populace in the town tribes, both soon ceased to have any local or territorial meaning, and all were so confused that the members of one could not be told from those of

20 another except by the registers; so that the idea of the word tribe became personal instead of real, or rather came to be little more than a chimera.

It happened in addition that the town tribes, being more on the spot, were often the stronger in the comitia and sold the State to those who stooped to buy the votes of the rabble composing them.

25 As the founder had set up ten curiæ in each tribe, the whole Roman people, which was then contained within the walls, consisted of thirty curiæ, each with its temples, its gods, its officers, its priests and its festivals, which were called compitalia and corresponded to the paganalia, held in later times by the rural tribes.

30 When Servius made his new division, as the thirty curiæ could not be shared equally between his four tribes, and as he was unwilling to interfere with them, they became a further division of the inhabitants of Rome, quite independent of the tribes: but in the case of the rural tribes and their members there was no question of curiæ, as the tribes had then become a purely civil

35 institution, and, a new system of levying troops having been introduced, the military divisions of Romulus were superfluous. Thus, although every citizen was enrolled in a tribe, there were very many who were not members of a curia.

Servius made yet a third division, quite distinct from the two we have mentioned, which became, in its effects, the most important of all. He

40 distributed the whole Roman people into six classes, distinguished neither by

place nor by person, but by wealth; the first classes included the rich, the last the poor, and those between persons of moderate means. These six classes were subdivided into one hundred and ninety-three other bodies, called centuries, which were so divided that the first class alone comprised more than half of
5   them, while the last comprised only one. Thus the class that had the smallest number of members had the largest number of centuries, and the whole of the last class only counted as a single subdivision, although it alone included more than half the inhabitants of Rome.

    In order that the people might have the less insight into the results of this
10 arrangement, Servius tried to give it a military tone: in the second class he inserted two centuries of armourers, and in the fourth two of makers of instruments of war: in each class, except the last, he distinguished young and old, that is, those who were under an obligation to bear arms and those whose age gave them legal exemption. It was this distinction, rather than that of wealth,
15 which required frequent repetition of the census or counting. Lastly, he ordered that the assembly should be held in the Campus Martius, and that all who were of age to serve should come there armed.

    The reason for his not making in the last class also the division of young and old was that the populace, of whom it was composed, was not given the
20 right to bear arms for its country: a man had to possess a hearth to acquire the right to defend it, and of all the troops of beggars who to-day lend lustre to the armies of kings, there is perhaps not one who would not have been driven with scorn out of a Roman cohort, at a time when soldiers were the defenders of liberty.
25   In this last class, however, proletarians were distinguished from capite censi. The former, not quite reduced to nothing, at least gave the State citizens, and sometimes, when the need was pressing, even soldiers. Those who had nothing at all, and could be numbered only by counting heads, were regarded as of absolutely no account, and Marius was the first who stooped to enrol them.
30   Without deciding now whether this third arrangement was good or bad in itself, I think I may assert that it could have been made practicable only by the simple morals, the disinterestedness, the liking for agriculture and the scorn for commerce and for love of gain which characterised the early Romans. Where is the modern people among whom consuming greed, unrest, intrigue, continual
35 removals, and perpetual changes of fortune, could let such a system last for twenty years without turning the State upside down? We must indeed observe that morality and the censorship, being stronger than this institution, corrected its defects at Rome, and that the rich man found himself degraded to the class of the poor for making too much display of his riches.

From all this it is easy to understand why only five classes are almost always mentioned, though there were really six. The sixth, as it furnished neither soldiers to the army nor votes in the Campus Martius,[39] and was almost without function in the State, was seldom regarded as of any account.

5 These were the various ways in which the Roman people was divided. Let us now see the effect on the assemblies. When lawfully summoned, these were called comitia: they were usually held in the public square at Rome or in the Campus Martius, and were distinguished as comitia curiata, comitia centuriata, and comitia tributa, according to the form under which they were convoked. The
10 comitia curiata were founded by Romulus; the centuriata by Servius; and the tributa by the tribunes of the people. No law received its sanction and no magistrate was elected, save in the comitia; and as every citizen was enrolled in a curia, a century, or a tribe, it follows that no citizen was excluded from the right of voting, and that the Roman people was truly sovereign both de jure and
15 de facto.

For the comitia to be lawfully assembled, and for their acts to have the force of law, three conditions were necessary. First, the body or magistrate convoking them had to possess the necessary authority; secondly, the assembly had to be held on a day allowed by law; and thirdly, the auguries had to be favourable.
20 The reason for the first regulation needs no explanation; the second is a matter of policy. Thus, the comitia might not be held on festivals or market-days, when the country-folk, coming to Rome on business, had not time to spend the day in the public square. By means of the third, the senate held in check the proud and restive people, and meetly restrained the ardour of seditious tribunes,
25 who, however, found more than one way of escaping this hindrance.

Laws and the election of rulers were not the only questions submitted to the judgment of the comitia: as the Roman people had taken on itself the most important functions of government, it may be said that the lot of Europe was regulated in its assemblies. The variety of their objects gave rise to the various
30 forms these took, according to the matters on which they had to pronounce.

In order to judge of these various forms, it is enough to compare them. Romulus, when he set up curia, had in view the checking of the senate by the people, and of the people by the senate, while maintaining his ascendancy over both alike. He therefore gave the people, by means of this assembly, all the
35 authority of numbers to balance that of power and riches, which he left to the patricians. But, after the spirit of monarchy, he left all the same a greater advantage to the patricians in the influence of their clients on the majority of votes. This excellent institution of patron and client was a masterpiece of statesmanship and humanity without which the patriciate, being flagrantly in
40 contradiction to the republican spirit, could not have survived. Rome alone has

the honour of having given to the world this great example, which never led to any abuse, and yet has never been followed.

As the assemblies by curiæ persisted under the kings till the time of Servius, and the reign of the later Tarquin was not regarded as legitimate, royal laws
5 were called generally leges curiatæ.

Under the Republic, the curiæ, still confined to the four urban tribes, and including only the populace of Rome, suited neither the senate, which led the patricians, nor the tribunes, who, though plebeians, were at the head of the well-to-do citizens. They therefore fell into disrepute, and their degradation was such,
10 that thirty lictors used to assemble and do what the comitia curiata should have done.

The division by centuries was so favourable to the aristocracy that it is hard to see at first how the senate ever failed to carry the day in the comitia bearing their name, by which the consuls, the censors and the other curule magistrates
15 were elected. Indeed, of the hundred and ninety-three centuries into which the six classes of the whole Roman people were divided, the first class contained ninety-eight; and, as voting went solely by centuries, this class alone had a majority over all the rest. When all these centuries were in agreement, the rest of the votes were not even taken; the decision of the smallest number passed for
20 that of the multitude, and it may be said that, in the comitia centuriata, decisions were regulated far more by depth of purses than by the number of votes.

But this extreme authority was modified in two ways. First, the tribunes as a rule, and always a great number of plebeians, belonged to the class of the rich, and so counterbalanced the influence of the patricians in the first class.
25 The second way was this. Instead of causing the centuries to vote throughout in order, which would have meant beginning always with the first, the Romans always chose one by lot which proceeded alone to the election; after this all the centuries were summoned another day according to their rank, and the same election was repeated, and as a rule confirmed. Thus the authority of
30 example was taken away from rank, and given to the lot on a democratic principle.

From this custom resulted a further advantage. The citizens from the country had time, between the two elections, to inform themselves of the merits of the candidate who had been provisionally nominated, and did not have to vote
35 without knowledge of the case. But, under the pretext of hastening matters, the abolition of this custom was achieved, and both elections were held on the same day.

The comitia tributa were properly the council of the Roman people. They were convoked by the tribunes alone; at them the tribunes were elected and
40 passed their plebiscita. The senate not only had no standing in them, but even no

right to be present; and the senators, being forced to obey laws on which they could not vote, were in this respect less free than the meanest citizens. This injustice was altogether ill-conceived, and was alone enough to invalidate the decrees of a body to which all its members were not admitted. Had all the patricians attended the comitia by virtue of the right they had as citizens, they would not, as mere private individuals, have had any considerable influence on a vote reckoned by counting heads, where the meanest proletarian was as good as the princeps senatus.

It may be seen, therefore, that besides the order which was achieved by these various ways of distributing so great a people and taking its votes, the various methods were not reducible to forms indifferent in themselves, but the results of each were relative to the objects which caused it to be preferred.

Without going here into further details, we may gather from what has been said above that the comitia tributa were the most favourable to popular government, and the comitia centuriata to aristocracy. The comitia curiata, in which the populace of Rome formed the majority, being fitted only to further tyranny and evil designs, naturally fell into disrepute, and even seditious persons abstained from using a method which too clearly revealed their projects. It is indisputable that the whole majesty of the Roman people lay solely in the comitia centuriata, which alone included all; for the comitia curiata excluded the rural tribes, and the comitia tributa the senate and the patricians.

As for the method of taking the vote, it was among the ancient Romans as simple as their morals, although not so simple as at Sparta. Each man declared his vote aloud, and a clerk duly wrote it down; the majority in each tribe determined the vote of the tribe, the majority of the tribes that of the people, and so with curiæ and centuries. This custom was good as long as honesty was triumphant among the citizens, and each man was ashamed to vote publicly in favour of an unjust proposal or an unworthy subject; but, when the people grew corrupt and votes were bought, it was fitting that voting should be secret in order that purchasers might be restrained by mistrust, and rogues be given the means of not being traitors.

I know that Cicero attacks this change, and attributes partly to it the ruin of the Republic. But though I feel the weight Cicero's authority must carry on such a point, I cannot agree with him; I hold, on the contrary, that, for want of enough such changes, the destruction of the State must be hastened. Just as the regimen of health does not suit the sick, we should not wish to govern a people that has been corrupted by the laws that a good people requires. There is no better proof of this rule than the long life of the Republic of Venice, of which the shadow still exists, solely because its laws are suitable only for men who are wicked.

The citizens were provided, therefore, with tablets by means of which each man could vote without any one knowing how he voted: new methods were also introduced for collecting the tablets, for counting voices, for comparing numbers, etc.; but all these precautions did not prevent the good faith of the officers charged with these functions[40] from being often suspect. Finally, to prevent intrigues and trafficking in votes, edicts were issued; but their very number proves how useless they were.

Towards the close of the Republic, it was often necessary to have recourse to extraordinary expedients in order to supplement the inadequacy of the laws. Sometimes miracles were supposed; but this method, while it might impose on the people, could not impose on those who governed. Sometimes an assembly was hastily called together, before the candidates had time to form their factions: sometimes a whole sitting was occupied with talk, when it was seen that the people had been won over and was on the point of taking up a wrong position. But in the end ambition eluded all attempts to check it; and the most incredible fact of all is that, in the midst of all these abuses, the vast people, thanks to its ancient regulations, never ceased to elect magistrates, to pass laws, to judge cases, and to carry through business both public and private, almost as easily as the senate itself could have done.

5. THE TRIBUNATE

WHEN an exact proportion cannot be established between the constituent parts of the State, or when causes that cannot be removed continually alter the relation of one part to another, recourse is had to the institution of a peculiar magistracy that enters into no corporate unity with the rest. This restores to each term its right relation to the others, and provides a link or middle term between either prince and people, or prince and Sovereign, or, if necessary, both at once.

This body, which I shall call the tribunate, is the preserver of the laws and of the legislative power. It serves sometimes to protect the Sovereign against the government, as the tribunes of the people did at Rome; sometimes to uphold the government against the people, as the Council of Ten now does at Venice; and sometimes to maintain the balance between the two, as the Ephors did at Sparta.

The tribunate is not a constituent part of the city, and should have no share in either legislative or executive power; but this very fact makes its own power the greater: for, while it can do nothing, it can prevent anything from being done. It is more sacred and more revered, as the defender of the laws, than the prince who executes them, or than the Sovereign which ordains them. This was seen very clearly at Rome, when the proud patricians, for all their scorn of the people, were forced to bow before one of its officers, who had neither auspices nor jurisdiction.

The tribunate, wisely tempered, is the strongest support a good constitution can have; but if its strength is ever so little excessive, it upsets the whole State. Weakness, on the other hand, is not natural to it: provided it is something, it is never less than it should be.

It degenerates into tyranny when it usurps the executive power, which it should confine itself to restraining, and when it tries to dispense with the laws, which it should confine itself to protecting. The immense power of the Ephors, harmless as long as Sparta preserved its morality, hastened corruption when once it had begun. The blood of Agis, slaughtered by these tyrants, was avenged by his successor; the crime and the punishment of the Ephors alike hastened the destruction of the republic, and after Cleomenes Sparta ceased to be of any account. Rome perished in the same way: the excessive power of the tribunes, which they had usurped by degrees, finally served, with the help of laws made to secure liberty, as a safeguard for the emperors who destroyed it. As for the Venetian Council of Ten, it is a tribunal of blood, an object of horror to patricians and people alike; and, so far from giving a lofty protection to the laws, it does nothing, now they have become degraded, but strike in the darkness blows of which no one dare take note.

The tribunate, like the government, grows weak as the number of its members increases. When the tribunes of the Roman people, who first numbered only two, and then five, wished to double that number, the senate let them do so, in the confidence that it could use one to check another, as indeed it afterwards freely did.

The best method of preventing usurpations by so formidable a body, though no government has yet made use of it, would be not to make it permanent, but to regulate the periods during which it should remain in abeyance. These intervals, which should not be long enough to give abuses time to grow strong, may be so fixed by law that they can easily be shortened at need by extraordinary commissions.

This method seems to me to have no disadvantages, because, as I have said, the tribunate, which forms no part of the constitution, can be removed without the constitution being affected. It seems to be also efficacious, because a newly restored magistrate starts not with the power his predecessor exercised, but with that which the law allows him.

6. THE DICTATORSHIP

THE inflexibility of the laws, which prevents them from adapting themselves to circumstances, may, in certain cases, render them disastrous, and make them bring about, at a time of crisis, the ruin of the State. The order and slowness of the forms they enjoin require a space of time which circumstances sometimes withhold. A thousand cases against which the legislator has made no provision may present themselves, and it is a highly necessary part of foresight to be conscious that everything cannot be foreseen.

It is wrong therefore to wish to make political institutions so strong as to
5 render it impossible to suspend their operation. Even Sparta allowed its laws to lapse.

However, none but the greatest dangers can counterbalance that of changing the public order, and the sacred power of the laws should never be arrested save when the existence of the country is at stake. In these rare and obvious cases,
10 provision is made for the public security by a particular act entrusting it to him who is most worthy. This commitment may be carried out in either of two ways, according to the nature of the danger.

If increasing the activity of the government is a sufficient remedy, power is concentrated in the hands of one or two of its members: in this case the change
15 is not in the authority of the laws, but only in the form of administering them. If, on the other hand, the peril is of such a kind that the paraphernalia of the laws are an obstacle to their preservation, the method is to nominate a supreme ruler, who shall silence all the laws and suspend for a moment the sovereign authority. In such a case, there is no doubt about the general will, and it is clear that the
20 people's first intention is that the State shall not perish. Thus the suspension of the legislative authority is in no sense its abolition; the magistrate who silences it cannot make it speak; he dominates it, but cannot represent it. He can do anything, except make laws.

The first method was used by the Roman senate when, in a consecrated
25 formula, it charged the consuls to provide for the safety of the Republic. The second was employed when one of the two consuls nominated a dictator:[41] a custom Rome borrowed from Alba.

During the first period of the Republic, recourse was very often had to the dictatorship, because the State had not yet a firm enough basis to be able to
30 maintain itself by the strength of its constitution alone. As the state of morality then made superfluous many of the precautions which would have been necessary at other times, there was no fear that a dictator would abuse his authority, or try to keep it beyond his term of office. On the contrary, so much power appeared to be burdensome to him who was clothed with it, and he made
35 all speed to lay it down, as if taking the place of the laws had been too troublesome and too perilous a position to retain.

It is therefore the danger not of its abuse, but of its cheapening, that makes me attack the indiscreet use of this supreme magistracy in the earliest times. For as long as it was freely employed at elections, dedications and purely formal
40 functions, there was danger of its becoming less formidable in time of need, and

of men growing accustomed to regarding as empty a title that was used only on occasions of empty ceremonial.

Towards the end of the Republic, the Romans, having grown more circumspect, were as unreasonably sparing in the use of the dictatorship as they had formerly been lavish. It is easy to see that their fears were without foundation, that the weakness of the capital secured it against the magistrates who were in its midst; that a dictator might, in certain cases, defend the public liberty, but could never endanger it; and that the chains of Rome would be forged, not in Rome itself, but in her armies. The weak resistance offered by Marius to Sulla, and by Pompey to Cæsar, clearly showed what was to be expected from authority at home against force from abroad.

This misconception led the Romans to make great mistakes; such, for example, as the failure to nominate a dictator in the Catilinarian conspiracy. For, as only the city itself, with at most some province in Italy, was concerned, the unlimited authority the laws gave to the dictator would have enabled him to make short work of the conspiracy, which was, in fact, stifled only by a combination of lucky chances human prudence had no right to expect.

Instead, the senate contented itself with entrusting its whole power to the consuls, so that Cicero, in order to take effective action, was compelled on a capital point to exceed his powers; and if, in the first transports of joy, his conduct was approved, he was justly called, later on, to account for the blood of citizens spilt in violation of the laws. Such a reproach could never have been levelled at a dictator. But the consul's eloquence carried the day; and he himself, Roman though he was, loved his own glory better than his country, and sought, not so much the most lawful and secure means of saving the State, as to get for himself the whole honour of having done so.[42] He was therefore justly honoured as the liberator of Rome, and also justly punished as a law-breaker. However brilliant his recall may have been, it was undoubtedly an act of pardon.

However this important trust be conferred, it is important that its duration should be fixed at a very brief period, incapable of being ever prolonged. In the crises which lead to its adoption, the State is either soon lost, or soon saved; and, the present need passed, the dictatorship becomes either tyrannical or idle. At Rome, where dictators held office for six months only, most of them abdicated before their time was up. If their term had been longer, they might well have tried to prolong it still further, as the decemvirs did when chosen for a year. The dictator had only time to provide against the need that had caused him to be chosen; he had none to think of further projects.

7. THE CENSORSHIP

AS the law is the declaration of the general will, the censorship is the declaration of the public judgment: public opinion is the form of law which the censor administers, and, like the prince, only applies to particular cases.

The censorial tribunal, so far from being the arbiter of the people's opinion,
5 only declares it, and, as soon as the two part company, its decisions are null and void.

It is useless to distinguish the morality of a nation from the objects of its esteem; both depend on the same principle and are necessarily indistinguishable. There is no people on earth the choice of whose pleasures is not decided by
10 opinion rather than nature. Right men's opinions, and their morality will purge itself. Men always love what is good or what they find good; it is in judging what is good that they go wrong. This judgment, therefore, is what must be regulated. He who judges of morality judges of honour; and he who judges of honour finds his law in opinion.

15 The opinions of a people are derived from its constitution; although the law does not regulate morality, it is legislation that gives it birth. When legislation grows weak, morality degenerates; but in such cases the judgment of the censors will not do what the force of the laws has failed to effect.

From this it follows that the censorship may be useful for the preservation
20 of morality, but can never be so for its restoration. Set up censors while the laws are vigorous; as soon as they have lost their vigour, all hope is gone; no legitimate power can retain force when the laws have lost it.

The censorship upholds morality by preventing opinion from growing corrupt, by preserving its rectitude by means of wise applications, and
25 sometimes even by fixing it when it is still uncertain. The employment of seconds in duels, which had been carried to wild extremes in the kingdom of France, was done away with merely by these words in a royal edict: "As for those who are cowards enough to call upon seconds." This judgment, in anticipating that of the public, suddenly decided it. But when edicts from the
30 same source tried to pronounce duelling itself an act of cowardice, as indeed it is, then, since common opinion does not regard it as such, the public took no notice of a decision on a point on which its mind was already made up.

I have stated elsewhere[43] that as public opinion is not subject to any constraint, there need be no trace of it in the tribunal set up to represent it. It is
35 impossible to admire too much the art with which this resource, which we moderns have wholly lost, was employed by the Romans, and still more by the Lacedæmonians.

A man of bad morals having made a good proposal in the Spartan Council, the Ephors neglected it, and caused the same proposal to be made by a virtuous citizen. What an honour for the one, and what a disgrace for the other, without praise or blame of either! Certain drunkards from Samos[44] polluted the tribunal of the Ephors: the next day, a public edict gave Samians permission to be filthy. An actual punishment would not have been so severe as such an impunity. When Sparta has pronounced on what is or is not right, Greece makes no appeal from her judgments.

8. CIVIL RELIGION

AT first men had no kings save the gods, and no government save theocracy. They reasoned like Caligula, and, at that period, reasoned aright. It takes a long time for feeling so to change that men can make up their minds to take their equals as masters, in the hope that they will profit by doing so.

From the mere fact that God was set over every political society, it followed that there were as many gods as peoples. Two peoples that were strangers the one to the other, and almost always enemies, could not long recognise the same master: two armies giving battle could not obey the same leader. National divisions thus led to polytheism, and this in turn gave rise to theological and civil intolerance, which, as we shall see hereafter, are by nature the same.

The fancy the Greeks had for rediscovering their gods among the barbarians arose from the way they had of regarding themselves as the natural Sovereigns of such peoples. But there is nothing so absurd as the erudition which in our days identifies and confuses gods of different nations. As if Moloch, Saturn, and Chronos could be the same god! As if the Phoenician Baal, the Greek Zeus, and the Latin Jupiter could be the same! As if there could still be anything common to imaginary beings with different names!

If it is asked how in pagan times, where each State had its cult and its gods, there were no wars of religion, I answer that it was precisely because each State, having its own cult as well as its own government, made no distinction between its gods and its laws. Political war was also theological; the provinces of the gods were, so to speak, fixed by the boundaries of nations. The god of one people had no right over another. The gods of the pagans were not jealous gods; they shared among themselves the empire of the world: even Moses and the Hebrews sometimes lent themselves to this view by speaking of the God of Israel. It is true, they regarded as powerless the gods of the Canaanites, a proscribed people condemned to destruction, whose place they were to take; but remember how they spoke of the divisions of the neighbouring peoples they were forbidden to attack! "Is not the possession of what belongs to your god Chamos lawfully your due?" said Jephthah to the Ammonites. "We have the same title to the lands our conquering God has made his own."[45] Here, I think, there is a recognition that the rights of Chamos and those of the God of Israel are of the same nature.

But when the Jews, being subject to the Kings of Babylon, and, subsequently, to those of Syria, still obstinately refused to recognise any god
5   save their own, their refusal was regarded as rebellion against their conqueror, and drew down on them the persecutions we read of in their history, which are without parallel till the coming of Christianity.[46]

Every religion, therefore, being attached solely to the laws of the State which prescribed it, there was no way of converting a people except by
10   enslaving it, and there could be no missionaries save conquerors. The obligation to change cults being the law to which the vanquished yielded, it was necessary to be victorious before suggesting such a change. So far from men fighting for the gods, the gods, as in Homer, fought for men; each asked his god for victory, and repaid him with new altars. The Romans, before taking a city, summoned
15   its gods to quit it; and, in leaving the Tarentines their outraged gods, they regarded them as subject to their own and compelled to do them homage. They left the vanquished their gods as they left them their laws. A wreath to the Jupiter of the Capitol was often the only tribute they imposed.

Finally, when, along with their empire, the Romans had spread their cult
20   and their gods, and had themselves often adopted those of the vanquished, by granting to both alike the rights of the city, the peoples of that vast empire insensibly found themselves with multitudes of gods and cults, everywhere almost the same; and thus paganism throughout the known world finally came to be one and the same religion.

25   It was in these circumstances that Jesus came to set up on earth a spiritual kingdom, which, by separating the theological from the political system, made the State no longer one, and brought about the internal divisions which have never ceased to trouble Christian peoples. As the new idea of a kingdom of the other world could never have occurred to pagans, they always looked on the
30   Christians as really rebels, who, while feigning to submit, were only waiting for the chance to make themselves independent and their masters, and to usurp by guile the authority they pretended in their weakness to respect. This was the cause of the persecutions.

What the pagans had feared took place. Then everything changed its aspect:
35   the humble Christians changed their language, and soon this so-called kingdom of the other world turned, under a visible leader, into the most violent of earthly despotisms.

However, as there have always been a prince and civil laws, this double power and conflict of jurisdiction have made all good polity impossible in

Christian States; and men have never succeeded in finding out whether they were bound to obey the master or the priest.

Several peoples, however, even in Europe and its neighbourhood, have desired without success to preserve or restore the old system: but the spirit of
5 Christianity has everywhere prevailed. The sacred cult has always remained or again become independent of the Sovereign, and there has been no necessary link between it and the body of the State. Mahomet held very sane views, and linked his political system well together; and, as long as the form of his government continued under the caliphs who succeeded him, that government
10 was indeed one, and so far good. But the Arabs, having grown prosperous, lettered, civilised, slack and cowardly, were conquered by barbarians: the division between the two powers began again; and, although it is less apparent among the Mahometans than among the Christians, it none the less exists, especially in the sect of Ali, and there are States, such as Persia, where it is
15 continually making itself felt.

Among us, the Kings of England have made themselves heads of the Church, and the Czars have done the same: but this title has made them less its masters than its ministers; they have gained not so much the right to change it, as the power to maintain it: they are not its legislators, but only its princes.
20 Wherever the clergy is a corporate body,[47] it is master and legislator in its own country. There are thus two powers, two Sovereigns, in England and in Russia, as well as elsewhere.

Of all Christian writers, the philosopher Hobbes alone has seen the evil and how to remedy it, and has dared to propose the reunion of the two heads of the
25 eagle, and the restoration throughout of political unity, without which no State or government will ever be rightly constituted. But he should have seen that the masterful spirit of Christianity is incompatible with his system, and that the priestly interest would always be stronger than that of the State. It is not so much what is false and terrible in his political theory, as what is just and true, that has
30 drawn down hatred on it.[48]

I believe that if the study of history were developed from this point of view, it would be easy to refute the contrary opinions of Bayle and Warburton, one of whom holds that religion can be of no use to the body politic, while the other, on the contrary, maintains that Christianity is its strongest support. We should
35 demonstrate to the former that no State has ever been founded without a religious basis, and to the latter, that the law of Christianity at bottom does more harm by weakening than good by strengthening the constitution of the State. To make myself understood, I have only to make a little more exact the too vague ideas of religion as relating to this subject.

170

Religion, considered in relation to society, which is either general or particular, may also be divided into two kinds: the religion of man, and that of the citizen. The first, which has neither temples, nor altars, nor rites, and is confined to the purely internal cult of the supreme God and the eternal

5 obligations of morality, is the religion of the Gospel pure and simple, the true theism, what may be called natural divine right or law. The other, which is codified in a single country, gives it its gods, its own tutelary patrons; it has its dogmas, its rites, and its external cult prescribed by law; outside the single nation that follows it, all the world is in its sight infidel, foreign and barbarous;

10 the duties and rights of man extend for it only as far as its own altars. Of this kind were all the religions of early peoples, which we may define as civil or positive divine right or law.

There is a third sort of religion of a more singular kind, which gives men two codes of legislation, two rulers, and two countries, renders them subject to

15 contradictory duties, and makes it impossible for them to be faithful both to religion and to citizenship. Such are the religions of the Lamas and of the Japanese, and such is Roman Christianity, which may be called the religion of the priest. It leads to a sort of mixed and anti-social code which has no name.

In their political aspect, all these three kinds of religion have their defects.

20 The third is so clearly bad, that it is waste of time to stop to prove it such. All that destroys social unity is worthless; all institutions that set man in contradiction to himself are worthless.

The second is good in that it unites the divine cult with love of the laws, and, making country the object of the citizens' adoration, teaches them that

25 service done to the State is service done to its tutelary god. It is a form of theocracy, in which there can be no pontiff save the prince, and no priests save the magistrates. To die for one's country then becomes martyrdom; violation of its laws, impiety; and to subject one who is guilty to public execration is to condemn him to the anger of the gods: Sacer estod.

30 On the other hand, it is bad in that, being founded on lies and error, it deceives men, makes them credulous and superstitious, and drowns the true cult of the Divinity in empty ceremonial. It is bad, again, when it becomes tyrannous and exclusive, and makes a people bloodthirsty and intolerant, so that it breathes fire and slaughter, and regards as a sacred act the killing of every one who does

35 not believe in its gods. The result is to place such a people in a natural state of war with all others, so that its security is deeply endangered.

There remains therefore the religion of man or Christianity – not the Christianity of to-day, but that of the Gospel, which is entirely different. By means of this holy, sublime, and real religion all men, being children of one

God, recognise one another as brothers, and the society that unites them is not dissolved even at death.

But this religion, having no particular relation to the body politic, leaves the laws in possession of the force they have in themselves without making any addition to it; and thus one of the great bonds that unite society considered in severally fails to operate. Nay, more, so far from binding the hearts of the citizens to the State, it has the effect of taking them away from all earthly things. I know of nothing more contrary to the social spirit.

We are told that a people of true Christians would form the most perfect society imaginable. I see in this supposition only one great difficulty: that a society of true Christians would not be a society of men.

I say further that such a society, with all its perfection, would be neither the strongest nor the most lasting: the very fact that it was perfect would rob it of its bond of union; the flaw that would destroy it would lie in its very perfection.

Every one would do his duty; the people would be law-abiding, the rulers just and temperate; the magistrates upright and incorruptible; the soldiers would scorn death; there would be neither vanity nor luxury. So far, so good; but let us hear more.

Christianity as a religion is entirely spiritual, occupied solely with heavenly things; the country of the Christian is not of this world. He does his duty, indeed, but does it with profound indifference to the good or ill success of his cares. Provided he has nothing to reproach himself with, it matters little to him whether things go well or ill here on earth. If the State is prosperous, he hardly dares to share in the public happiness, for fear he may grow proud of his country's glory; if the State is languishing, he blesses the hand of God that is hard upon His people.

For the State to be peaceable and for harmony to be maintained, all the citizens without exception would have to be good Christians; if by ill hap there should be a single self-seeker or hypocrite, a Catiline or a Cromwell, for instance, he would certainly get the better of his pious compatriots. Christian charity does not readily allow a man to think hardly of his neighbours. As soon as, by some trick, he has discovered the art of imposing on them and getting hold of a share in the public authority, you have a man established in dignity; it is the will of God that he be respected: very soon you have a power; it is God's will that it be obeyed: and if the power is abused by him who wields it, it is the scourge wherewith God punishes His children. There would be scruples about driving out the usurper: public tranquillity would have to be disturbed, violence would have to be employed, and blood spilt; all this accords ill with Christian meekness; and after all, in this vale of sorrows, what does it matter whether we are free men or serfs? The essential thing is to get to heaven, and resignation is only an additional means of doing so.

If war breaks out with another State, the citizens march readily out to battle; not one of them thinks of flight; they do their duty, but they have no passion for
5   victory; they know better how to die than how to conquer. What does it matter whether they win or lose? Does not Providence know better than they what is meet for them? Only think to what account a proud, impetuous and passionate enemy could turn their stoicism! Set over against them those generous peoples who were devoured by ardent love of glory and of their country, imagine your
10   Christian republic face to face with Sparta or Rome: the pious Christians will be beaten, crushed and destroyed, before they know where they are, or will owe their safety only to the contempt their enemy will conceive for them. It was to my mind a fine oath that was taken by the soldiers of Fabius, who swore, not to conquer or die, but to come back victorious – and kept their oath. Christians
15   would never have taken such an oath; they would have looked on it as tempting God.

But I am mistaken in speaking of a Christian republic; the terms are mutually exclusive. Christianity preaches only servitude and dependence. Its spirit is so favourable to tyranny that it always profits by such a régime. True
20   Christians are made to be slaves, and they know it and do not much mind: this short life counts for too little in their eyes.

I shall be told that Christian troops are excellent. I deny it. Show me an instance. For my part, I know of no Christian troops. I shall be told of the Crusades. Without disputing the valour of the Crusaders, I answer that, so far
25   from being Christians, they were the priests' soldiery, citizens of the Church. They fought for their spiritual country, which the Church had, somehow or other, made temporal. Well understood, this goes back to paganism: as the Gospel sets up no national religion, a holy war is impossible among Christians.

Under the pagan emperors, the Christian soldiers were brave; every
30   Christian writer affirms it, and I believe it: it was a case of honourable emulation of the pagan troops. As soon as the emperors were Christian, this emulation no longer existed, and, when the Cross had driven out the eagle, Roman valour wholly disappeared.

But, setting aside political considerations, let us come back to what is right,
35   and settle our principles on this important point. The right which the social compact gives the Sovereign over the subjects does not, we have seen, exceed the limits of public expediency.[49] The subjects then owe the Sovereign an account of their opinions only to such an extent as they matter to the community. Now, it matters very much to the community that each citizen
40   should have a religion. That will make him love his duty; but the dogmas of that

religion concern the State and its members only so far as they have reference to morality and to the duties which he who professes them is bound to do to others. Each man may have, over and above, what opinions he pleases, without it being the Sovereign's business to take cognisance of them; for, as the Sovereign has no authority in the other world, whatever the lot of its subjects may be in the life to come, that is not its business, provided they are good citizens in this life.

There is therefore a purely civil profession of faith of which the Sovereign should fix the articles, not exactly as religious dogmas, but as social sentiments without which a man cannot be a good citizen or a faithful subject.[50] While it can compel no one to believe them, it can banish from the State whoever does not believe them – it can banish him, not for impiety, but as an anti-social being, incapable of truly loving the laws and justice, and of sacrificing, at need, his life to his duty. If any one, after publicly recognising these dogmas, behaves as if he does not believe them, let him be punished by death: he has committed the worst of all crimes, that of lying before the law.

The dogmas of civil religion ought to be few, simple, and exactly worded, without explanation or commentary. The existence of a mighty, intelligent and beneficent Divinity, possessed of foresight and providence, the life to come, the happiness of the just, the punishment of the wicked, the sanctity of the social contract and the laws: these are its positive dogmas. Its negative dogmas I confine to one, intolerance, which is a part of the cults we have rejected.

Those who distinguish civil from theological intolerance are, to my mind, mistaken. The two forms are inseparable. It is impossible to live at peace with those we regard as damned; to love them would be to hate God who punishes them: we positively must either reclaim or torment them. Wherever theological intolerance is admitted, it must inevitably have some civil effect;[51] and as soon as it has such an effect, the Sovereign is no longer Sovereign even in the temporal sphere: thenceforce priests are the real masters, and kings only their ministers.

Now that there is and can be no longer an exclusive national religion, tolerance should be given to all religions that tolerate others, so long as their dogmas contain nothing contrary to the duties of citizenship. But whoever dares to say: Outside the Church is no salvation, ought to be driven from the State, unless the State is the Church, and the prince the pontiff. Such a dogma is good only in a theocratic government; in any other, it is fatal. The reason for which Henry IV is said to have embraced the Roman religion ought to make every honest man leave it, and still more any prince who knows how to reason.

9. CONCLUSION

Now that I have laid down the true principles of political right, and tried to give the State a basis of its own to rest on, I ought next to strengthen it by its external relations, which would include the law of nations, commerce, the right of war and conquest, public right, leagues, negotiations, treaties, etc. But all this
5   forms a new subject that is far too vast for my narrow scope. I ought throughout to have kept to a more limited sphere.

---

[1] "Learned inquiries into public right are often only the history of past abuses; and troubling to study them too deeply is a profitless infatuation" (*Essay on the Interests of France in Relation to its Neighbours*, by the Marquis d'Argenson). This is exactly what Grotius has done.

[2] See a short treatise of Plutarch's entitled *That Animals Reason*.

[3] The Romans, who understood and respected the right of war more than any other nation on earth, carried their scruples on this head so far that a citizen was not allowed to serve as a volunteer without engaging himself expressly against the enemy, and against such and such an enemy by name. A legion in which the younger Cato was seeing his first service under Popilius having been reconstructed, the elder Cato wrote to Popilius that, if he wished his son to continue serving under him, he must administer to him a new military oath, because, the first having been annulled, he was no longer able to bear arms against the enemy. The same Cato wrote to his son telling him to take great care not to go into battle before taking this new oath. I know that the siege of Clusium and other isolated events can be quoted against me; but I am citing laws and customs. The Romans are the people that least often transgressed its laws; and no other people has had such good ones.

[4] The real meaning of this word has been almost wholly lost in modern times; most people mistake a town for a city, and a townsman for a citizen. They do not know that houses make a town, but citizens a city. The same mistake long ago cost the Carthaginians dear. I have never read of the title of citizens being given to the subjects of any prince, not even the ancient Macedonians or the English of to-day, though they are nearer liberty than any one else. The French alone everywhere familiarly adopt the name of citizens, because, as can be seen from their dictionaries, they have no idea of its meaning; otherwise they would be guilty in usurping it, of the crime of lèse-majesté: among them, the name expresses a virtue, and not a right. When Bodin spoke of our citizens and townsmen, he fell into a bad blunder in taking the one class for the other. M. d'Alembert has avoided the error, and, in his article on Geneva, has clearly distinguished the four orders of men (or even five, counting mere foreigners) who dwell in our town, of which two only compose the Republic. No other French writer, to my knowledge, has understood the real meaning of the word citizen.

[5] Under bad governments, this equality is only apparent and illusory: it serves only to keep the pauper in his poverty and the rich man in the position he has usurped. In fact, laws are always of use to those who possess and harmful to those who have nothing: from which it follows that the social state is advantageous to men only when all have something and none too much.

[6] To be general, a will need not always be unanimous; but every vote must be counted: any exclusion is a breach of generality.

[7] "Every interest," says the Marquis d'Argenson, "has different principles. The agreement of two particular interests is formed by opposition to a third." He might have added that

the agreement of all interests is formed by opposition to that of each. If there were no different interests, the common interest would be barely felt, as it would encounter no obstacle; all would go on of its own accord, and politics would cease to be an art.

[8] "In fact," says Machiavelli, "there are some divisions that are harmful to a Republic and some that are advantageous. Those which stir up sects and parties are harmful; those attended by neither are advantageous. Since, then, the founder of a Republic cannot help enmities arising, he ought at least to prevent them from growing into sects" (*History of Florence*, Book vii).

[9] Attentive readers, do not, I pray, be in a hurry to charge me with contradicting myself. The terminology made it unavoidable, considering the poverty of the language; but wait and see.

[10] I understand by this word, not merely an aristocracy or a democracy, but generally any government directed by the general will, which is the law. To be legitimate, the government must be, not one with the Sovereign, but its minister. In such a case even a monarchy is a Republic. This will be made clearer in the following book.

[11] A people becomes famous only when its legislation begins to decline. We do not know for how many centuries the system of Lycurgus made the Spartans happy before the rest of Greece took any notice of it.

[12] Montesquieu, *The Greatness and Decadence of the Romans*, ch. i.

[13] Those who know Calvin only as a theologian much under-estimate the extent of his genius. The codification of our wise edicts, in which he played a large part, does him no less honour than his Institute. Whatever revolution time may bring in our religion, so long as the spirit of patriotism and liberty still lives among us, the memory of this great man will be for ever blessed.

[14] "In truth," says Machiavelli, "there has never been, in any country, an extraordinary legislator who has not had recourse to God; for otherwise his laws would not have been accepted: there are, in fact, many useful truths of which a wise man may have knowledge without their having in themselves such clear reasons for their being so as to be able to convince others" (*Discourses on Livy*, Bk. v, ch. xi).

[15] If there were two neighbouring peoples, one of which could not do without the other, it would be very hard on the former, and very dangerous for the latter. Every wise nation, in such a case, would make haste to free the other from dependence. The Republic of Thiascala, enclosed by the Mexican Empire, preferred doing without salt to buying from the Mexicans, or even getting it from them as a gift. The Thiascalans were wise enough to see the snare hidden under such liberality. They kept their freedom, and that little State, shut up in that great Empire, was finally the instrument of its ruin.

[16] If the object is to give the State consistency, bring the two extremes as near to each other as possible; allow neither rich men nor beggars. These two estates, which are naturally inseparable, are equally fatal to the common good; from the one come the friends of tyranny, and from the other tyrants. It is always between them that public liberty is put up to auction; the one buys, and the other sells.

[17] "Any branch of foreign commerce," says M. d'Argenson, "creates on the whole only apparent advantage for the kingdom in general; it may enrich some individuals, or even some towns; but the nation as a whole gains nothing by it, and the people is no better off."

[18] Thus at Venice the College, even in the absence of the Doge, is called "Most Serene Prince."

[19] [Montesquieu, *The Spirit of Laws*, III:3]

[20] The Palatine of Posen, father of the King of Poland, Duke of Lorraine.

[21] I prefer liberty with danger to peace with slavery.

[22] It is clear that the word optimales meant, among the ancients, not the best, but the most powerful.

[23] It is of great importance that the form of the election of magistrates should be regulated by law; for if it is left at the discretion of the prince, it is impossible to avoid falling into hereditary aristocracy, as the Republics of Venice and Berne actually did. The first of these has therefore long been a State dissolved; the second, however, is maintained by the extreme wisdom of the senate, and forms an honourable and highly dangerous exception.

[24] Machiavelli was a proper man and a good citizen; but, being attached to the court of the Medici, he could not help veiling his love of liberty in the midst of his country's oppression. The choice of his detestable hero, Caesar Borgia, clearly enough shows his hidden aim; and the contradiction between the teaching of the Prince and that of the Discourses on Livy and the History of Florence shows that this profound political thinker has so far been studied only by superficial or corrupt readers. The Court of Rome sternly prohibited his book. I can well believe it; for it is that Court it most clearly portrays.

[25] Tacitus, *Histories*, i. 16. "For the best, and also the shortest way of finding out what is good and what is bad is to consider what you would have wished to happen or not to happen, had another than you been Emperor."

[26] In the *Statesman*.

[27] [Montesquieu, *The Spirit of Laws*, XIV]

[28] This does not contradict what I said before (Book II, ch. 9) about the disadvantages of great States; for we were then dealing with the authority of the government over the members, while here we are dealing with its force against the subjects. Its scattered members serve it as rallying-points for action against the people at a distance, but it has no rallying-point for direct action on its members themselves. Thus the length of the lever is its weakness in the one case, and its strength in the other.

[29] On the same principle it should be judged what centuries deserve the preference for human prosperity. Those in which letters and arts have flourished have been too much admired, because the hidden object of their culture has not been fathomed, and their fatal effects not taken into account. "Idque apud imperitos humanitas vocabatur, cum pars servitutis esset." (Fools called "humanity" what was a part of slavery, Tacitus, *Agricola*, 31.) Shall we never see in the maxims books lay down the vulgar interest that makes their writers speak? No, whatever they may say, when, despite its renown, a country is depopulated, it is not true that all is well, and it is not enough that a poet should have an income of 100,000 francs to make his age the best of all. Less attention should be paid to the apparent repose and tranquillity of the rulers than to the well-being of their nations as wholes, and above all of the most numerous States. A hail-storm lays several cantons waste, but it rarely makes a famine. Outbreaks and civil wars give rulers rude shocks, but they are not the real ills of peoples, who may even get a respite, while there is a dispute as to who shall tyrannise over them. Their true prosperity and calamities come from their permanent condition: it is when the whole remains crushed beneath the yoke, that decay sets in, and that the rulers destroy them at will, and "ubi solitudinem faciunt, pacem appellant." (Where they create solitude, they call it peace, Tacitus, Agricola, 31.) When the bickerings of the great disturbed the kingdom of France, and the Coadjutor of Paris took a dagger in his pocket to the Parliament, these things did not prevent the people of France from prospering and multiplying in dignity, ease and freedom. Long ago Greece flourished in the midst of the most savage wars; blood ran in torrents, and yet the whole country was covered with inhabitants. It appeared, says Machiavelli, that in the midst of murder, proscription and civil war, our republic only throve: the virtue, morality and

independence of the citizens did more to strengthen it than all their dissensions had done to enfeeble it. A little disturbance gives the soul elasticity; what makes the race truly prosperous is not so much peace as liberty.

[30] The slow formation and the progress of the Republic of Venice in its lagoons are a notable instance of this sequence; and it is most astonishing that, after more than twelve hundred years' existence, the Venetians seem to be still at the second stage, which they reached with the Serrar di Consiglio in 1198. As for the ancient Dukes who are brought up against them, it is proved, whatever the Squittinio della libertà veneta may say of them, that they were in no sense sovereigns.

A case certain to be cited against my view is that of the Roman Republic, which, it will be said, followed exactly the opposite course, and passed from monarchy to aristocracy and from aristocracy to democracy. I by no means take this view of it.

What Romulus first set up was a mixed government, which soon deteriorated into despotism. From special causes, the State died an untimely death, as new-born children sometimes perish without reaching manhood. The expulsion of the Tarquins was the real period of the birth of the Republic. But at first it took on no constant form, because, by not abolishing the patriciate, it left half its work undone. For, by this means, hereditary aristocracy, the worst of all legitimate forms of administration, remained in conflict with democracy, and the form of the government, as Machiavelli has proved, was only fixed on the establishment of the tribunate: only then was there a true government and a veritable democracy. In fact, the people was then not only Sovereign, but also magistrate and judge; the senate was only a subordinate tribunal, to temper and concentrate the government, and the consuls themselves, though they were patricians, first magistrates, and absolute generals in war, were in Rome itself no more than presidents of the people.

From that point, the government followed its natural tendency, and inclined strongly to aristocracy. The patriciate, we may say, abolished itself, and the aristocracy was found no longer in the body of patricians as at Venice and Genoa, but in the body of the senate, which was composed of patricians and plebeians, and even in the body of tribunes when they began to usurp an active function: for names do not affect facts, and, when the people has rulers who govern for it, whatever name they bear, the government is an aristocracy.

The abuse of aristocracy led to the civil wars and the triumvirate. Sulla, Julius Caesar and Augustus became in fact real monarchs; and finally, under the despotism of Tiberius, the State was dissolved. Roman history then confirms, instead of invalidating, the principle I have laid down.

[31] "Omnes enim et habentur et dicuntur tyranni, qui potestate utuntur perpetua in ea civitate quæ libertate usa est" (Cornelius Nepos, *Life of Miltiades*). (For all those are called and considered tyrants, who hold perpetual power in a State that has known liberty.) It is true that Aristotle (*Ethics*, Book viii, chapter x) distinguishes the tyrant from the king by the fact that the former governs in his own interest, and the latter only for the good of his subjects; but not only did all Greek authors in general use the word tyrant in a different sense, as appears most clearly in Xenophon's *Hiero*, but also it would follow from Aristotle's distinction that, from the very beginning of the world, there has not yet been a single king.

[32] In nearly the same sense as this word has in the English Parliament. The similarity of these functions would have brought the consuls and the tribunes into conflict, even had all jurisdiction been suspended.

[33] To adopt in cold countries the luxury and effeminacy of the East is to desire to submit to its chains; it is indeed to bow to them far more inevitably in our case than in theirs.

[34] I had intended to do this in the sequel to this work, when in dealing with external relations I came to the subject of confederations. The subject is quite new, and its principles have still to be laid down.

[35] Provided, of course, he does not leave to escape his obligations and avoid having to serve his country in the hour of need. Flight in such a case would be criminal and punishable, and would be, not withdrawal, but desertion.

[36] This should of course be understood as applying to a free State; for elsewhere family, goods, lack of a refuge, necessity, or violence may detain a man in a country against his will; and then his dwelling there no longer by itself implies his consent to the contract or to its violation.

[37] At Genoa, the word Liberty may be read over the front of the prisons and on the chains of the galley-slaves. This application of the device is good and just. It is indeed only malefactors of all estates who prevent the citizen from being free. In the country in which all such men were in the galleys, the most perfect liberty would be enjoyed.

[38] [Montesquieu, The Spirit of Laws, II:2]

[39] I say "in the Campus Martius" because it was there that the comitia assembled by centuries; in its two other forms the people assembled in the forum or elsewhere; and then the capite censi had as much influence and authority as the foremost citizens.

[40] Custodes, diribitores, rogatores suffragiorum.

[41] The nomination was made secretly by night, as if there were something shameful in setting a man above the laws.

[42] That is what he could not be sure of, if he proposed a dictator; for he dared not nominate himself, and could not be certain that his colleague would nominate him.

[43] I merely call attention in this chapter to a subject with which I have dealt at greater length in my Letter to M. d'Alembert.

[44] They were from another island, which the delicacy of our language forbids me to name on this occasion.

[45] Nonne ea quæ possidet Chamos deus tuus, tibi jure debentur? (Judges, 11:24.) Such is the text in the Vulgate. Father de Carrières translates: "Do you not regard yourselves as having a right to what your god possesses?" I do not know the force of the Hebrew text: but I perceive that, in the Vulgate, Jephthah positively recognises the right of the god Chamos, and that the French translator weakened this admission by inserting an "according to you," which is not in the Latin.

[46] It is quite clear that the Phocian War, which was called "the Sacred War," was not a war of religion. Its object was the punishment of acts of sacrilege, and not the conquest of unbelievers.

[47] It should be noted that the clergy find their bond of union not so much in formal assemblies, as in the communion of Churches. Communion and excommunication are the social compact of the clergy, a compact which will always make them masters of peoples and kings. All priests who communicate together are fellow-citizens, even if they come from opposite ends of the earth. This invention is a masterpiece of statesmanship: there is nothing like it among pagan priests; who have therefore never formed a clerical corporate body.

[48] See, for instance, in a letter from Grotius to his brother (April 11, 1643), what that learned man found to praise and to blame in the *De Cive*. It is true that, with a bent for indulgence, he seems to pardon the writer the good for the sake of the bad; but all men are not so forgiving.

[49] "In the republic," says the Marquis d'Argenson, "each man is perfectly free in what does not harm others." This is the invariable limitation, which it is impossible to define

more exactly. I have not been able to deny myself the pleasure of occasionally quoting from this manuscript, though it is unknown to the public, in order to do honour to the memory of a good and illustrious man, who had kept even in the Ministry the heart of a good citizen, and views on the government of his country that were sane and right.

[50] Cæsar, pleading for Catiline, tried to establish the dogma that the soul is mortal: Cato and Cicero, in refutation, did not waste time in philosophising. They were content to show that Cæsar spoke like a bad citizen, and brought forward a doctrine that would have a bad effect on the State. This, in fact, and not a problem of theology, was what the Roman senate had to judge.

[51] Marriage, for instance, being a civil contract, has civil effects without which society cannot even subsist. Suppose a body of clergy should claim the sole right of permitting this act, a right which every intolerant religion must of necessity claim, is it not clear that in establishing the authority of the Church in this respect, it will be destroying that of the prince, who will have thenceforth only as many subjects as the clergy choose to allow him? Being in a position to marry or not to marry people according to their acceptance of such and such a doctrine, their admission or rejection of such and such a formula, their greater or less piety, the Church alone, by the exercise of prudence and firmness, will dispose of all inheritances, offices and citizens, and even of the State itself, which could not subsist if it were composed entirely of bastards? But, I shall be told, there will be appeals on the ground of abuse, summonses and decrees; the temporalities will be seized. How sad! The clergy, however little, I will not say courage, but sense it has, will take no notice and go its way: it will quietly allow appeals, summonses, decrees and seizures, and, in the end, will remain the master. It is not, I think, a great sacrifice to give up a part, when one is sure of securing all.

Adam Smith

Adam Smith (b. 1723, Kircaldy, d. 1790, Edinburgh) was a Scottish economist and moral philosopher. Smith studied moral philosopher under Francis Hutcheson, one of the founding figures of the Scottish Enlightenment – an intellectual movement that would eventually count Smith and his close friend David Hume as its leading lights. Although he served briefly as a commissioner of customs, Smith spent the bulk of his career as an academic, first as a lecturer at Edinburgh, and eventually as a holder of Hutcheson's Chair of Moral Philosophy at the University of Glasgow. Smith was a prolific writer, contributing to a wide range of topics, including political economy, moral philosophy, law and jurisprudence, logic, rhetoric, and history. Although his writings were primarily academic, they often addressed important policy debates of the day, including, notably, trade policy, and because of Smith's stature and popularity, became important points of reference in those debates.

Smith's *An Inquiry into the Nature and Causes of the Wealth of Nations* was widely read and admired during his lifetime and has become the single most influential piece of writing in the history of economic thought. His other most influential work, the earlier *The Theory of Moral Sentiments*, secured Smith's position alongside David Hume as one of the most influential modern theorists of the relationship between morality and individual human interests.

The most enduring political impact of Smith's work is in shaping the articulation of an economically grounded defense of limited government and political libertarianism.

Adam Smith
AN INQUIRY INTO THE NATURE AND CAUSES OF THE WEALTH OF NATIONS
(1776)

INTRODUCTION AND PLAN OF THE WORK
The annual labour of every nation is the fund which originally supplies it with all the necessaries and conveniences of life which it annually consumes, and which consist always, either in the immediate produce of that labour, or in what is purchased with that produce from other nations.

5   According therefore, as this produce, or what is purchased with it, bears a greater or smaller proportion to the number of those who are to consume it, the nation will be better or worse supplied with all the necessaries and conveniences for which it has occasion.

But this proportion must in every nation be regulated by two different
10   circumstances; first, by the skill, dexterity, and judgment with which its labour is generally applied; and, secondly, by the proportion between the number of those who are employed in useful labour, and that of those who are not so employed. Whatever be the soil, climate, or extent of territory of any particular nation, the abundance or scantiness of its annual supply must, in that particular situation, depend upon those
15   two circumstances.

The abundance or scantiness of this supply too seems to depend more upon the former of those two circumstances than upon the latter. Among the savage nations of hunters and fishers, every individual who is able to work, is more or less employed in useful labour, and endeavours to provide, as well as he can, the necessaries and
20   conveniencies of life, for himself, or such of his family or tribe as are either too old, or too young, or too infirm to go a hunting and fishing. Such nations, however, are so miserably poor, that, from mere want, they are frequently reduced, or, at least, think themselves reduced, to the necessity sometimes of directly destroying, and sometimes of abandoning their infants, their old people, and those afflicted with
25   lingering diseases, to perish with hunger, or to be devoured by wild beasts. Among civilized and thriving nations, on the contrary, though a great number of people do not labour at all, many of whom consume the produce of ten times, frequently of a hundred times more labour than the greater part of those who work; yet the produce of the whole labour of the society is so great, that all are often abundantly supplied,
30   and a workman, even of the lowest and poorest order, if he is frugal and industrious, may enjoy a greater share of the necessaries and conveniences of life than it is possible for any savage to acquire.

The causes of this improvement, in the productive powers of labour, and the order, according to which its produce is naturally distributed among the different ranks and conditions of men in the society, make the subject of the First Book of this Inquiry.

5   Whatever be the actual state of the skill, dexterity, and judgment with which labour is applied in any nation, the abundance or scantiness of its annual supply must depend, during the continuance of that state, upon the proportion between the number of those who are annually employed in useful labour, and that of those who are not so employed. The number of useful and productive labourers, it will hereafter

10   appear, is every where in proportion to the quantity of capital stock which is employed in setting them to work, and to the particular way in which it is so employed. The Second Book, therefore, treats of the nature of capital stock, of the manner in which it is gradually accumulated, and of the different quantities of labour which it puts into motion, according to the different ways in which it is employed.

15   Nations tolerably well advanced as to skill, dexterity, and judgment, in the application of labour, have followed very different plans in the general conduct or direction of it; and those plans have not all been equally favourable to the greatness of its produce. The policy of some nations has given extraordinary encouragement to the industry of the country; that of others to the industry of towns. Scarce any nation

20   has dealt equally and impartially with every sort of industry. Since the downfal of the Roman empire, the policy of Europe has been more favourable to arts, manufactures, and commerce, the industry of towns; than to agriculture, the industry of the country. The circumstances which seem to have introduced and established this policy are explained in the Third Book.

25   Though those different plans were, perhaps, first introduced by the private interests and prejudices of particular orders of men, without any regard to, or foresight of, their consequences upon the general welfare of the society; yet they have given occasion to very different theories of political œconomy; of which some magnify the importance of that industry which is carried on in towns, others of that

30   which is carried on in the country. Those theories have had a considerable influence, not only upon the opinions of men of learning, but upon the public conduct of princes and sovereign states. I have endeavoured, in the Fourth Book, to explain, as fully and distinctly as I can, those different theories, and the principal effects which they have produced in different ages and nations.

35   To explain in what has consisted the revenue of the great body of the people, or what has been the nature of those funds which, in different ages and nations, have supplied their annual consumption, is the object of these Four first Books. The Fifth and last Book treats of the revenue of the sovereign, or commonwealth. In this Book I have endeavoured to show; first, what are the necessary expences of the sovereign,

or commonwealth; which of those expences ought to be defrayed by the general contribution of the whole society; and which of them, by that of some particular part only, or of some particular members of it; secondly, what are the different methods in which the whole society may be made to contribute towards defraying the
5 expences incumbent on the whole society, and what are the principal advantages and inconveniencies of each of those methods: and, thirdly and lastly, what are the reasons and causes which have induced almost all modern governments to mortgage some part of this revenue, or to contract debts, and what have been the effects of those debts upon the real wealth, the annual produce of the land and labour of the
10 society.

OF THE DIVISION OF LABOUR

The greatest improvement in the productive powers of labour, and the greater part of the skill, dexterity, and judgment with which it is any where directed, or applied, seem to have been the effects of the division of labour.

The effects of the division of labour, in the general business of society, will be
15 more easily understood, by considering in what manner it operates in some particular manufactures. It is commonly supposed to be carried furthest in some very trifling ones; not perhaps that it really is carried further in them than in others of more importance: but in those trifling manufactures which are destined to supply the small wants of but a small number of people, the whole number of workmen must
20 necessarily be small; and those employed in every different branch of the work can often be collected into the same workhouse, and placed at once under the view of the spectator. In those great manufactures, on the contrary, which are destined to supply the great wants of the great body of the people, every different branch of the work employs so great a number of workmen, that it is impossible to collect them all into
25 the same workhouse. We can seldom see more, at one time, than those employed in one single branch. Though in such manufactures, therefore, the work may really be divided into a much greater number of parts, than in those of a more trifling nature, the division is not near so obvious, and has accordingly been much less observed.

To take an example, therefore, from a very trifling manufacture; but one in
30 which the division of labour has been very often taken notice of, the trade of the pin–maker; a workman not educated to this business (which the division of labour has rendered a distinct trade), nor acquainted with the use of the machinery employed in it (to the invention of which the same division of labour has probably given occasion), could scarce, perhaps, with his utmost industry, make one pin in a day,
35 and certainly could not make twenty. But in the way in which this business is now carried on, not only the whole work is a peculiar trade, but it is divided into a number

of branches, of which the greater part are likewise peculiar trades. One man draws out the wire, another straights it, a third cuts it, a fourth points it, a fifth grinds it at the top for receiving the head; to make the head requires two or three distinct operations; to put it on, is a peculiar business, to whiten the pins is another; it is even
5   a trade by itself to put them into the paper; and the important business of making a pin is, in this manner, divided into about eighteen distinct operations, which, in some manufactories, are all performed by distinct hands, though in others the same man will sometimes perform two or three of them. I have seen a small manufactory of this kind where ten men only were employed, and where some of them consequently
10   performed two or three distinct operations. But though they were very poor, and therefore but indifferently accommodated with the necessary machinery, they could, when they exerted themselves, make among them about twelve pounds of pins in a day. There are in a pound upwards of four thousand pins of a middling size. Those ten persons, therefore, could make among them upwards of forty–eight thousand pins
15   in a day. Each person, therefore, making a tenth part of forty–eight thousand pins, might be considered as making four thousand eight hundred pins in a day. But if they had all wrought separately and independently, and without any of them having been educated to this peculiar business, they certainly could not each of them have made twenty, perhaps not one pin in a day; that is, certainly, not the two hundred and
20   fortieth, perhaps not the four thousand eight hundredth part of what they are at present capable of performing, in consequence of a proper division and combination of their different operations.

     In every other art and manufacture, the effects of the division of labour are similar to what they are in this very trifling one; though, in many of them, the labour
25   can neither be so much subdivided, nor reduced to so great a simplicity of operation. The division of labour, however, so far as it can be introduced, occasions, in every art, a proportionable increase of the productive powers of labour. The separation of different trades and employments from one another, seems to have taken place, in consequence of this advantage. This separation too is generally carried furthest in
30   those countries which enjoy the highest degree of industry and improvement; what is the work of one man, in a rude state of society, being generally that of several in an improved one. In every improved society, the farmer is generally nothing but a farmer; the manufacturer, nothing but a manufacturer. The labour too which is necessary to produce any one complete manufacture, is almost always divided
35   among a great number of hands. How many different trades are employed in each branch of the linen and woollen manufactures, from the growers of the flax and the wool, to the bleachers and smoothers of the linen, or to the dyers and dressers of the cloth! The nature of agriculture, indeed, does not admit of so many subdivisions of labour, nor of so complete a separation of one business from another, as

manufactures. It is impossible to separate so entirely, the business of the grazier from that of the corn–farmer, as the trade of the carpenter is commonly separated from that of the smith. The spinner is almost always a distinct person from the weaver; but the ploughman, the harrower, the sower of the seed, and the reaper of the corn, are often the same. The occasions for those different sorts of labour returning with the different seasons of the year, it is impossible that one man should be constantly employed in any one of them. This impossibility of making so complete and entire a separation of all the different branches of labour employed in agriculture, is perhaps the reason why the improvement of the productive powers of labour in this art, does not always keep pace with their improvement in manufactures. The most opulent nations, indeed, generally excel all their neighbours in agriculture as well as in manufactures; but they are commonly more distinguished by their superiority in the latter than in the former. Their lands are in general better cultivated, and having more labour and expence bestowed upon them, produce more, in proportion to the extent and natural fertility of the ground. But this superiority of produce is seldom much more than in proportion to the superiority of labour and expence. In agriculture, the labour of the rich country is not always much more productive than that of the poor; or, at least, it is never so much more productive, as it commonly is in manufactures. The corn of the rich country, therefore, will not always, in the same degree of goodness, come cheaper to market than that of the poor. The corn of Poland, in the same degree of goodness, is as cheap as that of France, notwithstanding the superior opulence and improvement of the latter country. The corn of France is, in the corn provinces, fully as good, and in most years nearly about the same price with the corn of England, though, in opulence and improvement, France is perhaps inferior to England. The corn–lands of England, however, are better cultivated than those of France, and the corn–lands^e of France are said to be much better cultivated than those of Poland. But though the poor country, notwithstanding the inferiority of its cultivation, can, in some measure, rival the rich in the cheapness and goodness of its corn, it can pretend to no such competition in its manufactures; at least if those manufactures suit the soil, climate, and situation of the rich country. The silks of France are better and cheaper than those of England, because the silk manufacture, ^{f}at least under the present high duties upon the importation of raw silk, does not so well suit the climate of England as that of France. But the hard–ware and the coarse woollens of England are beyond all comparison superior to those of France, and much cheaper too in the same degree of goodness. In Poland there are said to be scarce any manufactures of any kind, a few of those coarser household manufactures excepted, without which no country can well subsist.

This great increase of the quantity of work, which, in consequence of the division of labour, the same number of people are capable of performing, is owing to three different circumstances; first, to the increase of dexterity in every particular workman; secondly, to the saving of the time which is commonly lost in passing from one species of work to another; and lastly, to the invention of a great number of machines which facilitate and abridge labour, and enable one man to do the work of

5   many.

First, the improvement of the dexterity of the workman necessarily increases the quantity of the work he can perform, and the division of labour, by reducing every man's business to some one simple operation, and by making this operation the sole employment of his life, necessarily increases very much the dexterity of the

10   workman. A common smith, who, though accustomed to handle the hammer, has never been used to make nails, if upon some particular occasion he is obliged to attempt it, will scarce, I am assured, be able to make above two or three hundred nails in a day, and those too very bad ones. A smith who has been accustomed to make nails, but whose sole or principal business has not been that of a nailer, can

15   seldom with his utmost diligence make more than eight hundred or a thousand nails in a day. I have seen several boys under twenty years of age who had never exercised any other trade but that of making nails, and who, when they exerted themselves, could make, each of them, upwards of two thousand three hundred nails in a day. The making of a nail, however, is by no means one of the simplest operations. The

20   same person blows the bellows, stirs or mends the fire as there is occasion, heats the iron, and forges every part of the nail: In forging the head too he is obliged to change his tools. The different operations into which the making of a pin, or of a metal button, is subdivided, are all of them much more simple, and the dexterity of the person, of whose life it has been the sole business to perform them, is usually much

25   greater. The rapidity with which some of the operations of those manufactures are performed, exceeds what the human hand could, by those who had never seen them, be supposed capable of acquiring.

Secondly, the advantage which is gained by saving the time commonly lost in passing from one sort of work to another, is much greater than we should at first

30   view be apt to imagine it. It is impossible to pass very quickly from one kind of work to another, that is carried on in a different place, and with quite different tools. A country weaver, who cultivates a small farm, must lose a good deal of time in passing from his loom to the field, and from the field to his loom. When the two trades can be carried on in the same workhouse, the loss of time is no doubt much

35   less. It is even in this case, however, very considerable. A man commonly saunters a little in turning his hand from one sort of employment to another. When he first begins the new work he is seldom very keen and hearty; his mind, as they say, does not go to it, and for some time he rather trifles than applies to good purpose. The habit of sauntering and of indolent careless application, which is naturally, or rather

necessarily acquired by every country workman who is obliged to change his work and his tools every half hour, and to apply his hand in twenty different ways almost every day of his life; renders him almost always slothful and lazy, and incapable of any vigorous application even on the most pressing occasions. Independent,
5 therefore, of his deficiency in point of dexterity, this cause alone must always reduce considerably the quantity of work which he is capable of performing.

Thirdly, and lastly, every body must be sensible how much labour is facilitated and abridged by the application of proper machinery. It is unnecessary to give any example I shall only observe, therefore, that the invention of all those machines by
10 which labour is so much facilitated and abridged, seems to have been originally owing to the division of labour. Men are much more likely to discover easier and readier methods of attaining any object, when the whole attention of their minds is directed towards that single object, than when it is dissipated among a great variety of things. But in consequence of the division of labour, the whole of every man's
15 attention comes naturally to be directed towards some one very simple object. It is naturally to be expected, therefore, that some one or other of those who are employed in each particular branch of labour should soon find out easier and readier methods of performing their own particular work, wherever the nature of it admits of such improvement. A great part of the machines made use of in those manufactures
20 in which labour is most subdivided, were originally the inventions of common workmen, who, being each of them employed in some very simple operation, naturally turned their thoughts towards finding out easier and readier methods of performing it. Whoever has been much accustomed to visit such manufactures, must frequently have been shewn very pretty machines, which were the inventions of such
25 workmen, in order to facilitate and quicken their own particular part of the work. In the first fire–engines, a boy was constantly employed to open and shut alternately the communication between the boiler and the cylinder, according as the piston either ascended or descended. One of those boys, who loved to play with his companions, observed that, by tying a string from the handle of the valve, which opened this
30 communication, to another part of the machine, the valve would open and shut without his assistance, and leave him at liberty to divert himself with his play– fellows. One of the greatest improvements that has been made upon this machine, since it was first invented, was in this manner the discovery of a boy who wanted to save his own labour.
35 All the improvements in machinery, however, have by no means been the inventions of those who had occasion to use the machines. Many improvements have been made by the ingenuity of the makers of the machines, when to make them became the business of a peculiar trade; and some by that of those who are called philosophers or men of speculation, whose trade it is, not to do any thing, but to

observe every thing; and who, upon that account, are often capable of combining together the powers of the most distant and dissimilar objects. In the progress of society, philosophy or speculation becomes, like every other employment, the principal or sole trade and occupation of a particular class of citizens. Like every
5   other employment too, it is subdivided into a great number of different branches, each of which affords occupation to a peculiar tribe or class of philosophers; and this subdivision of employment in philosophy, as well as in every other business, improves dexterity, and saves time. Each individual becomes more expert in his own peculiar branch, more work is done upon the whole, and the quantity of science is
10   considerably increased by it.

It is the great multiplication of the productions of all the different arts, in consequence of the division of labour, which occasions, in a well–governed society, that universal opulence which extends itself to the lowest ranks of the people. Every workman has a great quantity of his own work to dispose of beyond what he himself
15   has occasion for; and every other workman being exactly in the same situation, he is enabled to exchange a great quantity of his own goods for a great quantity, or, what comes to the same thing, for the price of a great quantity of theirs. He supplies them abundantly with what they have occasion for, and they accommodate him as amply with what he has occasion for, and a general plenty diffuses itself through all the
20   different ranks of the society.

Observe the accommodation of the most common artificer or daylabourer in a civilized and thriving country, and you will perceive that the number of people of whose industry a part, though but a small part, has been employed in procuring him this accommodation, exceeds all computation. The woollen coat, for example, which
25   covers the daylabourer, as coarse and rough as it may appear, is the produce of the joint labour of a great multitude of workmen. The shepherd, the sorter of the wool, the wool–comber or carder, the dyer, the scribbler, the spinner, the weaver, the fuller, the dresser, with many others, must all join their different arts in order to complete even this homely production. How many merchants and carriers, besides, must have
30   been employed in transporting the materials from some of those workmen to others who often live in a very distant part of the country! How much commerce and navigation in particular, how many ship–builders, sailors, sail–makers, rope–makers, must have been employed in order to bring together the different drugs made use of by the dyer, which often come from the remotest corners of the world! What a
35   variety of labour too is necessary in order to produce the tools of the meanest of those workmen! To say nothing of such complicated machines as the ship of the sailor, the mill of the fuller, or even the loom of the weaver, let us consider only what a variety of labour is requisite in order to form that very simple machine, the shears with which the shepherd clips the wool. The miner, the builder of the furnace

for smelting the ore, the feller of the timber, the burner of the charcoal to be made use of in the smelting–house, the brick–maker, the brick–layer, the workmen who attend the furnace, the mill–wright, the forger, the smith, must all of them join their different arts in order to produce them. Were we to examine, in the same manner, all the different parts of his dress and household furniture, the coarse linen shirt which he wears next his skin, the shoes which cover his feet, the bed which he lies on, and all the different parts which compose it, the kitchen–grate at which he prepares his victuals, the coals which he makes use of for that purpose, dug from the bowels of the earth, and brought to him perhaps by a long sea and a long land carriage, all the other utensils of his kitchen, all the furniture of his table, the knives and forks, the earthen or pewter plates upon which he serves up and divides his victuals, the different hands employed in preparing his bread and his beer, the glass window which lets in the heat and the light, and keeps out the wind and the rain, with all the knowledge and art requisite for preparing that beautiful and happy invention, without which these northern parts of the world could scarce have afforded a very comfortable habitation, together with the tools of all the different workmen employed in producing those different conveniencies; if we examine, I say, all these things, and consider what a variety of labour is employed about each of them, we shall be sensible that without the assistance and cooperation of many thousands, the very meanest person in a civilized country could not be provided, even according to, what we very falsely imagine, the easy and simple manner in which he is commonly accommodated. Compared, indeed, with the more extravagant luxury of the great, his accommodation must no doubt appear extremely simple and easy; and yet it may be true, perhaps, that the accommodation of an European prince does not always so much exceed that of an industrious and frugal peasant, as the accommodation of the latter exceeds that of many an African king, the absolute master of the lives and liberties of ten thousand naked savages.

OF THE PRINCIPLE WHICH GIVES OCCASION TO THE DIVISION OF LABOR

This division of labour, from which so many advantages are derived, is not originally the effect of any human wisdom, which foresees and intends that general opulence to which it gives occasion. It is the necessary, though very slow and gradual consequence of a certain propensity in human nature which has in view no such extensive utility; the propensity to truck, barter, and exchange one thing for another.

Whether this propensity be one of those original principles in human nature, of which no further account can be given; or whether, as seems more probable, it be the

necessary consequence of the faculties of reason and speech, it belongs not to our present subject to enquire. It is common to all men, and to be found in no other race of animals, which seem to know neither this nor any other species of contracts. Two greyhounds, in running down the same hare, have sometimes the appearance of
5   acting in some sort of concert. Each turns her towards his companion, or endeavours to intercept her when his companion turns her towards himself. This, however, is not the effect of any contract, but of the accidental concurrence of their passions in the same object at that particular time. Nobody ever saw a dog make a fair and deliberate exchange of one bone for another with another dog. Nobody ever saw one animal by
10   its gestures and natural cries signify to another, this is mine, that yours; I am willing to give this for that. When an animal wants to obtain something either of a man or of another animal, it has no other means of persuasion but to gain the favour of those whose service it requires. A puppy fawns upon its dam, and a spaniel endeavours by a thousand attractions to engage the attention of its master who is at dinner, when it
15   wants to be fed by him. Man sometimes uses the same arts with his brethren, and when he has no other means of engaging them to act according to his inclinations, endeavours by every servile and fawning attention to obtain their good will. He has not time, however, to do this upon every occasion. In civilized society he stands at all times in need of the co–operation and assistance of great multitudes, while his
20   whole life is scarce sufficient to gain the friendship of a few persons. In almost every other race of animals each individual, when it is grown up to maturity, is intirely independent, and in its natural state has occasion for the assistance of no other living creature. But man has almost constant occasion for the help of his brethren, and it is in vain for him to expect it from their benevolence only. He will be more likely to
25   prevail if he can interest their self–love in his favour, and shew them that it is for their own advantage to do for him what he requires of them. Whoever offers to another a bargain of any kind, proposes to do this. Give me that which I want, and you shall have this which you want, is the meaning of every such offer; and it is in this manner that we obtain from one another the far greater part of those good offices
30   which we stand in need of. It is not from the benevolence of the butcher, the brewer, or the baker, that we expect our dinner, but from their regard to their own interest. We address ourselves, not to their humanity but to their self–love, and never talk to them of our own necessities but of their advantages. Nobody but a beggar chuses to depend chiefly upon the benevolence of his fellow–citizens. Even a beggar does not
35   depend upon it entirely. The charity of well–disposed people, indeed, supplies him with the whole fund of his subsistence. But though this principle ultimately provides him with all the necessaries of life which he has occasion for, it neither does nor can provide him with them as he has occasion for them. The greater part of his occasional wants are supplied in the same manner as those of other people, by treaty,

by barter, and by purchase. With the money which one man gives him he purchases food. The old cloaths which another bestows upon him he exchanges for other old cloaths which suit him better, or for lodging, or for food, or for money, with which he can buy either food, cloaths, or lodging, as he has occasion.

5   As it is by treaty, by barter, and by purchase, that we obtain from one another the greater part of those mutual good offices which we stand in need of, so it is this same trucking disposition which originally gives occasion to the division of labour. In a tribe of hunters or shepherds a particular person makes bows and arrows, for example, with more readiness and dexterity than any other. He frequently exchanges

10   them for cattle or for venison with his companions; and he finds at last that he can in this manner get more cattle and venison, than if he himself went to the field to catch them. From a regard to his own interest, therefore, the making of bows and arrows grows to be his chief business, and he becomes a sort of armourer. Another excels in making the frames and covers of their little huts or moveable houses. He is

15   accustomed to be of use in this way to his neighbours, who reward him in the same manner with cattle and with venison, till at last he finds it his interest to dedicate himself entirely to this employment, and to become a sort of house–carpenter. In the same manner a third becomes a smith or a brazier, a fourth a tanner or dresser of hides or skins, the principal part of the clothing of savages. And thus the certainty of

20   being able to exchange all that surplus part of the produce of his own labour, which is over and above his own consumption, for such parts of the produce of other men's labour as he may have occasion for, encourages every man to apply himself to a particular occupation, and to cultivate and bring to perfection whatever talent or genius he may possess for that particular species of business.

25   The difference of natural talents in different men is, in reality, much less than we are aware of; and the very different genius which appears to distinguish men of different professions, when grown up to maturity, is not upon many occasions so much the cause, as the effect of the division of labour. The difference between the most dissimilar characters, between a philosopher and a common street porter, for

30   example, seems to arise not so much from nature, as from habit, custom, and education. When they came into the world, and for the first six or eight years of their existence, they were, perhaps very much alike, and neither their parents nor play–fellows could perceive any remarkable difference. About that age, or soon after, they come to be employed in very different occupations. The difference of talents comes

35   then to be taken notice of, and widens by degrees, till at last the vanity of the philosopher is willing to acknowledge scarce any resemblance. But without the disposition to truck, barter, and exchange, every man must have procured to himself every necessary and conveniency of life which he wanted. All must have had the same duties to perform, and the same work to do, and there could have been no such

difference of employment as could alone give occasion to any great difference of talents

As it is this disposition which forms that difference of talents, so remarkable among men of different professions, so it is this same disposition which renders that
5   difference useful. Many tribes of animals acknowledged to be all of the same species, derive from nature a much more remarkable distinction of genius, than what, antecedent to custom and education, appears to take place among men. By nature a philosopher is not in genius and disposition half so different from a street porter, as a mastiff is from a greyhound, or a greyhound from a spaniel, or this last from a
10 shepherd's dog. Those different tribes of animals, however, though all of the same species, are of scarce any use to one another. The strength of the mastiff is not, in the least, supported either by the swiftness of the greyhound, or by the sagacity of the spaniel, or by the docility of the shepherd's dog. The effects of those different geniuses and talents, for want of the power or disposition to barter and exchange,
15 cannot be brought into a common stock, and do not in the least contribute to the better accommodation and conveniency of the species. Each animal is still obliged to support and defend itself, separately and independently, and derives no sort of advantage from that variety of talents with which nature has distinguished its fellows. Among men, on the contrary, the most dissimilar geniuses are of use to one
20 another; the different produces of their respective talents, by the general disposition to truck, barter, and exchange, being brought, as it were, into a common stock, where every man may purchase whatever part of the produce of other men's talents he has occasion for.

****

HOW THE COMMERCE OF THE TOWNS CONRIBIUTED TO THE IMPROVEMENT OF THE COUNTRY

The increase and riches of commercial and manufacturing towns, contributed to
25 the improvement and cultivation of the countries to which they belonged, in three different ways.

First, by affording a great and ready market for the rude produce of the country, they gave encouragement to its cultivation and further improvement. This benefit was not even confined to the countries in which they were situated, but extended
30 more or less to all those with which they had any dealings. To all of them they afforded a market for some part either of their rude or manufactured produce, and consequently gave some encouragement to the industry and improvement of all. Their own country, however, on account of its neighbourhood, necessarily derived

the greatest benefit from this market. Its rude produce being charged with less carriage, the traders could pay the growers a better price for it, and yet afford it as cheap to the consumers as that of more distant countries.

Secondly, the wealth acquired by the inhabitants of cities was frequently employed in purchasing such lands as were to be sold, of which a great part would frequently be uncultivated. Merchants are commonly ambitious of becoming country gentlemen, and when they do, they are generally the best of all improvers. A merchant is accustomed to employ his money chiefly in profitable projects; whereas a mere country gentleman is accustomed to employ it chiefly in expence. The one often sees his money go from him and return to him again with a profit: the other, when once he parts with it, very seldom expects to see any more of it. Those different habits naturally affect their temper and disposition in every sort of business. A merchant is commonly a bold; a country gentleman, a timid undertaker. The one is not afraid to lay out at once a large capital upon the improvement of his land, when he has a probable prospect of raising the value of it in proportion to the expence. The other, if he has any capital, which is not always the case, seldom ventures to employ it in this manner. If he improves at all, it is commonly not with a capital, but with what he can save out of his annual revenue. Whoever has had the fortune to live in a mercantile town situated in an unimproved country, must have frequently observed how much more spirited the operations of merchants were in this way, than those of mere country gentlemen. The habits, besides, of order, œconomy and attention, to which mercantile business naturally forms a merchant, render him much fitter to execute, with profit and success, any project of improvement.

Thirdly, and lastly, commerce and manufactures gradually introduced order and good government, and with them, the liberty and security of individuals, among the inhabitants of the country, who had before lived almost in a continual state of war with their neighbours, and of servile dependency upon their superiors. This, though it has been the least observed, is by far the most important of all their effects. Mr. Hume is the only writer who, so far as I know, has hitherto taken notice of it.

In a country which has neither foreign commerce, nor any of the finer manufactures, a great proprietor, having nothing for which he can exchange the greater part of the produce of his lands which is over and above the maintenance of the cultivators, consumes the whole in rustick hospitality at home. If this surplus produce is sufficient to maintain a hundred or a thousand men, he can make use of it in no other way than by maintaining a hundred or a thousand men. He is at all times, therefore, surrounded with a multitude of retainers and dependants, who having no equivalent to give in return for their maintenance, but being fed entirely by his bounty, must obey him, for the same reason that soldiers must obey the prince who pays them. Therefore the extension of commerce and manufactures in Europe, the

196

hospitality of the rich and the great, from the sovereign down to the smallest baron, exceeded every thing which in the present times we can easily form a notion of. Westminster–hall was the dining–room of William Rufus, and might frequently, perhaps, not be too large for his company. It was reckoned a piece of magnificence
5   in Thomas Becket, that he strowed the floor of his hall with clean hay or rushes in the season, in order that the knights and squires, who could not get seats, might not spoil their fine cloaths when they sat down on the floor to eat their dinner. The great earl of Warwick is said to have entertained every day at his different manors, thirty thousand people; and though the number here may have been exaggerated, it must,
10 however, have been very great to admit of such exaggeration. A hospitality nearly of the same kind was exercised not many years ago in many different parts of the highlands of Scotland. It seems to be common in all nations to whom commerce and manufactures are little known. I have seen, says Doctor Pocock, an Arabian chief dine in the streets of a town where he had come to sell his cattle, and invite all
15 passengers, even common beggars, to sit down with him and partake of his banquet.

The occupiers of land were in every respect as dependent upon the great proprietor as his retainers. Even such of them as were not in a state of village, were tenants at will, who paid a rent in no respect equivalent to the subsistence which the land afforded them. A crown, half a crown, a sheep, a lamb, was some years ago in
20 the highlands of Scotland a common rent for lands which maintained a family. In some places it is so at this day; nor will money at present purchase a greater quantity of commodities there than in other places. In a country where the surplus produce of a large estate must be consumed upon the estate itself, it will frequently be more convenient for the proprietor, that part of it be consumed at a distance from his own
25 house, provided they who consume it are as dependent upon him as either his retainers or his menial servants. He is thereby saved from the embarrassment of either too large a company or too large a family. A tenant at will, who possesses land sufficient to maintain his family for little more than a quit–rent, is as dependent upon the proprietor as any servant or retainer whatever, and must obey him with as little
30 reserve. Such a proprietor, as he feeds his servants and retainers at his own house, so he feeds his tenants at their houses. The subsistence of both is derived from his bounty, and its continuance depends upon his good pleasure.

Upon the authority which the great proprietors necessarily had in such a state of things over their tenants and retainers, was founded the power of the antient barons.
35 They necessarily became the judges in peace, and the leaders in war, of all who dwelt upon their estates. They could maintain order and execute the law within their respective demesnes, because each of them could there turn the whole force of all the inhabitants against the injustice of any one. No other person had sufficient authority to do this. The king in particular had not. In those antient times he was little more

than the greatest proprietor in his dominions, to whom, for the sake of common defence against their common enemies, the other great proprietors paid certain respects. To have enforced payment of a small debt within the lands of a great proprietor, where all the inhabitants were armed and accustomed to stand by one
5 another, would have cost the king, had he attempted it by his own authority, almost the same effort as to extinguish a civil war. He was, therefore, obliged to abandon the administration of justice through the greater part of the country, to those who were capable of administering it; and for the same reason to leave the command of the country militia to those whom that militia would obey.
10   It is a mistake to imagine that those territorial jurisdictions took their origin from the feudal law. Not only the highest jurisdictions both civil and criminal, but the power of levying troops, of coining money, and even that of making bye–laws for the government of their own people, were all rights possessed allodially by the great proprietors of land several centuries before even the name of the feudal law was
15 known in Europe. The authority and jurisdiction of the Saxon lords in England, appear to have been as great before the conquest, as that of any of the Norman lords after it. But the feudal law is not supposed to have become the common law of England till after the conquest. That the most extensive authority and jurisdictions were possessed by the great lords in France allodially, long before the feudal law was
20 introduced into that country, is a matter of fact that admits of no doubt. That authority and those jurisdictions all necessarily flowed from the state of property and manners just now described. Without remounting to the remote antiquities of either the French or English monarchies, we may find in much later times many proofs that such effects must always flow from such causes. It is not thirty years ago since Mr.
25 Cameron of Lochiel, a gentleman of Lochabar in Scotland, without any legal warrant whatever, not being what was then called a lord of regality, nor even a tenant in chief, but a vassal of the duke of Argyle, and without being so much as a justice of peace, used, notwithstanding, to exercise the highest criminal jurisdiction over his own people. He is said to have done so with great equity, though without any of the
30 formalities of justice; and it is not improbable that the state of that part of the country at that time made it necessary for him to assume this authority in order to maintain the publick peace. That gentleman, whose rent never exceeded five hundred pounds a year, carried, in 1745, eight hundred of his own people into the rebellion with him.
    The introduction of the feudal law, so far from extending, may be regarded as an
35 attempt to moderate the authority of the great allodial lords. It established a regular subordination, accompanied with a long train of services and duties, from the king down to the smallest proprietor. During the minority of the proprietor, the rent, together with the management of his lands, fell into the hands of his immediate superior, and, consequently, those of all great proprietors into the hands of the king,

who was charged with the maintenance and education of the pupil, and who, from his authority as guardian, was supposed to have a right of disposing of him in marriage, provided it was in a manner not unsuitable to his rank. But though this institution necessarily tended to strengthen the authority of the king, and to weaken
5   that of the great proprietors, it could not do either sufficiently for establishing order and good government among the inhabitants of the country; because it could not alter sufficiently that state of property and manners from which the disorders arose. The authority of government still continued to be, as before, too weak in the head and too strong in the inferior members, and the excessive strength of the inferior members
10   was the cause of the weakness of the head. After the institution of feudal subordination, the king was as incapable of restraining the violence of the great lords as before. They still continued to make war according to their own discretion, almost continually upon one another, and very frequently upon the king; and the open country still continued to be a scene of violence, rapine, and disorder.
15   But what all the violence of the feudal institutions could never have effected, the silent and insensible operation of foreign commerce and manufactures gradually brought about. These gradually furnished the great proprietors with something for which they could exchange the whole surplus produce of their lands, and which they could consume themselves without sharing it either with tenants or retainers. All for
20   ourselves, and nothing for other people, seems, in every age of the world, to have been the vile maxim of the masters of mankind. As soon, therefore, as they could find a method of consuming the whole value of their rents themselves, they had no disposition to share them with any other persons. For a pair of diamond buckles perhaps, or for something as frivolous and useless, they exchanged the maintenance,
25   or what is the same thing, the price of the maintenance of a thousand men for a year, and with it the whole weight and authority which it could give them. The buckles, however, were to be all their own, and no other human creature was to have any share of them; whereas in the more antient method of expence they must have shared with at least a thousand people. With the judges that were to determine the
30   preference, this difference was perfectly decisive; and thus, for the gratification of the most childish, the meanest and the most sordid of all vanities, they gradually bartered their whole power and authority.
        In a country where there is no foreign commerce, nor any of the finer manufactures, a man of ten thousand a year cannot well employ his revenue in any
35   other way than in maintaining, perhaps, a thousand families, who are all of them necessarily at his command. In the present state of Europe, a man of ten thousand a year can spend his whole revenue, and he generally does so, without directly maintaining twenty people, or being able to command more than ten footmen not worth the commanding. Indirectly, perhaps, he maintains as great or even a greater

number of people than he could have done by the antient method of expence. For though the quantity of precious productions for which he exchanges his whole revenue be very small, the number of workmen employed in collecting and preparing it, must necessarily have been very great. Its great price generally arises from the wages of their labour, and the profits of all their immediate employers. By paying that price he indirectly pays all those wages and profits, and thus indirectly contributes to the maintenance of all the workmen and their employers. He generally contributes, however, but a very small proportion to that of each, to very few perhaps a tenth, to many not a hundredth, and to some not a thousandth, nor even a ten thousandth part of their whole annual maintenance. Though he contributes, therefore, to the maintenance of them all, they are all more or less independent of him, because generally they can all be maintained without him.

When the great proprietors of land spend their rents in maintaining their tenants and retainers, each of them maintains entirely all his own tenants and all his own retainers. But when they spend them in maintaining tradesmen and artificers, they may, all of them taken together, perhaps, maintain as great, or, on account of the waste which attends rustick hospitality, a greater number of people than before. Each of them, however, taken singly, contributes often but a very small share to the maintenance of any individual of this greater number. Each tradesman or artificer derives his subsistence from the employment, not of one, but of a hundred or a thousand different customers. Though in some measure obliged to them all, therefore, he is not absolutely dependent upon any one of them.

The personal expence of the great proprietors having in this manner gradually increased, it was impossible that the number of their retainers should not as gradually diminish, till they were at last dismissed altogether. The same cause gradually led them to dismiss the unnecessary part of their tenants. Farms were enlarged, and the occupiers of land, notwithstanding the complaints of depopulation, reduced to the number necessary for cultivating it, according to the imperfect state of cultivation and improvement in those times. By the removal of the unnecessary mouths, and by exacting from the farmer the full value of the farm, a greater surplus, or what is the same thing, the price of a greater surplus, was obtained for the proprietor, which the merchants and manufacturers soon furnished him with a method of spending upon his own person in the same manner as he had done the rest. The same cause continuing to operate, he was desirous to raise his rents above what his lands, in the actual state of their improvement, could afford. His tenants could agree to this upon one condition only, that they should be secured in their possession, for such a term of years as might give them time to recover with profit whatever they should lay out in the further improvement of the land. The expensive vanity of the landlord made him willing to accept of this condition; and hence the origin of long leases.

Even a tenant at will, who pays the full value of the land, is not altogether dependent upon the landlord. The pecuniary advantages which they receive from one another, are mutual and equal, and such a tenant will expose neither his life nor his fortune in the service of the proprietor. But if he has a lease for a long term of years,
5   he is altogether independent; and his landlord must not expect from him even the most trifling service beyond what is either expressly stipulated in the lease, or imposed upon him by the common and known law of the country.

The tenants having in this manner become independent, and the retainers being dismissed, the great proprietors were no longer capable of interrupting the regular
10   execution of justice, or of disturbing the peace of the country. Having sold their birth–right, not like Esau for a mess of pottage in time of hunger and necessity, but in the wantonness of plenty, for trinkets and baubles, fitter to be the play–things of children than the serious pursuits of men, they became as insignificant as any substantial burgher or tradesman in a city. A regular government was established in
15   the country as well as in the city, nobody having sufficient power to disturb its operations in the one, any more than in the other.

It does not, perhaps, relate to the present subject, but I cannot help remarking it, that very old families, such as have possessed some considerable estate from father to son for many successive generations, are very rare in commercial countries. In
20   countries which have little commerce, on the contrary, such as Wales or the highlands of Scotland, they are very common. The Arabian histories seem to be all full of genealogies, and there is a history written by a Tartar Khan, which has been translated into several European languages, and which contains scarce any thing else; a proof that antient families are very common among those nations. In countries
25   where a rich man can spend his revenue in no other way than by maintaining as many people as it can maintain, he is not apt to run out, and his benevolence it seems is seldom so violent as to attempt to maintain more than he can afford. But where he can spend the greatest revenue upon his own person, he frequently has no bounds to his expence, because he frequently has no bounds to his vanity, or to his affection for
30   his own person. In commercial countries, therefore, riches, in spite of the most violent regulations of law to prevent their dissipation, very seldom remain long in the same family. Among simple nations, on the contrary, they frequently do without any regulations of law; for among nations of shepherds, such as the Tartars and Arabs, the consumable nature of their property necessarily renders all such regulations
35   impossible.

A revolution of the greatest importance to the publick happiness, was in this manner brought about by two different orders of people, who had not the least intention to serve the publick. To gratify the most childish vanity was the sole motive of the great proprietors. The merchants and artificers, much less ridiculous, acted merely from a view to their own interest, and in pursuit of their own pedlar principle of turning a penny wherever a penny was to be got. Neither of them had either knowledge or foresight of that great revolution which the folly of the one, and the industry of the other, was gradually bringing about.

5   It is thus that through the greater part of Europe the commerce and manufactures of cities, instead of being the effect, have been the cause and occasion of the improvement and cultivation of the country.

This order, however, being contrary to the natural course of things, is necessarily both slow and uncertain. Compare the slow progress of those European
10   countries of which the wealth depends very much upon their commerce and manufactures, with the rapid advances of our North American colonies, of which the wealth is founded altogether in agriculture. Through the greater part of Europe, the number of inhabitants is not supposed to double in less than five hundred years. In several of our North American colonies, it is found to double in twenty or five–and–
15   twenty years. In Europe, the law of primogeniture, and perpetuities of different kinds, prevent the division of great estates, and thereby hinder the multiplication of small proprietors. A small proprietor, however, who knows every part of his little territory, who views it with all the affection which property, especially small property, naturally inspires, and who upon that account takes pleasure not only in
20   cultivating but in adorning it, is generally of all improvers the most industrious, the most intelligent, and the most successful. The same regulations, besides, keep so much land out of the market, that there are always more capitals to buy than there is land to sell, so that what is sold always sells at a monopoly price. The rent never pays the interest of the purchase–money, and is besides burdened with repairs and
25   other occasional charges, to which the interest of money is not liable. To purchase land is every where in Europe a most unprofitable employment of a small capital. For the sake of the superior security, indeed, a man of moderate circumstances, when he retires from business, will sometimes chuse to lay out his little capital in land. A man of profession too, whose revenue is derived from another source, often loves to
30   secure his savings in the same way. But a young man, who, instead of applying to trade or to some profession, should employ a capital of two or three thousand pounds in the purchase and cultivation of a small piece of land, might indeed expect to live very happily, and very independently, but must bid adieu, for ever, to all hope of either great fortune or great illustration, which by a different employment of his
35   stock he might have had the same chance of acquiring with other people. Such a person too, though he cannot aspire at being a proprietor, will often disdain to be a farmer. The small quantity of land, therefore, which is brought to market, and the high price of what is brought thither prevents a great number of capitals from being employed in its cultivation and improvement which would otherwise have taken that

direction. In North America, on the contrary, fifty or sixty pounds is often found a sufficient stock to begin a plantation with. The purchase and improvement of uncultivated land, is there the most profitable employment of the smallest as well as of the greatest capitals, and the most direct road to all the fortune and illustration
5 which can be acquired in that country. Such land, indeed, is in North America to be had almost for nothing, or at a price much below the value of the natural produce; a thing impossible in Europe, or, indeed, in any country where all lands have long been private property. If landed estates, however, were divided equally among all the children, upon the death of any proprietor who left a numerous family, the estate
10 would generally be sold. So much land would come to market, that it could no longer sell at a monopoly price. The free rent of the land would go nearer to pay the interest of the purchase–money, and a small capital might be employed in purchasing land as profitably as in any other way.

England, on account of the natural fertility of the soil, of the great extent of the
15 sea–coast in proportion to that of the whole country, and of the many navigable rivers which run through it, and afford the conveniency of water carriage to some of the most inland parts of it, is perhaps as well fitted by nature as any large country in Europe, to be the seat of foreign commerce, of manufactures for distant sale, and of all the improvements which these can occasion. From the beginning of the reign of
20 Elizabeth too, the English legislature has been peculiarly attentive to the interests of commerce and manufactures, and in reality there is no country in Europe, Holland itself not excepted, of which the law is, upon the whole, more favourable to this sort of industry. Commerce and manufactures have accordingly been continually advancing during all this period. The cultivation and improvement of the country
25 has, no doubt, been gradually advancing too: But it seems to have followed slowly, and at a distance, the more rapid progress of commerce and manufactures. The greater part of the country must probably have been cultivated before the reign of Elizabeth; and a very great part of it still remains uncultivated, and the cultivation of the far greater part, much inferior to what it might be. The law of England, however,
30 favours agriculture not only indirectly by the protection of commerce, but by several direct encouragements. Except in times of scarcity, the exportation of corn is not only free, but encouraged by a bounty. In times of moderate plenty, the importation of foreign corn is loaded with duties that amount to a prohibition. The importation of live cattle, except from Ireland, is prohibited at all times, and it is but of late that it
35 was permitted from thence. Those who cultivate the land, therefore, have a monopoly against their countrymen for the two greatest and most important articles of land produce, bread and butcher's meat. These encouragements, though at bottom, perhaps, as I shall endeavour to show hereafter, altogether illusory, sufficiently demonstrate at least the good intention of the legislature to favour agriculture. But

what is of much more importance than all of them, the yeomanry of England are rendered as secure, as independent, and as respectable as law can make them. No country, therefore, in which the right of primogeniture takes place, which pays tithes, and where perpetuities, though contrary to the spirit of the law, are admitted in some
5 cases, can give more encouragement to agriculture than England. Such, however, notwithstanding, is the state of its cultivation. What would it have been, had the law given no direct encouragement to agriculture besides what arises indirectly from the progress of commerce, and had left the yeomanry in the same condition as in most other countries of Europe? It is now more than two hundred years since the
10 beginning of the reign of Elizabeth, a period as long as the course of human prosperity usually endures.

France seems to have had a considerable share of foreign commerce near a century before England was distinguished as a commercial country. The marine of France was considerable, according to the notions of the times, before the expedition
15 of Charles the VIIIth to Naples. The cultivation and improvement of France, however, is, upon the whole, inferior to that of England. The law of the country has never given the same direct encouragement to agriculture.

The foreign commerce of Spain and Portugal to the other parts of Europe, though chiefly carried on in foreign ships, is very considerable. That to their colonies
20 is carried on in their own, and is much greater, on account of the great riches and extent of those colonies. But it has never introduced any considerable manufactures for distant sale into either of those countries, and the greater part of both still remains uncultivated. The foreign commerce of Portugal is of older standing than that of any great country in Europe, except Italy.
25 Italy is the only great country of Europe which seems to have been cultivated and im–proved in every part, by means of foreign commerce and manufactures for distant sale. Before the invasion of Charles the VIIIth, Italy, according to Guicciardin, was cultivated not less in the most mountainous and barren parts of the country, than in the plainest and most fertile. The advantageous situation of the
30 country, and the great number of independent states which at that time subsisted in it, probably contributed not a little to this general cultivation. It is not impossible too, notwithstanding this general expression of one of the most judicious and reserved of modern historians, that Italy was not at that time better cultivated than England is at present.
35 The capital, however, that is acquired to any country by commerce and manufactures, is all a very precarious and uncertain possession, till some part of it has been secured and realized in the cultivation and improvement of its lands. A merchant, it has been said very properly, is not necessarily the citizen of any particular country. It is in a great measure indifferent to him from what place he

carries on his trade; and a very trifling disgust will make him remove his capital, and together with it all the industry which it supports, from one country to another. No part of it can be said to belong to any particular country, till it has been spread as it were over the face of that country, either in buildings, or in the lasting improvement
5   of lands. No vestige now remains of the great wealth, said to have been possessed by the greater part of the Hans towns, except in the obscure histories of the thirteenth and fourteenth centuries. It is even uncertain where some of them were situated, or to what towns in Europe the Latin names given to some of them belong. But though the misfortunes of Italy in the end of the fifteenth and beginning of the sixteenth
10 centuries greatly diminished the commerce and manufactures of the cities of Lombardy and Tuscany, those countries still continue to be among the most populous and best cultivated in Europe. The civil wars of Flanders, and the Spanish government which succeeded them, chased away the great commerce of Antwerp, Ghent, and Bruges. But Flanders still continues to be one of the richest, best
15 cultivated, and most populous provinces of Europe. The ordinary revolutions of war and government easily dry up the sources of that wealth which arises from commerce only. That which arises from the more solid improvements of agriculture, is much more durable, and cannot be destroyed but by those more violent convulsions occasioned by the depredations of hostile and barbarous nations continued for a
20 century or two together; such as those that happened for some time before and after the fall of the Roman empire in the western provinces of Europe.

The Federalist Papers

The Federalist Papers were written by Alexander Hamilton (future first U.S. Secretary of the Treasury), James Madison (future fourth U.S. President, and the author of all the papers reprinted below), and John Jay (future first Chief Justice of the U.S. Supreme Court). Comprising a total of 85 articles, they were published serially in 1787 and 1788. Their immediate goal was to provide a series of arguments to further the ratification of the proposed constitution for the United States and to defend it against its critics, most notably the Anti-Federalists. A more distant goal was to aid in the interpretation of the Constitution. While their influence over the ratification is disputed, the Federalist Papers have unequivocally become one of the primary U.S. national documents, frequently invoked in the official opinions of the U.S. Supreme Court and by constitutional scholars seeking to evaluate the Court's actions.

THE FEDERALIST PAPERS
(1787-1788)

No. 9
The Utility of the Union as a Safeguard Against Domestic Faction and Insurrection

To the People of the State of New York:

A FIRM Union will be of the utmost moment to the peace and liberty of the States, as a barrier against domestic faction and insurrection. It is impossible to read the history of the petty republics of Greece and Italy without feeling
5   sensations of horror and disgust at the distractions with which they were continually agitated, and at the rapid succession of revolutions by which they were kept in a state of perpetual vibration between the extremes of tyranny and anarchy. If they exhibit occasional calms, these only serve as short-lived contrast to the furious storms that are to succeed. If now and then intervals of
10 felicity open to view, we behold them with a mixture of regret, arising from the reflection that the pleasing scenes before us are soon to be overwhelmed by the tempestuous waves of sedition and party rage. If momentary rays of glory break forth from the gloom, while they dazzle us with a transient and fleeting brilliancy, they at the same time admonish us to lament that the vices of
15 government should pervert the direction and tarnish the lustre of those bright talents and exalted endowments for which the favored soils that produced them have been so justly celebrated.

From the disorders that disfigure the annals of those republics the advocates of despotism have drawn arguments, not only against the forms of republican
20 government, but against the very principles of civil liberty. They have decried all free government as inconsistent with the order of society, and have indulged themselves in malicious exultation over its friends and partisans. Happily for mankind, stupendous fabrics reared on the basis of liberty, which have flourished for ages, have, in a few glorious instances, refuted their gloomy
25 sophisms. And, I trust, America will be the broad and solid foundation of other edifices, not less magnificent, which will be equally permanent monuments of their errors.

But it is not to be denied that the portraits they have sketched of republican government were too just copies of the originals from which they were taken. If
30 it had been found impracticable to have devised models of a more perfect structure, the enlightened friends to liberty would have been obliged to abandon the cause of that species of government as indefensible. The science of politics,

however, like most other sciences, has received great improvement. The efficacy of various principles is now well understood, which were either not known at all, or imperfectly known to the ancients. The regular distribution of power into distinct departments; the introduction of legislative balances and checks; the
5 institution of courts composed of judges holding their offices during good behavior; the representation of the people in the legislature by deputies of their own election: these are wholly new discoveries, or have made their principal progress towards perfection in modern times. They are means, and powerful means, by which the excellences of republican government may be retained and
10 its imperfections lessened or avoided. To this catalogue of circumstances that tend to the amelioration of popular systems of civil government, I shall venture, however novel it may appear to some, to add one more, on a principle which has been made the foundation of an objection to the new Constitution; I mean the ENLARGEMENT of the ORBIT within which such systems are to revolve,
15 either in respect to the dimensions of a single State or to the consolidation of several smaller States into one great Confederacy. The latter is that which immediately concerns the object under consideration. It will, however, be of use to examine the principle in its application to a single State, which shall be attended to in another place.
20 The utility of a Confederacy, as well to suppress faction and to guard the internal tranquillity of States, as to increase their external force and security, is in reality not a new idea. It has been practiced upon in different countries and ages, and has received the sanction of the most approved writers on the subject of politics. The opponents of the plan proposed have, with great assiduity, cited
25 and circulated the observations of Montesquieu on the necessity of a contracted territory for a republican government. But they seem not to have been apprised of the sentiments of that great man expressed in another part of his work, nor to have adverted to the consequences of the principle to which they subscribe with such ready acquiescence.
30 When Montesquieu recommends a small extent for republics, the standards he had in view were of dimensions far short of the limits of almost every one of these States. Neither Virginia, Massachusetts, Pennsylvania, New York, North Carolina, nor Georgia can by any means be compared with the models from which he reasoned and to which the terms of his description apply. If we
35 therefore take his ideas on this point as the criterion of truth, we shall be driven to the alternative either of taking refuge at once in the arms of monarchy, or of splitting ourselves into an infinity of little, jealous, clashing, tumultuous commonwealths, the wretched nurseries of unceasing discord, and the miserable objects of universal pity or contempt. Some of the writers who have come
40 forward on the other side of the question seem to have been aware of the

dilemma; and have even been bold enough to hint at the division of the larger States as a desirable thing. Such an infatuated policy, such a desperate expedient, might, by the multiplication of petty offices, answer the views of men who possess not qualifications to extend their influence beyond the narrow

5 circles of personal intrigue, but it could never promote the greatness or happiness of the people of America.

Referring the examination of the principle itself to another place, as has been already mentioned, it will be sufficient to remark here that, in the sense of the author who has been most emphatically quoted upon the occasion, it would

10 only dictate a reduction of the SIZE of the more considerable MEMBERS of the Union, but would not militate against their being all comprehended in one confederate government. And this is the true question, in the discussion of which we are at present interested.

So far are the suggestions of Montesquieu from standing in opposition to a

15 general Union of the States, that he explicitly treats of a CONFEDERATE REPUBLIC as the expedient for extending the sphere of popular government, and reconciling the advantages of monarchy with those of republicanism.

"It is very probable," (says he[1]) "that mankind would have been obliged at length to live constantly under the government of a SINGLE PERSON, had they

20 not contrived a kind of constitution that has all the internal advantages of a republican, together with the external force of a monarchical government. I mean a CONFEDERATE REPUBLIC.

"This form of government is a convention by which several smaller *states* agree to become members of a larger *one*, which they intend to form. It is a kind

25 of assemblage of societies that constitute a new one, capable of increasing, by means of new associations, till they arrive to such a degree of power as to be able to provide for the security of the united body.

"A republic of this kind, able to withstand an external force, may support itself without any internal corruptions. The form of this society prevents all

30 manner of inconveniences.

"If a single member should attempt to usurp the supreme authority, he could not be supposed to have an equal authority and credit in all the confederate states. Were he to have too great influence over one, this would alarm the rest. Were he to subdue a part, that which would still remain free might oppose him

35 with forces independent of those which he had usurped and overpower him before he could be settled in his usurpation.

"Should a popular insurrection happen in one of the confederate states the others are able to quell it. Should abuses creep into one part, they are reformed by those that remain sound. The state may be destroyed on one side, and not on the other; the confederacy may be dissolved, and the confederates preserve their sovereignty.

"As this government is composed of small republics, it enjoys the internal happiness of each; and with respect to its external situation, it is possessed, by
5   means of the association, of all the advantages of large monarchies.

I have thought it proper to quote at length these interesting passages, because they contain a luminous abridgment of the principal arguments in favor of the Union, and must effectually remove the false impressions which a misapplication of other parts of the work was calculated to make. They have, at
10   the same time, an intimate connection with the more immediate design of this paper; which is, to illustrate the tendency of the Union to repress domestic faction and insurrection.

A distinction, more subtle than accurate, has been raised between a *confederacy* and a *consolidation* of the States. The essential characteristic of the
15   first is said to be, the restriction of its authority to the members in their collective capacities, without reaching to the individuals of whom they are composed. It is contended that the national council ought to have no concern with any object of internal administration. An exact equality of suffrage between the members has also been insisted upon as a leading feature of a confederate
20   government. These positions are, in the main, arbitrary; they are supported neither by principle nor precedent. It has indeed happened, that governments of this kind have generally operated in the manner which the distinction taken notice of, supposes to be inherent in their nature; but there have been in most of them extensive exceptions to the practice, which serve to prove, as far as
25   example will go, that there is no absolute rule on the subject. And it will be clearly shown in the course of this investigation that as far as the principle contended for has prevailed, it has been the cause of incurable disorder and imbecility in the government.

The definition of a *confederate republic* seems simply to be "an assemblage
30   of societies," or an association of two or more states into one state. The extent, modifications, and objects of the federal authority are mere matters of discretion. So long as the separate organization of the members be not abolished; so long as it exists, by a constitutional necessity, for local purposes; though it should be in perfect subordination to the general authority of the union,
35   it would still be, in fact and in theory, an association of states, or a confederacy. The proposed Constitution, so far from implying an abolition of the State governments, makes them constituent parts of the national sovereignty, by allowing them a direct representation in the Senate, and leaves in their possession certain exclusive and very important portions of sovereign power.

This fully corresponds, in every rational import of the terms, with the idea of a federal government.

In the Lycian confederacy, which consisted of twenty-three CITIES or republics, the largest were entitled to *three* votes in the COMMON COUNCIL,
5 those of the middle class to *two*, and the smallest to *one*. The COMMON COUNCIL had the appointment of all the judges and magistrates of the respective CITIES. This was certainly the most, delicate species of interference in their internal administration; for if there be any thing that seems exclusively appropriated to the local jurisdictions, it is the appointment of their own officers.
10 Yet Montesquieu, speaking of this association, says: "Were I to give a model of an excellent Confederate Republic, it would be that of Lycia." Thus we perceive that the distinctions insisted upon were not within the contemplation of this enlightened civilian; and we shall be led to conclude, that they are the novel refinements of an erroneous theory.
15 PUBLIUS

No. 10
The Utility of the Union as a Safeguard Against Domestic Faction and Insurrection (continued)

To the People of the State of New York:
AMONG the numerous advantages promised by a well constructed Union, none deserves to be more accurately developed than its tendency to break and control the violence of faction. The friend of popular governments never finds
20 himself so much alarmed for their character and fate, as when he contemplates their propensity to this dangerous vice. He will not fail, therefore, to set a due value on any plan which, without violating the principles to which he is attached, provides a proper cure for it. The instability, injustice, and confusion introduced into the public councils, have, in truth, been the mortal diseases
25 under which popular governments have everywhere perished; as they continue to be the favorite and fruitful topics from which the adversaries to liberty derive their most specious declamations. The valuable improvements made by the American constitutions on the popular models, both ancient and modern, cannot certainly be too much admired; but it would be an unwarrantable partiality, to
30 contend that they have as effectually obviated the danger on this side, as was wished and expected. Complaints are everywhere heard from our most considerate and virtuous citizens, equally the friends of public and private faith, and of public and personal liberty, that our governments are too unstable, that the public good is disregarded in the conflicts of rival parties, and that measures

are too often decided, not according to the rules of justice and the rights of the minor party, but by the superior force of an interested and overbearing majority. However anxiously we may wish that these complaints had no foundation, the evidence, of known facts will not permit us to deny that they are in some degree
5   true. It will be found, indeed, on a candid review of our situation, that some of the distresses under which we labor have been erroneously charged on the operation of our governments; but it will be found, at the same time, that other causes will not alone account for many of our heaviest misfortunes; and, particularly, for that prevailing and increasing distrust of public engagements,
10   and alarm for private rights, which are echoed from one end of the continent to the other. These must be chiefly, if not wholly, effects of the unsteadiness and injustice with which a factious spirit has tainted our public administrations.

By a faction, I understand a number of citizens, whether amounting to a majority or a minority of the whole, who are united and actuated by some
15   common impulse of passion, or of interest, adversed to the rights of other citizens, or to the permanent and aggregate interests of the community.

There are two methods of curing the mischiefs of faction: the one, by removing its causes; the other, by controlling its effects.

There are again two methods of removing the causes of faction: the one, by
20   destroying the liberty which is essential to its existence; the other, by giving to every citizen the same opinions, the same passions, and the same interests.

It could never be more truly said than of the first remedy, that it was worse than the disease. Liberty is to faction what air is to fire, an aliment without which it instantly expires. But it could not be less folly to abolish liberty, which
25   is essential to political life, because it nourishes faction, than it would be to wish the annihilation of air, which is essential to animal life, because it imparts to fire its destructive agency.

The second expedient is as impracticable as the first would be unwise. As long as the reason of man continues fallible, and he is at liberty to exercise it,
30   different opinions will be formed. As long as the connection subsists between his reason and his self-love, his opinions and his passions will have a reciprocal influence on each other; and the former will be objects to which the latter will attach themselves. The diversity in the faculties of men, from which the rights of property originate, is not less an insuperable obstacle to a uniformity of interests.
35   The protection of these faculties is the first object of government. From the protection of different and unequal faculties of acquiring property, the possession of different degrees and kinds of property immediately results; and from the influence of these on the sentiments and views of the respective proprietors, ensues a division of the society into different interests and parties.

The latent causes of faction are thus sown in the nature of man; and we see them everywhere brought into different degrees of activity, according to the different circumstances of civil society. A zeal for different opinions concerning religion, concerning government, and many other points, as well of speculation as of practice; an attachment to different leaders ambitiously contending for preeminence and power; or to persons of other descriptions whose fortunes have been interesting to the human passions, have, in turn, divided mankind into parties, inflamed them with mutual animosity, and rendered them much more disposed to vex and oppress each other than to co-operate for their common good. So strong is this propensity of mankind to fall into mutual animosities, that where no substantial occasion presents itself, the most frivolous and fanciful distinctions have been sufficient to kindle their unfriendly passions and excite their most violent conflicts. But the most common and durable source of factions has been the various and unequal distribution of property. Those who hold and those who are without property have ever formed distinct interests in society. Those who are creditors, and those who are debtors, fall under a like discrimination. A landed interest, a manufacturing interest, a mercantile interest, a moneyed interest, with many lesser interests, grow up of necessity in civilized nations, and divide them into different classes, actuated by different sentiments and views. The regulation of these various and interfering interests forms the principal task of modern legislation, and involves the spirit of party and faction in the necessary and ordinary operations of the government.

No man is allowed to be a judge in his own cause, because his interest would certainly bias his judgment, and, not improbably, corrupt his integrity. With equal, nay with greater reason, a body of men are unfit to be both judges and parties at the same time; yet what are many of the most important acts of legislation, but so many judicial determinations, not indeed concerning the rights of single persons, but concerning the rights of large bodies of citizens? And what are the different classes of legislators but advocates and parties to the causes which they determine? Is a law proposed concerning private debts? It is a question to which the creditors are parties on one side and the debtors on the other. Justice ought to hold the balance between them. Yet the parties are, and must be, themselves the judges; and the most numerous party, or, in other words, the most powerful faction must be expected to prevail. Shall domestic manufactures be encouraged, and in what degree, by restrictions on foreign manufactures? are questions which would be differently decided by the landed and the manufacturing classes, and probably by neither with a sole regard to justice and the public good. The apportionment of taxes on the various descriptions of property is an act which seems to require the most exact impartiality; yet there is, perhaps, no legislative act in which greater opportunity and temptation are given to a predominant party to trample on the rules of justice. Every shilling with which they overburden the inferior number, is a shilling saved to their own pockets.

It is in vain to say that enlightened statesmen will be able to adjust these
5   clashing interests, and render them all subservient to the public good. Enlightened statesmen will not always be at the helm. Nor, in many cases, can such an adjustment be made at all without taking into view indirect and remote considerations, which will rarely prevail over the immediate interest which one party may find in disregarding the rights of another or the good of the whole.
10 The inference to which we are brought is, that the *causes* of faction cannot be removed, and that relief is only to be sought in the means of controlling its *effects*.

If a faction consists of less than a majority, relief is supplied by the republican principle, which enables the majority to defeat its sinister views by
15 regular vote. It may clog the administration, it may convulse the society; but it will be unable to execute and mask its violence under the forms of the Constitution. When a majority is included in a faction, the form of popular government, on the other hand, enables it to sacrifice to its ruling passion or interest both the public good and the rights of other citizens. To secure the
20 public good and private rights against the danger of such a faction, and at the same time to preserve the spirit and the form of popular government, is then the great object to which our inquiries are directed. Let me add that it is the great desideratum by which this form of government can be rescued from the opprobrium under which it has so long labored, and be recommended to the
25 esteem and adoption of mankind.

By what means is this object attainable? Evidently by one of two only. Either the existence of the same passion or interest in a majority at the same time must be prevented, or the majority, having such coexistent passion or interest, must be rendered, by their number and local situation, unable to concert
30 and carry into effect schemes of oppression. If the impulse and the opportunity be suffered to coincide, we well know that neither moral nor religious motives can be relied on as an adequate control. They are not found to be such on the injustice and violence of individuals, and lose their efficacy in proportion to the number combined together, that is, in proportion as their efficacy becomes
35 needful.

From this view of the subject it may be concluded that a pure democracy, by which I mean a society consisting of a small number of citizens, who assemble and administer the government in person, can admit of no cure for the mischiefs of faction. A common passion or interest will, in almost every case, be
40 felt by a majority of the whole; a communication and concert result from the

form of government itself; and there is nothing to check the inducements to sacrifice the weaker party or an obnoxious individual. Hence it is that such democracies have ever been spectacles of turbulence and contention; have ever been found incompatible with personal security or the rights of property; and
5   have in general been as short in their lives as they have been violent in their deaths. Theoretic politicians, who have patronized this species of government, have erroneously supposed that by reducing mankind to a perfect equality in their political rights, they would, at the same time, be perfectly equalized and assimilated in their possessions, their opinions, and their passions.
10   A republic, by which I mean a government in which the scheme of representation takes place, opens a different prospect, and promises the cure for which we are seeking. Let us examine the points in which it varies from pure democracy, and we shall comprehend both the nature of the cure and the efficacy which it must derive from the Union.
15   The two great points of difference between a democracy and a republic are: first, the delegation of the government, in the latter, to a small number of citizens elected by the rest; secondly, the greater number of citizens, and greater sphere of country, over which the latter may be extended.
The effect of the first difference is, on the one hand, to refine and enlarge
20   the public views, by passing them through the medium of a chosen body of citizens, whose wisdom may best discern the true interest of their country, and whose patriotism and love of justice will be least likely to sacrifice it to temporary or partial considerations. Under such a regulation, it may well happen that the public voice, pronounced by the representatives of the people, will be
25   more consonant to the public good than if pronounced by the people themselves, convened for the purpose. On the other hand, the effect may be inverted. Men of factious tempers, of local prejudices, or of sinister designs, may, by intrigue, by corruption, or by other means, first obtain the suffrages, and then betray the interests, of the people. The question resulting is, whether small or extensive
30   republics are more favorable to the election of proper guardians of the public weal; and it is clearly decided in favor of the latter by two obvious considerations:
In the first place, it is to be remarked that, however small the republic may be, the representatives must be raised to a certain number, in order to guard
35   against the cabals of a few; and that, however large it may be, they must be limited to a certain number, in order to guard against the confusion of a multitude. Hence, the number of representatives in the two cases not being in proportion to that of the two constituents, and being proportionally greater in the small republic, it follows that, if the proportion of fit characters be not less in the

large than in the small republic, the former will present a greater option, and consequently a greater probability of a fit choice.

In the next place, as each representative will be chosen by a greater number of citizens in the large than in the small republic, it will be more difficult for
5   unworthy candidates to practice with success the vicious arts by which elections are too often carried; and the suffrages of the people being more free, will be more likely to centre in men who possess the most attractive merit and the most diffusive and established characters.

It must be confessed that in this, as in most other cases, there is a mean, on
10   both sides of which inconveniences will be found to lie. By enlarging too much the number of electors, you render the representatives too little acquainted with all their local circumstances and lesser interests; as by reducing it too much, you render him unduly attached to these, and too little fit to comprehend and pursue great and national objects. The federal Constitution forms a happy combination
15   in this respect; the great and aggregate interests being referred to the national, the local and particular to the State legislatures.

The other point of difference is, the greater number of citizens and extent of territory which may be brought within the compass of republican than of democratic government; and it is this circumstance principally which renders
20   factious combinations less to be dreaded in the former than in the latter. The smaller the society, the fewer probably will be the distinct parties and interests composing it; the fewer the distinct parties and interests, the more frequently will a majority be found of the same party; and the smaller the number of individuals composing a majority, and the smaller the compass within which
25   they are placed, the more easily will they concert and execute their plans of oppression. Extend the sphere, and you take in a greater variety of parties and interests; you make it less probable that a majority of the whole will have a common motive to invade the rights of other citizens; or if such a common motive exists, it will be more difficult for all who feel it to discover their own
30   strength, and to act in unison with each other. Besides other impediments, it may be remarked that, where there is a consciousness of unjust or dishonorable purposes, communication is always checked by distrust in proportion to the number whose concurrence is necessary.

Hence, it clearly appears, that the same advantage which a republic has over
35   a democracy, in controlling the effects of faction, is enjoyed by a large over a small republic, – is enjoyed by the Union over the States composing it. Does the advantage consist in the substitution of representatives whose enlightened views and virtuous sentiments render them superior to local prejudices and schemes of injustice? It will not be denied that the representation of the Union will be most
40   likely to possess these requisite endowments. Does it consist in the greater

security afforded by a greater variety of parties, against the event of any one party being able to outnumber and oppress the rest? In an equal degree does the increased variety of parties comprised within the Union, increase this security. Does it, in fine, consist in the greater obstacles opposed to the concert and accomplishment of the secret wishes of an unjust and interested majority? Here, again, the extent of the Union gives it the most palpable advantage.

The influence of factious leaders may kindle a flame within their particular States, but will be unable to spread a general conflagration through the other States. A religious sect may degenerate into a political faction in a part of the Confederacy; but the variety of sects dispersed over the entire face of it must secure the national councils against any danger from that source. A rage for paper money, for an abolition of debts, for an equal division of property, or for any other improper or wicked project, will be less apt to pervade the whole body of the Union than a particular member of it; in the same proportion as such a malady is more likely to taint a particular county or district, than an entire State.

In the extent and proper structure of the Union, therefore, we behold a republican remedy for the diseases most incident to republican government. And according to the degree of pleasure and pride we feel in being republicans, ought to be our zeal in cherishing the spirit and supporting the character of Federalists.

PUBLIUS

No. 37
Concerning the Difficulties of the Convention in Devising a Proper Form of Government

To the People of the State of New York:

IN REVIEWING the defects of the existing Confederation, and showing that they cannot be supplied by a government of less energy than that before the public, several of the most important principles of the latter fell of course under consideration. But as the ultimate object of these papers is to determine clearly and fully the merits of this Constitution, and the expediency of adopting it, our plan cannot be complete without taking a more critical and thorough survey of the work of the convention, without examining it on all its sides, comparing it in all its parts, and calculating its probable effects. That this remaining task may be executed under impressions conducive to a just and fair result, some reflections must in this place be indulged, which candor previously suggests.

It is a misfortune, inseparable from human affairs, that public measures are rarely investigated with that spirit of moderation which is essential to a just estimate of their real tendency to advance or obstruct the public good; and that

this spirit is more apt to be diminished than promoted, by those occasions which require an unusual exercise of it. To those who have been led by experience to attend to this consideration, it could not appear surprising, that the act of the convention, which recommends so many important changes and innovations,
5   which may be viewed in so many lights and relations, and which touches the springs of so many passions and interests, should find or excite dispositions unfriendly, both on one side and on the other, to a fair discussion and accurate judgment of its merits. In some, it has been too evident from their own publications, that they have scanned the proposed Constitution, not only with a
10   predisposition to censure, but with a predetermination to condemn; as the language held by others betrays an opposite predetermination or bias, which must render their opinions also of little moment in the question. In placing, however, these different characters on a level, with respect to the weight of their opinions, I wish not to insinuate that there may not be a material difference in
15   the purity of their intentions. It is but just to remark in favor of the latter description, that as our situation is universally admitted to be peculiarly critical, and to require indispensably that something should be done for our relief, the predetermined patron of what has been actually done may have taken his bias from the weight of these considerations, as well as from considerations of a
20   sinister nature. The predetermined adversary, on the other hand, can have been governed by no venial motive whatever. The intentions of the first may be upright, as they may on the contrary be culpable. The views of the last cannot be upright, and must be culpable. But the truth is, that these papers are not addressed to persons falling under either of these characters. They solicit the
25   attention of those only, who add to a sincere zeal for the happiness of their country, a temper favorable to a just estimate of the means of promoting it.

Persons of this character will proceed to an examination of the plan submitted by the convention, not only without a disposition to find or to magnify faults; but will see the propriety of reflecting, that a faultless plan was not to be
30   expected. Nor will they barely make allowances for the errors which may be chargeable on the fallibility to which the convention, as a body of men, were liable; but will keep in mind, that they themselves also are but men, and ought not to assume an infallibility in rejudging the fallible opinions of others.

With equal readiness will it be perceived, that besides these inducements to
35   candor, many allowances ought to be made for the difficulties inherent in the very nature of the undertaking referred to the convention.

The novelty of the undertaking immediately strikes us. It has been shown in the course of these papers, that the existing Confederation is founded on principles which are fallacious; that we must consequently change this first
40   foundation, and with it the superstructure resting upon it. It has been shown, that

the other confederacies which could be consulted as precedents have been vitiated by the same erroneous principles, and can therefore furnish no other light than that of beacons, which give warning of the course to be shunned, without pointing out that which ought to be pursued. The most that the convention could do in such a situation, was to avoid the errors suggested by the past experience of other countries, as well as of our own; and to provide a convenient mode of rectifying their own errors, as future experiences may unfold them.

Among the difficulties encountered by the convention, a very important one must have lain in combining the requisite stability and energy in government, with the inviolable attention due to liberty and to the republican form. Without substantially accomplishing this part of their undertaking, they would have very imperfectly fulfilled the object of their appointment, or the expectation of the public; yet that it could not be easily accomplished, will be denied by no one who is unwilling to betray his ignorance of the subject. Energy in government is essential to that security against external and internal danger, and to that prompt and salutary execution of the laws which enter into the very definition of good government. Stability in government is essential to national character and to the advantages annexed to it, as well as to that repose and confidence in the minds of the people, which are among the chief blessings of civil society. An irregular and mutable legislation is not more an evil in itself than it is odious to the people; and it may be pronounced with assurance that the people of this country, enlightened as they are with regard to the nature, and interested, as the great body of them are, in the effects of good government, will never be satisfied till some remedy be applied to the vicissitudes and uncertainties which characterize the State administrations. On comparing, however, these valuable ingredients with the vital principles of liberty, we must perceive at once the difficulty of mingling them together in their due proportions. The genius of republican liberty seems to demand on one side, not only that all power should be derived from the people, but that those intrusted with it should be kept in independence on the people, by a short duration of their appointments; and that even during this short period the trust should be placed not in a few, but a number of hands. Stability, on the contrary, requires that the hands in which power is lodged should continue for a length of time the same. A frequent change of men will result from a frequent return of elections; and a frequent change of measures from a frequent change of men: whilst energy in government requires not only a certain duration of power, but the execution of it by a single hand.

How far the convention may have succeeded in this part of their work, will better appear on a more accurate view of it. From the cursory view here taken, it must clearly appear to have been an arduous part.

Not less arduous must have been the task of marking the proper line of partition between the authority of the general and that of the State governments. Every man will be sensible of this difficulty, in proportion as he has been accustomed to contemplate and discriminate objects extensive and complicated
5   in their nature. The faculties of the mind itself have never yet been distinguished and defined, with satisfactory precision, by all the efforts of the most acute and metaphysical philosophers. Sense, perception, judgment, desire, volition, memory, imagination, are found to be separated by such delicate shades and minute gradations that their boundaries have eluded the most subtle
10 investigations, and remain a pregnant source of ingenious disquisition and controversy. The boundaries between the great kingdom of nature, and, still more, between the various provinces, and lesser portions, into which they are subdivided, afford another illustration of the same important truth. The most sagacious and laborious naturalists have never yet succeeded in tracing with
15 certainty the line which separates the district of vegetable life from the neighboring region of unorganized matter, or which marks the ermination of the former and the commencement of the animal empire. A still greater obscurity lies in the distinctive characters by which the objects in each of these great departments of nature have been arranged and assorted.
20   When we pass from the works of nature, in which all the delineations are perfectly accurate, and appear to be otherwise only from the imperfection of the eye which surveys them, to the institutions of man, in which the obscurity arises as well from the object itself as from the organ by which it is contemplated, we must perceive the necessity of moderating still further our expectations and
25 hopes from the efforts of human sagacity. Experience has instructed us that no skill in the science of government has yet been able to discriminate and define, with sufficient certainty, its three great provinces the legislative, executive, and judiciary; or even the privileges and powers of the different legislative branches. Questions daily occur in the course of practice, which prove the obscurity which
30 reins in these subjects, and which puzzle the greatest adepts in political science.
        The experience of ages, with the continued and combined labors of the most enlightened legislatures and jurists, has been equally unsuccessful in delineating the several objects and limits of different codes of laws and different tribunals of justice. The precise extent of the common law, and the statute law, the maritime
35 law, the ecclesiastical law, the law of corporations, and other local laws and customs, remains still to be clearly and finally established in Great Britain, where accuracy in such subjects has been more industriously pursued than in any other part of the world. The jurisdiction of her several courts, general and local, of law, of equity, of admiralty, etc., is not less a source of frequent and
40 intricate discussions, sufficiently denoting the indeterminate limits by which

they are respectively circumscribed. All new laws, though penned with the greatest technical skill, and passed on the fullest and most mature deliberation, are considered as more or less obscure and equivocal, until their meaning be liquidated and ascertained by a series of particular discussions and

5   adjudications. Besides the obscurity arising from the complexity of objects, and the imperfection of the human faculties, the medium through which the conceptions of men are conveyed to each other adds a fresh embarrassment. The use of words is to express ideas. Perspicuity, therefore, requires not only that the ideas should be distinctly formed, but that they should be expressed by words

10   distinctly and exclusively appropriate to them. But no language is so copious as to supply words and phrases for every complex idea, or so correct as not to include many equivocally denoting different ideas. Hence it must happen that however accurately objects may be discriminated in themselves, and however accurately the discrimination may be considered, the definition of them may be

15   rendered inaccurate by the inaccuracy of the terms in which it is delivered. And this unavoidable inaccuracy must be greater or less, according to the complexity and novelty of the objects defined. When the Almighty himself condescends to address mankind in their own language, his meaning, luminous as it must be, is rendered dim and doubtful by the cloudy medium through which it is

20   communicated.

    Here, then, are three sources of vague and incorrect definitions: indistinctness of the object, imperfection of the organ of conception, inadequateness of the vehicle of ideas. Any one of these must produce a certain degree of obscurity. The convention, in delineating the boundary between the

25   federal and State jurisdictions, must have experienced the full effect of them all.

    To the difficulties already mentioned may be added the interfering pretensions of the larger and smaller States. We cannot err in supposing that the former would contend for a participation in the government, fully proportioned to their superior wealth and importance; and that the latter would not be less

30   tenacious of the equality at present enjoyed by them. We may well suppose that neither side would entirely yield to the other, and consequently that the struggle could be terminated only by compromise. It is extremely probable, also, that after the ratio of representation had been adjusted, this very compromise must have produced a fresh struggle between the same parties, to give such a turn to

35   the organization of the government, and to the distribution of its powers, as would increase the importance of the branches, in forming which they had respectively obtained the greatest share of influence. There are features in the Constitution which warrant each of these suppositions; and as far as either of them is well founded, it shows that the convention must have been compelled to

40   sacrifice theoretical propriety to the force of extraneous considerations.

Nor could it have been the large and small States only, which would marshal themselves in opposition to each other on various points. Other combinations, resulting from a difference of local position and policy, must have created additional difficulties. As every State may be divided into different
5   districts, and its citizens into different classes, which give birth to contending interests and local jealousies, so the different parts of the United States are distinguished from each other by a variety of circumstances, which produce a like effect on a larger scale. And although this variety of interests, for reasons sufficiently explained in a former paper, may have a salutary influence on the
10   administration of the government when formed, yet every one must be sensible of the contrary influence, which must have been experienced in the task of forming it.

Would it be wonderful if, under the pressure of all these difficulties, the convention should have been forced into some deviations from that artificial
15   structure and regular symmetry which an abstract view of the subject might lead an ingenious theorist to bestow on a Constitution planned in his closet or in his imagination? The real wonder is that so many difficulties should have been surmounted, and surmounted with a unanimity almost as unprecedented as it must have been unexpected. It is impossible for any man of candor to reflect on
20   this circumstance without partaking of the astonishment. It is impossible for the man of pious reflection not to perceive in it a finger of that Almighty hand which has been so frequently and signally extended to our relief in the critical stages of the revolution.

We had occasion, in a former paper, to take notice of the repeated trials
25   which have been unsuccessfully made in the United Netherlands for reforming the baneful and notorious vices of their constitution. The history of almost all the great councils and consultations held among mankind for reconciling their discordant opinions, assuaging their mutual jealousies, and adjusting their respective interests, is a history of factions, contentions, and disappointments,
30   and may be classed among the most dark and degraded pictures which display the infirmities and depravities of the human character. If, in a few scattered instances, a brighter aspect is presented, they serve only as exceptions to admonish us of the general truth; and by their lustre to darken the gloom of the adverse prospect to which they are contrasted. In revolving the causes from
35   which these exceptions result, and applying them to the particular instances before us, we are necessarily led to two important conclusions. The first is, that the convention must have enjoyed, in a very singular degree, an exemption from the pestilential influence of party animosities the disease most incident to deliberative bodies, and most apt to contaminate their proceedings. The second
40   conclusion is that all the deputations composing the convention were

satisfactorily accommodated by the final act, or were induced to accede to it by a deep conviction of the necessity of sacrificing private opinions and partial interests to the public good, and by a despair of seeing this necessity diminished by delays or by new experiments.

5   PUBLIUS

No. 47
The Particular Structure of the New Government and the Distribution of Power Among Its Different Parts

To the People of the State of New York:

HAVING reviewed the general form of the proposed government and the general mass of power allotted to it, I proceed to examine the particular structure of this government, and the distribution of this mass of power among its

10   constituent parts.

One of the principal objections inculcated by the more respectable adversaries to the Constitution, is its supposed violation of the political maxim, that the legislative, executive, and judiciary departments ought to be separate and distinct. In the structure of the federal government, no regard, it is said,

15   seems to have been paid to this essential precaution in favor of liberty. The several departments of power are distributed and blended in such a manner as at once to destroy all symmetry and beauty of form, and to expose some of the essential parts of the edifice to the danger of being crushed by the disproportionate weight of other parts.

20   No political truth is certainly of greater intrinsic value, or is stamped with the authority of more enlightened patrons of liberty, than that on which the objection is founded. The accumulation of all powers, legislative, executive, and judiciary, in the same hands, whether of one, a few, or many, and whether hereditary, selfappointed, or elective, may justly be pronounced the very

25   definition of tyranny. Were the federal Constitution, therefore, really chargeable with the accumulation of power, or with a mixture of powers, having a dangerous tendency to such an accumulation, no further arguments would be necessary to inspire a universal reprobation of the system. I persuade myself, however, that it will be made apparent to every one, that the charge cannot be

30   supported, and that the maxim on which it relies has been totally misconceived and misapplied. In order to form correct ideas on this important subject, it will be proper to investigate the sense in which the preservation of liberty requires that the three great departments of power should be separate and distinct.

The oracle who is always consulted and cited on this subject is the celebrated Montesquieu. If he be not the author of this invaluable precept in the science of politics, he has the merit at least of displaying and recommending it most effectually to the attention of mankind. Let us endeavor, in the first place,
5   to ascertain his meaning on this point.

The British Constitution was to Montesquieu what Homer has been to the didactic writers on epic poetry. As the latter have considered the work of the immortal bard as the perfect model from which the principles and rules of the epic art were to be drawn, and by which all similar works were to be judged, so
10   this great political critic appears to have viewed the Constitution of England as the standard, or to use his own expression, as the mirror of political liberty; and to have delivered, in the form of elementary truths, the several characteristic principles of that particular system. That we may be sure, then, not to mistake his meaning in this case, let us recur to the source from which the maxim was
15   drawn.

On the slightest view of the British Constitution, we must perceive that the legislative, executive, and judiciary departments are by no means totally separate and distinct from each other. The executive magistrate forms an integral part of the legislative authority. He alone has the prerogative of making treaties
20   with foreign sovereigns, which, when made, have, under certain limitations, the force of legislative acts. All the members of the judiciary department are appointed by him, can be removed by him on the address of the two Houses of Parliament, and form, when he pleases to consult them, one of his constitutional councils. One branch of the legislative department forms also a great
25   constitutional council to the executive chief, as, on another hand, it is the sole depositary of judicial power in cases of impeachment, and is invested with the supreme appellate jurisdiction in all other cases. The judges, again, are so far connected with the legislative department as often to attend and participate in its deliberations, though not admitted to a legislative vote.
30   From these facts, by which Montesquieu was guided, it may clearly be inferred that, in saying "There can be no liberty where the legislative and executive powers are united in the same person, or body of magistrates," or, "if the power of judging be not separated from the legislative and executive powers," he did not mean that these departments ought to have no *partial*
35   *agency* in, or no *control* over, the acts of each other. His meaning, as his own words import, and still more conclusively as illustrated by the example in his eye, can amount to no more than this, that where the *whole* power of one department is exercised by the same hands which possess the *whole* power of another department, the fundamental principles of a free constitution are
40   subverted. This would have been the case in the constitution examined by him,

225

if the king, who is the sole executive magistrate, had possessed also the complete legislative power, or the supreme administration of justice; or if the entire legislative body had possessed the supreme judiciary, or the supreme executive authority. This, however, is not among the vices of that constitution.

5 The magistrate in whom the whole executive power resides cannot of himself make a law, though he can put a negative on every law; nor administer justice in person, though he has the appointment of those who do administer it. The judges can exercise no executive prerogative, though they are shoots from the executive stock; nor any legislative function, though they may be advised with by the

10 legislative councils. The entire legislature can perform no judiciary act, though by the joint act of two of its branches the judges may be removed from their offices, and though one of its branches is possessed of the judicial power in the last resort. The entire legislature, again, can exercise no executive prerogative, though one of its branches constitutes the supreme executive magistracy, and

15 another, on the impeachment of a third, can try and condemn all the subordinate officers in the executive department.

The reasons on which Montesquieu grounds his maxim are a further demonstration of his meaning. "When the legislative and executive powers are united in the same person or body," says he, "there can be no liberty, because

20 apprehensions may arise lest *the same* monarch or senate should *enact* tyrannical laws to *execute* them in a tyrannical manner." Again: "Were the power of judging joined with the legislative, the life and liberty of the subject would be exposed to arbitrary control, for *the judge* would then be *the legislator*. Were it joined to the executive power, *the judge* might behave with all the

25 violence of *an oppressor*." Some of these reasons are more fully explained in other passages; but briefly stated as they are here, they sufficiently establish the meaning which we have put on this celebrated maxim of this celebrated author.

If we look into the constitutions of the several States, we find that, notwithstanding the emphatical and, in some instances, the unqualified terms in

30 which this axiom has been laid down, there is not a single instance in which the several departments of power have been kept absolutely separate and distinct. New Hampshire, whose constitution was the last formed, seems to have been fully aware of the impossibility and inexpediency of avoiding any mixture whatever of these departments, and has qualified the doctrine by declaring "that

35 the legislative, executive, and judiciary powers ought to be kept as separate from, and independent of, each other *as the nature of a free government will admit; or as is consistent with that chain of connection that binds the whole fabric of the constitution in one indissoluble bond of unity and amity.*" Her constitution accordingly mixes these departments in several respects. The

40 Senate, which is a branch of the legislative department, is also a judicial tribunal

for the trial of impeachments. The President, who is the head of the executive department, is the presiding member also of the Senate; and, besides an equal vote in all cases, has a casting vote in case of a tie. The executive head is himself eventually elective every year by the legislative department, and his
5   council is every year chosen by and from the members of the same department. Several of the officers of state are also appointed by the legislature. And the members of the judiciary department are appointed by the executive department.

     The constitution of Massachusetts has observed a sufficient though less pointed caution, in expressing this fundamental article of liberty. It declares
10 "that the legislative department shall never exercise the executive and judicial powers, or either of them; the executive shall never exercise the legislative and judicial powers, or either of them; the judicial shall never exercise the legislative and executive powers, or either of them." This declaration corresponds precisely with the doctrine of Montesquieu, as it has been explained, and is not in a single
15 point violated by the plan of the convention. It goes no farther than to prohibit any one of the entire departments from exercising the powers of another department. In the very Constitution to which it is prefixed, a partial mixture of powers has been admitted. The executive magistrate has a qualified negative on the legislative body, and the Senate, which is a part of the legislature, is a court
20 of impeachment for members both of the executive and judiciary departments. The members of the judiciary department, again, are appointable by the executive department, and removable by the same authority on the address of the two legislative branches. Lastly, a number of the officers of government are annually appointed by the legislative department. As the appointment to offices,
25 particularly executive offices, is in its nature an executive function, the compilers of the Constitution have, in this last point at least, violated the rule established by themselves.

     I pass over the constitutions of Rhode Island and Connecticut, because they were formed prior to the Revolution, and even before the principle under
30 examination had become an object of political attention.

     The constitution of New York contains no declaration on this subject; but appears very clearly to have been framed with an eye to the danger of improperly blending the different departments. It gives, nevertheless, to the executive magistrate, a partial control over the legislative department; and, what
35 is more, gives a like control to the judiciary department; and even blends the executive and judiciary departments in the exercise of this control. In its council of appointment members of the legislative are associated with the executive authority, in the appointment of officers, both executive and judiciary. And its court for the trial of impeachments and correction of errors is to consist of one
40 branch of the legislature and the principal members of the judiciary department.

The constitution of New Jersey has blended the different powers of government more than any of the preceding. The governor, who is the executive magistrate, is appointed by the legislature; is chancellor and ordinary, or surrogate of the State; is a member of the Supreme Court of Appeals, and

5   president, with a casting vote, of one of the legislative branches. The same legislative branch acts again as executive council of the governor, and with him constitutes the Court of Appeals. The members of the judiciary department are appointed by the legislative department and removable by one branch of it, on the impeachment of the other.

10   According to the constitution of Pennsylvania, the president, who is the head of the executive department, is annually elected by a vote in which the legislative department predominates. In conjunction with an executive council, he appoints the members of the judiciary department, and forms a court of impeachment for trial of all officers, judiciary as well as executive. The judges

15   of the Supreme Court and justices of the peace seem also to be removable by the legislature; and the executive power of pardoning in certain cases, to be referred to the same department. The members of the executive counoil are made EX-OFFICIO justices of peace throughout the State.

In Delaware, the chief executive magistrate is annually elected by the

20   legislative department. The speakers of the two legislative branches are vice-presidents in the executive department. The executive chief, with six others, appointed, three by each of the legislative branches constitutes the Supreme Court of Appeals; he is joined with the legislative department in the appointment of the other judges. Throughout the States, it appears that the members of the

25   legislature may at the same time be justices of the peace; in this State, the members of one branch of it are EX-OFFICIO justices of the peace; as are also the members of the executive council. The principal officers of the executive department are appointed by the legislative; and one branch of the latter forms a court of impeachments. All officers may be removed on address of the

30   legislature.

Maryland has adopted the maxim in the most unqualified terms; declaring that the legislative, executive, and judicial powers of government ought to be forever separate and distinct from each other. Her constitution, notwithstanding, makes the executive magistrate appointable by the legislative department; and

35   the members of the judiciary by the executive department.

The language of Virginia is still more pointed on this subject. Her constitution declares, "that the legislative, executive, and judiciary departments shall be separate and distinct; so that neither exercise the powers properly belonging to the other; nor shall any person exercise the powers of more than

40   one of them at the same time, except that the justices of county courts shall be

eligible to either House of Assembly." Yet we find not only this express exception, with respect to the members of the irferior courts, but that the chief magistrate, with his executive council, are appointable by the legislature; that two members of the latter are triennially displaced at the pleasure of the
5   legislature; and that all the principal offices, both executive and judiciary, are filled by the same department. The executive prerogative of pardon, also, is in one case vested in the legislative department.

     The constitution of North Carolina, which declares "that the legislative, executive, and supreme judicial powers of government ought to be forever
10 separate and distinct from each other," refers, at the same time, to the legislative department, the appointment not only of the executive chief, but all the principal officers within both that and the judiciary department.

     In South Carolina, the constitution makes the executive magistracy eligible by the legislative department. It gives to the latter, also, the appointment of the
15 members of the judiciary department, including even justices of the peace and sheriffs; and the appointment of officers in the executive department, down to captains in the army and navy of the State.

     In the constitution of Georgia, where it is declared "that the legislative, executive, and judiciary departments shall be separate and distinct, so that
20 neither exercise the powers properly belonging to the other," we find that the executive department is to be filled by appointments of the legislature; and the executive prerogative of pardon to be finally exercised by the same authority. Even justices of the peace are to be appointed by the legislature.

     In citing these cases, in which the legislative, executive, and judiciary
25 departments have not been kept totally separate and distinct, I wish not to be regarded as an advocate for the particular organizations of the several State governments. I am fully aware that among the many excellent principles which they exemplify, they carry strong marks of the haste, and still stronger of the inexperience, under which they were framed. It is but too obvious that in some
30 instances the fundamental principle under consideration has been violated by too great a mixture, and even an actual consolidation, of the different powers; and that in no instance has a competent provision been made for maintaining in practice the separation delineated on paper. What I have wished to evince is, that the charge brought against the proposed Constitution, of violating the sacred
35 maxim of free government, is warranted neither by the real meaning annexed to that maxim by its author, nor by the sense in which it has hitherto been understood in America. This interesting subject will be resumed in the ensuing paper.

    PUBLIUS

No. 48
These Departments Should Not Be So Far Separated as to Have No Constitutional Control Over Each Other

To the People of the State of New York:

IT WAS shown in the last paper that the political apothegm there examined does not require that the legislative, executive, and judiciary departments should be wholly unconnected with each other. I shall undertake, in the next place, to
5   show that unless these departments be so far connected and blended as to give to each a constitutional control over the others, the degree of separation which the maxim requires, as essential to a free government, can never in practice be duly maintained.

It is agreed on all sides, that the powers properly belonging to one of the
10 departments ought not to be directly and completely administered by either of the other departments. It is equally evident, that none of them ought to possess, directly or indirectly, an overruling influence over the others, in the administration of their respective powers. It will not be denied, that power is of an encroaching nature, and that it ought to be effectually restrained from passing
15 the limits assigned to it. After discriminating, therefore, in theory, the several classes of power, as they may in their nature be legislative, executive, or judiciary, the next and most difficult task is to provide some practical security for each, against the invasion of the others. What this security ought to be, is the great problem to be solved.
20   Will it be sufficient to mark, with precision, the boundaries of these departments, in the constitution of the government, and to trust to these parchment barriers against the encroaching spirit of power? This is the security which appears to have been principally relied on by the compilers of most of the American constitutions. But experience assures us, that the efficacy of the
25 provision has been greatly overrated; and that some more adequate defense is indispensably necessary for the more feeble, against the more powerful, members of the government. The legislative department is everywhere extending the sphere of its activity, and drawing all power into its impetuous vortex.
30   The founders of our republics have so much merit for the wisdom which they have displayed, that no task can be less pleasing than that of pointing out the errors into which they have fallen. A respect for truth, however, obliges us to remark, that they seem never for a moment to have turned their eyes from the danger to liberty from the overgrown and all-grasping prerogative of an
35 hereditary magistrate, supported and fortified by an hereditary branch of the legislative authority. They seem never to have recollected the danger from

legislative usurpations, which, by assembling all power in the same hands, must lead to the same tyranny as is threatened by executive usurpations.

In a government where numerous and extensive prerogatives are placed in the hands of an hereditary monarch, the executive department is very justly
5 regarded as the source of danger, and watched with all the jealousy which a zeal for liberty ought to inspire. In a democracy, where a multitude of people exercise in person the legislative functions, and are continually exposed, by their incapacity for regular deliberation and concerted measures, to the ambitious intrigues of their executive magistrates, tyranny may well be apprehended, on
10 some favorable emergency, to start up in the same quarter. But in a representative republic, where the executive magistracy is carefully limited; both in the extent and the duration of its power; and where the legislative power is exercised by an assembly, which is inspired, by a supposed influence over the people, with an intrepid confidence in its own strength; which is sufficiently
15 numerous to feel all the passions which actuate a multitude, yet not so numerous as to be incapable of pursuing the objects of its passions, by means which reason prescribes; it is against the enterprising ambition of this department that the people ought to indulge all their jealousy and exhaust all their precautions.

The legislative department derives a superiority in our governments from
20 other circumstances. Its constitutional powers being at once more extensive, and less susceptible of precise limits, it can, with the greater facility, mask, under complicated and indirect measures, the encroachments which it makes on the co-ordinate departments. It is not unfrequently a question of real nicety in legislative bodies, whether the operation of a particular measure will, or will not,
25 extend beyond the legislative sphere. On the other side, the executive power being restrained within a narrower compass, and being more simple in its nature, and the judiciary being described by landmarks still less uncertain, projects of usurpation by either of these departments would immediately betray and defeat themselves. Nor is this all: as the legislative department alone has access to the
30 pockets of the people, and has in some constitutions full discretion, and in all a prevailing influence, over the pecuniary rewards of those who fill the other departments, a dependence is thus created in the latter, which gives still greater facility to encroachments of the former.

I have appealed to our own experience for the truth of what I advance on
35 this subject. Were it necessary to verify this experience by particular proofs, they might be multiplied without end. I might find a witness in every citizen who has shared in, or been attentive to, the course of public administrations. I might collect vouchers in abundance from the records and archives of every State in the Union. But as a more concise, and at the same time equally

satisfactory, evidence, I will refer to the example of two States, attested by two unexceptionable authorities.

The first example is that of Virginia, a State which, as we have seen, has expressly declared in its constitution, that the three great departments ought not
5   to be intermixed. The authority in support of it is Mr. Jefferson, who, besides his other advantages for remarking the operation of the government, was himself the chief magistrate of it. In order to convey fully the ideas with which his experience had impressed him on this subject, it will be necessary to quote a passage of some length from his very interesting *Notes on the State of Virginia*,
10 p. 195. "All the powers of government, legislative, executive, and judiciary, result to the legislative body. The concentrating these in the same hands, is precisely the definition of despotic government. It will be no alleviation, that these powers will be exercised by a plurality of hands, and not by a single one. One hundred and seventy-three despots would surely be as oppressive as one.
15 Let those who doubt it, turn their eyes on the republic of Venice. As little will it avail us, that they are chosen by ourselves. An *elective despotism* was not the government we fought for; but one which should not only be founded on free principles, but in which the powers of government should be so divided and balanced among several bodies of magistracy, as that no one could transcend
20 their legal limits, without being effectually checked and restrained by the others. For this reason, that convention which passed the ordinance of government, laid its foundation on this basis, that the legislative, executive, and judiciary departments should be separate and distinct, so that no person should exercise the powers of more than one of them at the same time. *But no barrier was*
25 *provided between these several powers.* The judiciary and the executive members were left dependent on the legislative for their subsistence in office, and some of them for their continuance in it. If, therefore, the legislature assumes executive and judiciary powers, no opposition is likely to be made; nor, if made, can be effectual; because in that case they may put their proceedings
30 into the form of acts of Assembly, which will render them obligatory on the other branches. They have accordingly, *in many* instances, *decided rights* which should have been left to *judiciary controversy*, and *the direction of the executive, during the whole time of their session, is becoming habitual and familiar.*"

The other State which I shall take for an example is Pennsylvania; and the
35 other authority, the Council of Censors, which assembled in the years 1783 and 1784. A part of the duty of this body, as marked out by the constitution, was "to inquire whether the constitution had been preserved inviolate in every part; and whether the legislative and executive branches of government had performed their duty as guardians of the people, or assumed to themselves, or exercised,
40 other or greater powers than they are entitled to by the constitution. " In the

execution of this trust, the council were necessarily led to a comparison of both the legislative and executive proceedings, with the constitutional powers of these departments; and from the facts enumerated, and to the truth of most of which both sides in the council subscribed, it appears that the constitution had
5   been flagrantly violated by the legislature in a variety of important instances.

A great number of laws had been passed, violating, without any apparent necessity, the rule requiring that all bills of a public nature shall be previously printed for the consideration of the people; although this is one of the precautions chiefly relied on by the constitution against improper acts of
10 legislature.

The constitutional trial by jury had been violated, and powers assumed which had not been delegated by the constitution.

Executive powers had been usurped.

The salaries of the judges, which the constitution expressly requires to be
15 fixed, had been occasionally varied; and cases belonging to the judiciary department frequently drawn within legislative cognizance and determination.

Those who wish to see the several particulars falling under each of these heads, may consult the journals of the council, which are in print. Some of them, it will be found, may be imputable to peculiar circumstances connected with the
20 war; but the greater part of them may be considered as the spontaneous shoots of an ill-constituted government.

It appears, also, that the executive department had not been innocent of frequent breaches of the constitution. There are three observations, however, which ought to be made on this head: *first*, a great proportion of the instances
25 were either immediately produced by the necessities of the war, or recommended by Congress or the commander-in-chief; *second*, in most of the other instances, they conformed either to the declared or the known sentiments of the legislative department; *third*, the executive department of Pennsylvania is distinguished from that of the other States by the number of members
30 composing it. In this respect, it has as much affinity to a legislative assembly as to an executive council. And being at once exempt from the restraint of an individual responsibility for the acts of the body, and deriving confidence from mutual example and joint influence, unauthorized measures would, of course, be more freely hazarded, than where the executive department is administered by a
35 single hand, or by a few hands.

The conclusion which I am warranted in drawing from these observations is, that a mere demarcation on parchment of the constitutional limits of the several departments, is not a sufficient guard against those encroachments which lead to a tyrannical concentration of all the powers of government in the same hands.

PUBLIUS

No. 49

Method of Guarding Against the Encroachments of Any One Department of Government by Appealing to the People Through a Convention

To the People of the State of New York:

5   THE author of the *Notes on the State of Virginia*, quoted in the last paper, has subjoined to that valuable work the draught of a constitution, which had been prepared in order to be laid before a convention, expected to be called in 1783, by the legislature, for the establishment of a constitution for that commonwealth. The plan, like every thing from the same pen, marks a turn of

10   thinking, original, comprehensive, and accurate; and is the more worthy of attention as it equally displays a fervent attachment to republican government and an enlightened view of the dangerous propensities against which it ought to be guarded. One of the precautions which he proposes, and on which he appears ultimately to rely as a palladium to the weaker departments of power against the

15   invasions of the stronger, is perhaps altogether his own, and as it immediately relates to the subject of our present inquiry, ought not to be overlooked.

His proposition is, "that whenever any two of the three branches of government shall concur in opinion, each by the voices of two thirds of their whole number, that a convention is necessary for altering the constitution, or

20   *correcting breaches of it*, a convention shall be called for the purpose."

As the people are the only legitimate fountain of power, and it is from them that the constitutional charter, under which the several branches of government hold their power, is derived, it seems strictly consonant to the republican theory, to recur to the same original authority, not only whenever it may be necessary to

25   enlarge, diminish, or new-model the powers of the government, but also whenever any one of the departments may commit encroachments on the chartered authorities of the others. The several departments being perfectly co-ordinate by the terms of their common commission, none of them, it is evident, can pretend to an exclusive or superior right of settling the boundaries between

30   their respective powers; and how are the encroachments of the stronger to be prevented, or the wrongs of the weaker to be redressed, without an appeal to the people themselves, who, as the grantors of the commissions, can alone declare its true meaning, and enforce its observance?

There is certainly great force in this reasoning, and it must be allowed to prove that a constitutional road to the decision of the people ought to be marked out and kept open, for certain great and extraordinary occasions. But there appear to be insuperable objections against the proposed recurrence to the

5   people, as a provision in all cases for keeping the several departments of power within their constitutional limits.

In the first place, the provision does not reach the case of a combination of two of the departments against the third. If the legislative authority, which possesses so many means of operating on the motives of the other departments,

10   should be able to gain to its interest either of the others, or even one third of its members, the remaining department could derive no advantage from its remedial provision. I do not dwell, however, on this objection, because it may be thought to be rather against the modification of the principle, than against the principle itself.

15   In the next place, it may be considered as an objection inherent in the principle, that as every appeal to the people would carry an implication of some defect in the government, frequent appeals would, in a great measure, deprive the government of that veneration which time bestows on every thing, and without which perhaps the wisest and freest governments would not possess the

20   requisite stability. If it be true that all governments rest on opinion, it is no less true that the strength of opinion in each individual, and its practical influence on his conduct, depend much on the number which he supposes to have entertained the same opinion. The reason of man, like man himself, is timid and cautious when left alone, and acquires firmness and confidence in proportion to the

25   number with which it is associated. When the examples which fortify opinion are *ancient* as well as *numerous*, they are known to have a double effect. In a nation of philosophers, this consideration ought to be disregarded. A reverence for the laws would be sufficiently inculcated by the voice of an enlightened reason. But a nation of philosophers is as little to be expected as the

30   philosophical race of kings wished for by Plato. And in every other nation, the most rational government will not find it a superfluous advantage to have the prejudices of the community on its side.

The danger of disturbing the public tranquillity by interesting too strongly the public passions, is a still more serious objection against a frequent reference

35   of constitutional questions to the decision of the whole society. Notwithstanding the success which has attended the revisions of our established forms of government, and which does so much honor to the virtue and intelligence of the people of America, it must be confessed that the experiments are of too ticklish a nature to be unnecessarily multiplied. We are to recollect that all the existing

40   constitutions were formed in the midst of a danger which repressed the passions

most unfriendly to order and concord; of an enthusiastic confidence of the people in their patriotic leaders, which stifled the ordinary diversity of opinions on great national questions; of a universal ardor for new and opposite forms, produced by a universal resentment and indignation against the ancient
5 government; and whilst no spirit of party connected with the changes to be made, or the abuses to be reformed, could mingle its leaven in the operation. The future situations in which we must expect to be usually placed, do not present any equivalent security against the danger which is apprehended.

But the greatest objection of all is, that the decisions which would probably
10 result from such appeals would not answer the purpose of maintaining the constitutional equilibrium of the government. We have seen that the tendency of republican governments is to an aggrandizement of the legislative at the expense of the other departments. The appeals to the people, therefore, would usually be made by the executive and judiciary departments. But whether made by one side
15 or the other, would each side enjoy equal advantages on the trial? Let us view their different situations. The members of the executive and judiciary departments are few in number, and can be personally known to a small part only of the people. The latter, by the mode of their appointment, as well as by the nature and permanency of it, are too far removed from the people to share
20 much in their prepossessions. The former are generally the objects of jealousy, and their administration is always liable to be discolored and rendered unpopular. The members of the legislative department, on the other hand, are numberous. They are distributed and dwell among the people at large. Their connections of blood, of friendship, and of acquaintance embrace a great
25 proportion of the most influential part of the society. The nature of their public trust implies a personal influence among the people, and that they are more immediately the confidential guardians of the rights and liberties of the people. With these advantages, it can hardly be supposed that the adverse party would have an equal chance for a favorable issue.
30 But the legislative party would not only be able to plead their cause most successfully with the people. They would probably be constituted themselves the judges. The same influence which had gained them an election into the legislature, would gain them a seat in the convention. If this should not be the case with all, it would probably be the case with many, and pretty certainly with
35 those leading characters, on whom every thing depends in such bodies. The convention, in short, would be composed chiefly of men who had been, who actually were, or who expected to be, members of the department whose conduct was arraigned. They would consequently be parties to the very question to be decided by them.

It might, however, sometimes happen, that appeals would be made under circumstances less adverse to the executive and judiciary departments. The usurpations of the legislature might be so flagrant and so sudden, as to admit of no specious coloring. A strong party among themselves might take side with the
5   other branches. The executive power might be in the hands of a peculiar favorite of the people. In such a posture of things, the public decision might be less swayed by prepossessions in favor of the legislative party. But still it could never be expected to turn on the true merits of the question. It would inevitably be connected with the spirit of pre-existing parties, or of parties springing out of
10   the question itself. It would be connected with persons of distinguished character and extensive influence in the community. It would be pronounced by the very men who had been agents in, or opponents of, the measures to which the decision would relate. The PASSIONS, therefore, not the REASON, of the public would sit in judgment. But it is the reason, alone, of the public, that ought
15   to control and regulate the government. The passions ought to be controlled and regulated by the government.

   We found in the last paper, that mere declarations in the written constitution are not sufficient to restrain the several departments within their legal rights. It appears in this, that occasional appeals to the people would be neither a proper
20   nor an effectual provision for that purpose. How far the provisions of a different nature contained in the plan above quoted might be adequate, I do not examine. Some of them are unquestionably founded on sound political principles, and all of them are framed with singular ingenuity and precision.

   PUBLIUS

No. 50
Periodical Appeals to the People Considered

25   To the People of the State of New York:

   IT MAY be contended, perhaps, that instead of *occasional* appeals to the people, which are liable to the objections urged against them, *periodical* appeals are the proper and adequate means of *preventing and correcting infractions of the Constitution.*

30   It will be attended to, that in the examination of these expedients, I confine myself to their aptitude for *enforcing* the Constitution, by keeping the several departments of power within their due bounds, without particularly considering them as provisions for *altering* the Constitution itself. In the first view, appeals to the people at fixed periods appear to be nearly as ineligible as appeals on
35   particular occasions as they emerge. If the periods be separated by short

intervals, the measures to be reviewed and rectified will have been of recent date, and will be connected with all the circumstances which tend to vitiate and pervert the result of occasional revisions. If the periods be distant from each other, the same remark will be applicable to all recent measures; and in
5 proportion as the remoteness of the others may favor a dispassionate review of them, this advantage is inseparable from inconveniences which seem to counterbalance it. In the first place, a distant prospect of public censure would be a very feeble restraint on power from those excesses to which it might be urged by the force of present motives. Is it to be imagined that a legislative
10 assembly, consisting of a hundred or two hundred members, eagerly bent on some favorite object, and breaking through the restraints of the Constitution in pursuit of it, would be arrested in their career, by considerations drawn from a censorial revision of their conduct at the future distance of ten, fifteen, or twenty years? In the next place, the abuses would often have completed their
15 mischievous effects before the remedial provision would be applied. And in the last place, where this might not be the case, they would be of long standing, would have taken deep root, and would not easily be extirpated.

The scheme of revising the constitution, in order to correct recent breaches of it, as well as for other purposes, has been actually tried in one of the States.
20 One of the objects of the Council of Censors which met in Pennsylvania in 1783 and 1784, was, as we have seen, to inquire, "whether the constitution had been violated, and whether the legislative and executive departments had encroached upon each other." This important and novel experiment in politics merits, in several points of view, very particular attention. In some of them it may,
25 perhaps, as a single experiment, made under circumstances somewhat peculiar, be thought to be not absolutely conclusive. But as applied to the case under consideration, it involves some facts, which I venture to remark, as a complete and satisfactory illustration of the reasoning which I have employed.

First. It appears, from the names of the gentlemen who composed the
30 council, that some, at least, of its most active members had also been active and leading characters in the parties which pre-existed in the State.

Second. It appears that the same active and leading members of the council had been active and influential members of the legislative and executive branches, within the period to be reviewed; and even patrons or opponents of the
35 very measures to be thus brought to the test of the constitution. Two of the members had been vice-presidents of the State, and several other members of the executive council, within the seven preceding years. One of them had been speaker, and a number of others distinguished members, of the legislative assembly within the same period.

Third. Every page of their proceedings witnesses the effect of all these circumstances on the temper of their deliberations. Throughout the continuance of the council, it was split into two fixed and violent parties. The fact is acknowledged and lamented by themselves. Had this not been the case, the face
5   of their proceedings exhibits a proof equally satisfactory. In all questions, however unimportant in themselves, or unconnected with each other, the same names stand invariably contrasted on the opposite columns. Every unbiased observer may infer, without danger of mistake, and at the same time without meaning to reflect on either party, or any individuals of either party, that,
10 unfortunately, *passion*, not *reason*, must have presided over their decisions. When men exercise their reason coolly and freely on a variety of distinct questions, they inevitably fall into different opinions on some of them. When they are governed by a common passion, their opinions, if they are so to be called, will be the same.
15   *Fourth*. It is at least problematical, whether the decisions of this body do not, in several instances, misconstrue the limits prescribed for the legislative and executive departments, instead of reducing and limiting them within their constitutional places.
        Fifth. I have never understood that the decisions of the council on
20 constitutional questions, whether rightly or erroneously formed, have had any effect in varying the practice founded on legislative constructions. It even appears, if I mistake not, that in one instance the contemporary legislature denied the constructions of the council, and actually prevailed in the contest.
        This censorial body, therefore, proves at the same time, by its researches,
25 the existence of the disease, and by its example, the inefficacy of the remedy.
        This conclusion cannot be invalidated by alleging that the State in which the experiment was made was at that crisis, and had been for a long time before, violently heated and distracted by the rage of party. Is it to be presumed, that at any future septennial epoch the same State will be free from parties? Is it to be
30 presumed that any other State, at the same or any other given period, will be exempt from them? Such an event ought to be neither presumed nor desired; because an extinction of parties necessarily implies either a universal alarm for the public safety, or an absolute extinction of liberty.
        Were the precaution taken of excluding from the assemblies elected by the
35 people, to revise the preceding administration of the government, all persons who should have been concerned with the government within the given period, the difficulties would not be obviated. The important task would probably devolve on men, who, with inferior capacities, would in other respects be little better qualified. Although they might not have been personally concerned in the
40 administration, and therefore not immediately agents in the measures to be

examined, they would probably have been involved in the parties connected
with these measures, and have been elected under their auspices.

PUBLIUS

No. 51
The Structure of the Government Must Furnish the Proper Checks and Balances Between the Different Departments

To the People of the State of New York:

5 　　TO WHAT expedient, then, shall we finally resort, for maintaining in
practice the necessary partition of power among the several departments, as laid
down in the Constitution? The only answer that can be given is, that as all these
exterior provisions are found to be inadequate, the defect must be supplied, by
so contriving the interior structure of the government as that its several
10 constituent parts may, by their mutual relations, be the means of keeping each
other in their proper places. Without presuming to undertake a full development
of this important idea, I will hazard a few general observations, which may
perhaps place it in a clearer light, and enable us to form a more correct judgment
of the principles and structure of the government planned by the convention.
15 　　In order to lay a due foundation for that separate and distinct exercise of the
different powers of government, which to a certain extent is admitted on all
hands to be essential to the preservation of liberty, it is evident that each
department should have a will of its own; and consequently should be so
constituted that the members of each should have as little agency as possible in
20 the appointment of the members of the others. Were this principle rigorously
adhered to, it would require that all the appointments for the supreme executive,
legislative, and judiciary magistracies should be drawn from the same fountain
of authority, the people, through channels having no communication whatever
with one another. Perhaps such a plan of constructing the several departments
25 would be less difficult in practice than it may in contemplation appear. Some
difficulties, however, and some additional expense would attend the execution
of it. Some deviations, therefore, from the principle must be admitted. In the
constitution of the judiciary department in particular, it might be inexpedient to
insist rigorously on the principle: first, because peculiar qualifications being
30 essential in the members, the primary consideration ought to be to select that
mode of choice which best secures these qualifications; secondly, because the
permanent tenure by which the appointments are held in that department, must
soon destroy all sense of dependence on the authority conferring them.

It is equally evident, that the members of each department should be as little dependent as possible on those of the others, for the emoluments annexed to their offices. Were the executive magistrate, or the judges, not independent of the legislature in this particular, their independence in every other would be
5   merely nominal.

But the great security against a gradual concentration of the several powers in the same department, consists in giving to those who administer each department the necessary constitutional means and personal motives to resist encroachments of the others. The provision for defense must in this, as in all
10   other cases, be made commensurate to the danger of attack. Ambition must be made to counteract ambition. The interest of the man must be connected with the constitutional rights of the place. It may be a reflection on human nature, that such devices should be necessary to control the abuses of government. But what is government itself, but the greatest of all reflections on human nature? If men
15   were angels, no government would be necessary. If angels were to govern men, neither external nor internal controls on government would be necessary. In framing a government which is to be administered by men over men, the great difficulty lies in this: you must first enable the government to control the governed; and in the next place oblige it to control itself. A dependence on the
20   people is, no doubt, the primary control on the government; but experience has taught mankind the necessity of auxiliary precautions.

This policy of supplying, by opposite and rival interests, the defect of better motives, might be traced through the whole system of human affairs, private as well as public. We see it particularly displayed in all the subordinate
25   distributions of power, where the constant aim is to divide and arrange the several offices in such a manner as that each may be a check on the other – that the private interest of every individual may be a sentinel over the public rights. These inventions of prudence cannot be less requisite in the distribution of the supreme powers of the State.
30   But it is not possible to give to each department an equal power of self-defense. In republican government, the legislative authority necessarily predominates. The remedy for this inconveniency is to divide the legislature into different branches; and to render them, by different modes of election and different principles of action, as little connected with each other as the nature of
35   their common functions and their common dependence on the society will admit. It may even be necessary to guard against dangerous encroachments by still further precautions. As the weight of the legislative authority requires that it should be thus divided, the weakness of the executive may require, on the other hand, that it should be fortified. An absolute negative on the legislature appears,
40   at first view, to be the natural defense with which the executive magistrate

should be armed. But perhaps it would be neither altogether safe nor alone sufficient. On ordinary occasions it might not be exerted with the requisite firmness, and on extraordinary occasions it might be perfidiously abused. May not this defect of an absolute negative be supplied by some qualified connection

5   between this weaker department and the weaker branch of the stronger department, by which the latter may be led to support the constitutional rights of the former, without being too much detached from the rights of its own department?

If the principles on which these observations are founded be just, as I

10   persuade myself they are, and they be applied as a criterion to the several State constitutions, and to the federal Constitution it will be found that if the latter does not perfectly correspond with them, the former are infinitely less able to bear such a test.

There are, moreover, two considerations particularly applicable to the

15   federal system of America, which place that system in a very interesting point of view.

First. In a single republic, all the power surrendered by the people is submitted to the administration of a single government; and the usurpations are guarded against by a division of the government into distinct and separate

20   departments. In the compound republic of America, the power surrendered by the people is first divided between two distinct governments, and then the portion allotted to each subdivided among distinct and separate departments. Hence a double security arises to the rights of the people. The different governments will control each other, at the same time that each will be

25   controlled by itself.

Second. It is of great importance in a republic not only to guard the society against the oppression of its rulers, but to guard one part of the society against the injustice of the other part. Different interests necessarily exist in different classes of citizens. If a majority be united by a common interest, the rights of the

30   minority will be insecure. There are but two methods of providing against this evil: the one by creating a will in the community independent of the majority – that is, of the society itself; the other, by comprehending in the society so many separate descriptions of citizens as will render an unjust combination of a majority of the whole very improbable, if not impracticable. The first method

35   prevails in all governments possessing an hereditary or self-appointed authority. This, at best, is but a precarious security; because a power independent of the society may as well espouse the unjust views of the major, as the rightful interests of the minor party, and may possibly be turned against both parties. The second method will be exemplified in the federal republic of the United

40   States. Whilst all authority in it will be derived from and dependent on the

242

society, the society itself will be broken into so many parts, interests, and classes of citizens, that the rights of individuals, or of the minority, will be in little danger from interested combinations of the majority. In a free government the security for civil rights must be the same as that for religious rights. It consists in

5 the one case in the multiplicity of interests, and in the other in the multiplicity of sects. The degree of security in both cases will depend on the number of interests and sects; and this may be presumed to depend on the extent of country and number of people comprehended under the same government. This view of the subject must particularly recommend a proper federal system to all the

10 sincere and considerate friends of republican government, since it shows that in exact proportion as the territory of the Union may be formed into more circumscribed Confederacies, or States oppressive combinations of a majority will be facilitated: the best security, under the republican forms, for the rights of every class of citizens, will be diminished: and consequently the stability and

15 independence of some member of the government, the only other security, must be proportionately increased. Justice is the end of government. It is the end of civil society. It ever has been and ever will be pursued until it be obtained, or until liberty be lost in the pursuit. In a society under the forms of which the stronger faction can readily unite and oppress the weaker, anarchy may as truly

20 be said to reign as in a state of nature, where the weaker individual is not secured against the violence of the stronger; and as, in the latter state, even the stronger individuals are prompted, by the uncertainty of their condition, to submit to a government which may protect the weak as well as themselves; so, in the former state, will the more powerful factions or parties be gradnally

25 induced, by a like motive, to wish for a government which will protect all parties, the weaker as well as the more powerful. It can be little doubted that if the State of Rhode Island was separated from the Confederacy and left to itself, the insecurity of rights under the popular form of government within such narrow limits would be displayed by such reiterated oppressions of factious

30 majorities that some power altogether independent of the people would soon be called for by the voice of the very factions whose misrule had proved the necessity of it. In the extended republic of the United States, and among the great variety of interests, parties, and sects which it embraces, a coalition of a majority of the whole society could seldom take place on any other principles

35 than those of justice and the general good; whilst there being thus less danger to a minor from the will of a major party, there must be less pretext, also, to provide for the security of the former, by introducing into the government a will not dependent on the latter, or, in other words, a will independent of the society itself. It is no less certain than it is important, notwithstanding the contrary

40 opinions which have been entertained, that the larger the society, provided it lie

within a practical sphere, the more duly capable it will be of self-government. And happily for the *republican cause*, the practicable sphere may be carried to a very great extent, by a judicious modification and mixture of the *federal principle*.

5   PUBLIUS

---

[1] *Spirit of Laws*, Vol. I., Book IX., Chap. I.

Karl Marx

Karl Marx (b. 1818, Trier, d. 1883, London) was a German philosopher, sociologist, economist, and radical politician. Marx was educated first at the University of Bonn and then at the Friedrich-Wilhelms-Universität in Berlin, where he became active in a group called the Young Hegelians. The Young Hegelians were followers of the great German philosopher George Hegel, who interpreted his ideas as calling for a radical revision of society and the role of religion in it. Marx went on to become one of the leaders of the German Social Democratic Party and of the First International, an international union of socialist organizations. Along with his disciple, co-author, and benefactor Friedrich Engels, Marx was also active in publishing several radical newspapers. His political activism led to a number of trials and political exiles, which culminated with his settling in London, where he spent the last 33 years of his life.

Marx was a prolific author. Apart from explicitly political documents such as *The Communist Manifesto* and *Critique of the Gotha Program* (a critique of a platform for the Social Democratic Party proposed by the followers of the socialist leader Ferdinand Lassalle), Marx wrote several highly influential analytic works. The most prominent among them is *Capital*, which provides a comprehensive critique of capitalist relations of production from the standpoint of Marx's theory of surplus value, and *The German Ideology*, which presents Marx's critique of post-Hegelian German philosophy and develops his theory of historical materialism.

Marx championed revolutionary activism against capitalism. Although during his lifetime such activism achieved only intermittent successes (e.g., the Paris Commune), his ideas were highly influential among the socialist revolutionaries at the turn of the 20th century and provided a key ideological background for the Bolshevik revolution of 1917 in Russia.

Karl Marx
CRITIQUE OF THE GOTHA PROGRAM
(1875)

SECTION ONE

I.

1. *"Labor is the source of all wealth and of all civilization, and since useful labor is possible only in and through society, the proceeds of labor belong, unabridged and in equal right, to all the members of society."*

First part of the paragraph: *"Labor is the source of all wealth and of all*
5 *civilization."*

Labor is not the source of all wealth. Nature is just as much the source of use-values (and these, certainly, form the material elements of wealth) as labor, which is itself only the expression of a natural force, human labor-power. The above phrase is to be found in every child's primer and is correct in so far as it is
10 assumed that labor starts out equipped with the requisite materials and means. But a Socialist platform should not let such middle class phrases pass, and permit, by silence, the conditions that alone give sense thereto to be suppressed. And in so far as man stands toward Nature,—the first source of all the means and objects of labor—in the relation of proprietor, in so far as he treats Nature as
15 belonging to him, his labor becomes the source of use-values, hence also of wealth. The capitalists have very good reasons for imputing to labor supernatural creative powers, because from the nature-imposed necessity of labor it follows that the man who possesses no property but his labor-power must, under all conditions of society and civilization, be the slave of those other
20 men who have made themselves the possessors of the material conditions for labor. He can work only with their permission, hence live only with their permission.

But let us take the sentence as it runs, or rather limps. What should we have expected as the conclusion? Plainly this:
25 "Since labor is the source of all wealth, no one in society can acquire wealth except as the product of labor. Therefore, if he does not work himself, he lives upon the labor of others, and also acquires his share of civilization at the expense of others' labor."

Instead of this, another sentence is attached by means of the phrase "and
30 since," in order to draw a conclusion from this latter sentence, and not from the former.

Second part of the paragraph: *"Useful labor is possible only in and through society."*

According to the first proposition labor was the source of all wealth and civilization; hence no society was possible without labor. Now we learn, on the
5   contrary, that no "useful" labor is possible without society.

It would have been as sensible to say that only in society can useless and even publicly injurious labor become a branch of industry, that only in society can men live in idleness, etc., etc.–in short, to copy the whole of Rousseau.

And what is "useful" labor? Plainly, only the labor that produces the desired
10   serviceable effect. A savage–and man is a savage after he has ceased to be an ape–a savage who kills an animal with a stone, who gathers fruits, etc., performs "useful" labor.

Thirdly, the conclusion: "And since useful labor is possible only in and through society,–the proceeds of labor belong unabridged, in equal right, to all
15   the members of society."

A beautiful conclusion! If useful labor is possible only in and through society, then the proceeds of labor 'belong to society – and the individual laborer receives only so much as is not necessary for the maintenance of the "pre-requisite" of labor, society.
20   Indeed, this has been the regular claim made by the champions of each succeeding social system. First come the claims of the government and all that hangs thereby, since it is the social organ for the maintenance of the social order; next come the claims of the various sorts of private property, for the various sorts of private property are the foundations of society, etc. It is plain,
25   such hollow phrases can be turned and twisted at will.

The first and second parts of the paragraph can have any sensible connection only in the following form:

"Labor can become the source of wealth and civilization only as social labor," or, what amounts to the same thing, "only in and through society."
30   This proposition is indisputably correct, for, even if isolated labor (its material pre-requisites presupposed) can create use-values, it can nevertheless produce neither wealth nor civilization.

And just as indisputable is this other statement:

"In the measure that labor is developed socially, and thereby becomes the
35   source of wealth and civilization, to that extent are developed also poverty and degradation on the side of the laborer, wealth and civilization on the side of the non-laborer."

This is the law of all history up till now. Therefore, instead of talking in general terms about "labor" and "society," it should have been clearly pointed out how, under present capitalist society, the conditions, material and otherwise, are at last produced, which enable, and indeed compel, the laborers to break through that social curse.

But, in fact, the entire paragraph – faulty both in style and contents –
5 appears here only in order to inscribe the Lassallean catchword of the "unabridged proceeds of labor" as the watchword on the flag of the party. I shall come back later to the "proceeds of labor," the "equal right," etc., as the same thing recurs in somewhat different form.

2. *"In present society the means of labor are the monopoly of the capitalist*
10 *class. The dependence of 'the working class, flowing from this, is the cause of misery and servitude in all forms. "*

This proposition is borrowed from the constitution of the International, but in an "improved," version, which makes it false. In present society the means of labor are the monopoly of the landlords (the monopoly of land forms even the
15 basis of the monopoly of capital) AND of the capitalists. In the passage referred to the constitution of the International mentions neither the one nor the other class of monopolists. It speaks of "the monopoly in the means of labor, that is, in the sources of life." The addition, "sources of life," shows sufficiently that the soil is included under the means of labor.
20 The "improvement" was made because Lassalle, for reasons now generally known, attacked the capitalist class ONLY, not the landlords. In England the capitalist is in most cases not even the owner of the soil on which his factory stands.

3. *"The emancipation of labor demands the elevation of the means of labor*
25 *to the common property of society and the cooperative regulation of the total labor of society, together with a just distribution of the proceeds of labor. "*

By "elevation of the means of labor to common property" is probably meant their "transformation into common property." But this only in passing.

What are "proceeds of labor"? The product of labor or its value? And in the
30 latter case, are they the total value of the product or only that part of the value which labor has newly added to the value of the consumed means of production?

"Proceeds of labor" is a loose notion which Lassalle has inserted in place of definite economic conceptions.

What is "just distribution"? Do not the capitalists maintain that the
35 distribution now prevailing is "just"? And, in fact, is it not the only "just" distribution on the basis of the present mode of production? Are economic relations regulated by theories of law or do not the legal relations, on the

contrary, arise out of the economic relations? Do not the Utopian Socialists also entertain the most variegated notions of what constitutes a "just" distribution?

In order to know what the phrase "just distribution" means here, we must regard this paragraph in connection with the first. This paragraph assumes a
5 state of society in which "the means of labor are common property, and the total social labor is regulated cooperatively," from the first paragraph we learn that "the proceeds of labor belong to all the members of society, unabridged and in equal right."

"To all the members of society"? Even to those who do not work? What,
10 then, becomes of "the unabridged proceeds of labor"? Only to the working members of society? What becomes, then, of "the equal right" of all the members of society?

Obviously, "all members of society" and "the equal right" are only methods of expression. The gist of the matter consists in this, that in this communistic
15 society every workingman must receive the "unabridged" Lassallean "proceeds of labor."

If we now take the term "proceeds of labor" in the sense of the product of labor, then the cooperative proceeds of labor are the total social product.

From this is to be deducted:
20 First: The amount required for the replacement of the means of production used up.

Secondly: An additional portion for the expansion of production.

Thirdly: A reserve and insurance fund against mischance, disturbances through the forces of nature, etc.
25 These deductions from the "unabridged proceeds of labor" are an economic necessity, and their magnitude has to be determined according to the existing means and forces, in part by calculating the probabilities, but they can in no way be calculated from the idea of justice.

There remains the other portion of the total product, destined to serve as
30 means of consumption.

Before this can be distributed among the individuals there are again to be deducted from it:

First: The general administrative expenses that do not form a part of production. This portion is from the outset very considerably reduced in
35 comparison with present society, and diminishes in the same measure in which the new society develops.

Secondly: That portion which is destined for the satisfaction of common wants, such as schools, provision for the protection of the public health, etc.

This portion is, from the very outset, considerably larger than in the present society and increases in the same measure in which the new society develops.

Thirdly: Funds for those unable to work, etc., in short, for what now belongs to so-called public charity.

Only now do we come to that "distribution" which the platform, under Lassallean influence, stupidly has alone in view, namely, that portion of the means of consumption which is distributed among the individual producers of the community.

The "unabridged proceeds of labor" have in our hands changed to "abridged," although what escapes the producer as a private individual directly or indirectly benefits him as a member of society.

As the phrase, "unabridged proceeds of labor," has disappeared, so indeed the phrase "proceeds of labor" now disappears.

Within the cooperative society, based on the common ownership of the means of production, the producers do not exchange their products; just as little does the labor expended on the products appear here as the value of these products, as a material quality possessed by them, since now, in contradistinction to capitalist society, the separate labors form no longer indirectly, but directly, constituent parts of the total labor. The term, "proceeds of labor," even nowadays rejectable because of its ambiguity, loses thus all meaning.

What we are dealing with here is a Communist society, not as it has developed on its own basis, but, on the contrary, as it is just issuing out of capitalist society; hence, a society that still retains, in every respect, economic, moral and intellectual, the birthmarks of the old society from whose womb it is issuing. Accordingly, the individual producer gets back – after the deductions– exactly as much as he gives to it. What he has given to it is his individual share of labor. For instance, the social labor day consists of the sum of the individual labor hours; the individual labor time of the single producer is the fraction of the social labor day supplied by him, his share of it. He receives from the community a check showing that he has done so much labor (after deducting his labor due to the common fund), and with this check he draws from the common store as much of the means of consumption as costs an equal amount of labor. The same quantity of labor that he has give to society in one form, he receives back in another form.

Evidently, there prevails here the same principle that today regulates the exchange of commodities, in so far as it is an exchange of equivalents. Substance and form have changed, because under the changed conditions no one can give anything except his labor, and because, on the other hand, nothing can

go over into the possession of individuals, except individual means of consumption. But so far as the distribution of the latter among the individual consumers is concerned, the same principle prevails 'as in the exchange of commodity-equivalents; an equal quantity of labor in one form is exchanged for
5   an equal quantity of labor in another form.

      Equal right is here, therefore, still according to the: principle, capitalist right, although principle and practice are no longer in conflict with each other, while the exchange of equivalents in the exchange of commodities exists only on the average, not in the individual cases.

10   Notwithstanding this progress, the equal right is still tainted with a capitalist limitation. The right of the producers is proportional to their contribution of labor; the equality consists in this, that the right is measured by an equal standard: labor.

      However, one person is physically or intellectually superior to the other,
15   and furnishes, therefore, more labor in the same time, or can work a longer time; andin order to serve as a measure, labor must be determined according to duration or intensity, otherwise it would cease to serve as a standard. This equal right is unequal right for unequal labor. It does not recognize class distinctions, because every one is only a workingman like everybody else; but it tacitly
20   recognizes unequal individual endowment, and hence, efficiency, as natural privileges. It is, therefore, in its substance, a right of inequality, like all right. According to its nature, right can consist only in the application of a common standard; but the unequal individuals (and they would not be different individuals if they were not unequal ones) can be measured according to a
25   common standard only in so far as they are brought under the some point of view, or, are regarded from a particular side only. For example, in the given instance they are regarded only as workingmen; we see nothing more in them, we disregard everything else. Moreover, one workingman is married, the other is not married; one has more children than the other, etc., etc. Hence, with equal
30   contribution of labor and, therefore, equal shares in the social consumption-fund, the one receives actually more than the other, the one is richer than the other, etc. In order to avoid all these shortcomings right would have to be not equal, but unequal.

      But these shortcomings are unavoidable in the first phase of Communist
35   society, as it has just issued from capitalist society after long travail. Right can never be superior to the economic development and the stage of civilization conditioned thereby.

      In the higher phase of Communist society, after the enslaving subordination of the individual under the division of labor has disappeared, and therewith also the opposition between manual and intellectual labor; after labor has become not only a means of life, but also the highest want in life; when, with the development of all the faculties of the individual, the productive forces have correspondingly increased, and all the springs of social wealth flow more abundantly–only then may the limited horizon of capitalist right be left behind entirely, and society inscribe on its banners: "From everyone according to his faculties, to everyone according to his needs !"

5

I went rather extensively into the "unabridged proceeds of labor" upon the one hand, and "the 'equal right" and "the just distribution" upon the other, in order to show how mischievous it is on the one hand to attempt to foist upon our party, as axioms, notions that at one time had a meaning, but have now become mere antiquated rubbish; and, on the other hand, which pervert the realistic conception–which it has required such labor to impress upon the party, but has now struck root in it–with the ideological nonsense about justice, etc., which is so current among the Democrats and the French Utopians.

10

15

Aside from the above, it was altogether a mistake to make much of the so-called distribution, and to lay on this the chief emphasis. The distribution of the means of consumption is but the result of the distribution of the factors of production.

20

But the distribution of the latter is a characteristic of the very mode of production. For example, the capitalist mode of production rests on this, that the material factors of production are alloted to the non-workers in the form of capital and landed property, while the mass of the people are owners only of the personal factor of production: labor-power. Given such a distribution of the elements of production, there results automatically the present distribution of the means of consumption. Given the common ownership of the material factors of production, there follows in the same way a distribution of the means of consumption different from the present. Utopian Socialism (and from it, again, a section of the Democracy) followed the capitalist economists in regarding and treating distribution as independent of production, and hence represented Socialism as turning chiefly around the question of distribution. After the true relationship has long been made clear, why again this backward step?

25

30

4. *"The emancipation of work must be the work of the working class itself–relative to which all other classes are only one reactionary mass."*

35

The first part of the sentence is taken from the introductory words of the statutes of the International, only it is "improved." In those statutes it is stated: "The emancipation of the working class must be the work of the workingmen

themselves." Here, on the contrary, "the working class" has to emancipate–
what? "The work." Comprehend that who can.

As recompense for such a statement there is inserted the counter statement,
a Lassallean citation of purest water: "Opposed to which [the working class] all
5   other classes form only one reactionary mass."

The Communist Manifesto declares: "Of all the classes that stand face to
face with the bourgeoisie today, the proletariat alone is really a revolutionary
class. The other classes decay and 'finally disappear in the face of modern
industry; the proletariat is its special and essential product."

10   The bourgeoisie is here conceived as a revolutionary class, as the bearer of
large industry, in contradistinction to the feudal and the intermediate strata, who
would retain all social privileges and who are the reflex of the outgrown
methods of production. Therefore, they do not, together with the bourgeoisie,
form only one reactionary mass.

15   On the other hand, the proletariat is revolutionary as against the
bourgeoisie, because it, rising upon the foundation of large industry, seeks to
remove the capitalist character from production, which the bourgeoisie in turn
seeks to perpetuate. But the Manifesto adds that the "lower middle class ...
become revolutionary only in view of their impending transfer into the
20   proletariat."

From this standpoint it is therefore again nonsense to say that they, together
with the bourgeoisie, and on top of that the feudal class, "form only one
reactionary mass" relative to the working class.

Did we at the last elections shout at the artisans, the small manufacturers,
25   etc., and the peasants: "Relative to us you together with the bourgeoisie and the
feudal lords form only one reactionary mass"?

Lassalle knew the Communist Manifesto by heart, as his faithful followers
knew his writings which were to bring salvation. If he therefore grossly falsified
the Manifesto, that happened only that he might gloss over his alliance with the
30   absolutist and feudalist opponents as against the bourgeoisie.

In addition to that, his philosophical dictum is now dragged in by the hair in
the above paragraph, without the least connection with the garbled citation from
the statutes of the International. It is therefore simply a piece of impertinence,
and not at all displeasing to Bismarck – one of those cheap crudities in which
35   the Marat of Berlin indulges.

5. *"The working class strives for its emancipation next of all within the
confines of the present-day national state, conscious that the necessary result of*

its efforts–which is common to the workingmen of all civilized countries will be the international fraternization of peoples."

Lassalle, contrary to the Communist Manifesto and to all earlier Socialism, regarded the labor movement from the narrowest national standpoint. He is being followed in that respect, and this after the activity of the International!

It is self-evident that the working class, in order to be able to fight at all, must organize itself at home as a class, and that the home country is the immediate scene of action of its struggle. In so far its class struggle is, not in essence, but as the Communist Manifesto states, "in form," national. But the "confines of the present-day national State," – for instance, those of the German Empire – are again, economically, "within the confines" of the world market, politically, "within the confines" of the State system. The first worthy merchant knows that German trade is at the same time foreign trade, and the greatness of Herr Bismarck consists also of course in a kind of international politics.

And to what does the German Labor Party reduce its internationalism? To the consciousness that the result of its endeavors will be the "international fraternization of peoples" – a phrase borrowed from the bourgeois league of peace and freedom, which is supposed to pass as an equivalent for the international fraternization of the working classes in their common struggle against the ruling classes and their governments.

Of the international functions of the German working class not a word is said! And thus the working class is to oppose its own bourgeoisie which, with the bourgeoisie of all other countries and Bismarck's policy of international conspiracy, is leagued against it.

As a matter of fact that avowal of internationalism in the program is immeasurably below that contained in the party of free trade. This latter party also claims that the outcome of its efforts is the "international fraternization of peoples." But that party also does something in order to make commerce international, and in no way rests satisfied with the consciousness that all peoples carry on trade among themselves at home.

The international activity of the working classes in no way depends upon the existence of the "International Association of Workingmen." This latter was only the first attempt to furnish a central body for that activity; an attempt which, because of the impulse given, was of a lasting character, but which, in its first historical form, was no longer fulfillable after the fall of the Paris Commune.

Bismarck's "North German" paper was entirely in the right when it, to the satisfaction of its master, stated that the German Labor Party in its new program abjured internationalism.

II.

6. *"Starting from these principles, the German Labor Party aims with all lawful means to establish the free state – and – Socialist society; the abolition of the wage system with the iron law of wages – and– of exploitation in every form; the removing of all social and political inequality."*

5   Of the "free" State I shall speak later.

So the German Labor Party must henceforth believe in Lassalle's "iron law of wages"! And in order that it may not be passed over unnoticed, you commit the absurdity to speak of the "abolition of the wage system" (it should read: "system of wage-labor") with the "iron law of wages." If I abolish wage-labor, I,
10   of course, abolish also its laws, be they made of iron or of sponge. But Lassalle's warfare against wage-labor turns almost entirely around this so-called law. Hence, in order to prove the Lassallean sect has triumphed, the "wage-system" must be abolished "with the iron law of wages," and not without it.

It is well known that of the "iron law of wages" nothing belongs to Lassalle
15   but the word "iron," borrowed from Goethe's "eternal, iron, great laws." The word iron is the shibboleth by which the faithful recognize one another. But if I take the law with Lassalle's label, and therefore in his sense, I must also take it with his demonstration. And what is this? As Lange showed, shortly after Lassalle's death, it is the Malthusian theory of population (preached by Lange
20   himself).

But if this theory is correct, then I can not abolish the law, even if I abolish wage-labor a hundred times, since in that case the law controls not only the system of wage-labor, but every social system whatsoever. Relying on this very law, the economists have proven for the past fifty years and more that Socialism
25   cannot abolish nature-imposed misery, but can only generalize it, distribute it simultaneously over the whole body of society!

But all this is not the main thing. Disregarding entirely the false Lassallean conception of the law, the truly revolting retrogression consists in this:

Since Lassalle's death the scientific knowledge has made way in our party
30   that wages are not what they seem, namely, the value or price of labor, but only a disguised form for the value or price of labor-power.

Thereby the whole capitalist theory of wages, hitherto prevailing, together with all the criticism hitherto directed against it, was once and for all overthrown, and the fact clearly established that the laborer is only permitted to
35   work for his living, i.e., to live, so long as he works a certain time gratis for the capitalist (hence also for those who share the surplus-value with the latter); that

the pivot around which the entire capitalist system of production turns, is to increase this unpaid labor either by lengthening the working day, or by developing the productive powers of labor, or by straining the laborer to more intense exertion, etc., etc.; that, therefore, the system of wage-labor is a system of slavery, and indeed slavery, which, moreover, grows harder in proportion as the productive powers of labor are developed in society, no matter whether the laborer's pay is better or worse. And now after this conception has become more and more accepted in our party, you turn back to the dogmas of Lassalle, even though you must know that Lassalle did not know what wages were, but, following the capitalist economists, took the appearance for the essence.

It is just as if among slaves who had at last penetrated the mystery of slavery, and had risen in rebellion, a slave, imbued with superannuated notions, inscribed on the program of the rebellion: "Slavery must be abolished, because under the system of slavery the slaves' food can never exceed a certain low maximum."

Is not the mere fact that the representatives of our party were capable of committing such a monstrous outrage against the correct understanding prevailing among the rank and file of the party, enough to show with what frivolity they went at the drawing up of this compromise program!

Instead of the vague phrase at the conclusion of the paragraph : "to remove all social and political inequality" it should have been said that with the abolition of all class distinctions all social and political inequality springing from them will disappear of its own accord.

III.

7. *"The German Labor Party, in order to pave the way for the solution of the Social Question, demands the establishment of productive cooperative associations with state aid, under the democratic control of the working population. The productive cooperative associations are to be called into existence in such proportions in industry and agriculture that from them will arise the socialist organization of the totality of production."*

After the Lassallean "iron law of wages" there follows the cure-all of the prophet. The path thereto is being paved in a worthy manner. In place of the existing class struggle a newspaper-scribe's phrase steps up: "The Social Question," toward the solution of which the path is being paved. Instead of arising from the revolutionary transforming process of society, the "Socialist organization of the totality of production" arises from "the State aid" which the State gives to the productive cooperatives, and which it, not the worker, "calls into being." This is really worthy of the imagination of Lassalle, that one can build a new society with the aid of State loans as easily as one can build a new railroad.

Out of shame, the "State aid" is placed under the democratic control of the "working population."

5   First of all, "the working population" in Germany consists, in its majority, of peasants, and not of proletarians.

Secondly, "democratic" in German means "rule of the people." But what is the meaning of "the popular control of the working population"? And this with a working population which, in making such demands upon the State, expresses

10   its complete consciousness that it neither rules nor is ripe for rulership!

It is superfluous to enter upon a criticism here of the "prescription" written by Buchez, under Louis Philippe, in opposition to the French Socialists, and accepted by the reactionary workingmen of the "ateliers." Nor does the chief offense lie in the fact that the specific panacea was written into the program, but

15   rather in that the standpoint of the class movement is abandoned and one goes back to that of a sectarian movement.

That the workingmen desire to create the conditions of cooperative production upon a social scale, and first of all, among themselves, upon a national scale, means only that they are working upon the transformation of the

20   present conditions of production, and has nothing in common with the creation of cooperative societies by means of State aid. But so far as the present cooperative societies are concerned, they have value ONLY in so far as they are independent creations of workingmen, fostered neither by governments nor by the bourgeoisie.

SECTION TWO.

25   I come now to the democratic section.

A. Free Foundation of the State.

First of all, according to Part II, the German Labor Party aims at "the free State."

Free State – what does that mean?

30   It is in no way the aim of the workingmen, who have emancipated themselves from what has been called "the subject's limited intelligence," to make the State free. The State is almost as "free" in the German Empire as in Russia. Liberty consists in this, that the State is transformed from an organ superior to society into one subordinate to it; and even today State institutions

35   are more or less free in proportion as they limit the "freedom of the State."

259

The German Labor Party shows – at least, if it adopts this platform – that its Socialist ideas are not even skin-deep; since, instead of treating the society existing (and this applies to every future society) as the basis of the existing State (or of any future State in case of a future society), it, on the contrary, treats

5 the State as having independent existence, which possesses its own intellectual, moral, and free or unfree foundations.

The thing is made worse by the reckless misapplication of the words "present State," "present society," and the still more reckless misconception of the nature of that State to which the demands of this platform are addressed!

10 "Present society" is capitalist society, which exists in all civilized countries, more or less free from feudal alloy, more or less modified through the peculiar historical development of each country, more or less developed. On the other hand, the "present State" changes with the boundary line of each country. It is different in the Prusso-German Empire from Switzerland; different in England

15 from the United States. "The present State" is therefore a fiction.

In spite, however, of their manifold differences of form, the different States of the different civilized countries have this in common, that all of them stand upon the basis of modern capitalist society, though their capitalistic development be more or less advanced. Hence they also have certain essential

20 characteristics in common. In this sense one may speak of the present "State institution" as distinguished from that of the future, in which its present roots, capitalist society, will have decayed.

What, then, is the change which the institution of the State will undergo in a communistic society? In other words, what social functions, analogous to the

25 present functions of the State, will remain there? This question can be answered only by proceeding scientifically; the problem is not brought one flea's leap nearer its solution by a thousand combinations of the word "people" with the word "State."

Between the capitalist and the communist systems of society lies the period

30 of the revolutionary transformation of the one into the other. This corresponds to a political transition period, whose State can be nothing else but the revolutionary dictatorship of the proletariat.

But the platform applies neither to the latter, nor to the future State organization of communist society.

35 Its political demands contain nothing but the old democratic litany that the whole world knows: "universal suffrage, " "direct legislation, " "administration of justice by the people," "arming of the nation," etc. They are a mere echo of the middle-class People's Party, of the League for Freedom and Peace; they are all demands that, so far as they are not of an exaggerated–fantastic conception,

are realized now. Only the State, in which they are found, is not situated within the boundary lines of the German Empire, but in Switzerland, the United States, etc. This sort of "Future State" is present State, though existing outside the limits of the German Empire.

5 But one thing has been forgotten. Since the German Labor Party expressly declares that it is acting "within the present national State," ITS State, the Prusso-German Empire, it should not have forgotten the main thing, namely, that all these fine dainties rest on the recognition of the so-called sovereignty of the people, hence that they are in place only in a democratic republic – its

10 demands were certainly otherwise and for the greater part absurd, since one demands only what he has not got.

But since you are not in a position – and wisely so; for the circumstances demand caution–to demand the democratic republic, as the French labor programs did during the reigns of Louis Philippe and Louis Napoleon, you

15 should not have resorted to the. Subterfuge of demanding things that have a meaning only in a democratic republic from a State that is nothing else than a military despotism adorned with parliamentary forms alloyed with feudalism, influenced by the capitalist class, bureaucratically constructed and police protected.

20 Even vulgar democracy, which sees the millennium in the democratic republic and has no inkling of the fact that the class struggle is to be definitely fought out, under this final form of State organization of capitalist society – even vulgar democracy stands mountain-high above that kind of democracy that keeps within the limits of what the police permit and logic forbids.

25 You clearly show that you certainly mean by "State" nothing else but the Government machine, i.e., the State in so far as it constitutes a distinct organism, differentiated from society through the division of labor, when you use the words: "The German Labor Party demands as the economic foundation of the State a single progressive income tax, etc." Taxes are the foundation of the

30 governmental machinery and of nothing else. In that "future State" existing in Switzerland this demand is pretty well realized. An income tax presupposes the different sources of income of the different social classes, hence capitalist society. It is, therefore, not at all strange that the financial reformers of Liverpool–capitalists, with Gladstone's brother at their head–make the same

35 demand as this platform.

B. "The German Labor Party demands as the intellectual and moral foundation of the State:

I. Universal and equal popular education by the State; universal obligatory attendance at school; free tuition."

"Equal public education?" What do you imagine these words mean? Do you think that in present society (and this is the society we are concerned with)
5 education can be equal for all classes? Or is it demanded that the higher classes also, forcibly, be reduced to the modicum of education – common school that alone is compatible with the economic circumstances of, not only the wage workers, but also of the peasants?

"Universal obligatory attendance at school; free tuition." The former is to
10 be found even in Germany; the latter in Switzerland and in the United States. If in some of the states of the United States even the higher institutions of learning are "free," that means practically only that the educational expenses of the higher classes are defrayed by the general treasury. Incidentally, this same thing holds good with regard to the "free administration of justice," demanded in
15 clause A, section 5. Criminal justice is to be had free everywhere; civil justice turns almost exclusively around conflicts over property, and, accordingly, affects almost entirely the possessing classes. Are they to conduct their litigation at the expense of the common treasury?

The paragraph pertaining to schools should at least have demanded
20 technical schools (theoretical and practical) in conjunction with public schools.

"Public education by the State" is entirely to be rejected.

To determine by a general law the means for maintaining public schools, qualifications of the teaching staff, branches of instruction, etc., and, as happens in the instance of the United States, supervision of these legal requirements by
25 government inspectors to see that they are fulfilled, is an altogether different thing from appointing the State as educator of the people.

Moreover, the government and the church must equally be excluded from any influence upon the school. But in the Prussian-German Empire the case is just the other way about; there is just the State which needs a very severe
30 education by the people. One does not help his case any with the lame excuse that he has in mind a "future State"; we have seen what the outcome of that has been.

The entire program, however, despite its democratic trimmings, is tainted through and through with the Lassallean sectarian beliefs on subjection of the
35 State; or, what is no better, with beliefs in democratic miracles; or rather, it is a compromise between these two sorts of miracle-working beliefs, both of them equally foreign to Socialism.

"Freedom of science" – that is found in one of the paragraphs of the Prussian Constitution. Why also here?

"Freedom of conscience"! If one at this juncture of the "Kultur kampf" (the struggle of the liberal bourgeoisie against clerical political influence in the State) desired to bring home to liberalism its old slogans, that could really only be done in this form: "Everyone must be permitted to satisfy his religious ... needs
5 ... without the Prussian police poking its nose into them." But in that case the Labor Party would have to declare its consciousness that "bourgeois freedom of conscience" is nothing else than toleration of all possible kinds of religious freedom of conscience, and that it, moreover, was striving to free the conscience from the religious superstition. But one does not like to rise above the bourgeois
10 level.

I have reached the end, for that addition which now follows in the program forms no characteristic part thereof. I may therefore say briefly:

II. *"Normal working day."*

The Labor Party of no other country has limited itself to such an indefinite
15 demand, but has always fixed upon the length of the working day which it considered normal for the given conditions.

III. *"Restriction of woman, and prohibition of child labor."*

The fixing of a normal working day must first of all include the restriction of woman labor, in so far as this relates to duration, intermission, etc., of the
20 working day; otherwise it can only mean the exclusion of woman labor from branches of industry which are particularly detrimental to the health of women or which are dangerous to the morals of the female sex. If that was meant, it should have been stated.

"Prohibition of child labor." Here it was absolutely necessary to state the
25 age limit. General prohibition of the labor of children is irreconcilable with the existence of large industry, and is therefore an empty, pious wish.

The introduction of the same – if possible – would be reactionary, since, with a rigid regulation of the working time according to the different age periods and the other precautionary measures for the protection of children, an early
30 combining of productive labor with instruction is one of the mightiest means of the transformation of present-day society.

IV. *"State supervision of factories, workshops, and home industry."*

As against the Prussian-German State it was absolutely necessary to demand that the inspectors could only be removed by the courts; that any
35 workingman could report them to the court for violation of duty; and that they must belong to the medical profession.

V. *"Regulation of prison labor."*

A paltry demand in a general labor program. At all events it should have been clearly stated that common criminals should not be treated like cattle, and that their only means of redemption, productive labor, should not, for fear of competition, be denied them. That is certainly the least that one could expect of Socialists.

VI. *"An effective employers' liability law."*

5   It should have been stated how an "effective" liability law; was to be conceived.

Incidentally, in considering the normal working day, that part of factory legislation which deals with health and safety measures was overlooked. The law providing for employers' liability comes into operation only when these

10   regulations are violated…

Dixi et salvavi animam meam.
["I have spoken and saved my soul."]

Karl Marx and Friedrich Engels
MANIFESTO OF THE COMMUNIST PARTY
(1848)

A spectre is haunting Europe — the spectre of communism. All the powers of old Europe have entered into a holy alliance to exorcise this spectre: Pope and Tsar, Metternich and Guizot, French Radicals and German police-spies.

Where is the party in opposition that has not been decried as communistic
5 by its opponents in power? Where is the opposition that has not hurled back the branding reproach of communism, against the more advanced opposition parties, as well as against its reactionary adversaries?

Two things result from this fact:

I.   Communism is already acknowledged by all European
10 powers to be itself a power.

II.   It is high time that Communists should openly, in the face of the whole world, publish their views, their aims, their tendencies, and meet this nursery tale of the Spectre of Communism with a manifesto of the party itself.

15 To this end, Communists of various nationalities have assembled in London and sketched the following manifesto, to be published in the English, French, German, Italian, Flemish and Danish languages.

I. BOURGEOIS AND PROLETARIANS

The history of all hitherto existing society is the history of class struggles.

Freeman and slave, patrician and plebeian, lord and serf, guild-master and
20 journeyman, in a word, oppressor and oppressed, stood in constant opposition to one another, carried on an uninterrupted, now hidden, now open fight, a fight that each time ended, either in a revolutionary reconstitution of society at large, or in the common ruin of the contending classes.

In the earlier epochs of history, we find almost everywhere a complicated
25 arrangement of society into various orders, a manifold gradation of social rank. In ancient Rome we have patricians, knights, plebeians, slaves; in the Middle Ages, feudal lords, vassals, guild-masters, journeymen, apprentices, serfs; in almost all of these classes, again, subordinate gradations.

The modern bourgeois society that has sprouted from the ruins of feudal
30 society has not done away with class antagonisms. It has but established new classes, new conditions of oppression, new forms of struggle in place of the old ones.

Our epoch, the epoch of the bourgeoisie, possesses, however, this distinct feature: it has simplified class antagonisms. Society as a whole is more and more splitting up into two great hostile camps, into two great classes directly facing each other — Bourgeoisie and Proletariat.

5   From the serfs of the Middle Ages sprang the chartered burghers of the earliest towns. From these burgesses the first elements of the bourgeoisie were developed.

The discovery of America, the rounding of the Cape, opened up fresh ground for the rising bourgeoisie. The East-Indian and Chinese markets, the

10 colonisation of America, trade with the colonies, the increase in the means of exchange and in commodities generally, gave to commerce, to navigation, to industry, an impulse never before known, and thereby, to the revolutionary element in the tottering feudal society, a rapid development.

The feudal system of industry, in which industrial production was

15 monopolised by closed guilds, now no longer sufficed for the growing wants of the new markets. The manufacturing system took its place. The guild-masters were pushed on one side by the manufacturing middle class; division of labour between the different corporate guilds vanished in the face of division of labour in each single workshop.

20 Meantime the markets kept ever growing, the demand ever rising. Even manufacturer no longer sufficed. Thereupon, steam and machinery revolutionised industrial production. The place of manufacture was taken by the giant, Modern Industry; the place of the industrial middle class by industrial millionaires, the leaders of the whole industrial armies, the modern bourgeois.

25 Modern industry has established the world market, for which the discovery of America paved the way. This market has given an immense development to commerce, to navigation, to communication by land. This development has, in its turn, reacted on the extension of industry; and in proportion as industry, commerce, navigation, railways extended, in the same proportion the

30 bourgeoisie developed, increased its capital, and pushed into the background every class handed down from the Middle Ages.

We see, therefore, how the modern bourgeoisie is itself the product of a long course of development, of a series of revolutions in the modes of production and of exchange.

35 Each step in the development of the bourgeoisie was accompanied by a corresponding political advance of that class. An oppressed class under the sway of the feudal nobility, an armed and self-governing association in the medieval commune : here independent urban republic (as in Italy and Germany); there taxable "third estate" of the monarchy (as in France); afterwards, in the period of

manufacturing proper, serving either the semi-feudal or the absolute monarchy as a counterpoise against the nobility, and, in fact, cornerstone of the great monarchies in general, the bourgeoisie has at last, since the establishment of Modern Industry and of the world market, conquered for itself, in the modern
5 representative State, exclusive political sway. The executive of the modern state is but a committee for managing the common affairs of the whole bourgeoisie.

The bourgeoisie, historically, has played a most revolutionary part.

The bourgeoisie, wherever it has got the upper hand, has put an end to all feudal, patriarchal, idyllic relations. It has pitilessly torn asunder the motley
10 feudal ties that bound man to his "natural superiors", and has left remaining no other nexus between man and man than naked self-interest, than callous "cash payment". It has drowned the most heavenly ecstasies of religious fervour, of chivalrous enthusiasm, of philistine sentimentalism, in the icy water of egotistical calculation. It has resolved personal worth into exchange value, and
15 in place of the numberless indefeasible chartered freedoms, has set up that single, unconscionable freedom — Free Trade. In one word, for exploitation, veiled by religious and political illusions, it has substituted naked, shameless, direct, brutal exploitation.

The bourgeoisie has stripped of its halo every occupation hitherto honoured
20 and looked up to with reverent awe. It has converted the physician, the lawyer, the priest, the poet, the man of science, into its paid wage labourers.

The bourgeoisie has torn away from the family its sentimental veil, and has reduced the family relation to a mere money relation.

The bourgeoisie has disclosed how it came to pass that the brutal display of
25 vigour in the Middle Ages, which reactionaries so much admire, found its fitting complement in the most slothful indolence. It has been the first to show what man's activity can bring about. It has accomplished wonders far surpassing Egyptian pyramids, Roman aqueducts, and Gothic cathedrals; it has conducted expeditions that put in the shade all former Exoduses of nations and crusades.
30 The bourgeoisie cannot exist without constantly revolutionising the instruments of production, and thereby the relations of production, and with them the whole relations of society. Conservation of the old modes of production in unaltered form, was, on the contrary, the first condition of existence for all earlier industrial classes. Constant revolutionising of
35 production, uninterrupted disturbance of all social conditions, everlasting uncertainty and agitation distinguish the bourgeois epoch from all earlier ones. All fixed, fast-frozen relations, with their train of ancient and venerable prejudices and opinions, are swept away, all new-formed ones become antiquated before they can ossify. All that is solid melts into air, all that is holy

is profaned, and man is at last compelled to face with sober senses his, real conditions of life, and his relations with his kind.

The need of a constantly expanding market for its products chases the bourgeoisie over the entire surface of the globe. It must nestle everywhere, settle
5 everywhere, establish connexions everywhere.

The bourgeoisie has through its exploitation of the world market given a cosmopolitan character to production and consumption in every country. To the great chagrin of Reactionists, it has drawn from under the feet of industry the national ground on which it stood. All old-established national industries have
10 been destroyed or are daily being destroyed. They are dislodged by new industries, whose introduction becomes a life and death question for all civilised nations, by industries that no longer work up indigenous raw material, but raw material drawn from the remotest zones; industries whose products are consumed, not only at home, but in every quarter of the globe. In place of the
15 old wants, satisfied by the production of the country, we find new wants, requiring for their satisfaction the products of distant lands and climes. In place of the old local and national seclusion and self-sufficiency, we have intercourse in every direction, universal inter-dependence of nations. And as in material, so also in intellectual production. The intellectual creations of individual nations
20 become common property. National one-sidedness and narrow-mindedness become more and more impossible, and from the numerous national and local literatures, there arises a world literature.

The bourgeoisie, by the rapid improvement of all instruments of production, by the immensely facilitated means of communication, draws all, even the most
25 barbarian, nations into civilisation. The cheap prices of commodities are the heavy artillery with which it batters down all Chinese walls, with which it forces the barbarians' intensely obstinate hatred of foreigners to capitulate. It compels all nations, on pain of extinction, to adopt the bourgeois mode of production; it compels them to introduce what it calls civilisation into their midst, i.e., to
30 become bourgeois themselves. In one word, it creates a world after its own image.

The bourgeoisie has subjected the country to the rule of the towns. It has created enormous cities, has greatly increased the urban population as compared with the rural, and has thus rescued a considerable part of the population from
35 the idiocy of rural life. Just as it has made the country dependent on the towns, so it has made barbarian and semi-barbarian countries dependent on the civilised ones, nations of peasants on nations of bourgeois, the East on the West.

The bourgeoisie keeps more and more doing away with the scattered state of the population, of the means of production, and of property. It has

269

agglomerated population, centralised the means of production, and has concentrated property in a few hands. The necessary consequence of this was political centralisation. Independent, or but loosely connected provinces, with separate interests, laws, governments, and systems of taxation, became lumped
5   together into one nation, with one government, one code of laws, one national class-interest, one frontier, and one customs-tariff.

     The bourgeoisie, during its rule of scarce one hundred years, has created more massive and more colossal productive forces than have all preceding generations together. Subjection of Nature's forces to man, machinery,
10 application of chemistry to industry and agriculture, steam-navigation, railways, electric telegraphs, clearing of whole continents for cultivation, canalisation or rivers, whole populations conjured out of the ground — what earlier century had even a presentiment that such productive forces slumbered in the lap of social labour?
15   We see then: the means of production and of exchange, on whose foundation the bourgeoisie built itself up, were generated in feudal society. At a certain stage in the development of these means of production and of exchange, the conditions under which feudal society produced and exchanged, the feudal organisation of agriculture and manufacturing industry, in one word, the feudal
20 relations of property became no longer compatible with the already developed productive forces; they became so many fetters. They had to be burst asunder; they were burst asunder.

     Into their place stepped free competition, accompanied by a social and political constitution adapted in it, and the economic and political sway of the
25 bourgeois class.

     A similar movement is going on before our own eyes. Modern bourgeois society, with its relations of production, of exchange and of property, a society that has conjured up such gigantic means of production and of exchange, is like the sorcerer who is no longer able to control the powers of the nether world
30 whom he has called up by his spells. For many a decade past the history of industry and commerce is but the history of the revolt of modern productive forces against modern conditions of production, against the property relations that are the conditions for the existence of the bourgeois and of its rule. It is enough to mention the commercial crises that by their periodical return put the
35 existence of the entire bourgeois society on its trial, each time more threateningly. In these crises, a great part not only of the existing products, but also of the previously created productive forces, are periodically destroyed. In these crises, there breaks out an epidemic that, in all earlier epochs, would have seemed an absurdity — the epidemic of over-production. Society suddenly finds

itself put back into a state of momentary barbarism; it appears as if a famine, a universal war of devastation, had cut off the supply of every means of subsistence; industry and commerce seem to be destroyed; and why? Because there is too much civilisation, too much means of subsistence, too much
5   industry, too much commerce. The productive forces at the disposal of society no longer tend to further the development of the conditions of bourgeois property; on the contrary, they have become too powerful for these conditions, by which they are fettered, and so soon as they overcome these fetters, they bring disorder into the whole of bourgeois society, endanger the existence of
10 bourgeois property. The conditions of bourgeois society are too narrow to comprise the wealth created by them. And how does the bourgeoisie get over these crises? On the one hand by enforced destruction of a mass of productive forces; on the other, by the conquest of new markets, and by the more thorough exploitation of the old ones. That is to say, by paving the way for more
15 extensive and more destructive crises, and by diminishing the means whereby crises are prevented.

The weapons with which the bourgeoisie felled feudalism to the ground are now turned against the bourgeoisie itself.

But not only has the bourgeoisie forged the weapons that bring death to
20 itself; it has also called into existence the men who are to wield those weapons — the modern working class — the proletarians.

In proportion as the bourgeoisie, i.e., capital, is developed, in the same proportion is the proletariat, the modern working class, developed — a class of labourers, who live only so long as they find work, and who find work only so
25 long as their labour increases capital. These labourers, who must sell themselves piecemeal, are a commodity, like every other article of commerce, and are consequently exposed to all the vicissitudes of competition, to all the fluctuations of the market.

Owing to the extensive use of machinery, and to the division of labour, the
30 work of the proletarians has lost all individual character, and, consequently, all charm for the workman. He becomes an appendage of the machine, and it is only the most simple, most monotonous, and most easily acquired knack, that is required of him. Hence, the cost of production of a workman is restricted, almost entirely, to the means of subsistence that he requires for maintenance, and for
35 the propagation of his race. But the price of a commodity, and therefore also of labour, is equal to its cost of production. In proportion, therefore, as the repulsiveness of the work increases, the wage decreases. Nay more, in proportion as the use of machinery and division of labour increases, in the same proportion the burden of toil also increases, whether by prolongation of the

working hours, by the increase of the work exacted in a given time or by increased speed of machinery, etc.

Modern Industry has converted the little workshop of the patriarchal master into the great factory of the industrial capitalist. Masses of labourers, crowded
5 into the factory, are organised like soldiers. As privates of the industrial army they are placed under the command of a perfect hierarchy of officers and sergeants. Not only are they slaves of the bourgeois class, and of the bourgeois State; they are daily and hourly enslaved by the machine, by the overlooker, and, above all, by the individual bourgeois manufacturer himself. The more openly
10 this despotism proclaims gain to be its end and aim, the more petty, the more hateful and the more embittering it is.

The less the skill and exertion of strength implied in manual labour, in other words, the more modern industry becomes developed, the more is the labour of men superseded by that of women. Differences of age and sex have no longer
15 any distinctive social validity for the working class. All are instruments of labour, more or less expensive to use, according to their age and sex.

No sooner is the exploitation of the labourer by the manufacturer, so far, at an end, that he receives his wages in cash, than he is set upon by the other portions of the bourgeoisie, the landlord, the shopkeeper, the pawnbroker, etc.
20 The lower strata of the middle class — the small tradespeople, shopkeepers, and retired tradesmen generally, the handicraftsmen and peasants — all these sink gradually into the proletariat, partly because their diminutive capital does not suffice for the scale on which Modern Industry is carried on, and is swamped in the competition with the large capitalists, partly because their
25 specialised skill is rendered worthless by new methods of production. Thus the proletariat is recruited from all classes of the population.

The proletariat goes through various stages of development. With its birth begins its struggle with the bourgeoisie. At first the contest is carried on by individual labourers, then by the workpeople of a factory, then by the operative
30 of one trade, in one locality, against the individual bourgeois who directly exploits them. They direct their attacks not against the bourgeois conditions of production, but against the instruments of production themselves; they destroy imported wares that compete with their labour, they smash to pieces machinery, they set factories ablaze, they seek to restore by force the vanished status of the
35 workman of the Middle Ages.

At this stage, the labourers still form an incoherent mass scattered over the whole country, and broken up by their mutual competition. If anywhere they unite to form more compact bodies, this is not yet the consequence of their own active union, but of the union of the bourgeoisie, which class, in order to attain

its own political ends, is compelled to set the whole proletariat in motion, and is moreover yet, for a time, able to do so. At this stage, therefore, the proletarians do not fight their enemies, but the enemies of their enemies, the remnants of absolute monarchy, the landowners, the non-industrial bourgeois, the petty
5   bourgeois. Thus, the whole historical movement is concentrated in the hands of the bourgeoisie; every victory so obtained is a victory for the bourgeoisie.

But with the development of industry, the proletariat not only increases in number; it becomes concentrated in greater masses, its strength grows, and it feels that strength more. The various interests and conditions of life within the
10   ranks of the proletariat are more and more equalised, in proportion as machinery obliterates all distinctions of labour, and nearly everywhere reduces wages to the same low level. The growing competition among the bourgeois, and the resulting commercial crises, make the wages of the workers ever more fluctuating. The increasing improvement of machinery, ever more rapidly
15   developing, makes their livelihood more and more precarious; the collisions between individual workmen and individual bourgeois take more and more the character of collisions between two classes. Thereupon, the workers begin to form combinations (Trades' Unions) against the bourgeois; they club together in order to keep up the rate of wages; they found permanent associations in order to
20   make provision beforehand for these occasional revolts. Here and there, the contest breaks out into riots.

Now and then the workers are victorious, but only for a time. The real fruit of their battles lies, not in the immediate result, but in the ever expanding union of the workers. This union is helped on by the improved means of
25   communication that are created by modern industry, and that place the workers of different localities in contact with one another. It was just this contact that was needed to centralise the numerous local struggles, all of the same character, into one national struggle between classes. But every class struggle is a political struggle. And that union, to attain which the burghers of the Middle Ages, with
30   their miserable highways, required centuries, the modern proletarian, thanks to railways, achieve in a few years.

This organisation of the proletarians into a class, and, consequently into a political party, is continually being upset again by the competition between the workers themselves. But it ever rises up again, stronger, firmer, mightier. It
35   compels legislative recognition of particular interests of the workers, by taking advantage of the divisions among the bourgeoisie itself. Thus, the ten-hours' bill in England was carried.

Altogether collisions between the classes of the old society further, in many ways, the course of development of the proletariat. The bourgeoisie finds itself

involved in a constant battle. At first with the aristocracy; later on, with those portions of the bourgeoisie itself, whose interests have become antagonistic to the progress of industry; at all time with the bourgeoisie of foreign countries. In all these battles, it sees itself compelled to appeal to the proletariat, to ask for
5 help, and thus, to drag it into the political arena. The bourgeoisie itself, therefore, supplies the proletariat with its own elements of political and general education, in other words, it furnishes the proletariat with weapons for fighting the bourgeoisie.

Further, as we have already seen, entire sections of the ruling class are, by
10 the advance of industry, precipitated into the proletariat, or are at least threatened in their conditions of existence. These also supply the proletariat with fresh elements of enlightenment and progress.

Finally, in times when the class struggle nears the decisive hour, the progress of dissolution going on within the ruling class, in fact within the whole
15 range of old society, assumes such a violent, glaring character, that a small section of the ruling class cuts itself adrift, and joins the revolutionary class, the class that holds the future in its hands. Just as, therefore, at an earlier period, a section of the nobility went over to the bourgeoisie, so now a portion of the bourgeoisie goes over to the proletariat, and in particular, a portion of the
20 bourgeois ideologists, who have raised themselves to the level of comprehending theoretically the historical movement as a whole.

Of all the classes that stand face to face with the bourgeoisie today, the proletariat alone is a really revolutionary class. The other classes decay and finally disappear in the face of Modern Industry; the proletariat is its special and
25 essential product.

The lower middle class, the small manufacturer, the shopkeeper, the artisan, the peasant, all these fight against the bourgeoisie, to save from extinction their existence as fractions of the middle class. They are therefore not revolutionary, but conservative. Nay more, they are reactionary, for they try to roll back the
30 wheel of history. If by chance, they are revolutionary, they are only so in view of their impending transfer into the proletariat; they thus defend not their present, but their future interests, they desert their own standpoint to place themselves at that of the proletariat.

The "dangerous class", [lumpenproletariat] the social scum, that passively
35 rotting mass thrown off by the lowest layers of the old society, may, here and there, be swept into the movement by a proletarian revolution; its conditions of life, however, prepare it far more for the part of a bribed tool of reactionary intrigue.

In the condition of the proletariat, those of old society at large are already virtually swamped. The proletarian is without property; his relation to his wife and children has no longer anything in common with the bourgeois family relations; modern industry labour, modern subjection to capital, the same in England as in France, in America as in Germany, has stripped him of every trace of national character. Law, morality, religion, are to him so many bourgeois prejudices, behind which lurk in ambush just as many bourgeois interests.

All the preceding classes that got the upper hand sought to fortify their already acquired status by subjecting society at large to their conditions of appropriation. The proletarians cannot become masters of the productive forces of society, except by abolishing their own previous mode of appropriation, and thereby also every other previous mode of appropriation. They have nothing of their own to secure and to fortify; their mission is to destroy all previous securities for, and insurances of, individual property.

All previous historical movements were movements of minorities, or in the interest of minorities. The proletarian movement is the self-conscious, independent movement of the immense majority, in the interest of the immense majority. The proletariat, the lowest stratum of our present society, cannot stir, cannot raise itself up, without the whole superincumbent strata of official society being sprung into the air.

Though not in substance, yet in form, the struggle of the proletariat with the bourgeoisie is at first a national struggle. The proletariat of each country must, of course, first of all settle matters with its own bourgeoisie.

In depicting the most general phases of the development of the proletariat, we traced the more or less veiled civil war, raging within existing society, up to the point where that war breaks out into open revolution, and where the violent overthrow of the bourgeoisie lays the foundation for the sway of the proletariat.

Hitherto, every form of society has been based, as we have already seen, on the antagonism of oppressing and oppressed classes. But in order to oppress a class, certain conditions must be assured to it under which it can, at least, continue its slavish existence. The serf, in the period of serfdom, raised himself to membership in the commune, just as the petty bourgeois, under the yoke of the feudal absolutism, managed to develop into a bourgeois. The modern labourer, on the contrary, instead of rising with the process of industry, sinks deeper and deeper below the conditions of existence of his own class. He becomes a pauper, and pauperism develops more rapidly than population and wealth. And here it becomes evident, that the bourgeoisie is unfit any longer to be the ruling class in society, and to impose its conditions of existence upon society as an over-riding law. It is unfit to rule because it is incompetent to assure an existence to its slave within his slavery, because it cannot help letting him sink into such a state, that it has to feed him, instead of being fed by him. Society can no longer live under this bourgeoisie, in other words, its existence is no longer compatible with society.

5   The essential conditions for the existence and for the sway of the bourgeois class is the formation and augmentation of capital; the condition for capital is wage-labour. Wage-labour rests exclusively on competition between the labourers. The advance of industry, whose involuntary promoter is the bourgeoisie, replaces the isolation of the labourers, due to competition, by the
10 revolutionary combination, due to association. The development of Modern Industry, therefore, cuts from under its feet the very foundation on which the bourgeoisie produces and appropriates products. What the bourgeoisie therefore produces, above all, are its own grave-diggers. Its fall and the victory of the proletariat are equally inevitable.

II. PROLETARIANS AND COMMUNISTS

15   In what relation do the Communists stand to the proletarians as a whole? The Communists do not form a separate party opposed to the other working-class parties.

They have no interests separate and apart from those of the proletariat as a whole.

20   They do not set up any sectarian principles of their own, by which to shape and mould the proletarian movement.

The Communists are distinguished from the other working-class parties by this only:

(1) In the national struggles of the proletarians of the different countries,
25 they point out and bring to the front the common interests of the entire proletariat, independently of all nationality.

(2) In the various stages of development which the struggle of the working class against the bourgeoisie has to pass through, they always and everywhere represent the interests of the movement as a whole.

30   The Communists, therefore, are on the one hand, practically, the most advanced and resolute section of the working-class parties of every country, that section which pushes forward all others; on the other hand, theoretically, they have over the great mass of the proletariat the advantage of clearly understanding the lines of march, the conditions, and the ultimate general results
35 of the proletarian movement.

The immediate aim of the Communists is the same as that of all other proletarian parties: formation of the proletariat into a class, overthrow of the bourgeois supremacy, conquest of political power by the proletariat.

The theoretical conclusions of the Communists are in no way based on ideas or principles that have been invented, or discovered, by this or that would-be universal reformer.

They merely express, in general terms, actual relations springing from an existing class struggle, from a historical movement going on under our very eyes. The abolition of existing property relations is not at all a distinctive feature of communism.

All property relations in the past have continually been subject to historical change consequent upon the change in historical conditions.

The French Revolution, for example, abolished feudal property in favour of bourgeois property.

The distinguishing feature of Communism is not the abolition of property generally, but the abolition of bourgeois property. But modern bourgeois private property is the final and most complete expression of the system of producing and appropriating products, that is based on class antagonisms, on the exploitation of the many by the few.

In this sense, the theory of the Communists may be summed up in the single sentence: Abolition of private property.

We Communists have been reproached with the desire of abolishing the right of personally acquiring property as the fruit of a man's own labour, which property is alleged to be the groundwork of all personal freedom, activity and independence.

Hard-won, self-acquired, self-earned property! Do you mean the property of petty artisan and of the small peasant, a form of property that preceded the bourgeois form? There is no need to abolish that; the development of industry has to a great extent already destroyed it, and is still destroying it daily.

Or do you mean the modern bourgeois private property?

But does wage-labour create any property for the labourer? Not a bit. It creates capital, i.e., that kind of property which exploits wage-labour, and which cannot increase except upon condition of begetting a new supply of wage-labour for fresh exploitation. Property, in its present form, is based on the antagonism of capital and wage labour. Let us examine both sides of this antagonism.

To be a capitalist, is to have not only a purely personal, but a social status in production. Capital is a collective product, and only by the united action of many members, nay, in the last resort, only by the united action of all members of society, can it be set in motion.

Capital is therefore not only personal; it is a social power.

When, therefore, capital is converted into common property, into the property of all members of society, personal property is not thereby transformed into social property. It is only the social character of the property that is
5 changed. It loses its class character.

Let us now take wage-labour.

The average price of wage-labour is the minimum wage, i.e., that quantum of the means of subsistence which is absolutely requisite to keep the labourer in bare existence as a labourer. What, therefore, the wage-labourer appropriates by
10 means of his labour, merely suffices to prolong and reproduce a bare existence. We by no means intend to abolish this personal appropriation of the products of labour, an appropriation that is made for the maintenance and reproduction of human life, and that leaves no surplus wherewith to command the labour of others. All that we want to do away with is the miserable character of this
15 appropriation, under which the labourer lives merely to increase capital, and is allowed to live only in so far as the interest of the ruling class requires it.

In bourgeois society, living labour is but a means to increase accumulated labour. In Communist society, accumulated labour is but a means to widen, to enrich, to promote the existence of the labourer.
20   In bourgeois society, therefore, the past dominates the present; in Communist society, the present dominates the past. In bourgeois society capital is independent and has individuality, while the living person is dependent and has no individuality.

And the abolition of this state of things is called by the bourgeois, abolition
25 of individuality and freedom! And rightly so. The abolition of bourgeois individuality, bourgeois independence, and bourgeois freedom is undoubtedly aimed at.

By freedom is meant, under the present bourgeois conditions of production, free trade, free selling and buying.
30   But if selling and buying disappears, free selling and buying disappears also. This talk about free selling and buying, and all the other "brave words" of our bourgeois about freedom in general, have a meaning, if any, only in contrast with restricted selling and buying, with the fettered traders of the Middle Ages, but have no meaning when opposed to the Communistic abolition of buying and
35 selling, of the bourgeois conditions of production, and of the bourgeoisie itself.

You are horrified at our intending to do away with private property. But in your existing society, private property is already done away with for nine-tenths of the population; its existence for the few is solely due to its non-existence in the hands of those nine-tenths. You reproach us, therefore, with intending to do away with a form of property, the necessary condition for whose existence is the non-existence of any property for the immense majority of society.

In one word, you reproach us with intending to do away with your property. Precisely so; that is just what we intend.

5 From the moment when labour can no longer be converted into capital, money, or rent, into a social power capable of being monopolised, i.e., from the moment when individual property can no longer be transformed into bourgeois property, into capital, from that moment, you say, individuality vanishes.

You must, therefore, confess that by "individual" you mean no other person 10 than the bourgeois, than the middle-class owner of property. This person must, indeed, be swept out of the way, and made impossible.

Communism deprives no man of the power to appropriate the products of society; all that it does is to deprive him of the power to subjugate the labour of others by means of such appropriations.

15 It has been objected that upon the abolition of private property, all work will cease, and universal laziness will overtake us.

According to this, bourgeois society ought long ago to have gone to the dogs through sheer idleness; for those those of its members who work, acquire nothing, and those who acquire anything do not work. The whole of this 20 objection is but another expression of the tautology: that there can no longer be any wage-labour when there is no longer any capital.

All objections urged against the Communistic mode of producing and appropriating material products, have, in the same way, been urged against the Communistic mode of producing and appropriating intellectual products. Just as, 25 to the bourgeois, the disappearance of class property is the disappearance of production itself, so the disappearance of class culture is to him identical with the disappearance of all culture.

That culture, the loss of which he laments, is, for the enormous majority, a mere training to act as a machine.

30 But don't wrangle with us so long as you apply, to our intended abolition of bourgeois property, the standard of your bourgeois notions of freedom, culture, law, &c. Your very ideas are but the outgrowth of the conditions of your bourgeois production and bourgeois property, just as your jurisprudence is but the will of your class made into a law for all, a will whose essential character 35 and direction are determined by the economical conditions of existence of your class.

The selfish misconception that induces you to transform into eternal laws of nature and of reason, the social forms springing from your present mode of production and form of property – historical relations that rise and disappear in the progress of production – this misconception you share with every ruling class that has preceded you. What you see clearly in the case of ancient property, what you admit in the case of feudal property, you are of course forbidden to admit in the case of your own bourgeois form of property.

5   Abolition [Aufhebung] of the family! Even the most radical flare up at this infamous proposal of the Communists.

On what foundation is the present family, the bourgeois family, based? On capital, on private gain. In its completely developed form, this family exists only among the bourgeoisie. But this state of things finds its complement in the practical absence of the family among the proletarians, and in public prostitution.

The bourgeois family will vanish as a matter of course when its complement vanishes, and both will vanish with the vanishing of capital.

Do you charge us with wanting to stop the exploitation of children by their parents? To this crime we plead guilty.

But, you say, we destroy the most hallowed of relations, when we replace home education by social.

And your education! Is not that also social, and determined by the social conditions under which you educate, by the intervention direct or indirect, of society, by means of schools, &c.? The Communists have not invented the intervention of society in education; they do but seek to alter the character of that intervention, and to rescue education from the influence of the ruling class.

The bourgeois clap-trap about the family and education, about the hallowed co-relation of parents and child, becomes all the more disgusting, the more, by the action of Modern Industry, all the family ties among the proletarians are torn asunder, and their children transformed into simple articles of commerce and instruments of labour.

But you Communists would introduce community of women, screams the bourgeoisie in chorus.

The bourgeois sees his wife a mere instrument of production. He hears that the instruments of production are to be exploited in common, and, naturally, can come to no other conclusion that the lot of being common to all will likewise fall to the women.

He has not even a suspicion that the real point aimed at is to do away with the status of women as mere instruments of production.

For the rest, nothing is more ridiculous than the virtuous indignation of our bourgeois at the community of women which, they pretend, is to be openly and officially established by the Communists. The Communists have no need to introduce community of women; it has existed almost from time immemorial.

Our bourgeois, not content with having wives and daughters of their proletarians at their disposal, not to speak of common prostitutes, take the greatest pleasure in seducing each other's wives.

Bourgeois marriage is, in reality, a system of wives in common and thus, at

5　the most, what the Communists might possibly be reproached with is that they desire to introduce, in substitution for a hypocritically concealed, an openly legalised community of women. For the rest, it is self-evident that the abolition of the present system of production must bring with it the abolition of the community of women springing from that system, i.e., of prostitution both

10　public and private.

The Communists are further reproached with desiring to abolish countries and nationality.

The working men have no country. We cannot take from them what they have not got. Since the proletariat must first of all acquire political supremacy,

15　must rise to be the leading class of the nation, must constitute itself the nation, it is so far, itself national, though not in the bourgeois sense of the word.

National differences and antagonism between peoples are daily more and more vanishing, owing to the development of the bourgeoisie, to freedom of commerce, to the world market, to uniformity in the mode of production and in

20　the conditions of life corresponding thereto.

The supremacy of the proletariat will cause them to vanish still faster. United action, of the leading civilised countries at least, is one of the first conditions for the emancipation of the proletariat.

In proportion as the exploitation of one individual by another will also be

25　put an end to, the exploitation of one nation by another will also be put an end to. In proportion as the antagonism between classes within the nation vanishes, the hostility of one nation to another will come to an end.

The charges against Communism made from a religious, a philosophical and, generally, from an ideological standpoint, are not deserving of serious

30　examination.

Does it require deep intuition to comprehend that man's ideas, views, and conception, in one word, man's consciousness, changes with every change in the conditions of his material existence, in his social relations and in his social life?

What else does the history of ideas prove, than that intellectual production

35　changes its character in proportion as material production is changed? The ruling ideas of each age have ever been the ideas of its ruling class.

When people speak of the ideas that revolutionise society, they do but express that fact that within the old society the elements of a new one have been created, and that the dissolution of the old ideas keeps even pace with the dissolution of the old conditions of existence.

When the ancient world was in its last throes, the ancient religions were overcome by Christianity. When Christian ideas succumbed in the 18th century
5 to rationalist ideas, feudal society fought its death battle with the then revolutionary bourgeoisie. The ideas of religious liberty and freedom of conscience merely gave expression to the sway of free competition within the domain of knowledge.

"Undoubtedly," it will be said, "religious, moral, philosophical, and
10 juridical ideas have been modified in the course of historical development. But religion, morality, philosophy, political science, and law, constantly survived this change."

"There are, besides, eternal truths, such as Freedom, Justice, etc., that are common to all states of society. But Communism abolishes eternal truths, it
15 abolishes all religion, and all morality, instead of constituting them on a new basis; it therefore acts in contradiction to all past historical experience."

What does this accusation reduce itself to? The history of all past society has consisted in the development of class antagonisms, antagonisms that assumed different forms at different epochs.
20 But whatever form they may have taken, one fact is common to all past ages, viz., the exploitation of one part of society by the other. No wonder, then, that the social consciousness of past ages, despite all the multiplicity and variety it displays, moves within certain common forms, or general ideas, which cannot completely vanish except with the total disappearance of class antagonisms.
25 The Communist revolution is the most radical rupture with traditional relations; no wonder that its development involved the most radical rupture with traditional ideas.

But let us have done with the bourgeois objections to Communism.

We have seen above, that the first step in the revolution by the working
30 class is to raise the proletariat to the position of ruling class to win the battle of democracy.

The proletariat will use its political supremacy to wrest, by degree, all capital from the bourgeoisie, to centralise all instruments of production in the hands of the State, i.e., of the proletariat organised as the ruling class; and to
35 increase the total productive forces as rapidly as possible.

Of course, in the beginning, this cannot be effected except by means of despotic inroads on the rights of property, and on the conditions of bourgeois production; by means of measures, therefore, which appear economically insufficient and untenable, but which, in the course of the movement, outstrip themselves, necessitate further inroads upon the old social order, and are unavoidable as a means of entirely revolutionising the mode of production.

These measures will, of course, be different in different countries.

Nevertheless, in most advanced countries, the following will be pretty
5   generally applicable:

1. Abolition of property in land and application of all rents of land to public purposes.

2. A heavy progressive or graduated income tax.

3. Abolition of all rights of inheritance.
10   4. Confiscation of the property of all emigrants and rebels.

5. Centralisation of credit in the banks of the state, by means of a national bank with State capital and an exclusive monopoly.

6. Centralisation of the means of communication and transport in the hands of the State.
15   7. Extension of factories and instruments of production owned by the State; the bringing into cultivation of waste-lands, and the improvement of the soil generally in accordance with a common plan.

8. Equal liability of all to work. Establishment of industrial armies, especially for agriculture.
20   9. Combination of agriculture with manufacturing industries; gradual abolition of all the distinction between town and country by a more equable distribution of the populace over the country.

10. Free education for all children in public schools. Abolition of children's factory labour in its present form. Combination of education with
25   industrial production, &c, &c.

When, in the course of development, class distinctions have disappeared, and all production has been concentrated in the hands of a vast association of the whole nation, the public power will lose its political character. Political power, properly so called, is merely the organised power of one class for oppressing
30   another. If the proletariat during its contest with the bourgeoisie is compelled, by the force of circumstances, to organise itself as a class, if, by means of a revolution, it makes itself the ruling class, and, as such, sweeps away by force the old conditions of production, then it will, along with these conditions, have swept away the conditions for the existence of class antagonisms and of classes
35   generally, and will thereby have abolished its own supremacy as a class.

In place of the old bourgeois society, with its classes and class antagonisms, we shall have an association, in which the free development of each is the condition for the free development of all.

III. SOCIALIST AND COMMUNIST LITERATURE
1. Reactionary Socialism
A. Feudal Socialism

Owing to their historical position, it became the vocation of the aristocracies of France and England to write pamphlets against modern bourgeois society. In the French Revolution of July 1830, and in the English reform agitation[A], these aristocracies again succumbed to the hateful upstart.
5 Thenceforth, a serious political struggle was altogether out of the question. A literary battle alone remained possible. But even in the domain of literature the old cries of the restoration period had become impossible.

In order to arouse sympathy, the aristocracy was obliged to lose sight, apparently, of its own interests, and to formulate their indictment against the
10 bourgeoisie in the interest of the exploited working class alone. Thus, the aristocracy took their revenge by singing lampoons on their new masters and whispering in his ears sinister prophesies of coming catastrophe.

In this way arose feudal Socialism: half lamentation, half lampoon; half an echo of the past, half menace of the future; at times, by its bitter, witty and
15 incisive criticism, striking the bourgeoisie to the very heart's core; but always ludicrous in its effect, through total incapacity to comprehend the march of modern history.

The aristocracy, in order to rally the people to them, waved the proletarian alms-bag in front for a banner. But the people, so often as it joined them, saw on
20 their hindquarters the old feudal coats of arms, and deserted with loud and irreverent laughter.

One section of the French Legitimists and "Young England" exhibited this spectacle.

In pointing out that their mode of exploitation was different to that of the
25 bourgeoisie, the feudalists forget that they exploited under circumstances and conditions that were quite different and that are now antiquated. In showing that, under their rule, the modern proletariat never existed, they forget that the modern bourgeoisie is the necessary offspring of their own form of society.

For the rest, so little do they conceal the reactionary character of their
30 criticism that their chief accusation against the bourgeois amounts to this, that under the bourgeois régime a class is being developed which is destined to cut up root and branch the old order of society.

What they upbraid the bourgeoisie with is not so much that it creates a proletariat as that it creates a revolutionary proletariat.
35   In political practice, therefore, they join in all coercive measures against the working class; and in ordinary life, despite their high-falutin phrases, they stoop

284

to pick up the golden apples dropped from the tree of industry, and to barter truth, love, and honour, for traffic in wool, beetroot-sugar, and potato spirits.

As the parson has ever gone hand in hand with the landlord, so has Clerical Socialism with Feudal Socialism.

5   Nothing is easier than to give Christian asceticism a Socialist tinge. Has not Christianity declaimed against private property, against marriage, against the State? Has it not preached in the place of these, charity and poverty, celibacy and mortification of the flesh, monastic life and Mother Church? Christian Socialism is but the holy water with which the priest consecrates the heart-
10 burnings of the aristocrat.

B. Petty-Bourgeois Socialism

The feudal aristocracy was not the only class that was ruined by the bourgeoisie, not the only class whose conditions of existence pined and perished in the atmosphere of modern bourgeois society. The medieval burgesses and the small peasant proprietors were the precursors of the modern bourgeoisie. In
15 those countries which are but little developed, industrially and commercially, these two classes still vegetate side by side with the rising bourgeoisie.

In countries where modern civilisation has become fully developed, a new class of petty bourgeois has been formed, fluctuating between proletariat and bourgeoisie, and ever renewing itself as a supplementary part of bourgeois
20 society. The individual members of this class, however, are being constantly hurled down into the proletariat by the action of competition, and, as modern industry develops, they even see the moment approaching when they will completely disappear as an independent section of modern society, to be replaced in manufactures, agriculture and commerce, by overlookers, bailiffs
25 and shopmen.

In countries like France, where the peasants constitute far more than half of the population, it was natural that writers who sided with the proletariat against the bourgeoisie should use, in their criticism of the bourgeois régime, the standard of the peasant and petty bourgeois, and from the standpoint of these
30 intermediate classes, should take up the cudgels for the working class. Thus arose petty-bourgeois Socialism. Sismondi was the head of this school, not only in France but also in England.

This school of Socialism dissected with great acuteness the contradictions in the conditions of modern production. It laid bare the hypocritical apologies of
35 economists. It proved, incontrovertibly, the disastrous effects of machinery and division of labour; the concentration of capital and land in a few hands; overproduction and crises; it pointed out the inevitable ruin of the petty

bourgeois and peasant, the misery of the proletariat, the anarchy in production, the crying inequalities in the distribution of wealth, the industrial war of extermination between nations, the dissolution of old moral bonds, of the old family relations, of the old nationalities.

5   In its positive aims, however, this form of Socialism aspires either to restoring the old means of production and of exchange, and with them the old property relations, and the old society, or to cramping the modern means of production and of exchange within the framework of the old property relations that have been, and were bound to be, exploded by those means. In either case, it
10 is both reactionary and Utopian.

    Its last words are: corporate guilds for manufacture; patriarchal relations in agriculture.

    Ultimately, when stubborn historical facts had dispersed all intoxicating effects of self-deception, this form of Socialism ended in a miserable hangover.

C. German or "True" Socialism

15   The Socialist and Communist literature of France, a literature that originated under the pressure of a bourgeoisie in power, and that was the expressions of the struggle against this power, was introduced into Germany at a time when the bourgeoisie, in that country, had just begun its contest with feudal absolutism.

20   German philosophers, would-be philosophers, and beaux esprits (men of letters), eagerly seized on this literature, only forgetting, that when these writings immigrated from France into Germany, French social conditions had not immigrated along with them. In contact with German social conditions, this French literature lost all its immediate practical significance and assumed a
25 purely literary aspect. Thus, to the German philosophers of the Eighteenth Century, the demands of the first French Revolution were nothing more than the demands of "Practical Reason" in general, and the utterance of the will of the revolutionary French bourgeoisie signified, in their eyes, the laws of pure Will, of Will as it was bound to be, of true human Will generally.

30   The work of the German literati consisted solely in bringing the new French ideas into harmony with their ancient philosophical conscience, or rather, in annexing the French ideas without deserting their own philosophic point of view.

    This annexation took place in the same way in which a foreign language is
35 appropriated, namely, by translation.

    It is well known how the monks wrote silly lives of Catholic Saints over the manuscripts on which the classical works of ancient heathendom had been written. The German literati reversed this process with the profane French literature. They wrote their philosophical nonsense beneath the French original. For instance, beneath the French criticism of the economic functions of money, they wrote "Alienation of Humanity", and beneath the French criticism of the

5   bourgeois state they wrote "Dethronement of the Category of the General", and so forth.

     The introduction of these philosophical phrases at the back of the French historical criticisms, they dubbed "Philosophy of Action", "True Socialism", "German Science of Socialism", "Philosophical Foundation of Socialism", and

10   so on.

     The French Socialist and Communist literature was thus completely emasculated. And, since it ceased in the hands of the German to express the struggle of one class with the other, he felt conscious of having overcome "French one-sidedness" and of representing, not true requirements, but the

15   requirements of Truth; not the interests of the proletariat, but the interests of Human Nature, of Man in general, who belongs to no class, has no reality, who exists only in the misty realm of philosophical fantasy.

     This German socialism, which took its schoolboy task so seriously and solemnly, and extolled its poor stock-in-trade in such a mountebank fashion,

20   meanwhile gradually lost its pedantic innocence.

     The fight of the Germans, and especially of the Prussian bourgeoisie, against feudal aristocracy and absolute monarchy, in other words, the liberal movement, became more earnest.

     By this, the long-wished for opportunity was offered to "True" Socialism of

25   confronting the political movement with the Socialist demands, of hurling the traditional anathemas against liberalism, against representative government, against bourgeois competition, bourgeois freedom of the press, bourgeois legislation, bourgeois liberty and equality, and of preaching to the masses that they had nothing to gain, and everything to lose, by this bourgeois movement.

30   German Socialism forgot, in the nick of time, that the French criticism, whose silly echo it was, presupposed the existence of modern bourgeois society, with its corresponding economic conditions of existence, and the political constitution adapted thereto, the very things those attainment was the object of the pending struggle in Germany.

35   To the absolute governments, with their following of parsons, professors, country squires, and officials, it served as a welcome scarecrow against the threatening bourgeoisie.

It was a sweet finish, after the bitter pills of flogging and bullets, with which these same governments, just at that time, dosed the German working-class risings.

While this "True" Socialism thus served the government as a weapon for fighting the German bourgeoisie, it, at the same time, directly represented a reactionary interest, the interest of German Philistines. In Germany, the petty-bourgeois class, a relic of the sixteenth century, and since then constantly cropping up again under the various forms, is the real social basis of the existing state of things.

To preserve this class is to preserve the existing state of things in Germany. The industrial and political supremacy of the bourgeoisie threatens it with certain destruction — on the one hand, from the concentration of capital; on the other, from the rise of a revolutionary proletariat. "True" Socialism appeared to kill these two birds with one stone. It spread like an epidemic.

The robe of speculative cobwebs, embroidered with flowers of rhetoric, steeped in the dew of sickly sentiment, this transcendental robe in which the German Socialists wrapped their sorry "eternal truths", all skin and bone, served to wonderfully increase the sale of their goods amongst such a public.

And on its part German Socialism recognised, more and more, its own calling as the bombastic representative of the petty-bourgeois Philistine.

It proclaimed the German nation to be the model nation, and the German petty Philistine to be the typical man. To every villainous meanness of this model man, it gave a hidden, higher, Socialistic interpretation, the exact contrary of its real character. It went to the extreme length of directly opposing the "brutally destructive" tendency of Communism, and of proclaiming its supreme and impartial contempt of all class struggles. With very few exceptions, all the so-called Socialist and Communist publications that now (1847) circulate in Germany belong to the domain of this foul and enervating literature.

2. Conservative or Bourgeois Socialism

A part of the bourgeoisie is desirous of redressing social grievances in order to secure the continued existence of bourgeois society.

To this section belong economists, philanthropists, humanitarians, improvers of the condition of the working class, organisers of charity, members of societies for the prevention of cruelty to animals, temperance fanatics, hole-and-corner reformers of every imaginable kind. This form of socialism has, moreover, been worked out into complete systems.

We may cite Proudhon's Philosophis de la Misère as an example of this form.

The Socialistic bourgeois want all the advantages of modern social conditions without the struggles and dangers necessarily resulting therefrom. They desire the existing state of society, minus its revolutionary and disintegrating elements. They wish for a bourgeoisie without a proletariat. The
5   bourgeoisie naturally conceives the world in which it is supreme to be the best; and bourgeois Socialism develops this comfortable conception into various more or less complete systems. In requiring the proletariat to carry out such a system, and thereby to march straightway into the social New Jerusalem, it but requires in reality, that the proletariat should remain within the bounds of existing
10   society, but should cast away all its hateful ideas concerning the bourgeoisie.
       A second, and more practical, but less systematic, form of this Socialism sought to depreciate every revolutionary movement in the eyes of the working class by showing that no mere political reform, but only a change in the material conditions of existence, in economical relations, could be of any advantage to
15   them. By changes in the material conditions of existence, this form of Socialism, however, by no means understands abolition of the bourgeois relations of production, an abolition that can be affected only by a revolution, but administrative reforms, based on the continued existence of these relations; reforms, therefore, that in no respect affect the relations between capital and
20   labour, but, at the best, lessen the cost, and simplify the administrative work, of bourgeois government.
       Bourgeois Socialism attains adequate expression when, and only when, it becomes a mere figure of speech.
       Free trade: for the benefit of the working class. Protective duties: for the
25   benefit of the working class. Prison Reform: for the benefit of the working class. This is the last word and the only seriously meant word of bourgeois socialism.
       It is summed up in the phrase: the bourgeois is a bourgeois — for the benefit of the working class.

3. Critical-Utopian Socialism and Communism
       We do not here refer to that literature which, in every great modern
30   revolution, has always given voice to the demands of the proletariat, such as the writings of Babeuf and others.
       The first direct attempts of the proletariat to attain its own ends, made in times of universal excitement, when feudal society was being overthrown, necessarily failed, owing to the then undeveloped state of the proletariat, as well
35   as to the absence of the economic conditions for its emancipation, conditions that had yet to be produced, and could be produced by the impending bourgeois epoch alone. The revolutionary literature that accompanied these first

movements of the proletariat had necessarily a reactionary character. It inculcated universal asceticism and social levelling in its crudest form.

The Socialist and Communist systems, properly so called, those of Saint-Simon, Fourier, Owen, and others, spring into existence in the early undeveloped period, described above, of the struggle between proletariat and bourgeoisie (see Section 1. Bourgeois and Proletarians).

The founders of these systems see, indeed, the class antagonisms, as well as the action of the decomposing elements in the prevailing form of society. But the proletariat, as yet in its infancy, offers to them the spectacle of a class without any historical initiative or any independent political movement.

Since the development of class antagonism keeps even pace with the development of industry, the economic situation, as they find it, does not as yet offer to them the material conditions for the emancipation of the proletariat. They therefore search after a new social science, after new social laws, that are to create these conditions.

Historical action is to yield to their personal inventive action; historically created conditions of emancipation to fantastic ones; and the gradual, spontaneous class organisation of the proletariat to an organisation of society especially contrived by these inventors. Future history resolves itself, in their eyes, into the propaganda and the practical carrying out of their social plans.

In the formation of their plans, they are conscious of caring chiefly for the interests of the working class, as being the most suffering class. Only from the point of view of being the most suffering class does the proletariat exist for them.

The undeveloped state of the class struggle, as well as their own surroundings, causes Socialists of this kind to consider themselves far superior to all class antagonisms. They want to improve the condition of every member of society, even that of the most favoured. Hence, they habitually appeal to society at large, without the distinction of class; nay, by preference, to the ruling class. For how can people, when once they understand their system, fail to see in it the best possible plan of the best possible state of society?

Hence, they reject all political, and especially all revolutionary action; they wish to attain their ends by peaceful means, necessarily doomed to failure, and by the force of example, to pave the way for the new social Gospel.

Such fantastic pictures of future society, painted at a time when the proletariat is still in a very undeveloped state and has but a fantastic conception of its own position, correspond with the first instinctive yearnings of that class for a general reconstruction of society.

But these Socialist and Communist publications contain also a critical element. They attack every principle of existing society. Hence, they are full of the most valuable materials for the enlightenment of the working class. The practical measures proposed in them — such as the abolition of the distinction
5 between town and country, of the family, of the carrying on of industries for the account of private individuals, and of the wage system, the proclamation of social harmony, the conversion of the function of the state into a more superintendence of production — all these proposals point solely to the disappearance of class antagonisms which were, at that time, only just cropping
10 up, and which, in these publications, are recognised in their earliest indistinct and undefined forms only. These proposals, therefore, are of a purely Utopian character.

The significance of Critical-Utopian Socialism and Communism bears an inverse relation to historical development. In proportion as the modern class
15 struggle develops and takes definite shape, this fantastic standing apart from the contest, these fantastic attacks on it, lose all practical value and all theoretical justification. Therefore, although the originators of these systems were, in many respects, revolutionary, their disciples have, in every case, formed mere reactionary sects. They hold fast by the original views of their masters, in
20 opposition to the progressive historical development of the proletariat. They, therefore, endeavour, and that consistently, to deaden the class struggle and to reconcile the class antagonisms. They still dream of experimental realisation of their social Utopias, of founding isolated "phalansteres", of establishing "Home Colonies", or setting up a "Little Icaria" — duodecimo editions of the New
25 Jerusalem — and to realise all these castles in the air, they are compelled to appeal to the feelings and purses of the bourgeois. By degrees, they sink into the category of the reactionary [or] conservative Socialists depicted above, differing from these only by more systematic pedantry, and by their fanatical and superstitious belief in the miraculous effects of their social science.
30 They, therefore, violently oppose all political action on the part of the working class; such action, according to them, can only result from blind unbelief in the new Gospel.

The Owenites in England, and the Fourierists in France, respectively, oppose the Chartists and the Réformistes.

IV. POSITION OF THE COMMUNISTS IN RELATION TO THE VARIOUS EXISTING OPPOSITION PARTIES

Section II has made clear the relations of the Communists to the existing working-class parties, such as the Chartists in England and the Agrarian Reformers in America.

5 The Communists fight for the attainment of the immediate aims, for the enforcement of the momentary interests of the working class; but in the movement of the present, they also represent and take care of the future of that movement. In France, the Communists ally with the Social-Democrats against the conservative and radical bourgeoisie, reserving, however, the right to take up a critical position in regard to phases and illusions traditionally handed down

10 from the great Revolution.

In Switzerland, they support the Radicals, without losing sight of the fact that this party consists of antagonistic elements, partly of Democratic Socialists, in the French sense, partly of radical bourgeois.

In Poland, they support the party that insists on an agrarian revolution as the

15 prime condition for national emancipation, that party which fomented the insurrection of Cracow in 1846.

In Germany, they fight with the bourgeoisie whenever it acts in a revolutionary way, against the absolute monarchy, the feudal squirearchy, and the petty bourgeoisie.

20 But they never cease, for a single instant, to instill into the working class the clearest possible recognition of the hostile antagonism between bourgeoisie and proletariat, in order that the German workers may straightway use, as so many weapons against the bourgeoisie, the social and political conditions that the bourgeoisie must necessarily introduce along with its supremacy, and in order

25 that, after the fall of the reactionary classes in Germany, the fight against the bourgeoisie itself may immediately begin.

The Communists turn their attention chiefly to Germany, because that country is on the eve of a bourgeois revolution that is bound to be carried out under more advanced conditions of European civilisation and with a much more

30 developed proletariat than that of England was in the seventeenth, and France in the eighteenth century, and because the bourgeois revolution in Germany will be but the prelude to an immediately following proletarian revolution.

In short, the Communists everywhere support every revolutionary movement against the existing social and political order of things.

35 In all these movements, they bring to the front, as the leading question in each, the property question, no matter what its degree of development at the time.

Finally, they labour everywhere for the union and agreement of the democratic parties of all countries.

The Communists disdain to conceal their views and aims. They openly declare that their ends can be attained only by the forcible overthrow of all
5   existing social conditions. Let the ruling classes tremble at a Communistic revolution. The proletarians have nothing to lose but their chains. They have a world to win.

WORKING MEN OF ALL COUNTRIES, UNITE!

John Stuart Mill

John Stuart Mill (b. 1806, London, d. 1873, Avignon) was an English philosopher, journalist, and politician. His early life was deeply influenced by the classic utilitarians' ideas on progressive (scientific) education, advocated by his father, a key utilitarian philosopher and a close disciple of Jeremy Bentham. Although a prolific writer, Mill had a parallel successful career as an administrator in the British East India Company and served briefly as a member of Parliament. Mill's late marriage to Harriett Taylor brought him a measure of personal happiness that had remained unfilled by his professional successes. Taylor's feminism, which he wholeheartedly embraced, and classic utilitarianism, with which Mill had been engaged in dialogue since his teenage rebellion against his father's ideas, became two of the most lasting influences on his work. He admired the convictions of socialists like Marx but, in the end, was skeptical both about the practicality of their ideas and about their possible effect on individual liberty.

Mill's most important contributions to political philosophy include *On Liberty*, *Utilitarianism*, and *Considerations on Representative Government*. He was also the author of a highly influential economic text of his day, *Principles of Political Economy*, and of *A System of Logic* – a systematic analysis of inductive proofs.

Mill's most enduring political contribution is his defense of the open society, which has made his name synonymous with classical liberalism and his work a key resource for the critics of Soviet totalitarianism such as F. von Hayek and others.

John Stuart Mill
ON LIBERTY
(1879)

The grand, leading principle, towards which every argument; unfolded in
these pages directly converges, is the absolute and essential importance of
human development in its richest diversity.
Wilhelm von Humboldt: *Sphere and Duties of Government.*

TO the beloved and deplored memory of her who was the inspirer, and in
part the author, of all that is best in my writings — the friend and wife whose
5   exalted sense of truth and right was my strongest incitement, and whose
approbation was my chief reward — I dedicate this volume. Like all that I have
written for many years, it belongs as much to her as to me; but the work as it
stands has had, in a very insufficient degree, the inestimable advantage of her
revision; some of the most important portions having been reserved for a more
10   careful reexamination, which they are now never destined to receive. Were I but
capable of interpreting to the world one half the great thoughts and noble
feelings which are buried in her grave, I should be the medium of a greater
benefit to it, than is ever likely to arise from anything that I can write,
unprompted and unassisted by her all but unrivalled wisdom.

CHAPTER I.
Introductory.
15   THE subject of this Essay is not the so-called Liberty of the Will, so
unfortunately opposed to the misnamed doctrine of Philosophical Necessity; but
Civil, or Social Liberty: the nature and limits of the power which can be
legitimately exercised by society over the individual. A question seldom stated,
and hardly ever discussed, in general terms, but which profoundly influences the
20   practical controversies of the age by its latent presence, and is likely soon to
make itself recognized as the vital question of the future. It is so far from being
new, that, in a certain sense, it has divided mankind, almost from the remotest
ages, but in the stage of progress into which the more civilized portions of the
species have now entered, it presents itself under new conditions, and requires a
25   different and more fundamental treatment.
      The struggle between Liberty and Authority is the most conspicuous feature
in the portions of history with which we are earliest familiar, particularly in that
of Greece, Rome, and England. But in old times this contest was between

subjects, or some classes of subjects, and the government. By liberty, was meant protection against the tyranny of the political rulers. The rulers were conceived (except in some of the popular governments of Greece) as in a necessarily antagonistic position to the people whom they ruled. They consisted of a
5   governing One, or a governing tribe or caste, who derived their authority from inheritance or conquest; who, at all events, did not hold it at the pleasure of the governed, and whose supremacy men did not venture, perhaps did not desire, to contest, whatever precautions might be taken against its oppressive exercise. Their power was regarded as necessary, but also as highly dangerous; as a
10   weapon which they would attempt to use against their subjects, no less than against external enemies. To prevent the weaker members of the community from being preyed upon by innumerable vultures, it was needful that there should be an animal of prey stronger than the rest, commissioned to keep them down. But as the king of the vultures would be no less bent upon preying on the
15   flock than any of the minor harpies, it was indispensable to be in a perpetual attitude of defence against his beak and claws. The aim, therefore, of patriots, was to set limits to the power which the ruler should be suffered to exercise over the community; and this limitation was what they meant by liberty. It was attempted in two ways. First, by obtaining a recognition of certain immunities,
20   called political liberties or rights, which it was to be regarded as a breach of duty in the ruler to infringe, and which, if he did infringe, specific resistance, or general rebellion, was held to be justifiable. A second, and generally a later expedient, was the establishment of constitutional checks; by which the consent of the community, or of a body of some sort supposed to represent its interests,
25   was made a necessary condition to some of the more important acts of the governing power. To the first of these modes of limitation, the ruling power, in most European countries, was compelled, more or less, to submit. It was not so with the second; and to attain this, or when already in some degree possessed, to attain it more completely, became everywhere the principal object of the lovers
30   of liberty. And so long as mankind were content to combat one enemy by another, and to be ruled by a master, on condition of being guaranteed more or less efficaciously against his tyranny, they did not carry their aspirations beyond this point.

     A time, however, came, in the progress of human affairs, when men ceased
35   to think it a necessity of nature that their governors should be an independent power, opposed in interest to themselves. It appeared to them much better that the various magistrates of the State should be their tenants or delegates, revocable at their pleasure. In that way alone, it seemed, could they have complete security that the powers of government would never be abused to their
40   disadvantage. By degrees, this new demand for elective and temporary rulers

became the prominent object of the exertions of the popular party, wherever any such party existed; and superseded, to a considerable extent, the previous efforts to limit the power of rulers. As the struggle proceeded for making the ruling power emanate from the periodical choice of the ruled, some persons began to
5 think that too much importance had been attached to the limitation of the power itself. *That* (it might seem) was a resource against rulers whose interests were habitually opposed to those of the people. What was now wanted was, that the rulers should be identified with the people; that their interest and will should be the interest and will of the nation. The nation did not need to be protected
10 against its own will. There was no fear of its tyrannizing over itself. Let the rulers be effectually responsible to it, promptly removable by it, and it could afford to trust them with power of which it could itself dictate the use to be made. Their power was but the nation's own power, concentrated, and in a form convenient for exercise. This mode of thought, or rather perhaps of feeling, was
15 common among the last generation of European liberalism, in the Continental section of which, it still apparently predominates. Those who admit any limit to what a government may do, except in the case of such governments as they think ought not to exist, stand out as brilliant exceptions among the political thinkers of the Continent. A similar tone of sentiment might by this time have
20 been prevalent in our own country, if the circumstances which for a time encouraged it had continued unaltered.

But, in political and philosophical theories, as well as in persons, success discloses faults and infirmities which failure might have concealed from observation. The notion, that the people have no need to limit their power over
25 themselves, might seem axiomatic, when popular government was a thing only dreamed about, or read of as having existed at some distant period of the past. Neither was that notion necessarily disturbed by such temporary aberrations as those of the French Revolution, the worst of which were the work of an usurping few, and which, in any case, belonged, not to the permanent working of popular
30 institutions, but to a sudden and convulsive outbreak against monarchical and aristocratic despotism. In time, however, a democratic republic came to occupy a large portion of the earth's surface, and made itself felt as one of the most powerful members of the community of nations; and elective and responsible government became subject to the observations and criticisms which wait upon
35 a great existing fact. It was now perceived that such phrases as "self-government," and "the power of the people over themselves," do not express the true state of the case. The "people" who exercise the power, are not always the same people with those over whom it is exercised, and the "self-government" spoken of, is not the government of each by himself, but of each by all the rest.
40 The will of the people, moreover, practically means, the will of the most

numerous or the most active *part* of the people; the majority, or those who
succeed in making themselves accepted as the majority: the people,
consequently, *may* desire to oppress a part of their number; and precautions are
as much needed against this, as against any other abuse of power. The limitation,
5   therefore, of the power of government over individuals, loses none of its
importance when the holders of power are regularly accountable to the
community, that is, to the strongest party therein. This view of things,
recommending itself equally to the intelligence of thinkers and to the inclination
of those important classes in European society to whose real or supposed
10   interests democracy is adverse, has had no difficulty in establishing itself; and in
political speculations "the tyranny of the majority" is now generally included
among the evils against which society requires to be on its guard.

Like other tyrannies, the tyranny of the majority was at first, and is still
vulgarly, held in dread, chiefly as operating through the acts of the public
15   authorities. But reflecting persons perceived that when society is itself the tyrant
— society collectively, over the separate individuals who compose it — its
means of tyrannizing are not restricted to the acts which it may do by the hands
of its political functionaries. Society can and does execute its own mandates:
and if it issues wrong mandates instead of right, or any mandates at all in things
20   with which it ought not to meddle, it practises a social tyranny more formidable
than many kinds of political oppression, since, though not usually upheld by
such extreme penalties, it leaves fewer means of escape, penetrating much more
deeply into the details of life, and enslaving the soul itself. Protection, therefore,
against the tyranny of the magistrate is not enough; there needs protection also
25   against the tyranny of the prevailing opinion and feeling; against the tendency of
society to impose, by other means than civil penalties, its own ideas and
practices as rules of conduct on those who dissent from them; to fetter the
development, and, if possible, prevent the formation, of any individuality not in
harmony with its ways, and compel all characters to fashion themselves upon
30   the model of its own. There is a limit to the legitimate interference of collective
opinion with individual independence; and to find that limit, and maintain it
against encroachment, is as indispensable to a good condition of human affairs,
as protection against political despotism.

But though this proposition is not likely to be contested in general terms,
35   the practical question, where to place the limit — how to make the fitting
adjustment between individual independence and social control — is a subject
on which nearly everything remains to be done. All that makes existence
valuable to any one, depends on the enforcement of restraints upon the actions
of other people. Some rules of conduct, therefore, must be imposed, by law in
40   the first place, and by opinion on many things which are not fit subjects for the

operation of law. What these rules should be, is the principal question in human affairs; but if we except a few of the most obvious cases, it is one of those which least progress has been made in resolving. No two ages, and scarcely any two countries, have decided it alike; and the decision of one age or country is a

5 wonder to another. Yet the people of any given age and country no more suspect any difficulty in it, than if it were a subject on which mankind had always been agreed. The rules which obtain among themselves appear to them self-evident and self-justifying. This all but universal illusion is one of the examples of the magical influence of custom, which is not only, as the proverb says, a second

10 nature, but is continually mistaken for the first. The effect of custom, in preventing any misgiving respecting the rules of conduct which mankind impose on one another, is all the more complete because the subject is one on which it is not generally considered necessary that reasons should be given, either by one person to others, or by each to himself. People are accustomed to believe, and

15 have been encouraged in the belief by some who aspire to the character of philosophers, that their feelings, on subjects of this nature, are better than reasons, and render reasons unnecessary. The practical principle which guides them to their opinions on the regulation of human conduct, is the feeling in each person's mind that everybody should be required to act as he, and those with

20 whom he sympathizes, would like them to act. No one, indeed, acknowledges to himself that his standard of judgment is his own liking; but an opinion on a point of conduct, not supported by reasons, can only count as one person's preference; and if the reasons, when given, are a mere appeal to a similar preference felt by other people, it is still only many people's liking instead of one. To an ordinary

25 man, however, his own preference, thus supported, is not only a perfectly satisfactory reason, but the only one he generally has for any of his notions of morality, taste, or propriety, which are not expressly written in his religious creed; and his chief guide in the interpretation even of that. Men's opinions, accordingly, on what is laudable or blameable, are affected by all the

30 multifarious causes which influence their wishes in regard to the conduct of others, and which are as numerous as those which determine their wishes on any other subject. Sometimes their reason — at other times their prejudices or superstitions: often their social affections, not seldom their antisocial ones, their envy or jealousy, their arrogance or contemptuousness: but most commonly,

35 their desires or fears for themselves — their legitimate or illegitimate self-interest. Wherever there is an ascendant class, a large portion of the morality of the country emanates from its class interests, and its feelings of class superiority. The morality between Spartans and Helots, between planters and negroes, between princes and subjects, between nobles and roturiers, between men and

40 women, has been for the most part the creation of these class interests and

feelings: and the sentiments thus generated, react in turn upon the moral feelings of the members of the ascendant class, in their relations among themselves. Where, on the other hand, a class, formerly ascendant, has lost its ascendency, or where its ascendency is unpopular, the prevailing moral sentiments frequently
5   bear the impress of an impatient dislike of superiority Another grand determining principle of the rules of conduct, both in act and forbearance which have been enforced by law or opinion, has been the servility of mankind towards the supposed preferences or aversions of their temporal masters, or of their gods. This servility, though essentially selfish, is not hypocrisy; it gives rise to
10   perfectly genuine sentiments of abhorrence; it made men burn magicians and heretics. Among so many baser influences, the general and obvious interests of society have of course had a share, and a large one, in the direction of the moral sentiments: less, however, as a matter of reason, and on their own account, than as a consequence of the sympathies and antipathies which grew out of them: and
15   sympathies and antipathies which had little or nothing to do with the interests of society, have made themselves felt in the establishment of moralities with quite as great force.

     The likings and dislikings of society, or of some powerful portion of it, are thus the main thing which has practically determined the rules laid down for
20   general observance, under the penalties of law or opinion. And in general, those who have been in advance of society in thought and feeling, have left this condition of things unassailed in principle, however they may have come into conflict with it in some of its details. They have occupied themselves rather in inquiring what things society ought to like or dislike, than in questioning
25   whether its likings or dislikings should be a law to individuals. They preferred endeavoring to alter the feelings of mankind on the particular points on which they were themselves heretical, rather than make common cause in defence of freedom, with heretics generally. The only case in which the higher ground has been taken on principle and maintained with consistency, by any but an
30   individual here and there, is that of religious belief: a case instructive in many ways, and not least so as forming a most striking instance of the fallibility of what is called the moral sense: for the *odium theologicum,* in a sincere bigot, is one of the most unequivocal cases of moral feeling. Those who first broke the yoke of what called itself the Universal Church, were in general as little willing
35   to permit difference of religious opinion as that church itself. But when the heat of the conflict was over, without giving a complete victory to any party, and each church or sect was reduced to limit its hopes to retaining possession of the ground it already occupied; minorities, seeing that they had no chance of becoming majorities, were under the necessity of pleading to those whom they
40   could not convert, for permission to differ. It is accordingly on this battle-field,

almost solely, that the rights of the individual against society have been asserted on broad grounds of principle, and the claim of society to exercise authority over dissentients openly controverted. The great writers to whom the world owes what religious liberty it possesses, have mostly asserted freedom of conscience as an indefeasible right, and denied absolutely that a human being is accountable to others for his religious belief Yet so natural to mankind is intolerance in whatever they really care about, that religious freedom has hardly anywhere been practically realized, except where religious indifference, which dislikes to have its peace disturbed by theological quarrels, has added its weight to the scale. In the minds of almost all religious persons, even in the most tolerant countries, the duty of toleration is admitted with tacit reserves. One person will bear with dissent in matters of church government, but not of dogma; another can tolerate everybody, short of a Papist or an Unitarian; another, every one who believes in revealed religion; a few extend their charity a little further, but stop at the belief in a God and in a future state. Wherever the sentiment of the majority is still genuine and intense, it is found to have abated little of its claim to be obeyed.

In England, from the peculiar circumstances of our political history, though the yoke of opinion is perhaps heavier, that of law is lighter, than in most other countries of Europe; and there is considerable jealousy of direct interference, by the legislative or the executive power with private conduct; not so much from any just regard for the independence of the individual, as from the still subsisting habit of looking on the government as representing an opposite interest to the public. The majority have not yet learnt to feel the power of the government their power, or its opinions their opinions. When they do so, individual liberty will probably be as much exposed to invasion from the government, as it already is from public opinion. But, as yet, there is a considerable amount of feeling ready to be called forth against any attempt of the law to control individuals in things in which they have not hitherto been accustomed to be controlled by it; and this with very little discrimination as to whether the matter is, or is not, within the legitimate sphere of legal control; insomuch that the feeling, highly salutary on the whole, is perhaps quite as often misplaced as well grounded in the particular instances of its application. There is, in fact, no recognized principle by which the propriety or impropriety of government interference is customarily tested. People decide according to their personal preferences. Some, whenever they see any good to be done, or evil to be remedied, would willingly instigate the government to undertake the business; while others prefer to bear almost any amount of social evil, rather than add one to the departments of human interests amenable to governmental control. And men range themselves on one or the other side in any particular

case, according to this general direction of their sentiments; or according to the degree of interest which they feel in the particular thing which it is proposed that the government should do; or according to the belief they entertain that the government would, or would not, do it in the manner they prefer; but very rarely
5 on account of any opinion to which they consistently adhere, as to what things are fit to be done by a government. And it seems to me that, in consequence of this absence of rule or principle, one side is at present as often wrong as the other; the interference of government is, with about equal frequency, improperly invoked and improperly condemned.
10   The object of this Essay is to assert one very simple principle, as entitled to govern absolutely the dealings of society with the individual in the way of compulsion and control, whether the means used be physical force in the form of legal penalties, or the moral coercion of public opinion. That principle is, that the sole end for which mankind are warranted, individually or collectively, in
15 interfering with the liberty of action of any of their number, is self-protection. That the only purpose for which power can be rightfully exercised over any member of a civilized community, against his will, is to prevent harm to others. His own good, either physical or moral, is not a sufficient warrant. He cannot rightfully be compelled to do or forbear because it will be better for him to do
20 so, because it will make him happier, because, in the opinions of others, to do so would be wise, or even right These are good reasons for remonstrating with him, or reasoning with him, or persuading him or entreating him, but not for compelling him, or visiting him with any evil, in case he do other wise. To justify that, the conduct from which it is desired to deter him must be calculated
25 to produce evil to some one else. The only part of the conduct of any one, for which he is amenable to society, is that which concerns others. In the part which merely concerns himself, his independence is, of right, absolute. Over himself, over his own body and mind, the individual is sovereign.
     It is, perhaps, hardly necessary to say that this doctrine is meant to apply
30 only to human beings in the maturity of their faculties. We are not speaking of children, or of young persons below the age which the law may fix as that of manhood or womanhood. Those who are still in a state to require being taken care of by others, must be protected against their own actions as well as against external injury. For the same reason, we may leave out of consideration those
35 backward states of society in which the race itself may be considered as in its nonage. The early difficulties in the way of spontaneous progress are so great, that there is seldom any choice of means for overcoming them; and a ruler full of the spirit of improvement is warranted in the use of any expedients that will attain an end, perhaps otherwise unattainable. Despotism is a legitimate mode of
40 government in dealing with barbarians, provided the end be their improvement,

and the means justified by actually effecting that end. Liberty, as a principle, has no application to any state of things anterior to the time when mankind have become capable of being improved by free and equal discussion. Until then, there is nothing for them but implicit obedience to an Akbar or a Charlemagne, if they are so fortunate as to find one. But as soon as mankind have attained the capacity of being guided to their own improvement by conviction or persuasion (a period long since reached in all nations with whom we need here concern ourselves), compulsion, either in the direct form or in that of pains and penalties for non-compliance, is no longer admissible as a means to their own good, and justifiable only for the security of others.

It is proper to state that I forego any advantage which could be derived to my argument from the idea of abstract right, as a thing independent of utility. I regard utility as the ultimate appeal on all ethical questions; but it must be utility in the largest sense, grounded on the permanent interests of man as a progressive being. Those interests, I contend, authorize the subjection of individual spontaneity to external control, only in respect to those actions of each, which concern the interest of other people. If any one does an act hurtful to others, there is a *primâ facie* case for punishing him, by law, or, where legal penalties are not safely applicable, by general disapprobation. There are also many positive acts for the benefit of others, which he may rightfully be compelled to perform; such as, to give evidence in a court of justice; to bear his fair share in the common defence, or in any other joint work necessary to the interest of the society of which he enjoys the protection; and to perform certain acts of individual beneficence, such as saving a fellow creature's life, or interposing to protect the defenceless against ill-usage, things which whenever it is obviously a man's duty to do, he may rightfully be made responsible to society for not doing A person may cause evil to others not only by his actions but by his inaction, and in either case he is justly accountable to them for the injury. The latter case, it is true, requires a much more cautious exercise of compulsion than the former. To make any one answerable for doing evil to others, is the rule; to make him answerable for not preventing evil, is, comparatively speaking, the exception. Yet there are many cases clear enough and grave enough to justify that exception. In all things which regard the external relations of the individual, he is *de jure* amenable to those whose interests are concerned, and if need be, to society as their protector. There are often good reasons for not holding him to the responsibility; but these reasons must arise from the special expediencies of the case: either because it is a kind of case in which he is on the whole likely to act better, when left to his own discretion, than when controlled in any way in which society have it in their power to control him; or because the attempt to exercise control would produce other evils, greater than those which it would prevent. When such reasons as these preclude the enforcement of responsibility, the conscience of the agent himself should step into the vacant judgment-seat, and protect those interests of others which have no external protection; judging himself all the more rigidly, because the case does not admit of his being made

5   accountable to the judgment of his fellow-creatures.

But there is a sphere of action in which society, as distinguished from the individual, has, if any, only an indirect interest; comprehending all that portion of a person's life and conduct which affects only himself, or, if it also affects others, only with their free, voluntary, and undeceived consent and participation.

10   When I say only himself, I mean directly, and in the first instance: for whatever affects himself, may affect others *through* himself; and the objection which may be grounded on this contingency, will receive consideration in the sequel. This, then, is the appropriate region of human liberty. It comprises, first, the inward domain of consciousness; demanding liberty of conscience, in the most

15   comprehensive sense; liberty of thought and feeling; absolute freedom of opinion and sentiment on all subjects, practical or speculative, scientific, moral, or theological. The liberty of expressing and publishing opinions may seem to fall under a different principle, since it belongs to that part of the conduct of an individual which concerns other people; but, being almost of as much

20   importance as the liberty of thought itself, and resting in great part on the same reasons, is practically inseparable from it. Secondly, the principle requires liberty of tastes and pursuits; of framing the plan of our life to suit our own character; of doing as we like, subject to such consequences as may follow; without impediment from our fellow-creatures, so long as what we do does not

25   harm them, even though they should think our conduct foolish, perverse, or wrong. Thirdly, from this liberty of each individual, follows the liberty, within the same limits, of combination among individuals; freedom to unite, for any purpose not involving harm to others: the persons combining being supposed to be of full age, and not forced or deceived.

30   No society in which these liberties are not, on the whole, respected, is free, whatever may be its form of government; and none is completely free in which they do not exist absolute and unqualified. The only freedom which deserves the name, is that of pursuing our own good in our own way, so long as we do not attempt to deprive others of theirs, or impede their efforts to obtain it. Each is

35   the proper guardian of his own health, whether bodily, or mental and spiritual. Mankind are greater gainers by suffering each other to live as seems good to themselves, than by compelling each to live as seems good to the rest.

Though this doctrine is anything but new, and, to some persons, may have the air of a truism, there is no doctrine which stands more directly opposed to

40   the general tendency of existing opinion and practice. Society has expended

fully as much effort in the attempt (according to its lights) to compel people to conform to its notions of personal, as of social excellence. The ancient commonwealths thought themselves entitled to practise, and the ancient philosophers countenanced, the regulation of every part of private conduct by
5   public authority, on the ground that the State had a deep interest in the whole bodily and mental discipline of every one of its citizens; a mode of thinking which may have been admissible in small republics surrounded by powerful enemies, in constant peril of being subverted by foreign attack or internal commotion, and to which even a short interval of relaxed energy and self-
10 command might so easily be fatal, that they could not afford to wait for the salutary permanent effects of freedom. In the modern world, the greater size of political communities, and above all, the separation between the spiritual and temporal authority (which placed the direction of men's consciences in other hands than those which controlled their worldly affairs), prevented so great an
15 interference by law in the details of private life; but the engines of moral repression have been wielded more strenuously against divergence from the reigning opinion in self-regarding, than even in social matters; religion, the most powerful of the elements which have entered into the formation of moral feeling, having almost always been governed either by the ambition of a
20 hierarchy, seeking control over every department of human conduct, or by the spirit of Puritanism. And some of those modern reformers who have placed themselves in strongest opposition to the religions of the past, have been noway behind either churches or sects in their assertion of the right of spiritual domination: M. Comte, in particular, whose social system, as unfolded in his
25 *Traité de Politique Positive,* aims at establishing (though by moral more than by legal appliances) a despotism of society over the individual, surpassing anything contemplated in the political ideal of the most rigid disciplinarian among the ancient philosophers.

Apart from the peculiar tenets of individual thinkers, there is also in the
30 world at large an increasing inclination to stretch unduly the powers of society over the individual, both by the force of opinion and even by that of legislation: and as the tendency of all the changes taking place in the world is to strengthen society, and diminish the power of the individual, this encroachment is not one of the evils which tend spontaneously to disappear, but, on the contrary, to grow
35 more and more formidable. The disposition of mankind, whether as rulers or as fellow-citizens, to impose their own opinions and inclinations as a rule of conduct on others, is so energetically supported by some of the best and by some of the worst feelings incident to human nature, that it is hardly ever kept under restraint by anything but want of power; and as the power is not declining, but
40 growing, unless a strong barrier of moral conviction can be raised against the

mischief, we must expect, in the present circumstances of the world, to see it increase.

It will be convenient for the argument, if, instead of at once entering upon the general thesis, we confine ourselves in the first instance to a single branch of
5   it, on which the principle here stated is, if not fully, yet to a certain point, recognized by the current opinions. This one branch is the Liberty of Thought: from which it is impossible to separate the cognate liberty of speaking and of writing. Although these liberties, to some considerable amount, form part of the political morality of all countries which profess religious toleration and free
10 institutions, the grounds, both philosophical and practical, on which they rest, are perhaps not so familiar to the general mind, nor so thoroughly appreciated by many even of the leaders of opinion, as might have been expected. Those grounds, when rightly understood, are of much wider application than to only one division of the subject, and a thorough consideration of this part of the
15 question will be found the best introduction to the remainder. Those to whom nothing which I am about to say will be new, may therefore, I hope, excuse me, if on a subject which for now three centuries has been so often discussed, I venture on one discussion more.

CHAPTER II.
Of the liberty of thought and discussion.

THE time, it is to be hoped, is gone by when any defence would be
20 necessary of the "liberty of the press" as one of the securities against corrupt or tyrannical government. No argument, we may suppose, can now be needed, against permitting a legislature or an executive, not identified in interest with the people, to prescribe opinions to them, and determine what doctrines or what arguments they shall be allowed to hear. This aspect of the question, besides, has
25 been so often and so triumphantly enforced by preceding writers, that it needs not be specially insisted on in this place. Though the law of England, on the subject of the press, is as servile to this day as it was in the time of the Tudors, there is little danger of its being actually put in force against political discussion, except during some temporary panic, when fear of insurrection drives ministers
30 and judges from their propriety;[1] and, speaking generally, it is not, in constitutional countries, to be apprehended, that the government, whether completely responsible to the people or not, will often attempt to control the expression of opinion, except when in doing so it makes itself the organ of the general intolerance of the public. Let us suppose, therefore, that the government
35 is entirely at one with the people, and never thinks of exerting any power of coercion unless in agreement with what it conceives to be their voice. But I deny

the right of the people to exercise such coercion, either by themselves or by their government. The power itself is illegitimate. The best government has no more title to it than the worst. It is as noxious, or more noxious, when exerted in accordance with public opinion, than when in opposition to it. If all mankind
5 minus one, were of one opinion, and only one person were of the contrary opinion, mankind would be no more justified in silencing that one person, than he, if he had the power, would be justified in silencing mankind. Were an opinion a personal possession of no value except to the owner; if to be obstructed in the enjoyment of it were simply a private injury, it would make
10 some difference whether the injury was inflicted only on a few persons or on many. But the peculiar evil of silencing the expression of an opinion is, that it is robbing the human race; posterity as well as the existing generation; those who dissent from the opinion, still more than those who hold it. If the opinion is right, they are deprived of the opportunity of exchanging error for truth: if
15 wrong, they lose, what is almost as great a benefit, the clearer perception and livelier impression of truth, produced by its collision with error.

It is necessary to consider separately these two hypotheses, each of which has a distinct branch of the argument corresponding to it. We can never be sure that the opinion we are endeavoring to stifle is a false opinion; and if we were
20 sure, stifling it would be an evil still.

First: the opinion which it is attempted to suppress by authority may possibly be true. Those who desire to suppress it, of course deny its truth; but they are not infallible. They have no authority to decide the question for all mankind, and exclude every other person from the means of judging. To refuse a
25 hearing to an opinion, because they are sure that it is false, is to assume that *their* certainty is the same thing as *absolute* certainty. All silencing of discussion is an assumption of infallibility. Its condemnation may be allowed to rest on this common argument, not the worse for being common.

Unfortunately for the good sense of mankind, the fact of their fallibility is
30 far from carrying the weight in their practical judgment, which is always allowed to it in theory; for while every one well knows himself to be fallible, few think it necessary to take any precautions against their own fallibility, or admit the supposition that any opinion, of which they feel very certain, may be one of the examples of the error to which they acknowledge themselves to be
35 liable. Absolute princes, or others who are accustomed to unlimited deference, usually feel this complete confidence in their own opinions on nearly all subjects. People more happily situated, who sometimes hear their opinions disputed, and are not wholly unused to be set right when they are wrong, place the same unbounded reliance only on such of their opinions as are shared by all
40 who surround them, or to whom they habitually defer: for in proportion to a

man's want of confidence in his own solitary judgment, does he usually repose, with implicit trust, on the infallibility of "the world" in general. And the world, to each individual, means the part of it with which he comes in contact; his party, his sect, his church, his class of society: the man may be called, by
5 comparison, almost liberal and large-minded to whom it means anything so comprehensive as his own country or his own age. Nor is his faith in this collective authority at all shaken by his being aware that other ages, countries, sects, churches, classes, and parties have thought, and even now think, the exact reverse. He devolves upon his own world the responsibility of being in the right
10 against the dissentient worlds of other people; and it never troubles him that mere accident has decided which of these numerous worlds is the object of his reliance, and that the same causes which make him a Churchman in London, would have made him a Buddhist or a Confucian in Pekin. Yet it is as evident in itself, as any amount of argument can make it, that ages are no more infallible
15 than individuals; every age having held many opinions which subsequent ages have deemed not only false but absurd; and it is as certain that many opinions, now general, will be rejected by future ages, as it is that many, once general, are rejected by the present.

The objection likely to be made to this argument, would probably take some
20 such form as the following. There is no greater assumption of infallibility in forbidding the propagation of error, than in any other thing which is done by public authority on its own judgment and responsibility. Judgment is given to men that they may use it. Because it may be used erroneously, are men to be told that they ought not to use it at all? To prohibit what they think pernicious, is not
25 claiming exemption from error, but fulfilling the duty incumbent on them, although fallible, of acting on their conscientious conviction. If we were never to act on our opinions, because those opinions may be wrong, we should leave all our interests uncared for, and all our duties unperformed. An objection which applies to all conduct, can be no valid objection to any conduct in particular. It is
30 the duty of governments, and of individuals, to form the truest opinions they can; to form them carefully, and never impose them upon others unless they are quite sure of being right. But when they are sure (such reasoners may say), it is not conscientiousness but cowardice to shrink from acting on their opinions, and allow doctrines which they honestly think dangerous to the welfare of mankind,
35 either in this life or in another, to be scattered abroad without restraint, because other people, in less enlightened times, have persecuted opinions now believed to be true. Let us take care, it may be said, not to make the same mistake: but governments and nations have made mistakes in other things, which are not denied to be fit subjects for the exercise of authority: they have laid on bad
40 taxes, made unjust wars. Ought we therefore to lay on no taxes, and, under

whatever provocation, make no wars? Men, and governments, must act to the best of their ability. There is no such thing as absolute certainty, but there is assurance sufficient for the purposes of human life. We may, and must, assume our opinion to be true for the guidance of our own conduct: and it is assuming
5 no more when we forbid bad men to pervert society by the propagation of opinions which we regard as false and pernicious.

I answer, that it is assuming very much more. There is the greatest difference between presuming an opinion to be true, because, with every opportunity for contesting it, it has not been refuted, and assuming its truth for
10 the purpose of not permitting its refutation. Complete liberty of contradicting and disproving our opinion, is the very condition which justifies us in assuming its truth for purposes of action; and on no other terms can a being with human faculties have any rational assurance of being right.

When we consider either the history of opinion, or the ordinary conduct of
15 human life, to what is it to be ascribed that the one and the other are no worse than they are? Not certainly to the inherent force of the human understanding; for, on any matter not self-evident, there are ninety-nine persons totally incapable of judging of it, for one who is capable; and the capacity of the hundredth person is only comparative; for the majority of the eminent men of
20 every past generation held many opinions now known to be erroneous, and did or approved numerous things which no one will now justify. Why is it, then, that there is on the whole a preponderance among mankind of rational opinions and rational conduct? If there really is this preponderance — which there must be, unless human affairs are, and have always been, in an almost desperate state —
25 it is owing to a quality of the human mind, the source of everything respectable in man either as an intellectual or as a moral being, namely, that his errors are corrigible. He is capable of rectifying his mistakes, by discussion and experience. Not by experience alone There must be discussion, to show how experience is to be interpreted. Wrong opinions and practices gradually yield to
30 fact and argument: but facts and arguments, to produce any effect on the mind, must be brought before it. Very few facts are able to tell their own story, without comments to bring out their meaning. The whole strength and value, then, of human judgment, depending on the one property, that it can be set right when it is wrong, reliance can be placed on it only when the means of setting it right are
35 kept constantly at hand. In the case of any person whose judgment is really deserving of confidence, how has it become so? Because he has kept his mind open to criticism of his opinions and conduct. Because it has been his practice to listen to all that could be said against him; to profit by as much of it as was just, and expound to himself, and upon occasion to others, the fallacy of what was
40 fallacious. Because he has felt, that the only way in which a human being can

make some approach to knowing the whole of a subject, is by hearing what can be said about it by persons of every variety of opinion, and studying all modes in which it can be looked at by every character of mind. No wise man ever acquired his wisdom in any mode but this; nor is it in the nature of human
5   intellect to become wise in any other manner. The steady habit of correcting and completing his own opinion by collating it with those of others, so far from causing doubt and hesitation in carrying it into practice, is the only stable foundation for a just reliance on it: for, being cognizant of all that can, at least obviously, be said against him, and having taken up his position against all
10   gainsayers knowing that he has sought for objections and difficulties, instead of avoiding them, and has shut out no light which can be thrown upon the subject from any quarter — he has a right to think his judgment better than that of any person, or any multitude, who have not gone through a similar process.

      It is not too much to require that what the wisest of mankind, those who are
15   best entitled to trust their own judgment, find necessary to warrant their relying on it, should be submitted to by that miscellaneous collection of a few wise and many foolish individuals, called the public. The most intolerant of churches, the Roman Catholic Church, even at the canonization of a saint, admits, and listens patiently to, a "devil's advocate." The holiest of men, it appears, cannot be
20   admitted to posthumous honors, until all that the devil could say against him is known and weighed. If even the Newtonian philosophy were not permitted to be questioned, mankind could not feel as complete assurance of its truth as they now do. The beliefs which we have most warrant for, have no safeguard to rest on, but a standing invitation to the whole world to prove them unfounded. If the
25   challenge is not accepted, or is accepted and the attempt fails, we are far enough from certainty still; but we have done the best that the existing state of human reason admits of; we have neglected nothing that could give the truth a chance of reaching us: if the lists are kept open, we may hope that if there be a better truth, it will be found when the human mind is capable of receiving it; and in the
30   mean time we may rely on having attained such approach to truth, as is possible in our own day. This is the amount of certainty attainable by a fallible being, and this the sole way of attaining it.

      Strange it is, that men should admit the validity of the arguments for free discussion, but object to their being "pushed to an extreme;" not seeing that
35   unless the reasons are good for an extreme case, they are not good for any case. Strange that they should imagine that they are not assuming infallibility, when they acknowledge that there should be free discussion on all subjects which can possibly be *doubtful,* but think that some particular principle or doctrine should be forbidden to be questioned because it is *so certain,* that is, because *they are*
40   *certain* that it is certain. To call any proposition certain, while there is any one

who would deny its certainty if permitted, but who is not permitted, is to assume that we ourselves, and those who agree with us, are the judges of certainty, and judges without hearing the other side.

In the present age — which has been described as "destitute of faith, but
5   terrified at scepticism," — in which people feel sure, not so much that their opinions are true, as that they should not know what to do without them — the claims of an opinion to be protected from public attack are rested not so much on its truth, as on its importance to society. There are, it is alleged, certain beliefs, so useful, not to say indispensable to well-being, that it is as much the
10 duty of governments to uphold those beliefs, as to protect any other of the interests of society. In a case of such necessity, and so directly in the line of their duty, something less than infallibility may, it is maintained, warrant, and even bind, governments, to act on their own opinion, confirmed by the general opinion of mankind. It is also often argued, and still oftener thought, that none
15 but bad men would desire to weaken these salutary beliefs; and there can be nothing wrong, it is thought, in restraining bad men, and prohibiting what only such men would wish to practise. This mode of thinking makes the justification of restraints on discussion not a question of the truth of doctrines, but of their usefulness; and flatters itself by that means to escape the responsibility of
20 claiming to be an infallible judge of opinions. But those who thus satisfy themselves, do not perceive that the assumption of infallibility is merely shifted from one point to another. The usefulness of an opinion is itself matter of opinion: as disputable, as open to discussion and requiring discussion as much, as the opinion itself. There is the same need of an infallible judge of opinions to
25 decide an opinion to be noxious, as to decide it to be false, unless the opinion condemned has full opportunity of defending itself. And it will not do to say that the heretic may be allowed to maintain the utility or harmlessness of his opinion, though forbidden to maintain its truth. The truth of an opinion is part of its utility. If we would know whether or not it is desirable that a proposition should
30 be believed, is it possible to exclude the consideration of whether or not it is true? In the opinion, not of bad men, but of the best men, no belief which is contrary to truth can be really useful: and can you prevent such men from urging that plea, when they are charged with culpability for denying some doctrine which they are told is useful, but which they believe to be false? Those who are
35 on the side of received opinions, never fail to take all possible advantage of this plea; you do not find *them* handling the question of utility as if it could be completely abstracted from that of truth: on the contrary, it is, above all, because their doctrine is "the truth," that the knowledge or the belief of it is held to be so indispensable. There can be no fair discussion of the question of usefulness,
40 when an argument so vital may be employed on one side, but not on the other.

And in point of fact, when law or public feeling do not permit the truth of an opinion to be disputed, they are just as little tolerant of a denial of its usefulness. The utmost they allow is an extenuation of its absolute necessity, or of the positive guilt of rejecting it.

5   In order more fully to illustrate the mischief of denying a hearing to opinions because we, in our own judgment, have condemned them, it will be desirable to fix down the discussion to a concrete case; and I choose, by preference, the cases which are least favorable to me — in which the argument against freedom of opinion, both on the score of truth and on that of utility, is

10 considered the strongest. Let the opinions impugned be the belief in a God and in a future state, or any of the commonly received doctrines of morality. To fight the battle on such ground, gives a great advantage to an unfair antagonist; since he will be sure to say (and many who have no desire to be unfair will say it internally), Are these the doctrines which you do not deem sufficiently certain to

15 be taken under the protection of law? Is the belief in a God one of the opinions, to feel sure of which, you hold to be assuming infallibility? But I must be permitted to observe, that it is not the feeling sure of a doctrine (be it what it may) which I call an assumption of infallibility. It is the undertaking to decide that question *for others,* without allowing them to hear what can be said on the

20 contrary side. And I denounce and reprobate this pretension not the less, if put forth on the side of my most solemn convictions. How ever positive any one's persuasion may be, not only of the falsity, but of the pernicious consequences — not only of the pernicious consequences, but (to adopt expressions which I altogether condemn) the immorality and impiety of an opinion; yet if, in

25 pursuance of that private judgment, though backed by the public judgment of his country or his cotemporaries, he prevents the opinion from being heard in its defence, he assumes infallibility. And so far from the assumption being less objectionable or less dangerous because the opinion is called immoral or impious, this is the case of all others in which it is most fatal. These are exactly

30 the occasions on which the men of one generation commit those dreadful mistakes, which excite the astonishment and horror of posterity. It is among such that we find the instances memorable in history, when the arm of the law has been employed to root out the best men and the noblest doctrines; with deplorable success as to the men, though some of the doctrines have survived to

35 be (as if in mockery) invoked, in defence of similar conduct towards those who dissent from *them,* or from their received interpretation.

     Mankind can hardly be too often reminded, that there was once a man named Socrates, between whom and the legal authorities and public opinion of his time, there took place a memorable collision. Born in an age and country

40 abounding in individual greatness, this man has been handed down to us by

those who best knew both him and the age, as the most virtuous man in it; while *we* know him as the head and prototype of all subsequent teachers of virtue, the source equally of the lofty inspiration of Plato and the judicious utilitarianism of Aristotle, "*i maëstri di color che sanno,*" the two headsprings of ethical as of all
5 other philosophy. This acknowledged master of all the eminent thinkers who have since lived — whose fame, still growing after more than two thousand years, all but outweighs the whole remainder of the names which make his native city illustrious — was put to death by his countrymen, after a judicial conviction, for impiety and immorality. Impiety, in denying the gods recognized
10 by the State; indeed his accuser asserted (see the "Apologia") that he believed in no gods at all. Immorality, in being, by his doctrines and instructions, a "corruptor of youth." Of these charges the tribunal, there is every ground for believing, honestly found him guilty, and condemned the man who probably of all then born had deserved best of mankind, to be put to death as a criminal.
15   To pass from this to the only other instance of judicial iniquity, the mention of which, after the condemnation of Socrates, would not be an anti-climax: the event which took place on Calvary rather more than eighteen hundred years ago. The man who left on the memory of those who witnessed his life and conversation, such an impression of his moral grandeur, that eighteen
20 subsequent centuries have done homage to him as the Almighty in person, was ignominiously put to death, as what? As a blasphemer. Men did not merely mistake their benefactor; they mistook him for the exact contrary of what he was, and treated him as that prodigy of impiety, which they themselves are now held to be, for their treatment of him. The feelings with which mankind now
25 regard these lamentable transactions, especially the later of the two, render them extremely unjust in their judgment of the unhappy actors These were, to all appearance, not bad men — not worse than men commonly are, but rather the contrary; men who possessed in a full, or somewhat more than a full measure, the religious, moral, and patriotic feelings of their time and people: the very kind
30 of men who, in all times, our own included, have every chance of passing through life blameless and respected. The high-priest who rent his garments when the words were pronounced, which, according to all the ideas of his country, constituted the blackest guilt, was in all probability quite as sincere in his horror and indignation, as the generality of respectable and pious men now
35 are in the religious and moral sentiments they profess; and most of those who now shudder at his conduct, if they had lived in his time, and been born Jews, would have acted precisely as he did. Orthodox Christians who are tempted to think that those who stoned to death the first martyrs must have been worse men than they themselves are, ought to remember that one of those persecutors was
40 Saint Paul.

Let us add one more example, the most striking of all, if the impressiveness of an error is measured by the wisdom and virtue of him who falls into it. If ever any one, possessed of power, had grounds for thinking himself the best and most enlightened among his cotemporaries, it was the Emperor Marcus Aurelius.

5   Absolute monarch of the whole civilized world, he preserved through life not only the most unblemished justice, but what was less to be expected from his Stoical breeding, the tenderest heart. The few failings which are attributed to him, were all on the side of indulgence: while his writings, the highest ethical product of the ancient mind, differ scarcely perceptibly, if they differ at all, from

10   the most characteristic teachings of Christ. This man, a better Christian in all but the dogmatic sense of the word, than almost any of the ostensibly Christian sovereigns who have since reigned, persecuted Christianity. Placed at the summit of all the previous attainments of humanity, with an open, unfettered intellect, and a character which led him of himself to embody in his moral

15   writings the Christian ideal, he yet failed to see that Christianity was to be a good and not an evil to the world, with his duties to which he was so deeply penetrated. Existing society he knew to be in a deplorable state. But such as it was, he saw or thought he saw, that it was held together and prevented from being worse, by belief and reverence of the received divinities. As a ruler of

20   mankind, he deemed it his duty not to suffer society to fall in pieces; and saw not how, if its existing ties were removed, any others could be formed which could again knit it together. The new religion openly aimed at dissolving these ties: unless, therefore, it was his duty to adopt that religion, it seemed to be his duty to put it down. Inasmuch then as the theology of Christianity did not appear

25   to him true or of divine origin; inasmuch as this strange history of a crucified God was not credible to him, and a system which purported to rest entirely upon a foundation to him so wholly unbelievable, could not be foreseen by him to be that renovating agency which, after all abatements, it has in fact proved to be; the gentlest and most amiable of philosophers and rulers, under a solemn sense

30   of duty, authorized the persecution of Christianity. To my mind this is one of the most tragical facts in all history. It is a bitter thought, how different a thing the Christianity of the world might have been, if the Christian faith had been adopted as the religion of the empire under the auspices of Marcus Aurelius instead of those of Constantine. But it would be equally unjust to him and false

35   to truth, to deny, that no one plea which can be urged for punishing anti-Christian teaching, was wanting to Marcus Aurelius for punishing, as he did, the propagation of Christianity. No Christian more firmly believes that Atheism is false, and tends to the dissolution of society, than Marcus Aurelius believed the same things of Christianity; he who, of all men then living, might have been

40   thought the most capable of appreciating it. Unless any one who approves of

punishment for the promulgation of opinions, flatters himself that he is a wiser
and better man than Marcus Aurelius — more deeply versed in the wisdom of
his time, more elevated in his intellect above it — more earnest in his search for
truth, or more single-minded in his devotion to it when found; — let him abstain
5 from that assumption of the joint infallibility of himself and the multitude,
which the great Antoninus made with so unfortunate a result.

Aware of the impossibility of defending the use of punishment for
restraining irreligious opinions, by any argument which will not justify Marcus
Antoninus, the enemies of religious freedom, when hard pressed, occasionally
10 accept this consequence, and say, with Dr. Johnson, that the persecutors of
Christianity were in the right; that persecution is an ordeal through which truth
ought to pass, and always passes successfully, legal penalties being, in the end,
powerless against truth, though sometimes beneficially effective against
mischievous errors. This is a form of the argument for religious intolerance,
15 sufficiently remarkable not to be passed without notice.

A theory which maintains that truth may justifiably be persecuted because
persecution cannot possibly do it any harm, cannot be charged with being
intentionally hostile to the reception of new truths; but we cannot commend the
generosity of its dealing with the persons to whom mankind are indebted for
20 them. To discover to the world something which deeply concerns it, and of
which it was previously ignorant; to prove to it that it had been mistaken on
some vital point of temporal or spiritual interest, is as important a service as a
human being can render to his fellow-creatures, and in certain cases, as in those
of the early Christians and of the Reformers, those who think with Dr. Johnson
25 believe it to have been the most precious gift which could be bestowed on
mankind. That the authors of such splendid benefits should be requited by
martyrdom; that their reward should be to be dealt with as the vilest of
criminals, is not, upon this theory, a deplorable error and misfortune, for which
humanity should mourn in sackcloth and ashes, but the normal and justifiable
30 state of things. The propounder of a new truth according to this doctrine, should
stand, as stood, in the legislation of the Locrians, the proposer of a new law,
with a halter round his neck, to be instantly tightened if the public assembly did
not, on hearing his reasons, then and there adopt his proposition. People who
defend this mode of treating benefactors, cannot be supposed to set much value
35 on the benefit; and I believe this view of the subject is mostly confined to the
sort of persons who think that new truths may have been desirable once, but that
we have had enough of them now.

But, indeed, the dictum that truth always triumphs over persecution, is one
of those pleasant falsehoods which men repeat after one another till they pass
40 into commonplaces, but which all experience refutes. History teems with

instances of truth put down by persecution. If not suppressed forever, it may be thrown back for centuries. To speak only of religious opinions: the Reformation broke out at least twenty times before Luther, and was put down. Arnold of Brescia was put down Fra Dolcino was put down. Savonarola was put down.
5   The Albigeois were put down. The Vaudois were put down. The Lollards were put down. The Hussites were put down. Even after the era of Luther, wherever persecution was persisted in, it was successful. In Spain, Italy, Flanders, the Austrian empire, Protestanism was rooted out; and, most likely, would have been so in England, had Queen Mary lived, or Queen Elizabeth died.
10   Persecution has always succeeded, save where the heretics were too strong a party to be effectually persecuted. No reasonable person can doubt that Christianity might have been extirpated in the Roman empire. It spread, and became predominant, because the persecutions were only occasional, lasting but a short time, and separated by long intervals of almost undisturbed
15   propagandism. It is a piece of idle sentimentality that truth, merely as truth, has any inherent power denied to error, of prevailing against the dungeon and the stake. Men are not more zealous for truth than they often are for error, and a sufficient application of legal or even of social penalties will generally succeed in stopping the propagation of either. The real advantage which truth has,
20   consists in this, that when an opinion is true, it may be extinguished once, twice, or many times, but in the course of ages there will generally be found persons to rediscover it, until some one of its reappearances falls on a time when from favorable circumstances it escapes persecution until it has made such head as to withstand all subsequent attempts to suppress it.
25   It will be said, that we do not now put to death the introducers of new opinions: we are not like our fathers who slew the prophets, we even build sepulchres to them. It is true we no longer put heretics to death; and the amount of penal infliction which modern feeling would probably tolerate, even against the most obnoxious opinions, is not sufficient to extirpate them. But let us not
30   flatter ourselves that we are yet free from the stain even of legal persecution. Penalties for opinion, or at least for its expression, still exist by law; and their enforcement is not, even in these times, so unexampled as to make it at all incredible that they may some day be revived in full force. In the year 1857, at the summer assizes of the county of Cornwall, an unfortunate man,[2] said to be
35   of unexceptionable conduct in all relations of life, was sentenced to twenty-one months imprisonment, for uttering, and writing on a gate, some offensive words concerning Christianity. Within a month of the same time, at the Old Bailey, two persons, on two separate occasions,[3] were rejected as jurymen, and one of them grossly insulted by the judge and by one of the counsel, because they honestly
40   declared that they had no theological belief; and a third, a foreigner,[4] for the

same reason, was denied justice against a thief. This refusal of redress took place in virtue of the legal doctrine, that no person can be allowed to give evidence in a court of justice, who does not profess belief in a God (any god is sufficient) and in a future state; which is equivalent to declaring such persons to
5 be outlaws, excluded from the protection of the tribunals; who may not only be robbed or assaulted with impunity, if no one but themselves, or persons of similar opinions, be present but any one else may be robbed or assaulted with impunity, if the proof of the fact depends on their evidence. The assumption on which this is grounded, is that the oath is worthless, of a person who does not
10 believe in a future state; a proposition which betokens much ignorance of history in those who assent to it (since it is historically true that a large proportion of infidels in all ages have been persons of distinguished integrity and honor); and would be maintained by no one who had the smallest conception how many of the persons in greatest repute with the world, both for virtues and for
15 attainments, are well known, at least to their intimates, to be unbelievers. The rule, besides, is suicidal, and cuts away its own foundation. Under pretence that atheists must be liars, it admits the testimony of all atheists who are willing to lie, and rejects only those who brave the obloquy of publicly confessing a detested creed rather than affirm a falsehood. A rule thus self-convicted of
20 absurdity so far as regards its professed purpose, can be kept in force only as a badge of hatred, a relic of persecution; a persecution, too, having the peculiarity, that the qualification for undergoing it, is the being clearly proved not to deserve it. The rule, and the theory it implies, are hardly less insulting to believers than to infidels. For if he who does not believe in a future state necessarily lies, it
25 follows that they who do believe are only prevented from lying, if prevented they are, by the fear of hell. We will not do the authors and abettors of the rule the injury of supposing, that the conception which they have formed of Christian virtue is drawn from their own consciousness.

These, indeed, are but rags and remnants of persecution, and may be
30 thought to be not so much an indication of the wish to persecute, as an example of that very frequent infirmity of English minds, which makes them take a preposterous pleasure in the assertion of a bad principle, when they are no longer bad enough to desire to carry it really into practice. But unhappily there is no security in the state of the public mind, that the suspension of worse forms of
35 legal persecution, which has lasted for about the space of a generation, will continue. In this age the quiet surface of routine is as often ruffled by attempts to resuscitate past evils, as to introduce new benefits. What is boasted of at the present time as the revival of religion, is always, in narrow and uncultivated minds, at least as much the revival of bigotry; and where there is the strong
40 permanent leaven of intolerance in the feelings of a people, which at all times

318

abides in the middle classes of this country, it needs but little to provoke them into actively persecuting those whom they have never ceased to think proper objects of persecution.[5] For it is this — it is the opinions men entertain, and the feelings they cherish, respecting those who disown the beliefs they deem

5 important, which makes this country not a place of mental freedom. For a long time past, the chief mischief of the legal penalties is that they strengthen the social stigma. It is that stigma which is really effective, and so effective is it, that the profession of opinions which are under the ban of society is much less common in England, than is, in many other countries, the avowal of those which

10 incur risk of judicial punishment. In respect to all persons but those whose pecuniary circumstances make them independent of the good will of other people, opinion, on this subject, is as efficacious as law; men might as well be imprisoned, as excluded from the means of earning their bread. Those whose bread is already secured, and who desire no favors from men in power, or from

15 bodies of men, or from the public, have nothing to fear from the open avowal of any opinions, but to be ill-thought of and ill-spoken of, and this it ought not to require a very heroic mould to enable them to bear. There is no room for any appeal *ad misericordiam* in behalf of such persons. But though we do not now inflict so much evil on those who think differently from us, as it was formerly

20 our custom to do, it may be that we do ourselves as much evil as ever by our treatment of them. Socrates was put to death, but the Socratic philosophy rose like the sun in heaven, and spread its illumination over the whole intellectual firmament. Christians were cast to the lions, but the Christian Church grew up a stately and spreading tree, overtopping the older and less vigorous growths, and

25 stifling them by its shade. Our merely social intolerance, kills no one, roots out no opinions, but induces men to disguise them, or to abstain from any active effort for their diffusion. With us, heretical opinions do not perceptibly gain, or even lose, ground in each decade or generation; they never blaze out far and wide, but continue to smoulder in the narrow circles of thinking and studious

30 persons among whom they originate, without ever lighting up the general affairs of mankind with either a true or a deceptive light. And thus is kept up a state of things very satisfactory to some minds, because, without the unpleasant process of fining or imprisoning anybody, it maintains all prevailing opinions outwardly undisturbed, while it does not absolutely interdict the exercise of reason by

35 dissentients afflicted with the malady of thought. A convenient plan for having peace in the intellectual world, and keeping all things going on therein very much as they do already. But the price paid for this sort of intellectual pacification, is the sacrifice of the entire moral courage of the human mind. A state of things in which a large portion of the most active and inquiring intellects

40 find it advisable to keep the genuine principles and grounds of their convictions

within their own breasts, and attempt, in what they address to the public, to fit as much as they can of their own conclusions to premises which they have internally renounced, cannot send forth the open, fearless characters, and logical, consistent intellects who once adorned the thinking world. The sort of men who
5 can be looked for under it, are either mere conformers to commonplace, or time-servers for truth whose arguments on all great subjects are meant for their hearers, and are not those which have convinced themselves. Those who avoid this alternative, do so by narrowing their thoughts and interest to things which can be spoken of without venturing within the region of principles, that is, to
10 small practical matters, which would come right of themselves, if but the minds of mankind were strengthened and enlarged, and which will never be made effectually right until then; while that which would strengthen and enlarge men's minds, free and daring speculation on the highest subjects, is abandoned.
      Those in whose eyes this reticence on the part of heretics is no evil, should
15 consider in the first place, that in consequence of it there is never any fair and thorough discussion of heretical opinions; and that such of them as could not stand such a discussion, though they may be prevented from spreading, do not disappear. But it is not the minds of heretics that are deteriorated most, by the ban placed on all inquiry which does not end in the orthodox conclusions. The
20 greatest harm done is to those who are not heretics, and whose whole mental development is cramped, and their reason cowed, by the fear of heresy. Who can compute what the world loses in the multitude of promising intellects combined with timid characters, who dare not follow out any bold, vigorous, independent train of thought, lest it should land them in something which would admit of
25 being considered irreligious or immoral? Among them we may occasionally see some man of deep conscientiousness, and subtle and refined understanding, who spends a life in sophisticating with an intellect which he cannot silence, and exhausts the resources of ingenuity in attempting to reconcile the promptings of his conscience and reason with orthodoxy, which yet he does not, perhaps, to the
30 end succeed in doing. No one can be a great thinker who does not recognize, that as a thinker it is his first duty to follow his intellect to whatever conclusions it may lead. Truth gains more even by the errors of one who, with due study and preparation, thinks for himself, than by the true opinions of those who only hold them because they do not suffer themselves to think. Not that it is solely, or
35 chiefly, to form great thinkers, that freedom of thinking is required. On the contrary, it is as much, and even more indispensable, to enable average human beings to attain the mental stature which they are capable of. There have been, and may again be, great individual thinkers, in a general atmosphere of mental slavery. But there never has been, nor ever will be, in that atmosphere, an
40 intellectually active people. Where any people has made a temporary approach

to such a character, it has been because the dread of heterodox speculation was for a time suspended. Where there is a tacit convention that principles are not to be disputed; where the discussion of the greatest questions which can occupy humanity is considered to be closed, we cannot hope to find that generally high

5   scale of mental activity which has made some periods of history so remarkable. Never when controversy avoided the subjects which are large and important enough to kindle enthusiasm, was the mind of a people stirred up from its foundations, and the impulse given which raised even persons of the most ordinary intellect to something of the dignity of thinking beings. Of such we

10   have had an example in the condition of Europe during the times immediately following the Reformation; another, though limited to the Continent and to a more cultivated class, in the speculative movement of the latter half of the eighteenth century; and a third, of still briefer duration, in the intellectual fermentation of Germany during the Goethian and Fichtean period. These

15   periods differed widely in the particular opinions which they developed; but were alike in this, that during all three the yoke of authority was broken. In each, an old mental despotism had been thrown off, and no new one had yet taken its place. The impulse given at these three periods has made Europe what it now is. Every single improvement which has taken place either in the human mind or in

20   institutions, may be traced distinctly to one or other of them. Appearances have for some time indicated that all three impulses are well-nigh spent; and we can expect no fresh start, until we again assert our mental freedom.

Let us now pass to the second division of the argument, and dismissing the supposition that any of the received opinions may be false, let us assume them to

25   be true, and examine into the worth of the manner in which they are likely to be held, when their truth is not freely and openly canvassed. However unwillingly a person who has a strong opinion may admit the possibility that his opinion may be false, he ought to be moved by the consideration that however true it may be, if it is not fully, frequently, and fearlessly discussed, it will be held as a dead

30   dogma, not a living truth.

There is a class of persons (happily not quite so numerous as formerly) who think it enough if a person assents undoubtingly to what they think true, though he has no knowledge whatever of the grounds of the opinion, and could not make a tenable defence of it against the most superficial objections. Such

35   persons, if they can once get their creed taught from authority, naturally think that no good, and some harm, comes of its being allowed to be questioned. Where their influence prevails, they make it nearly impossible for the received opinion to be rejected wisely and considerately, though it may still be rejected rashly and ignorantly; for to shut out discussion entirely is seldom possible, and

40   when it once gets in, beliefs not grounded on conviction are apt to give way

before the slightest semblance of an argument. Waiving, however, this possibility — assuming that the true opinion abides in the mind, but abides as a prejudice, a belief independent of, and proof against, argument — this is not the way in which truth ought to be held by a rational being. This is not knowing the truth. Truth, thus held, is but one superstition the more, accidentally clinging to the words which enunciate a truth.

If the intellect and judgment of mankind ought to be cultivated, a thing which Protestants at least do not deny, on what can these faculties be more appropriately exercised by any one, than on the things which concern him so much that it is considered necessary for him to hold opinions on them? If the cultivation of the understanding consists in one thing more than in another, it is surely in learning the grounds of one's own opinions. Whatever people believe, on subjects on which it is of the first importance to believe rightly, they ought to be able to defend against at least the common objections. But, some one may say, "Let them be *taught* the grounds of their opinions. It does not follow that opinions must be merely parroted because they are never heard controverted. Persons who learn geometry do not simply commit the theorems to memory, but understand and learn likewise the demonstrations; and it would be absurd to say that they remain ignorant of the grounds of geometrical truths, because they never hear any one deny, and attempt to disprove them." Undoubtedly: and such teaching suffices on a subject like mathematics, where there is nothing at all to be said on the wrong side of the question. The peculiarity of the evidence of mathematical truths is, that all the argument is on one side. There are no objections, and no answers to objections. But on every subject on which difference of opinion is possible, the truth depends on a balance to be struck between two sets of conflicting reasons. Even in natural philosophy, there is always some other explanation possible of the same facts; some geocentric theory instead of heliocentric, some phlogiston instead of oxygen; and it has to be shown why that other theory cannot be the true one: and until this is shown, and until we know how it is shown, we do not understand the grounds of our opinion. But when we turn to subjects infinitely more complicated, to morals, religion, politics, social relations, and the business of life, three-fourths of the arguments for every disputed opinion consist in dispelling the appearances which favor some opinion different from it. The greatest orator, save one, of antiquity, has left it on record that he always studied his adversary's case with as great, if not with still greater, intensity than even his own. What Cicero practised as the means of forensic success, requires to be imitated by all who study any subject in order to arrive at the truth. He who knows only his own side of the case, knows little of that. His reasons may be good, and no one may have been able to refute them. But if he is equally unable to refute the reasons on the opposite side; if he does not so much as know what they are, he has no ground for preferring either opinion. The rational position for him would be suspension of judgment, and unless he contents himself with that, he is either led by authority, or adopts, like the generality of the world, the side to which he feels

5   most inclination. Nor is it enough that he should hear the arguments of adversaries from his own teachers, presented as they state them, and accompanied by what they offer as refutations. That is not the way to do justice to the arguments, or bring them into real contact with his own mind. He must be able to hear them from persons who actually believe them; who defend them in

10   earnest, and do their very utmost for them. He must know them in their most plausible and persuasive form; he must feel the whole force of the difficulty which the true view of the subject has to encounter and dispose of; else he will never really possess himself of the portion of truth which meets and removes that difficulty. Ninety-nine in a hundred of what are called educated men are in

15   this condition, even of those who can argue fluently for their opinions. Their conclusion may be true, but it might be false for anything they know: they have never thrown themselves into the mental position of those who think differently from them, and considered what such persons may have to say; and consequently they do not, in any proper sense of the word, know the doctrine

20   which they themselves profess. They do not know those parts of it which explain and justify the remainder; the considerations which show that a fact which seemingly conflicts with another is reconcilable with it, or that, of two apparently strong reasons, one and not the other ought to be preferred. All that part of the truth which turns the scale, and decides the judgment of a completely

25   informed mind, they are strangers to; nor is it ever really known, but to those who have attended equally and impartially to both sides, and endeavored to see the reasons of both in the strongest light. So essential is this discipline to a real understanding of moral and human subjects, that if opponents of all important truths do not exist, it is indispensable to imagine them, and supply them with the

30   strongest arguments which the most skilful devil's advocate can conjure up.

     To abate the force of these considerations, an enemy of free discussion may be supposed to say, that there is no necessity for mankind in general to know and understand all that can be said against or for their opinions by philosophers and theologians. That it is not needful for common men to be able to expose all

35   the misstatements or fallacies of an ingenious opponent. That it is enough if there is always somebody capable of answering them, so that nothing likely to mislead uninstructed persons remains unrefuted. That simple minds, having been taught the obvious grounds of the truths inculcated on them, may trust to authority for the rest, and being aware that they have neither knowledge nor

40   talent to resolve every difficulty which can be raised, may repose in the

assurance that all those which have been raised have been or can be answered, by those who are specially trained to the task.

Conceding to this view of the subject the utmost that can be claimed for it by those most easily satisfied with the amount of understanding of truth which
5 ought to accompany the belief of it; even so, the argument for free discussion is no way weakened. For even this doctrine acknowledges that mankind ought to have a rational assurance that all objections have been satisfactorily answered; and how are they to be answered if that which requires to be answered is not spoken? or how can the answer be known to be satisfactory, if the objectors
10 have no opportunity of showing that it is unsatisfactory? If not the public, at least the philosophers and theologians who are to resolve the difficulties, must make themselves familiar with those difficulties in their most puzzling form; and this cannot be accomplished unless they are freely stated, and placed in the most advantageous light which they admit of. The Catholic Church has its own
15 way of dealing with this embarrassing problem. It makes a broad separation between those who can be permitted to receive its doctrines on conviction, and those who must accept them on trust. Neither, indeed, are allowed any choice as to what they will accept; but the clergy, such at least as can be fully confided in, may admissibly and meritoriously make themselves acquainted with the
20 arguments of opponents, in order to answer them, and may, therefore, read heretical books; the laity, not unless by special permission, hard to be obtained. This discipline recognizes a knowledge of the enemy's case as beneficial to the teachers, but finds means, consistent with this, of denying it to the rest of the world: thus giving to the *élite* more mental culture, though not more mental
25 freedom, than it allows to the mass. By this device it succeeds in obtaining the kind of mental superiority which its purposes require; for though culture without freedom never made a large and liberal mind, it can make a clever *nisi prius* advocate of a cause. But in countries professing Protestantism, this resource is denied; since Protestants hold, at least in theory, that the responsibility for the
30 choice of a religion must be borne by each for himself, and cannot be thrown off upon teachers. Besides, in the present state of the world, it is practically impossible that writings which are read by the instructed can be kept from the uninstructed. If the teachers of mankind are to be cognizant of all that they ought to know, everything must be free to be written and published without restraint.
35 If, however, the mischievous operation of the absence of free discussion, when the received opinions are true, were confined to leaving men ignorant of the grounds of those opinions, it might be thought that this, if an intellectual, is no moral evil, and does not affect the worth of the opinions, regarded in their influence on the character. The fact, however, is, that not only the grounds of the
40 opinion are forgotten in the absence of discussion, but too often the meaning of

the opinion itself. The words which convey it, cease to suggest ideas, or suggest only a small portion of those they were originally employed to communicate. Instead of a vivid conception and a living belief, there remain only a few phrases retained by rote; or, if any part, the shell and husk only of the meaning is
5   retained, the finer essence being lost. The great chapter in human history which this fact occupies and fills, cannot be too earnestly studied and meditated on.

It is illustrated in the experience of almost all ethical doctrines and religious creeds. They are all full of meaning and vitality to those who originate them, and to the direct disciples of the originators. Their meaning continues to be felt in
10   undiminished strength, and is perhaps brought out into even fuller consciousness, so long as the struggle lasts to give the doctrine or creed an ascendency over other creeds. At last it either prevails, and becomes the general opinion, or its progress stops; it keeps possession of the ground it has gained, but ceases to spread further. When either of these results has become apparent,
15   controversy on the subject flags, and gradually dies away. The doctrine has taken its place, if not as a received opinion, as one of the admitted sects or divisions of opinion: those who hold it have generally inherited, not adopted it; and conversion from one of these doctrines to another, being now an exceptional fact, occupies little place in the thoughts of their professors. Instead of being, as
20   at first, constantly on the alert either to defend themselves against the world, or to bring the world over to them, they have subsided into acquiescence, and neither listen, when they can help it, to arguments against their creed, nor trouble dissentients (if there be such) with arguments in its favor. From this time may usually be dated the decline in the living power of the doctrine. We often
25   hear the teachers of all creeds lamenting the difficulty of keeping up in the minds of believers a lively apprehension of the truth which they nominally recognize, so that it may penetrate the feelings, and acquire a real mastery over the conduct. No such difficulty is complained of while the creed is still fighting for its existence: even the weaker combatants then know and feel what they are
30   fighting for, and the difference between it and other doctrines; and in that period of every creed's existence, not a few persons may be found, who have realized its fundamental principles in all the forms of thought, have weighed and considered them in all their important bearings, and have experienced the full effect on the character, which belief in that creed ought to produce in a mind
35   thoroughly imbued with it. But when it has come to be an hereditary creed, and to be received passively, not actively — when the mind is no longer compelled, in the same degree as at first, to exercise its vital powers on the questions which its belief presents to it, there is a progressive tendency to forget all of the belief except the formularies, or to give it a dull and torpid assent, as if accepting it on
40   trust dispensed with the necessity of realizing it in consciousness, or testing it by

personal experience; until it almost ceases to connect itself at all with the inner life of the human being. Then are seen the cases, so frequent in this age of the world as almost to form the majority, in which the creed remains as it were outside the mind, encrusting and petrifying it against all other influences
5   addressed to the higher parts of our nature; manifesting its power by not suffering any fresh and living conviction to get in, but itself doing nothing for the mind or heart, except standing sentinel over them to keep them vacant.

To what an extent doctrines intrinsically fitted to make the deepest impression upon the mind may remain in it as dead beliefs, without being ever
10 realized in the imagination, the feelings, or the understanding, is exemplified by the manner in which the majority of believers hold the doctrines of Christianity. By Christianity I here mean what is accounted such by all churches and sects — the maxims and precepts contained in the New Testament. These are considered sacred, and accepted as laws, by all professing Christians. Yet it is scarcely too
15 much to say that not one Christian in a thousand guides or tests his individual conduct by reference to those laws. The standard to which he does refer it, is the custom of his nation, his class, or his religious profession. He has thus, on the one hand, a collection of ethical maxims, which he believes to have been vouchsafed to him by infallible wisdom as rules for his government; and on the
20 other, a set of every-day judgments and practices, which go a certain length with some of those maxims, not so great a length with others, stand in direct opposition to some, and are, on the whole, a compromise between the Christian creed and the interests and suggestions of worldly life. To the first of these standards he gives his homage; to the other his real allegiance. All Christians
25 believe that the blessed are the poor and humble, and those who are ill-used by the world; that it is easier for a camel to pass through the eye of a needle than for a rich man to enter the kingdom of heaven; that they should judge not, lest they be judged; that they should swear not at all that they should love their neighbor as themselves; that if one take their cloak, they should give him their coat also;
30 that they should take no thought for the morrow; that if they would be perfect, they should sell all that they have and give it to the poor. They are not insincere when they say that they believe these things. They do believe them, as people believe what they have always heard lauded and never discussed. But in the sense of that living belief which regulates conduct, they believe these doctrines
35 just up to the point to which it is usual to act upon them. The doctrines in their integrity are serviceable to pelt adversaries with; and it is understood that they are to be put forward (when possible) as the reasons for whatever people do that they think laudable. But any one who reminded them that the maxims require an infinity of things which they never even think of doing, would gain nothing but
40 to be classed among those very unpopular characters who affect to be better than

other people. The doctrines have no hold on ordinary believers — are not a power in their minds. They have an habitual respect for the sound of them, but no feeling which spreads from the words to the things signified, and forces the mind to take *them* in, and make them conform to the formula. Whenever
5 conduct is concerned, they look round for Mr. A and B to direct them how far to go in obeying Christ.

Now we may be well assured that the case was not thus, but far otherwise, with the early Christians. Had it been thus, Christianity never would have expanded from an obscure sect of the despised Hebrews into the religion of the
10 Roman empire. When their enemies said, "See how these Christians love one another" (a remark not likely to be made by anybody now), they assuredly had a much livelier feeling of the meaning of their creed than they have ever had since. And to this cause, probably, it is chiefly owing that Christianity now makes so little progress in extending its domain, and after eighteen centuries, is
15 still nearly confined to Europeans and the descendants of Europeans. Even with the strictly religious, who are much in earnest about their doctrines, and attach a greater amount of meaning to many of them than people in general, it commonly happens that the part which is thus comparatively active in their minds is that which was made by Calvin, or Knox, or some such person much nearer in
20 character to themselves. The sayings of Christ coexist passively in their minds, producing hardly any effect beyond what is caused by mere listening to words so amiable and bland. There are many reasons, doubtless, why doctrines which are the badge of a sect retain more of their vitality than those common to all recognized sects, and why more pains are taken by teachers to keep their
25 meaning alive; but one reason certainly is, that the peculiar doctrines are more questioned, and have to be oftener defended against open gainsayers. Both teachers and learners go to sleep at their post, as soon as there is no enemy in the field.

The same thing holds true, generally speaking, of all traditional doctrines —
30 those of prudence and knowledge of life, as well as of morals or religion. All languages and literatures are full of general observations on life, both as to what it is, and how to conduct oneself in it; observations which everybody knows, which everybody repeats, or hears with acquiescence, which are received as truisms, yet of which most people first truly learn the meaning, when
35 experience, generally of a painful kind, has made it a reality to them. How often, when smarting under some unforeseen misfortune or disappointment, does a person call to mind some proverb or common saying, familiar to him all his life, the meaning of which, if he had ever before felt it as he does now, would have saved him from the calamity. There are indeed reasons for this, other than the
40 absence of discussion: there are many truths of which the full meaning *cannot*

be realized, until personal experience has brought it home. But much more of the meaning even of these would have been understood and what was understood would have been far more deeply impressed on the mind, if the man had been accustomed to hear it argued *pro* and *con* by people who did understand it. The fatal tendency of mankind to leave off thinking about a thing when it is no longer doubtful, is the cause of half their errors. A cotemporary author has well spoken of "the deep slumber of a decided opinion."

But what! (it may be asked) Is the absence of unanimity an indispensable condition of true knowledge? Is it necessary that some part of mankind should persist in error, to enable any to realize the truth? Does a belief cease to be real and vital as soon as it is generally received — and is a proposition never thoroughly understood and felt unless some doubt of it remains? As soon as mankind have unanimously accepted a truth, does the truth perish within them? The highest aim and best result of improved intelligence, it has hitherto been thought, is to unite mankind more and more in the acknowledgment of all important truths: and does the intelligence only last as long as it has not achieved its object? Do the fruits of conquest perish by the very completeness of the victory?

I affirm no such thing. As mankind improve, the number of doctrines which are no longer disputed or doubted will be constantly on the increase: and the well-being of mankind may almost be measured by the number and gravity of the truths which have reached the point of being uncontested. The cessation, on one question after another, of serious controversy, is one of the necessary incidents of the consolidation of opinion; a consolidation as salutary in the case of true opinions, as it is dangerous and noxious when the opinions are erroneous. But though this gradual narrowing of the bounds of diversity of opinion is necessary in both senses of the term, being at once inevitable and indispensable, we are not therefore obliged to conclude that all its consequences must be beneficial. The loss of so important an aid to the intelligent and living apprehension of a truth, as is afforded by the necessity of explaining it to, or defending it against, opponents, though not sufficient to outweigh, is no trifling drawback from, the benefit of its universal recognition. Where this advantage can no longer be had, I confess I should like to see the teachers of mankind endeavoring to provide a substitute for it; some contrivance for making the difficulties of the question as present to the learner's consciousness, as if they were pressed upon him by a dissentient champion, eager for his conversion.

But instead of seeking contrivances for this purpose, they have lost those they formerly had. The Socratic dialectics, so magnificently exemplified in the dialogues of Plato, were a contrivance of this description. They were essentially a negative discussion of the great questions of philosophy and life, directed with

consummate skill to the purpose of convincing any one who had merely adopted the commonplaces of received opinion, that he did not understand the subject — that he as yet attached no definite meaning to the doctrines he professed; in order that, becoming aware of his ignorance, he might be put in the way to attain
5 a stable belief, resting on a clear apprehension both of the meaning of doctrines and of their evidence. The school disputations of the Middle Ages had a somewhat similar object. They were intended to make sure that the pupil understood his own opinion, and (by necessary correlation) the opinion opposed to it, and could enforce the grounds of the one and confute those of the other.
10 These last-mentioned contests had indeed the incurable defect, that the premises appealed to were taken from authority, not from reason; and, as a discipline to the mind, they were in every respect inferior to the powerful dialectics which formed the intellects of the "Socratici viri:" but the modern mind owes far more to both than it is generally willing to admit, and the present modes of education
15 contain nothing which in the smallest degree supplies the place either of the one or of the other. A person who derives all his instruction from teachers or books, even if he escape the besetting temptation of contenting himself with cram, is under no compulsion to hear both sides; accordingly it is far from a frequent accomplishment, even among thinkers, to know both sides; and the weakest part
20 of what everybody says in defence of his opinion, is what he intends as a reply to antagonists. It is the fashion of the present time to disparage negative logic — that which points out weaknesses in theory or errors in practice, without establishing positive truths. Such negative criticism would indeed be poor enough as an ultimate result; but as a means to attaining any positive knowledge
25 or conviction worthy the name, it cannot be valued too highly; and until people are again systematically trained to it, there will be few great thinkers, and a low general average of intellect, in any but the mathematical and physical departments of speculation. On any other subject no one's opinions deserve the name of knowledge, except so far as he has either had forced upon him by
30 others, or gone through of himself the same mental process which would have been required of him in carrying on an active controversy with opponents. That, therefore, which when absent, it is so indispensable, but so difficult, to create, how worse than absurd is it to forego, when spontaneously offering itself! If there are any persons who contest a received opinion, or who will do so if law or
35 opinion will let them, let us thank them for it, open our minds to listen to them, and rejoice that there is some one to do for us what we otherwise ought, if we have any regard for either the certainty or the vitality of our convictions, to do with much greater labor for ourselves.

It still remains to speak of one of the principal causes which make diversity
40 of opinion advantageous, and will continue to do so until mankind shall have

entered a stage of intellectual advancement which at present seems at an incalculable distance. We have hitherto considered only two possibilities: that the received opinion may be false, and some other opinion, consequently, true; or that, the received opinion being true, a conflict with the opposite error is essential to a clear apprehension and deep feeling of its truth. But there is a commoner case than either of these; when the conflicting doctrines, instead of being one true and the other false, share the truth between them; and the nonconforming opinion is needed to supply the remainder of the truth, of which the received doctrine embodies only a part. Popular opinions, on subjects not palpable to sense, are often true, but seldom or never the whole truth. They are a part of the truth; sometimes a greater, sometimes a smaller part, but exaggerated, distorted, and disjoined from the truths by which they ought to be accompanied and limited. Heretical opinions, on the other hand, are generally some of these suppressed and neglected truths, bursting the bonds which kept them down, and either seeking reconciliation with the truth contained in the common opinion, or fronting it as enemies, and setting themselves up, with similar exclusiveness, as the whole truth. The latter case is hitherto the most frequent, as, in the human mind, one-sidedness has always been the rule, and many-sidedness the exception. Hence, even in revolutions of opinion, one part of the truth usually sets while another rises. Even progress, which ought to superadd, for the most part only substitutes one partial and incomplete truth for another; improvement consisting chiefly in this, that the new fragment of truth is more wanted, more adapted to the needs of the time, than that which it displaces. Such being the partial character of prevailing opinions, even when resting on a true foundation; every opinion which embodies somewhat of the portion of truth which the common opinion omits, ought to be considered precious, with whatever amount of error and confusion that truth may be blended. No sober judge of human affairs will feel bound to be indignant because those who force on our notice truths which we should otherwise have overlooked, overlook some of those which we see. Rather, he will think that so long as popular truth is one-sided, it is more desirable than otherwise that unpopular truth should have one-sided asserters too; such being usually the most energetic, and the most likely to compel reluctant attention to the fragment of wisdom which they proclaim as if it were the whole.

Thus, in the eighteenth century, when nearly all the instructed, and all those of the uninstructed who were led by them, were lost in admiration of what is called civilization, and of the marvels of modern science, literature, and philosophy, and while greatly overrating the amount of unlikeness between the men of modern and those of ancient times, indulged the belief that the whole of the difference was in their own favor; with what a salutary shock did the paradoxes of Rousseau explode like bombshells in the midst, dislocating the compact mass of one-sided opinion, and forcing its elements to recombine in a better form and with additional ingredients. Not that the current opinions were on the whole farther from the truth than Rousseau's were; on the contrary, they

5 were nearer to it; they contained more of positive truth, and very much less of error. Nevertheless there lay in Rousseau's doctrine, and has floated down the stream of opinion along with it, a considerable amount of exactly those truths which the popular opinion wanted; and these are the deposit which was left behind when the flood subsided. The superior worth of simplicity of life, the

10 enervating and demoralizing effect of the trammels and hypocrisies of artificial society, are ideas which have never been entirely absent from cultivated minds since Rousseau wrote; and they will in time produce their due effect, though at present needing to be asserted as much as ever, and to be asserted by deeds, for words, on this subject, have nearly exhausted their power.

15   In politics, again, it is almost a commonplace, that a party of order or stability, and a party of progress or reform, are both necessary elements of a healthy state of political life; until the one or the other shall have so enlarged its mental grasp as to be a party equally of order and of progress, knowing and distinguishing what is fit to be preserved from what ought to be swept away.

20 Each of these modes of thinking derives its utility from the deficiencies of the other; but it is in a great measure the opposition of the other that keeps each within the limits of reason and sanity. Unless opinions favorable to democracy and to aristocracy, to property and to equality, to cooperation and to competition, to luxury and to abstinence, to sociality and individuality, to liberty

25 and discipline, and all the other standing antagonisms of practical life, are expressed with equal freedom, and enforced and defended with equal talent and energy, there is no chance of both elements obtaining their due; one scale is sure to go up, and the other down. Truth, in the great practical concerns of life, is so much a question of the reconciling and combining of opposites, that very few

30 have minds sufficiently capacious and impartial to make the adjustment with an approach to correctness, and it has to be made by the rough process of a struggle between combatants fighting under hostile banners. On any of the great open questions just enumerated, if either of the two opinions has a better claim than the other, not merely to be tolerated, but to be encouraged and countenanced, it

35 is the one which happens at the particular time and place to be in a minority. That is the opinion which, for the time being, represents the neglected interests, the side of human well-being which is in danger of obtaining less than its share. I am aware that there is not, in this country, any intolerance of differences of opinion on most of these topics. They are adduced to show, by admitted and

40 multiplied examples, the universality of the fact, that only through diversity of

opinion is there, in the existing state of human intellect, a chance of fair play to all sides of the truth. When there are persons to be found, who form an exception to the apparent unanimity of the world on any subject, even if the world is in the right, it is always probable that dissentients have something
5 worth hearing to say for themselves, and that truth would lose something by their silence.

It may be objected, "But *some* received principles, especially on the highest and most vital subjects, are more than half-truths. The Christian morality, for instance, is the whole truth on that subject, and if any one teaches a morality
10 which varies from it, he is wholly in error." As this is of all cases the most important in practice, none can be fitter to test the general maxim. But before pronouncing what Christian morality is or is not, it would be desirable to decide what is meant by Christian morality. If it means the morality of the New Testament, I wonder that any one who derives his knowledge of this from the
15 book itself, can suppose that it was announced, or intended, as a complete doctrine of morals. The Gospel always refers to a preexisting morality, and confines its precepts to the particulars in which that morality was to be corrected, or superseded by a wider and higher; expressing itself, moreover, in terms most general, often impossible to be interpreted literally, and possessing
20 rather the impressiveness of poetry or eloquence than the precision of legislation. To extract from it a body of ethical doctrine, has never been possible without eking it out from the Old Testament, that is, from a system elaborate indeed, but in many respects barbarous, and intended only for a barbarous people. St. Paul, a declared enemy to this Judaical mode of interpreting the
25 doctrine and filling up the scheme of his Master, equally assumes a preexisting morality, namely, that of the Greeks and Romans; and his advice to Christians is in a great measure a system of accommodation to that; even to the extent of giving an apparent sanction to slavery. What is called Christian, but should rather be termed theological, morality, was not the work of Christ or the
30 Apostles, but is of much later origin, having been gradually built up by the Catholic Church of the first five centuries, and though not implicitly adopted by moderns and Protestants, has been much less modified by them than might have been expected. For the most part, indeed, they have contented themselves with cutting off the additions which had been made to it in the Middle Ages, each
35 sect supplying the place by fresh additions, adapted to its own character and tendencies. That mankind owe a great debt to this morality, and to its early teachers, I should be the last person to deny; but I do not scruple to say of it, that it is, in many important points, incomplete and one-sided, and that unless ideas and feelings, not sanctioned by it, had contributed to the formation of European
40 life and character, human affairs would have been in a worse condition than they

now are. Christian morality (so called) has all the characters of a reaction it is, in great part, a protest against Paganism. Its ideal is negative rather than positive; passive rather than active; Innocence rather than Nobleness; Abstinence from Evil, rather than energetic Pursuit of Good: in its precepts (as has been well
5   said) "thou shalt not" predominates unduly over "thou shalt." In its horror of sensuality, it made an idol of asceticism, which has been gradually compromised away into one of legality. It holds out the hope of heaven and the threat of hell, as the appointed and appropriate motives to a virtuous life: in this falling far below the best of the ancients, and doing what lies in it to give to human
10   morality an essentially selfish character, by disconnecting each man's feelings of duty from the interests of his fellow-creatures, except so far as a self-interested inducement is offered to him for consulting them. It is essentially a doctrine of passive obedience; it inculcates submission to all authorities found established; who indeed are not to be actively obeyed when they command what
15   religion forbids, but who are not to be resisted, far less rebelled against, for any amount of wrong to ourselves. And while, in the morality of the best Pagan nations, duty to the State holds even a disproportionate place, infringing on the just liberty of the individual; in purely Christian ethics, that grand department of duty is scarcely noticed or acknowledged. It is in the Koran, not the New
20   Testament, that we read the maxim — "A ruler who appoints any man to an office, when there is in his dominions an other man better qualified for it, sins against God and against the State." What little recognition the idea of obligation to the public obtains in modern morality, is derived from Greek and Roman sources, not from Christian; as, even in the morality of private life, whatever
25   exists of magnanimity, high-mindedness, personal dignity, even the sense of honor, is derived from the purely human, not the religious part of our education, and never could have grown out of a standard of ethics in which the only worth, professedly recognized, is that of obedience.

I am as far as any one from pretending that these defects are necessarily
30   inherent in the Christian ethics, in every manner in which it can be conceived, or that the many requisites of a complete moral doctrine which it does not contain, do not admit of being reconciled with it. Far less would I insinuate this of the doctrines and precepts of Christ himself. I believe that the sayings of Christ are all, that I can see any evidence of their having been intended to be; that they are
35   irreconcilable with nothing which a comprehensive morality requires; that everything which is excellent in ethics may be brought within them, with no greater violence to their language than has been done to it by all who have attempted to deduce from them any practical system of conduct whatever. But it is quite consistent with this, to believe that they contain, and were meant to
40   contain, only a part of the truth; that many essential elements of the highest

morality are among the things which are not provided for, nor intended to be provided for in the recorded deliverances of the Founder of Christianity, and which have been entirely thrown aside in the system of ethics erected on the basis of those deliverances by the Christian Church. And this being so, I think it
5 a great error to persist in attempting to find in the Christian doctrine that complete rule for our guidance, which its author intended it to sanction and enforce, but only partially to provide. I believe, too, that this narrow theory is becoming a grave practical evil, detracting greatly from the value of the moral training and instruction, which so many well-meaning persons are now at length
10 exerting themselves to promote. I much fear that by attempting to form the mind and feelings on an exclusively religious type, and discarding those secular standards (as for want of a better name they may be called) which heretofore coexisted with and supplemented the Christian ethics, receiving some of its spirit, and infusing into it some of theirs, there will result, and is even now
15 resulting, a low, abject, servile type of character, which, submit itself as it may to what it deems the Supreme Will, is incapable of rising to or sympathizing in the conception of Supreme Goodness. I believe that other ethics than any which can be evolved from exclusively Christian sources, must exist side by side with Christian ethics to produce the moral regeneration of mankind; and that the
20 Christian system is no exception to the rule, that in an imperfect state of the human mind, the interests of truth require a diversity of opinions. It is not necessary that in ceasing to ignore the moral truths not contained in Christianity, men should ignore any of those which it does contain. Such prejudice, or oversight, when it occurs, is altogether an evil; but it is one from which we
25 cannot hope to be always exempt, and must be regarded as the price paid for an inestimable good. The exclusive pretension made by a part of the truth to be the whole, must and ought to be protested against, and if a reactionary impulse should make the protestors unjust in their turn, this one-sidedness, like the others, may be lamented, but must be tolerated. If Christians would teach
30 infidels to be just to Christianity, they should themselves be just to in fidelity. It can do truth no service to blink the fact, known to all who have the most ordinary acquaintance with literary history, that a large portion of the noblest and most valuable moral teaching has been the work, not only of men who did not know, but of men who knew and rejected, the Christian faith.
35   I do not pretend that the most unlimited use of the freedom of enunciating all possible opinions would put an end to the evils of religious or philosophical sectarianism. Every truth which men of narrow capacity are in earnest about, is sure to be asserted, inculcated, and in many ways even acted on, as if no other truth existed in the world, or at all events none that could limit or qualify the
40 first. I acknowledge that the tendency of all opinions to become sectarian is not

cured by the freest discussion, but is often heightened and exacerbated thereby; the truth which ought to have been, but was not, seen, being rejected all the more violently because proclaimed by persons regarded as opponents. But it is not on the impassioned partisan, it is on the calmer and more disinterested by-
5   stander, that this collision of opinions works its salutary effect. Not the violent conflict between parts of the truth, but the quiet suppression of half of it, is the formidable evil: there is always hope when people are forced to listen to both sides; it is when they attend only to one that errors harden into prejudices, and truth itself ceases to have the effect of truth, by being exaggerated into
10   falsehood. And since there are few mental attributes more rare than that judicial faculty which can sit in intelligent judgment between two sides of a question, of which only one is represented by an advocate before it, truth has no chance but in proportion as every side of it, every opinion which embodies any fraction of the truth, not only finds advocates, but is so advocated as to be listened to.

15   We have now recognized the necessity to the mental well-being of mankind (on which all their other well-being depends) of freedom of opinion, and freedom of the expression of opinion, on four distinct grounds; which we will now briefly recapitulate.

       First, if any opinion is compelled to silence, that opinion may, for aught we
20   can certainly know, be true. To deny this is to assume our own infallibility.

       Secondly, though the silenced opinion be an error, it may, and very commonly does, contain a portion of truth; and since the general or prevailing opinion on any subject is rarely or never the whole truth, it is only by the collision of adverse opinions that the remainder of the truth has any chance of
25   being supplied.

       Thirdly, even if the received opinion be not only true, but the whole truth; unless it is suffered to be, and actually is, vigorously and earnestly contested, it will, by most of those who receive it, be held in the manner of a prejudice, with little comprehension or feeling of its rational grounds. And not only this, but,
30   fourthly, the meaning of the doctrine itself will be in danger of being lost, or enfeebled, and deprived of its vital effect on the character and conduct: the dogma becoming a mere formal profession, inefficacious for good, but cumbering the ground, and preventing the growth of any real and heartfelt conviction, from reason or personal experience.

35   Before quitting the subject of freedom of opinion, it is fit to take some notice of those who say, that the free expression of all opinions should be permitted, on condition that the manner be temperate, and do not pass the bounds of fair discussion. Much might be said on the impossibility of fixing where these supposed bounds are to be placed; for if the test be offence to those
40   whose opinion is attacked, I think experience testifies that this offence is given

whenever the attack is telling and powerful, and that every opponent who pushes them hard, and whom they find it difficult to answer, appears to them, if he shows any strong feeling on the subject, an intemperate opponent. But this, though an important consideration in a practical point of view, merges in a more
5 fundamental objection. Undoubtedly the manner of asserting an opinion, even though it be a true one, may be very objectionable, and may justly incur severe censure. But the principal offences of the kind are such as it is mostly impossible, unless by accidental self-betrayal, to bring home to conviction. The gravest of them is, to argue sophistically, to suppress facts or arguments, to
10 misstate the elements of the case, or misrepresent the opposite opinion. But all this, even to the most aggravated degree, is so continually done in perfect good faith, by persons who are not considered, and in many other respects may not deserve to be considered, ignorant or incompetent, that it is rarely possible on adequate grounds conscientiously to stamp the misrepresentation as morally
15 culpable; and still less could law presume to interfere with this kind of controversial misconduct. With regard to what is commonly meant by intemperate discussion, namely, invective, sarcasm, personality, and the like, the denunciation of these weapons would deserve more sympathy if it were ever proposed to interdict them equally to both sides; but it is only desired to restrain
20 the employment of them against the prevailing opinion: against the unprevailing they may not only be used without general disapproval, but will be likely to obtain for him who uses them the praise of honest zeal and righteous indignation. Yet whatever mischief arises from their use, is greatest when they are employed against the comparatively defenceless; and whatever unfair
25 advantage can be derived by any opinion from this mode of asserting it, accrues almost exclusively to received opinions. The worst offence of this kind which can be committed by a polemic, is to stigmatize those who hold the contrary opinion as bad and immoral men. To calumny of this sort, those who hold any unpopular opinion are peculiarly exposed, because they are in general few and
30 uninfluential, and nobody but themselves feels much interest in seeing justice done them; but this weapon is, from the nature of the case, denied to those who attack a prevailing opinion: they can neither use it with safety to themselves, nor, if they could, would it do anything but recoil on their own cause. In general, opinions contrary to those commonly received can only obtain a hearing by
35 studied moderation of language, and the most cautious avoidance of unnecessary offence, from which they hardly ever deviate even in a slight degree without losing ground: while unmeasured vituperation employed on the side of the prevailing opinion, really does deter people from professing contrary opinions, and from listening to those who profess them. For the interest, therefore, of truth
40 and justice, it is far more important to restrain this employment of vituperative

language than the other; and, for example, if it were necessary to choose, there would be much more need to discourage offensive attacks on infidelity, than on religion. It is, however, obvious that law and authority have no business with restraining either, while opinion ought, in every instance, to determine its verdict
5   by the circumstances of the individual case; condemning every one, on whichever side of the argument he places himself, in whose mode of advocacy either want of candor, or malignity, bigotry, or intolerance of feeling manifest themselves; but not inferring these vices from the side which a person takes, though it be the contrary side of the question to our own: and giving merited
10 honor to every one, whatever opinion he may hold, who has calmness to see and honesty to state what his opponents and their opinions really are, exaggerating nothing to their discredit, keeping nothing back which tells, or can be supposed to tell, in their favor. This is the real morality of public discussion; and if often violated, I am happy to think that there are many controversialists who to a great
15 extent observe it, and a still greater number who conscientiously strive towards it.

CHAPTER III.
Of individuality, as one of the elements of well-being.

SUCH being the reasons which make it imperative that human beings should be free to form opinions, and to express their opinions without reserve; and such the baneful consequences to the intellectual, and through that to the
20 moral nature of man, unless this liberty is either conceded, or asserted in spite of prohibition; let us next examine whether the same reasons do not require that men should be free to act upon their opinions — to carry these out in their lives, without hindrance, either physical or moral, from their fellow-men, so long as it is at their own risk and peril. This last proviso is of course indispensable. No one
25 pretends that actions should be as free as opinions. On the contrary, even opinions lose their immunity, when the circumstances in which they are expressed are such as to constitute their expression a positive instigation to some mischievous act. An opinion that corn-dealers are starvers of the poor, or that private property is robbery, ought to be unmolested when simply circulated
30 through the press, but may justly incur punishment when delivered orally to an excited mob assembled before the house of a corn-dealer, or when handed about among the same mob in the form of a placard. Acts, of whatever kind, which, without justifiable cause, do harm to others, may be, and in the more important cases absolutely require to be, controlled by the unfavorable sentiments, and,
35 when needful, by the active interference of mankind. The liberty of the individual must be thus far limited; he must not make himself a nuisance to

other people. But if he refrains from molesting others in what concerns them, and merely acts according to his own inclination and judgment in things which concern himself, the same reasons which show that opinion should be free, prove also that he should be allowed, without molestation, to carry his opinions
5 into practice at his own cost. That mankind are not infallible; that their truths, for the most part, are only half-truths; that unity of opinion, unless resulting from the fullest and freest comparison of opposite opinions, is not desirable, and diversity not an evil, but a good, until mankind are much more capable than at present of recognizing all sides of the truth, are principles applicable to men's
10 modes of action, not less than to their opinions. As it is useful that while mankind are imperfect there should be different opinions, so is it that there should be different experiments of living; that free scope should be given to varieties of character, short of injury to others; and that the worth of different modes of life should be proved practically, when any one thinks fit to try them.
15 It is desirable, in short, that in things which do not primarily concern others, individuality should assert itself. Where, not the person's own character, but the traditions or customs of other people are the rule of conduct, there is wanting one of the principal ingredients of human happiness, and quite the chief ingredient of individual and social progress.
20 In maintaining this principle, the greatest difficulty to be encountered does not lie in the appreciation of means towards an acknowledged end, but in the indifference of persons in general to the end itself. If it were felt that the free development of individuality is one of the leading essentials of well-being; that it is not only a coordinate element with all that is designated by the terms
25 civilization, instruction, education, culture, but is itself a necessary part and condition of all those things; there would be no danger that liberty should be undervalued, and the adjustment of the boundaries between it and social control would present no extraordinary difficulty. But the evil is, that individual spontaneity is hardly recognized by the common modes of thinking as having
30 any intrinsic worth, or deserving any regard on its own account. The majority, being satisfied with the ways of mankind as they now are (for it is they who make them what they are), cannot comprehend why those ways should not be good enough for everybody; and what is more, spontaneity forms no part of the ideal of the majority of moral and social reformers, but is rather looked on with
35 jealousy, as a troublesome and perhaps rebellious obstruction to the general acceptance of what these reformers, in their own judgment, think would be best for mankind. Few persons, out of Germany, even comprehend the meaning of the doctrine which Wilhelm von Humboldt, so eminent both as a *savant* and as a politician, made the text of a treatise — that "the end of man, or that which is
40 prescribed by the eternal or immutable dictates of reason, and not suggested by

338

vague and transient desires, is the highest and most harmonious development of his powers to a complete and consistent whole;" that, therefore, the object "towards which every human being must ceaselessly direct his efforts, and on which especially those who design to influence their fellow-men must ever keep
5   their eyes, is the individuality of power and development;" that for this there are two requisites, "freedom, and a variety of situations;" and that from the union of these arise "individual vigor and manifold diversity," which combine themselves in "originality."[6]

Little, however, as people are accustomed to a doctrine like that of Von
10   Humboldt, and surprising as it may be to them to find so high a value attached to individuality, the question, one must nevertheless think, can only be one of degree. No one's idea of excellence in conduct is that people should do absolutely nothing but copy one another. No one would assert that people ought not to put into their mode of life, and into the conduct of their concerns, any
15   impress whatever of their own judgment, or of their own individual character. On the other hand, it would be absurd to pretend that people ought to live as if nothing whatever had been known in the world before they came into it; as if experience had as yet done nothing towards showing that one mode of existence, or of conduct, is preferable to another. Nobody denies that people should be so
20   taught and trained in youth, as to know and benefit by the ascertained results of human experience. But it is the privilege and proper condition of a human being, arrived at the maturity of his faculties, to use and interpret experience in his own way. It is for him to find out what part of recorded experience is properly applicable to his own circumstances and character. The traditions and customs
25   of other people are, to a certain extent, evidence of what their experience has taught *them;* presumptive evidence, and as such, have a claim to his deference: but, in the first place, their experience may be too narrow; or they may not have interpreted it rightly. Secondly, their interpretation of experience may be correct but unsuitable to him. Customs are made for customary circumstances, and
30   customary characters: and his circumstances or his character may be uncustomary. Thirdly, though the customs be both good as customs, and suitable to him, yet to conform to custom, merely *as* custom, does not educate or develop in him any of the qualities which are the distinctive endowment of a human being. The human faculties of perception, judgment, discriminative feeling,
35   mental activity, and even moral preference, are exercised only in making a choice. He who does anything because it is the custom, makes no choice. He gains no practice either in discerning or in desiring what is best. The mental and moral, like the muscular powers, are improved only by being used. The faculties are called into no exercise by doing a thing merely because others do it, no more
40   than by believing a thing only because others believe it. If the grounds of an

opinion are not conclusive to the person's own reason, his reason cannot be strengthened, but is likely to be weakened by his adopting it: and if the inducements to an act are not such as are consentaneous to his own feelings and character (where affection, or the rights of others, are not concerned), it is so
5 much done towards rendering his feelings and character inert and torpid, instead of active and energetic.

He who lets the world, or his own portion of it, choose his plan of life for him, has no need of any other faculty than the ape-like one of imitation. He who chooses his plan for himself, employs all his faculties. He must use observation
10 to see, reasoning and judgment to foresee, activity to gather materials for decision, discrimination to decide, and when he has decided, firmness and self-control to hold to his deliberate decision. And these qualities he requires and exercises exactly in proportion as the part of his conduct which he determines according to his own judgment and feelings is a large one. It is possible that he
15 might be guided in some good path, and kept out of harm's way, without any of these things. But what will be his comparative worth as a human being? It really is of importance, not only what men do, but also what manner of men they are that do it. Among the works of man, which human life is rightly employed in perfecting and beautifying, the first in importance surely is man himself.
20 Supposing it were possible to get houses built, corn grown, battles fought, causes tried, and even churches erected and prayers said, by machinery — by automatons in human form — it would be a considerable loss to exchange for these automatons even the men and women who at present inhabit the more civilized parts of the world, and who assuredly are but starved specimens of
25 what nature can and will produce. Human nature is not a machine to be built after a model, and set to do exactly the work prescribed for it, but a tree, which requires to grow and develop itself on all sides, according to the tendency of the inward forces which make it a living thing.

It will probably be conceded that it is desirable people should exercise their
30 understandings, and that an intelligent following of custom, or even occasionally an intelligent deviation from custom, is better than a blind and simply mechanical adhesion to it. To a certain extent it is admitted, that our understanding should be our own: but there is not the same willingness to admit that our desires and impulses should be our own likewise; or that to possess
35 impulses of our own, and of any strength, is anything but a peril and a snare. Yet desires and impulses are as much a part of a perfect human being, as beliefs and restraints: and strong impulses are only perilous when not properly balanced; when one set of aims and inclinations is developed into strength, while others, which ought to coexist with them, remain weak and inactive. It is not because
40 men's desires are strong that they act ill; it is because their consciences are

340

weak. There is no natural connection between strong impulses and a weak
conscience. The natural connection is the other way. To say that one person's
desires and feelings are stronger and more various than those of another, is
merely to say that he has more of the raw material of human nature, and is
5   therefore capable, perhaps of more evil, but certainly of more good. Strong
impulses are but another name for energy. Energy may be turned to bad uses;
but more good may always be made of an energetic nature, than of an indolent
and impassive one. Those who have most natural feeling, are always those
whose cultivated feelings may be made the strongest. The same strong
10   susceptibilities which make the personal impulses vivid and powerful, are also
the source from whence are generated the most passionate love of virtue, and the
sternest self-control. It is through the cultivation of these, that society both does
its duty and protects its interests: not by rejecting the stuff of which heroes are
made, because it knows not how to make them. A person whose desires and
15   impulses are his own — are the expression of his own nature, as it has been
developed and modified by his own culture — is said to have a character. One
whose desires and impulses are not his own, has no character, no more than a
steam-engine has a character. If, in addition to being his own, his impulses are
strong, and are under the government of a strong will, he has an energetic
20   character. Whoever thinks that individuality of desires and impulses should not
be encouraged to unfold itself, must maintain that society has no need of strong
natures — is not the better for containing many persons who have much
character — and that a high general average of energy is not desirable.

    In some early states of society, these forces might be, and were, too much
25   ahead of the power which society then possessed of disciplining and controlling
them. There has been a time when the element of spontaneity and individuality
was in excess, and the social principle had a hard struggle with it. The difficulty
then was, to induce men of strong bodies or minds to pay obedience to any rules
which required them to control their impulses. To overcome this difficulty, law
30   and discipline, like the Popes struggling against the Emperors, asserted a power
over the whole man, claiming to control all his life in order to control his
character — which society had not found any other sufficient means of binding.
But society has now fairly got the better of individuality; and the danger which
threatens human nature is not the excess, but the deficiency, of personal
35   impulses and preferences. Things are vastly changed, since the passions of those
who were strong by station or by personal endowment were in a state of habitual
rebellion against laws and ordinances, and required to be rigorously chained up
to enable the persons within their reach to enjoy any particle of security. In our
times, from the highest class of society down to the lowest every one lives as
40   under the eye of a hostile and dreaded censorship. Not only in what concerns

others, but in what concerns only themselves, the individual, or the family, do not ask themselves — what do I prefer? or, what would suit my character and disposition? or, what would allow the best and highest in me to have fair play, and enable it to grow and thrive? They ask themselves, what is suitable to my

5 position? what is usually done by persons of my station and pecuniary circumstances? or (worse still) what is usually done by persons of a station and circumstances superior to mine? I do not mean that they choose what is customary, in preference to what suits their own inclination. It does not occur to them to have any inclination, except for what is customary. Thus the mind itself

10 is bowed to the yoke: even in what people do for pleasure, conformity is the first thing thought of; they like in crowds; they exercise choice only among things commonly done: peculiarity of taste, eccentricity of conduct, are shunned equally with crimes: until by dint of not following their own nature, they have no nature to follow: their human capacities are withered and starved: they

15 become incapable of any strong wishes or native pleasures, and are generally without either opinions or feelings of home growth, or properly their own. Now is this, or is it not, the desirable condition of human nature?

It is so, on the Calvinistic theory. According to that, the one great offence of man is Self-will. All the good of which humanity is capable, is comprised in

20 Obedience. You have no choice; thus you must do, and no otherwise: "whatever is not a duty is a sin." Human nature being radically corrupt, there is no redemption for any one until human nature is killed within him. To one holding this theory of life, crushing out any of the human faculties, capacities, and susceptibilities, is no evil: man needs no capacity, but that of surrendering

25 himself to the will of God: and if he uses any of his faculties for any other purpose but to do that supposed will more effectually, he is better without them. That is the theory of Calvinism; and it is held, in a mitigated form, by many who do not consider themselves Calvinists; the mitigation consisting in giving a less ascetic interpretation to the alleged will of God; asserting it to be his will that

30 mankind should gratify some of their inclinations; of course not in the manner they themselves prefer, but in the way of obedience, that is, in a way prescribed to them by authority; and, therefore, by the necessary conditions of the case, the same for all.

In some such insidious form there is at present a strong tendency to this

35 narrow theory of life, and to the pinched and hidebound type of human character which it patronizes. Many persons, no doubt, sincerely think that human beings thus cramped and dwarfed, are as their Maker designed them to be; just as many have thought that trees are a much finer thing when clipped into pollards, or cut out into figures of animals, than as nature made them. But if it be any part of

40 religion to believe that man was made by a good Being, it is more consistent

with that faith to believe, that this Being gave all human faculties that they might be cultivated and unfolded, not rooted out and consumed, and that he takes delight in every nearer approach made by his creatures to the ideal conception embodied in them, every increase in any of their capabilities of
5   comprehension, of action, or of enjoyment. There is a different type of human excellence from the Calvinistic; a conception of humanity as having its nature bestowed on it for other purposes than merely to be abnegated. "Pagan self-assertion" is one of the elements of human worth, as well as "Christian self-denial."[7] There is a Greek ideal of self-development, which the Platonic and
10 Christian ideal of self-government blends with, but does not supersede. It may be better to be a John Knox than an Alcibiades, but it is better to be a Pericles than either; nor would a Pericles, if we had one in these days, be without anything good which belonged to John Knox.

     It is not by wearing down into uniformity all that is individual in
15 themselves, but by cultivating it and calling it forth, within the limits imposed by the rights and interests of others, that human beings become a noble and beautiful object of contemplation; and as the works partake the character of those who do them, by the same process human life also becomes rich, diversified, and animating, furnishing more abundant aliment to high thoughts
20 and elevating feelings, and strengthening the tie which binds every individual to the race, by making the race infinitely better worth belonging to. In proportion to the development of his individuality, each person becomes more valuable to himself, and is therefore capable of being more valuable to others. There is a greater fullness of life about his own existence, and when there is more life in
25 the units there is more in the mass which is composed of them. As much compression as is necessary to prevent the stronger specimens of human nature from encroaching on the rights of others, cannot be dispensed with; but for this there is ample compensation even in the point of view of human development. The means of development which the individual loses by being prevented from
30 gratifying his inclinations to the injury of others, are chiefly obtained at the expense of the development of other people. And even to himself there is a full equivalent in the better development of the social part of his nature, rendered possible by the restraint put upon the selfish part. To be held to rigid rules of justice for the sake of others, develops the feelings and capacities which have
35 the good of others for their object. But to be restrained in things not affecting their good, by their mere displeasure, develops nothing valuable, except such force of character as may unfold itself in resisting the restraint. If acquiesced in, it dulls and blunts the whole nature. To give any fair play to the nature of each, it is essential that different persons should be allowed to lead different lives. In
40 proportion as this latitude has been exercised in any age, has that age been

noteworthy to posterity. Even despotism does not produce its worst effects, so long as Individuality exists under it; and whatever crushes individuality is despotism, by whatever name it may be called, and whether it professes to be enforcing the will of God or the injunctions of men.

5   Having said that Individuality is the same thing with development, and that it is only the cultivation of individuality which produces, or can produce, well-developed human beings, I might here close the argument: for what more or better can be said of any condition of human affairs, than that it brings human beings themselves nearer to the best thing they can be? or what worse can be
10 said of any obstruction to good, than that it prevents this? Doubtless, however, these considerations will not suffice to convince those who most need convincing; and it is necessary further to show, that these developed human beings are of some use to the undeveloped — to point out to those who do not desire liberty, and would not avail themselves of it, that they may be in some
15 intelligible manner rewarded for allowing other people to make use of it without hindrance.

    In the first place, then, I would suggest that they might possibly learn something from them. It will not be denied by anybody, that originality is a valuable element in human affairs. There is always need of persons not only to
20 discover new truths, and point out when what were once truths are true no longer, but also to commence new practices, and set the example of more enlightened conduct, and better taste and sense in human life. This cannot well be gainsaid by anybody who does not believe that the world has already attained perfection in all its ways and practices. It is true that this benefit is not capable
25 of being rendered by everybody alike: there are but few persons, in comparison with the whole of mankind, whose experiments, if adopted by others, would be likely to be any improvement on established practice. But these few are the salt of the earth; without them, human life would become a stagnant pool. Not only is it they who introduce good things which did not before exist; it is they who
30 keep the life in those which already existed. If there were nothing new to be done, would human intellect cease to be necessary? Would it be a reason why those who do the old things should forget why they are done, and do them like cattle, not like human beings? There is only too great a tendency in the best beliefs and practices to degenerate into the mechanical; and unless there were a
35 succession of persons whose ever-recurring originality prevents the grounds of those beliefs and practices from becoming merely traditional, such dead matter would not resist the smallest shock from anything really alive, and there would be no reason why civilization should not die out, as in the Byzantine Empire. Persons of genius, it is true, are, and are always likely to be, a small minority;
40 but in order to have them, it is necessary to preserve the soil in which they grow.

344

Genius can only breathe freely in an *atmosphere* of freedom. Persons of genius are, *ex vi termini, more* individual than any other people — less capable, consequently, of fitting themselves, without hurtful compression, into any of the small number of moulds which society provides in order to save its members the
5   trouble of forming their own character. If from timidity they consent to be forced into one of these moulds, and to let all that part of themselves which cannot expand under the pressure remain unexpanded, society will be little the better for their genius. If they are of a strong character, and break their fetters, they become a mark for the society which has not succeeded in reducing them to
10   commonplace, to point at with solemn warning as "wild," "erratic," and the like; much as if one should complain of the Niagara river for not flowing smoothly between its banks like a Dutch canal.

       I insist thus emphatically on the importance of genius, and the necessity of allowing it to unfold itself freely both in thought and in practice, being well
15   aware that no one will deny the position in theory, but knowing also that almost every one, in reality, is totally indifferent to it. People think genius a fine thing if it enables a man to write an exciting poem, or paint a picture. But in its true sense, that of originality in thought and action, though no one says that it is not a thing to be admired, nearly all, at heart, think that they can do very well without
20   it. Unhappily this is too natural to be wondered at. Originality is the one thing which unoriginal minds cannot feel the use of. They cannot see what it is to do for them: how should they? If they could see what it would do for them, it would not be originality. The first service which originality has to render them, is that of opening their eyes: which being once fully done, they would have a chance of
25   being themselves original. Meanwhile, recollecting that nothing was ever yet done which some one was not the first to do, and that all good things which exist are the fruits of originality, let them be modest enough to believe that there is something still left for it to accomplish, and assure themselves that they are more in need of originality, the less they are conscious of the want.

30   In sober truth, whatever homage may be professed, or even paid, to real or supposed mental superiority, the general tendency of things throughout the world is to render mediocrity the ascendant power among mankind. In ancient history, in the Middle Ages, and in a diminishing degree through the long transition from feudality to the present time, the individual was a power in
35   himself; and if he had either great talents or a high social position, he was a considerable power. At present individuals are lost in the crowd. In politics it is almost a triviality to say that public opinion now rules the world. The only power deserving the name is that of masses, and of governments while they make themselves the organ of the tendencies and instincts of masses. This is as
40   true in the moral and social relations of private life as in public transactions.

Those whose opinions go by the name of public opinion, are not always the same sort of public: in America, they are the whole white population in England, chiefly the middle class. But they are always a mass, that is to say, collective mediocrity. And what is a still greater novelty, the mass do not now take their opinions from dignitaries in Church or State, from ostensible leaders, or from books. Their thinking is done for them by men much like themselves, addressing them or speaking in their name, on the spur of the moment, through the newspapers. I am not complaining of all this. I do not assert that anything better is compatible, as a general rule, with the present low state of the human mind. But that does not hinder the government of mediocrity from being mediocre government. No government by a democracy or a numerous aristocracy, either in its political acts or in the opinions, qualities, and tone of mind which it fosters, ever did or could rise above mediocrity, except in so far as the sovereign Many have let themselves be guided (which in their best times they always have done) by the counsels and influence of a more highly gifted and instructed One or Few. The initiation of all wise or noble things, comes and must come from individuals; generally at first from some one individual. The honor and glory of the average man is that he is capable of following that initiative; that he can respond internally to wise and noble things, and be led to them with his eyes open. I am not countenancing the sort of "hero-worship" which applauds the strong man of genius for forcibly seizing on the government of the world and making it do his bidding in spite of itself. All he can claim is, freedom to point out the way. The power of compelling others into it, is not only inconsistent with the freedom and development of all the rest, but corrupting to the strong man himself. It does seem, however, that when the opinions of masses of merely average men are everywhere become or becoming the dominant power, the counterpoise and corrective to that tendency would be, the more and more pronounced individuality of those who stand on the higher eminences of thought. It is in these circumstances most especially, that exceptional individuals, instead of being deterred, should be encouraged in acting differently from the mass. In other times there was no advantage in their doing so, unless they acted not only differently, but better. In this age the mere example of non-conformity, the mere refusal to bend the knee to custom, is itself a service. Precisely because the tyranny of opinion is such as to make eccentricity a reproach, it is desirable, in order to break through that tyranny, that people should be eccentric. Eccentricity has always abounded when and where strength of character has abounded; and the amount of eccentricity in a society has generally been proportional to the amount of genius, mental vigor, and moral courage which it contained. That so few now dare to be eccentric, marks the chief danger of the time.

I have said that it is important to give the freest scope possible to uncustomary things, in order that it may in time appear which of these are fit to be converted into customs. But independence of action, and disregard of custom are not solely deserving of encouragement for the chance they afford that better
5   modes of action, and customs more worthy of general adoption, may be struck out; nor is it only persons of decided mental superiority who have a just claim to carry on their lives in their own way. There is no reason that all human existences should be constructed on some one, or some small number of patterns. If a person possesses any tolerable amount of common sense and
10   experience, his own mode of laying out his existence is the best, not because it is the best in itself, but because it is his own mode. Human beings are not like sheep; and even sheep are not undistinguishably alike. A man cannot get a coat or a pair of boots to fit him, unless they are either made to his measure, or he has a whole warehouse full to choose from: and is it easier to fit him with a life than
15   with a coat, or are human beings more like one another in their whole physical and spiritual conformation than in the shape of their feet? If it were only that people have diversities of taste, that is reason enough for not attempting to shape them all after one model. But different persons also require different conditions for their spiritual development; and can no more exist healthily in the same
20   moral, than all the variety of plants can in the same physical, atmosphere and climate. The same things which are helps to one person towards the cultivation of his higher nature, are hindrances to another. The same mode of life is a healthy excitement to one, keeping all his faculties of action and enjoyment in their best order, while to another it is a distracting burden, which suspends or
25   crushes all internal life. Such are the differences among human beings in their sources of pleasure, their susceptibilities of pain, and the operation on them of different physical and moral agencies, that unless there is a corresponding diversity in their modes of life, they neither obtain their fair share of happiness, nor grow up to the mental, moral, and aesthetic stature of which their nature is
30   capable. Why then should tolerance, as far as the public sentiment is concerned, extend only to tastes and modes of life which extort acquiescence by the multitude of their adherents? Nowhere (except in some monastic institutions) is diversity of taste entirely unrecognized; a person may without blame, either like or dislike rowing, or smoking, or music, or athletic exercises, or chess, or cards,
35   or study, because both those who like each of these things, and those who dislike them, are too numerous to be put down. But the man, and still more the woman, who can be accused either of doing "what nobody does," or of not doing "what everybody does," is the subject of as much depreciatory remark as if he or she had committed some grave moral delinquency. Persons require to possess a title,
40   or some other badge of rank, or the consideration of people of rank, to be able to

indulge somewhat in the luxury of doing as they like without detriment to their estimation. To indulge somewhat, I repeat: for whoever allow themselves much of that indulgence, incur the risk of something worse than disparaging speeches — they are in peril of a commission *de lunatico,* and of having their property taken from them and given to their relations.[8]

There is one characteristic of the present direction of public opinion, peculiarly calculated to make it intolerant of any marked demonstration of individuality. The general average of mankind are not only moderate in intellect, but also moderate in inclinations: they have no tastes or wishes strong enough to incline them to do anything unusual, and they consequently do not understand those who have, and class all such with the wild and intemperate whom they are accustomed to look down upon. Now, in addition to this fact which is general, we have only to suppose that a strong movement has set in towards the improvement of morals, and it is evident what we have to expect. In these days such a movement has set in; much has actually been effected in the way of increased regularity of conduct, and discouragement of excesses; and there is a philanthropic spirit abroad, for the exercise of which there is no more inviting field than the moral and prudential improvement of our fellow-creatures. These tendencies of the times cause the public to be more disposed than at most former periods to prescribe general rules of conduct, and endeavor to make every one conform to the approved standard. And that standard, express or tacit, is to desire nothing strongly. Its ideal of character is to be without any marked character; to maim by compression, like a Chinese lady's foot, every part of human nature which stands out prominently, and tends to make the person markedly dissimilar in outline to commonplace humanity.

As is usually the case with ideals which exclude one half of what is desirable, the present standard of approbation produces only an inferior imitation of the other half. Instead of great energies guided by vigorous reason, and strong feelings strongly controlled by a conscientious will, its result is weak feelings and weak energies, which therefore can be kept in outward conformity to rule without any strength either of will or of reason. Already energetic characters on any large scale are becoming merely traditional. There is now scarcely any outlet for energy in this country except business. The energy expended in that may still be regarded as considerable. What little is left from that employment, is expended on some hobby; which may be a useful, even a philanthropic hobby, but is always some one thing, and generally a thing of small dimensions. The greatness of England is now all collective: individually small, we only appear capable of anything great by our habit of combining; and with this our moral and religious philanthropists are perfectly contented. But it was men of another stamp than this that made England what it has been; and men of another stamp will be needed to prevent its decline.

The despotism of custom is everywhere the standing hindrance to human advancement, being in unceasing antagonism to that disposition to aim at
5   something better than customary, which is called, according to circumstances, the spirit of liberty, or that of progress or improvement. The spirit of improvement is not always a spirit of liberty, for it may aim at forcing improvements on an unwilling people; and the spirit of liberty, in so far as it resists such attempts, may ally itself locally and temporarily with the opponents
10   of improvement; but the only unfailing and permanent source of improvement is liberty, since by it there are as many possible independent centres of improvement as there are individuals. The progressive principle, however, in either shape, whether as the love of liberty or of improvement, is antagonistic to the sway of Custom, involving at least emancipation from that yoke; and the
15   contest between the two constitutes the chief interest of the history of mankind. The greater part of the world has, properly speaking, no history, because the despotism of Custom is complete. This is the case over the whole East. Custom is there, in all things, the final appeal; justice and right mean conformity to custom; the argument of custom no one, unless some tyrant intoxicated with
20   power, thinks of resisting. And we see the result. Those nations must once have had originality; they did not start out of the ground populous, lettered, and versed in many of the arts of life they made themselves all this, and were then the greatest and most powerful nations in the world. What are they now? The subjects or dependents of tribes whose forefathers wandered in the forests when
25   theirs had magnificent palaces and gorgeous temples, but over whom custom exercised only a divided rule with liberty and progress. A people, it appears, may be progressive for a certain length of time, and then stop: when does it stop? When it ceases to possess individuality. If a similar change should befall the nations of Europe, it will not be in exactly the same shape: the despotism of
30   custom with which these nations are threatened is not precisely stationariness. It proscribes singularity, but it does not preclude change, provided all change together. We have discarded the fixed costumes of our fore-fathers; every one must still dress like other people, but the fashion may change once or twice a year. We thus take care that when there is change, it shall be for change's sake,
35   and not from any idea of beauty or convenience; for the same idea of beauty or convenience would not strike all the world at the same moment, and be simultaneously thrown aside by all at another moment. But we are progressive as well as changeable: we continually make new inventions in mechanical things, and keep them until they are again superseded by better; we are eager for
40   improvement in politics, in education, even in morals, though in this last our

idea of improvement chiefly consists in persuading or forcing other people to be as good as ourselves. It is not progress that we object to; on the contrary, we flatten ourselves that we are the most progressive people who ever lived. It is individuality that we war against: we should think we had done wonders if we had made ourselves all alike; forgetting that the unlikeness of one person to another is generally the first thing which draws the attention of either to the imperfection of his own type, and the superiority of another, or the possibility, by combining the advantages of both, of producing something better than either. We have a warning example in China — a nation of much talent, and, in some respects, even wisdom, owing to the rare good fortune of having been provided at an early period with a particularly good set of customs, the work, in some measure, of men to whom even the most enlightened European must accord, under certain limitations, the title of sages and philosophers. They are remarkable, too, in the excellence of their apparatus for impressing, as far as possible, the best wisdom they possess upon every mind in the community, and securing that those who have appropriated most of it shall occupy the posts of honor and power. Surely the people who did this have discovered the secret of human progressiveness, and must have kept themselves steadily at the head of the movement of the world. On the contrary, they have become stationary — have remained so for thousands of years; and if they are ever to be farther improved, it must be by foreigners. They have succeeded beyond all hope in what English philanthropists are so industriously working at — in making a people all alike, all governing their thoughts and conduct by the same maxims and rules; and these are the fruits. The modern *régime* of public opinion is, in an unorganized form, what the Chinese educational and political systems are in an organized; and unless individuality shall be able successfully to assert itself against this yoke, Europe, notwithstanding its noble antecedents and its professed Christianity, will tend to become another China.

What is it that has hitherto preserved Europe from this lot? What has made the European family of nations an improving, instead of a stationary portion of mankind? Not any superior excellence in them, which when it exists, exists as the effect, not as the cause; but their remarkable diversity of character and culture. Individuals, classes, nations, have been extremely unlike one another: they have struck out a great variety of paths, each leading to something valuable; and although at every period those who traveled in different paths have been intolerant of one another, and each would have thought it an excellent thing if all the rest could have been compelled to travel his road, their attempts to thwart each other's development have rarely had any permanent success, and each has in time endured to receive the good which the others have offered. Europe is, in my judgment, wholly indebted to this plurality of paths for its progressive and

many-sided development. But it already begins to possess this benefit in a considerably less degree. It is decidedly advancing towards the Chinese ideal of making all people alike. M. de Tocqueville, in his last important work, remarks how much more the Frenchmen of the present day resemble one another, than
5   did those even of the last generation. The same remark might be made of Englishmen in a far greater degree. In a passage already quoted from Wilhelm von Humboldt, he points out two things as necessary conditions of human development, because necessary to render people unlike one another; namely, freedom, and variety of situations. The second of these two conditions is in this
10   country every day diminishing. The circumstances which surround different classes and individuals, and shape their characters, are daily becoming more assimilated. Formerly, different ranks, different neighborhoods, different trades and professions, lived in what might be called different worlds at present, to a great degree in the same Comparatively speaking, they now read the same
15   things, listen to the same things, see the same things, go to the same places, have their hopes and fears directed to the same objects, have the same rights and liberties, and the same means of asserting them. Great as are the differences of position which remain, they are nothing to those which have ceased. And the assimilation is still proceeding. All the political changes of the age promote it,
20   since they all tend to raise the low and to lower the high. Every extension of education promotes it, because education brings people under common influences, and gives them access to the general stock of facts and sentiments. Improvements in the means of communication promote it, by bringing the inhabitants of distant places into personal contact, and keeping up a rapid flow
25   of changes of residence between one place and another. The increase of commerce and manufactures promotes it, by diffusing more widely the advantages of easy circumstances, and opening all objects of ambition, even the highest, to general competition, whereby the desire of rising becomes no longer the character of a particular class, but of all classes. A more powerful agency
30   than even all these, in bringing about a general similarity among mankind, is the complete establishment, in this and other free countries, of the ascendency of public opinion in the State. As the various social eminences which enabled persons entrenched on them to disregard the opinion of the multitude, gradually become leveled; as the very idea of resisting the will of the public, when it is
35   positively known that they have a will, disappears more and more from the minds of practical politicians; there ceases to be any social support for non-conformity — any substantive power in society, which, itself opposed to the ascendancy of numbers, is interested in taking under its protection opinions and tendencies at variance with those of the public.

The combination of all these causes forms so great a mass of influences hostile to Individuality, that it is not easy to see how it can stand its ground. It will do so with increasing difficulty, unless the intelligent part of the public can be made to feel its value — to see that it is good there should be differences, even though not for the better, even though, as it may appear to them, some should be for the worse. If the claims of Individuality are ever to be asserted, the time is now, while much is still wanting to complete the enforced assimilation. It is only in the earlier stages that any stand can be successfully made against the encroachment. The demand that all other people shall resemble ourselves, grows by what it feeds on. If resistance waits till life is reduced *nearly* to one uniform type, all deviations from that type will come to be considered impious, immoral, even monstrous and contrary to nature. Mankind speedily become unable to conceive diversity, when they have been for some time unaccustomed to see it.

CHAPTER IV.
Of the limits to the authority of society over the individual.

WHAT, then, is the rightful limit to the sovereignty of the individual over himself? Where does the authority of society begin? How much of human life should be assigned to individuality, and how much to society?

Each will receive its proper share, if each has that which more particularly concerns it. To individuality should belong the part of life in which it is chiefly the individual that is interested; to society, the part which chiefly interests society.

Though society is not founded on a contract, and though no good purpose is answered by inventing a contract in order to deduce social obligations from it, every one who receives the protection of society owes a return for the benefit, and the fact of living in society renders it indispensable that each should be bound to observe a certain line of conduct towards the rest. This conduct consists, first, in not injuring the interests of one another; or rather certain interests, which, either by express legal provision or by tacit understanding, ought to be considered as rights; and secondly, in each person's bearing his share (to be fixed on some equitable principle) of the labors and sacrifices incurred for defending the society or its members from injury and molestation. These conditions society is justified in enforcing, at all costs to those who endeavor to withhold fulfillment. Nor is this all that society may do. The acts of an individual may be hurtful to others, or wanting in due consideration for their welfare, without going the length of violating any of their constituted rights. The offender may then be justly punished by opinion, though not by law. As soon as any part of a person's conduct affects prejudicially the interests of others,

society has jurisdiction over it, and the question whether the general welfare will or will not be promoted by interfering with it, becomes open to discussion. But there is no room for entertaining any such question when a person's conduct affects the interests of no persons besides himself, or needs not affect them
5   unless they like (all the persons concerned being of full age, and the ordinary amount of understanding). In all such cases there should be perfect freedom, legal and social, to do the action and stand the consequences.

It would be a great misunderstanding of this doctrine, to suppose that it is one of selfish indifference, which pretends that human beings have no business
10 with each other's conduct in life, and that they should not concern themselves about the well-doing or well-being of one another, unless their own interest is involved. Instead of any diminution, there is need of a great increase of disinterested exertion to promote the good of others. But disinterested benevolence can find other instruments to persuade people to their good, than
15 whips and scourges, either of the literal or the metaphorical sort. I am the last person to undervalue the self-regarding virtues; they are only second in importance, if even second, to the social. It is equally the business of education to cultivate both. But even education works by conviction and persuasion as well as by compulsion, and it is by the former only that, when the period of
20 education is past, the self-regarding virtues should be inculcated Human beings owe to each other help to distinguish the better from the worse, and encouragement to choose the former and avoid the latter. They should be forever stimulating each other to increased exercise of their higher faculties, and increased direction of their feelings and aims towards wise instead of foolish,
25 elevating instead of degrading, objects and contemplations. But neither one person, nor any number of persons, is warranted in saying to another human creature of ripe years, that he shall not do with his life for his own benefit what he chooses to do with it. He is the person most interested in his own well-being the interest which any other person, except in cases of strong personal
30 attachment, can have in it, is trifling, compared with that which he himself has; the interest which society has in him individually (except as to his conduct to others) is fractional, and altogether indirect: while, with respect to his own feelings and circumstances, the most ordinary man or woman has means of knowledge immeasurably surpassing those that can be possessed by any one
35 else. The interference of society to overrule his judgment and purposes in what only regards himself, must be grounded on general presumptions; which may be altogether wrong, and even if right, are as likely as not to be misapplied to individual cases, by persons no better acquainted with the circumstances of such cases than those are who look at them merely from without. In this department,
40 therefore, of human affairs, Individuality has its proper field of action. In the

conduct of human beings towards one another, it is necessary that general rules should for the most part be observed, in order that people may know what they have to expect; but in each person's own concerns, his individual spontaneity is entitled to free exercise. Considerations to aid his judgment, exhortations to
5   strengthen his will, may be offered to him, even obtruded on him, by others; but he, himself, is the final judge. All errors which he is likely to commit against advice and warning, are far outweighed by the evil of allowing others to constrain him to what they deem his good.

I do not mean that the feelings with which a person is regarded by others,
10 ought not to be in any way affected by his self-regarding qualities or deficiencies. This is neither possible nor desirable. If he is eminent in any of the qualities which conduce to his own good, he is, so far, a proper object of admiration. He is so much the nearer to the ideal perfection of human nature. If he is grossly deficient in those qualities, a sentiment the opposite of admiration
15 will follow. There is a degree of folly, and a degree of what may be called (though the phrase is not unobjectionable) lowness or depravation of taste, which, though it cannot justify doing harm to the person who manifests it, renders him necessarily and properly a subject of distaste, or, in extreme cases, even of contempt: a person could not have the opposite qualities in due strength
20 without entertaining these feelings. Though doing no wrong to any one, a person may so act as to compel us to judge him, and feel to him, as a fool, or as a being of an inferior order: and since this judgment and feeling are a fact which he would prefer to avoid, it is doing him a service to warn him of it beforehand, as of any other disagreeable consequence to which he exposes himself. It would be
25 well, indeed, if this good office were much more freely rendered than the common notions of politeness at present permit, and if one person could honestly point out to another that he thinks him in fault, without being considered unmannerly or presuming. We have a right, also, in various ways, to act upon our unfavorable opinion of any one, not to the oppression of his
30 individuality, but in the exercise of ours. We are not bound, for example, to seek his society; we have a right to avoid it (though not to parade the avoidance), for we have a right to choose the society most acceptable to us. We have a right, and it may be our duty to caution others against him, if we think his example or conversation likely to have a pernicious effect on those with whom he
35 associates. We may give others a preference over him in optional good offices, except those which tend to his improvement. In these various modes a person may suffer very severe penalties at the hands of others, for faults which directly concern only himself; but he suffers these penalties only in so far as they are the natural, and, as it were, the spontaneous consequences of the faults themselves,
40 not because they are purposely inflicted on him for the sake of punishment. A

person who shows rashness, obstinacy, self-conceit — who cannot live within moderate means — who cannot restrain himself from hurtful indulgences — who pursues animal pleasures at the expense of those of feeling and intellect — must expect to be lowered in the opinion of others, and to have a less share of their favorable sentiments, but of this he has no right to complain, unless he has merited their favor by special excellence in his social relations, and has thus established a title to their good offices, which is not affected by his demerits towards himself.

What I contend for is, that the inconveniences which are strictly inseparable from the unfavorable judgment of others, are the only ones to which a person should ever be subjected for that portion of his conduct and character which concerns his own good, but which does not affect the interests of others in their relations with him. Acts injurious to others require a totally different treatment. Encroachment on their rights; infliction on them of any loss or damage not justified by his own rights; falsehood or duplicity in dealing with them; unfair or ungenerous use of advantages over them; even selfish abstinence from defending them against injury — these are fit objects of moral reprobation, and, in grave cases, of moral retribution and punishment. And not only these acts, but the dispositions which lead to them, are properly immoral, and fit subjects of disapprobation which may rise to abhorrence. Cruelty of disposition; malice and ill-nature; that most anti-social and odious of all passions, envy; dissimulation and insincerity; irascibility on insufficient cause, and resentment disproportioned to the provocation; the love of domineering over others; the desire to engross more than one's share of advantages (the πλεονεξία of the Greeks); the pride which derives gratification from the abasement of others; the egotism which thinks self and its concerns more important than everything else, and decides all doubtful questions in his own favor; — these are moral vices, and constitute a bad and odious moral character: unlike the self-regarding faults previously mentioned, which are not properly immoralities, and to whatever pitch they may be carried, do not constitute wickedness. They may be proofs of any amount of folly, or want of personal dignity and self-respect; but they are only a subject of moral reprobation when they involve a breach of duty to others, for whose sake the individual is bound to have care for himself. What are called duties to ourselves are not socially obligatory, unless circumstances render them at the same time duties to others. The term duty to oneself, when it means anything more than prudence, means self-respect or self-development; and for none of these is any one accountable to his fellow-creatures, because for none of them is it for the good of mankind that he be held accountable to them.

The distinction between the loss of consideration which a person may rightly incur by defect of prudence or of personal dignity, and the reprobation which is due to him for an offence against the rights of others, is not a merely nominal distinction. It makes a vast difference both in our feelings and in our conduct towards him, whether he displeases us in things in which we think we have a right to control him, or in things in which we know that we have not. If

5   he displeases us, we may express our distaste, and we may stand aloof from a person as well as from a thing that displeases us; but we shall not therefore feel called on to make his life uncomfortable. We shall reflect that he already bears, or will bear, the whole penalty of his error; if he spoils his life by mismanagement, we shall not, for that reason, desire to spoil it still further:

10 instead of wishing to punish him, we shall rather endeavor to alleviate his punishment, by showing him how he may avoid or cure the evils his conduct tends to bring upon him. He may be to us an object of pity, perhaps of dislike, but not of anger or resentment; we shall not treat him like an enemy of society: the worst we shall think ourselves justified in doing is leaving him to himself, if

15 we do not interfere benevolently by showing interest or concern for him. It is far otherwise if he has infringed the rules necessary for the protection of his fellow-creatures, individually or collectively. The evil consequences of his acts do not then fall on himself, but on others; and society, as the protector of all its members, must retaliate on him; must inflict pain on him for the express purpose

20 of punishment, and must take care that it be sufficiently severe. In the one case, he is an offender at our bar, and we are called on not only to sit in judgment on him, but, in one shape or another, to execute our own sentence: in the other case, it is not our part to inflict any suffering on him, except what may incidentally follow from our using the same liberty in the regulation of our own affairs,

25 which we allow to him in his.

The distinction here pointed out between the part of a person's life which concerns only himself, and that which concerns others, many persons will refuse to admit. How (it may be asked) can any part of the conduct of a member of society be a matter of indifference to the other members? No person is an

30 entirely isolated being; it is impossible for a person to do anything seriously or permanently hurtful to himself, without mischief reaching at least to his near connections, and often far beyond them. If he injures his property, he does harm to those who directly or indirectly derived support from it, and usually diminishes, by a greater or less amount, the general resources of the community.

35 If he deteriorates his bodily or mental faculties, he not only brings evil upon all who depended on him for any portion of their happiness, but disqualifies himself for rendering the services which he owes to his fellow-creatures generally; perhaps becomes a burden on their affection or benevolence; and if such conduct were very frequent, hardly any offence that is committed would detract more

40 from the general sum of good. Finally, if by his vices or follies a person does no

356

direct harm to others, he is nevertheless (it may be said) injurious by his example; and ought to be compelled to control himself, for the sake of those whom the sight or knowledge of his conduct might corrupt or mislead.

And even (it will be added) if the consequences of misconduct could be
5   confined to the vicious or thoughtless individual, ought society to abandon to their own guidance those who are manifestly unfit for it? If protection against themselves is confessedly due to children and persons under age, is not society equally bound to afford it to persons of mature years who are equally incapable of self-government? If gambling, or drunkenness, or incontinence, or idleness,
10   or uncleanliness, are as injurious to happiness, and as great a hindrance to improvement, as many or most of the acts prohibited by law, why (it may be asked) should not law, so far as is consistent with practicability and social convenience, endeavor to repress these also? And as a supplement to the unavoidable imperfections of law, ought not opinion at least to organize a
15   powerful police against these vices, and visit rigidly with social penalties those who are known to practise them? There is no question here (it may be said) about restricting individuality, or impeding the trial of new and original experiments in living. The only things it is sought to prevent are things which have been tried and condemned from the beginning of the world until now;
20   things which experience has shown not to be useful or suitable to any person's individuality. There must be some length of time and amount of experience, after which a moral or prudential truth may be regarded as established: and it is merely desired to prevent generation after generation from falling over the same precipice which has been fatal to their predecessors.
25   I fully admit that the mischief which a person does to himself, may seriously affect, both through their sympathies and their interests, those nearly connected with him, and in a minor degree, society at large. When, by conduct of this sort, a person is led to violate a distinct and assignable obligation to any other person or persons, the case is taken out of the self-regarding class, and
30   becomes amenable to moral disapprobation in the proper sense of the term. If, for example, a man, through intemperance or extravagance, becomes unable to pay his debts, or, having undertaken the moral responsibility of a family, becomes from the same cause incapable of supporting or educating them, he is deservedly reprobated, and might be justly punished; but it is for the breach of
35   duty to his family or creditors, not for the extravagance. If the resources which ought to have been devoted to them, had been diverted from them for the most prudent investment, the moral culpability would have been the same. George Barnwell murdered his uncle to get money for his mistress, but if he had done it to set himself up in business, he would equally have been hanged. Again, in the
40   frequent case of a man who causes grief to his family by addiction to bad habits,

he deserves reproach for his unkindness or ingratitude; but so he may for cultivating habits not in themselves vicious, if they are painful to those with whom he passes his life, or who from personal ties are dependent on him for their comfort. Whoever fails in the consideration generally due to the interests and feelings of others, not being compelled by some more imperative duty, or justified by allowable self-preference, is a subject of moral disapprobation for that failure, but not for the cause of it, nor for the errors, merely personal to himself, which may have remotely led to it. In like manner, when a person disables himself, by conduct purely self-regarding, from the performance of some definite duty incumbent on him to the public, he is guilty of a social offence. No person ought to be punished simply for being drunk; but a soldier or a policeman should be punished for being drunk on duty. Whenever, in short, there is a definite damage, or a definite risk of damage, either to an individual or to the public, the case is taken out of the province of liberty, and placed in that of morality or law.

But with regard to the merely contingent, or, as it may be called, constructive injury which a person causes to society, by conduct which neither violates any specific duty to the public, nor occasions perceptible hurt to any assignable individual except himself; the inconvenience is one which society can afford to bear, for the sake of the greater good of human freedom. If grown persons are to be punished for not taking proper care of themselves, I would rather it were for their own sake, than under pretence of preventing them from impairing their capacity of rendering to society benefits which society does not pretend it has a right to exact. But I cannot consent to argue the point as if society had no means of bringing its weaker members up to its ordinary standard of rational conduct, except waiting till they do something irrational, and then punishing them, legally or morally, for it. Society has had absolute power over them during all the early portion of their existence: it has had the whole period of childhood and nonage in which to try whether it could make them capable of rational conduct in life. The existing generation is master both of the training and the entire circumstances of the generation to come; it cannot indeed make them perfectly wise and good, because it is itself so lamentably deficient in goodness and wisdom; and its best efforts are not always, in individual cases, its most successful ones; but it is perfectly well able to make the rising generation, as a whole, as good as, and a little better than, itself. If society lets any considerable number of its members grow up mere children, incapable of being acted on by rational consideration of distant motives, society has itself to blame for the consequences. Armed not only with all the powers of education, but with the ascendency which the authority of a received opinion always exercises over the minds who are least fitted to judge for themselves; and aided by the *natural*

penalties which cannot be prevented from falling on those who incur the distaste or the contempt of those who know them; let not society pretend that it needs, besides all this, the power to issue commands and enforce obedience in the personal concerns of individuals, in which, on all principles of justice and
5 policy, the decision ought to rest with those who are to abide the consequences. Nor is there anything which tends more to discredit and frustrate the better means of influencing conduct, than a resort to the worse. If there be among those whom it is attempted to coerce into prudence or temperance, any of the material of which vigorous and independent characters are made, they will infallibly
10 rebel against the yoke. No such person will ever feel that others have a right to control him in his concerns, such as they have to prevent him from injuring them in theirs; and it easily comes to be considered a mark of spirit and courage to fly in the face of such usurped authority, and do with ostentation the exact opposite of what it enjoins; as in the fashion of grossness which succeeded, in the time of
15 Charles II., to the fanatical moral intolerance of the Puritans With respect to what is said of the necessity of protecting society from the bad example set to others by the vicious or the self-indulgent; it is true that bad example may have a pernicious effect, especially the example of doing wrong to others with impunity to the wrongdoer. But we are now speaking of conduct which, while it does no
20 wrong to others, is supposed to do great harm to the agent himself: and I do not see how those who believe this, can think otherwise than that the example, on the whole, must be more salutary than hurtful, since, if it displays the misconduct, it displays also the painful or degrading consequences which, if the conduct is justly censured, must be supposed to be in all or most cases attendant
25 on it.

But the strongest of all the arguments against the interference of the public with purely personal conduct, is that when it does interfere, the odds are that it interferes wrongly, and in the wrong place. On questions of social morality, of duty to others, the opinion of the public, that is, of an overruling majority,
30 though often wrong, is likely to be still oftener right; because on such questions they are only required to judge of their own interests; of the manner in which some mode of conduct, if allowed to be practised, would affect themselves. But the opinion of a similar majority, imposed as a law on the minority, on questions of self-regarding conduct, is quite as likely to be wrong as right; for in these
35 cases public opinion means, at the best, some people's opinion of what is good or bad for other people; while very often it does not even mean that; the public, with the most perfect indifference, passing over the pleasure or convenience of those whose conduct they censure, and considering only their own preference. There are many who consider as an injury to themselves any conduct which they
40 have a distaste for, and resent it as an outrage to their feelings; as a religious

bigot, when charged with disregarding the religious feelings of others, has been known to retort that they disregard his feelings, by persisting in their abominable worship or creed. But there is no parity between the feeling of a person for his own opinion, and the feeling of another who is offended at his holding it; no
5   more than between the desire of a thief to take a purse, and the desire of the right owner to keep it. And a person's taste is as much his own peculiar concern as his opinion or his purse. It is easy for any one to imagine an ideal public, which leaves the freedom and choice of individuals in all uncertain matters undisturbed, and only requires them to abstain from modes of conduct which
10 universal experience has condemned. But where has there been seen a public which set any such limit to its censorship? or when does the public trouble itself about universal experience? In its interferences with personal conduct it is seldom thinking of anything but the enormity of acting or feeling differently from itself; and this standard of judgment, thinly disguised, is held up to
15 mankind as the dictate of religion and philosophy, by nine tenths of all moralists and speculative writers. These teach that things are right because they are right; because we feel them to be so. They tell us to search in our own minds and hearts for laws of conduct binding on ourselves and on all others. What can the poor public do but apply these instructions, and make their own personal
20 feelings of good and evil, if they are tolerably unanimous in them, obligatory on all the world?

     The evil here pointed out is not one which exists only in theory; and it may perhaps be expected that I should specify the instances in which the public of this age and country improperly invests its own preferences with the character of
25 moral laws. I am not writing an essay on the aberrations of existing moral feeling. That is too weighty a subject to be discussed parenthetically, and by way of illustration. Yet examples are necessary, to show that the principle I maintain is of serious and practical moment, and that I am not endeavoring to erect a barrier against imaginary evils. And it is not difficult to show, by
30 abundant instances, that to extend the bounds of what may be called moral police, until it encroaches on the most unquestionably legitimate liberty of the individual, is one of the most universal of all human propensities.

     As a first instance, consider the antipathies which men cherish on no better grounds than that persons whose religious opinions are different from theirs, do
35 not practise their religious observances, especially their religious abstinences. To cite a rather trivial example, nothing in the creed or practice of Christians does more to envenom the hatred of Mahomedans against them, than the fact of their eating pork. There are few acts which Christians and Europeans regard with more unaffected disgust, than Mussulmans regard this particular mode of
40 satisfying hunger. It is, in the first place, an offence against their religion; but

this circumstance by no means explains either the degree or the kind of their repugnance; for wine also is forbidden by their religion, and to partake of it is by all Mussulmans accounted wrong, but not disgusting. Their aversion to the flesh of the "unclean beast" is, on the contrary, of that peculiar character, resembling
5 an instinctive antipathy, which the idea of uncleanness, when once it thoroughly sinks into the feelings, seems always to excite even in those whose personal habits are anything but scrupulously cleanly, and of which the sentiment of religious impurity, so intense in the Hindoos, is a remarkable example. Suppose now that in a people, of whom the majority were Mussulmans, that majority
10 should insist upon not permitting pork to be eaten within the limits of the country. This would be nothing new in Mahomedan countries.[9] Would it be a legitimate exercise of the moral authority of public opinion? and if not, why not? The practice is really revolting to such a public. They also sincerely think that it is forbidden and abhorred by the Deity. Neither could the prohibition be
15 censured as religious persecution. It might be religious in its origin, but it would not be persecution for religion, since nobody's religion makes it a duty to eat pork. The only tenable ground of condemnation would be, that with the personal tastes and self-regarding concerns of individuals the public has no business to interfere.
20 To come somewhat nearer home: the majority of Spaniards consider it a gross impiety, offensive in the highest degree to the Supreme Being, to worship him in any other manner than the Roman Catholic; and no other public worship is lawful on Spanish soil. The people of all Southern Europe look upon a married clergy as not only irreligious, but unchaste, indecent, gross, disgusting.
25 What do Protestants think of these perfectly sincere feelings, and of the attempt to enforce them against non-Catholics? Yet, if mankind are justified in interfering with each other's liberty in things which do not concern the interests of others, on what principle is it possible consistently to exclude these cases? or who can blame people for desiring to suppress what they regard as a scandal in
30 the sight of God and man? No stronger case can be shown for prohibiting anything which is regarded as a personal immorality, than is made out for suppressing these practices in the eyes of those who regard them as impieties; and unless we are willing to adopt the logic of persecutors, and to say that we may persecute others because we are right, and that they must not persecute us
35 because they are wrong, we must beware of admitting a principle of which we should resent as a gross injustice the application to ourselves.
The preceding instances may be objected to, although unreasonably, as drawn from contingencies impossible among us: opinion, in this country, not being likely to enforce abstinence from meats, or to interfere with people for
40 worshipping, and for either marrying or not marrying, according to their creed or

inclination. The next example, however, shall be taken from an interference with liberty which we have by no means passed all danger of. Wherever the Puritans have been sufficiently powerful, as in New England, and in Great Britain at the time of the Commonwealth, they have endeavored, with considerable success, to
5   put down all public, and nearly all private, amusements: especially music, dancing, public games, or other assemblages for purposes of diversion, and the theatre. There are still in this country large bodies of persons by whose notions of morality and religion these recreations are condemned; and those persons belonging chiefly to the middle class, who are the ascendant power in the
10   present social and political condition of the kingdom, it is by no means impossible that persons of these sentiments may at some time or other command a majority in Parliament. How will the remaining portion of the community like to have the amusements that shall be permitted to them regulated by the religious and moral sentiments of the stricter Calvinists and Methodists? Would
15   they not, with considerable peremptoriness, desire these intrusively pious members of society to mind their own business? This is precisely what should be said to every government and every public, who have the pretension that no person shall enjoy any pleasure which they think wrong. But if the principle of the pretension be admitted, no one can reasonably object to its being acted on in
20   the sense of the majority, or other preponderating power in the country; and all persons must be ready to conform to the idea of a Christian commonwealth, as understood by the early settlers in New England, if a religious profession similar to theirs should ever succeed in regaining its lost ground, as religions supposed to be declining have so often been known to do.
25   To imagine another contingency, perhaps more likely to be realized than the one last mentioned. There is confessedly a strong tendency in the modern world towards a democratic constitution of society, accompanied or not by popular political institutions. It is affirmed that in the country where this tendency is most completely realized — where both society and the government are most
30   democratic — the United States — the feeling of the majority, to whom any appearance of a more showy or costly style of living than they can hope to rival is disagreeable, operates as a tolerably effectual sumptuary law, and that in many parts of the Union it is really difficult for a person possessing a very large income, to find any mode of spending it, which will not incur popular
35   disapprobation. Though such statements as these are doubtless much exaggerated as a representation of existing facts, the state of things they describe is not only a conceivable and possible, but a probable result of democratic feeling, combined with the notion that the public has a right to a veto on the manner in which individuals shall spend their incomes. We have only further to
40   suppose a considerable diffusion of Socialist opinions, and it may become

infamous in the eyes of the majority to possess more property than some very small amount, or any income not earned by manual labor. Opinions similar in principle to these, already prevail widely among the artisan class, and weigh oppressively on those who are amenable to the opinion chiefly of that class,
5   namely, its own members. It is known that the bad workmen who form the majority of the operatives in many branches of industry, are decidedly of opinion that bad workmen ought to receive the same wages as good, and that no one ought to be allowed, through piecework or otherwise, to earn by superior skill or industry more than others can without it. And they employ a moral
10   police, which occasionally becomes a physical one, to deter skilful workmen from receiving, and employers from giving, a larger remuneration for a more useful service. If the public have any jurisdiction over private concerns, I cannot see that these people are in fault, or that any individual's particular public can be blamed for asserting the same authority over his individual conduct, which the
15   general public asserts over people in general.

     But, without dwelling upon supposititious cases, there are, in our own day, gross usurpations upon the liberty of private life actually practised, and still greater ones threatened with some expectation of success, and opinions proposed which assert an unlimited right in the public not only to prohibit by
20   law everything which it thinks wrong, but in order to get at what it thinks wrong, to prohibit any number of things which it admits to be innocent.

     Under the name of preventing intemperance, the people of one English colony, and of nearly half the United States, have been interdicted by law from making any use whatever of fermented drinks, except for medical purposes: for
25   prohibition of their sale is in fact, as it is intended to be, prohibition of their use. And though the impracticability of executing the law has caused its repeal in several of the States which had adopted it, including the one from which it derives its name, an attempt has notwithstanding been commenced, and is prosecuted with considerable zeal by many of the professed philanthropists, to
30   agitate for a similar law in this country. The association, or "Alliance" as it terms itself, which has been formed for this purpose, has acquired some notoriety through the publicity given to a correspondence between its Secretary and one of the very few English public men who hold that a politician's opinions ought to be founded on principles. Lord Stanley's share in this correspondence
35   is calculated to strengthen the hopes already built on him, by those who know how rare such qualities as are manifested in some of his public appearances, unhappily are among those who figure in political life. The organ of the Alliance, who would "deeply deplore the recognition of any principle which could be wrested to justify bigotry and persecution," undertakes to point out the
40   "broad and impassable barrier" which divides such principles from those of the

association. "All matters relating to thought, opinion, conscience, appear to me," he says, "to be without the sphere of legislation; all pertaining to social act, habit, relation, subject only to a discretionary power vested in the State itself, and not in the individual, to be within it." No mention is made of a third class,
5 different from either of these, viz., acts and habits which are not social, but individual; although it is to this class, surely, that the act of drinking fermented liquors belongs. Selling fermented liquors, however, is trading, and trading is a social act. But the infringement complained of is not on the liberty of the seller, but on that of the buyer and consumer; since the State might just as well forbid
10 him to drink wine, as purposely make it impossible for him to obtain it. The Secretary, however, says, "I claim, as a citizen, a right to legislate whenever my social rights are invaded by the social act of another." And now for the definition of these "social rights." "If anything invades my social rights, certainly the traffic in strong drink does. It destroys my primary right of
15 security, by constantly creating and stimulating social disorder. It invades my right of equality, by deriving a profit from the creation of a misery, I am taxed to support. It impedes my right to free moral and intellectual development, by surrounding my path with dangers, and by weakening and demoralizing society, from which I have a right to claim mutual aid and intercourse." A theory of
20 "social rights," the like of which probably never before found its way into distinct language — being nothing short of this — that it is the absolute social right of every individual, that every other individual shall act in every respect exactly as he ought; that whosoever fails thereof in the smallest particular, violates my social right, and entitles me to demand from the legislature the
25 removal of the grievance. So monstrous a principle is far more dangerous than any single interference with liberty; there is no violation of liberty which it would not justify; it acknowledges no right to any freedom whatever, except perhaps to that of holding opinions in secret, without ever disclosing them: for the moment an opinion which I consider noxious, passes any one's lips, it
30 invades all the "social rights" attributed to me by the Alliance. The doctrine ascribes to all mankind a vested interest in each other's moral, intellectual, and even physical perfection, to be defined by each claimant according to his own standard.

Another important example of illegitimate interference with the rightful
35 liberty of the individual, not simply threatened, but long since carried into triumphant effect, is Sabbatarian legislation. Without doubt, abstinence on one day in the week, so far as the exigencies of life permit, from the usual daily occupation, though in no respect religiously binding on any except Jews, is a highly beneficial custom. And inasmuch as this custom cannot be observed
40 without a general consent to that effect among the industrious classes, therefore,

in so far as some persons by working may impose the same necessity on others, it may be allowable and right that the law should guarantee to each, the observance by others of the custom, by suspending the greater operations of industry on a particular day. But this justification, grounded on the direct interest
5   which others have in each individual's observance of the practice, does not apply to the self-chosen occupations in which a person may think fit to employ his leisure; nor does it hold good, in the smallest degree, for legal restrictions on amusements. It is true that the amusement of some is the day's work of others; but the pleasure not to say the useful recreation, of many, is worth the labor of a
10   few, provided the occupation is freely chosen, and can be freely resigned. The operatives are perfectly right in thinking that if all worked on Sunday seven days' work would have to be given for six days' wages: but so long as the great mass of employments are suspended, the small number who for the enjoyment of others must still work, obtain a proportional increase of earnings; and they are
15   not obliged to follow those occupations, if they prefer leisure to emolument. If a further remedy is sought, it might be found in the establishment by custom of a holiday on some other day of the week for those particular classes of persons. The only ground, therefore, on which restrictions on Sunday amusements can be defended, must be that they are religiously wrong; a motive of legislation which
20   never can be too earnestly protested against. "Deorum injuriæ Diis curæ." It remains to be proved that society or any of its officers holds a commission from on high to avenge any supposed offence to Omnipotence, which is not also a wrong to our fellow-creatures. The notion that it is one man's duty that another should be religious, was the foundation of all the religious persecutions ever
25   perpetrated, and if admitted, would fully justify them. Though the feeling which breaks out in the repeated attempts to stop railway traveling on Sunday, in the resistance to the opening of Museums, and the like, has not the cruelty of the old persecutors, the state of mind indicated by it is fundamentally the same. It is a determination not to tolerate others in doing what is permitted by their religion,
30   because it is not permitted by the persecutor's religion. It is a belief that God not only abominates the act of the misbeliever, but will not hold us guiltless if we leave him unmolested.

    I cannot refrain from adding to these examples of the little account commonly made of human liberty, the language of downright persecution which
35   breaks out from the press of this country, whenever it feels called on to notice the remarkable phenomenon of Mormonism. Much might be said on the unexpected and instructive fact, that an alleged new revelation, and a religion founded on it, the product of palpable imposture, not even supported by the *prestige* of extraordinary qualities in its founder, is believed by hundreds of
40   thousands, and has been made the foundation of a society, in the age of

newspapers, railways, and the electric telegraph. What here concerns us is, that this religion, like other and better religions, has its martys; that its prophet and founder was, for his teaching, put to death by a mob; that others of its adherents lost their lives by the same lawless violence; that they were forcibly expelled, in

5   a body, from the country in which they first grew up; while, now that they have been chased into a solitary recess in the midst of a desert, many in this country openly declare that it would be right (only that it is not convenient) to send an expedition against them, and compel them by force to conform to the opinions of other people. The article of the Mormonite doctrine which is the chief

10   provocative to the antipathy which thus breaks through the ordinary restraints of religious tolerance, is its sanction of polygamy; which, though permitted to Mahomedans, and Hindoos, and Chinese, seems to excite unquenchable animosity when practised by persons who speak English, and profess to be a kind of Christians. No one has a deeper disapprobation than I have of this

15   Mormon institution; both for other reasons, and because, far from being in any way countenanced by the principle of liberty, it is a direct infraction of that principle, being a mere riveting of the chains of one half of the community, and an emancipation of the other from reciprocity of obligation towards them. Still, it must be remembered that this relation is as much voluntary on the part of the

20   women concerned in it, and who may be deemed the sufferers by it, as is the case with any other form of the marriage institution; and however surprising this fact may appear, it has its explanation in the common ideas and customs of the world, which teaching women to think marriage the one thing needful, make it intelligible that many a woman should prefer being one of several wives, to not

25   being a wife at all. Other countries are not asked to recognize such unions, or release any portion of their inhabitants from their own laws on the score of Mormonite opinions. But when the dissentients have conceded to the hostile sentiments of others, far more than could justly be demanded; when they have left the countries to which their doctrines were unacceptable, and established

30   themselves in a remote corner of the earth, which they have been the first to render habitable to human beings; it is difficult to see on what principles but those of tyranny they can be prevented from living there under what laws they please, provided they commit no aggression on other nations, and allow perfect freedom of departure to those who are dissatisfied with their ways. A recent

35   writer, in some respects of considerable merit, proposes (to use his own words,) not a crusade, but a *civilizade,* against this polygamous community, to put an end to what seems to him a retrograde step in civilization. It also appears so to me, but I am not aware that any community has a right to force another to be civilized. So long as the sufferers by the bad law do not invoke assistance from

40   other communities, I cannot admit that persons entirely unconnected with them

ought to step in and require that a condition of things with which all who are directly interested appear to be satisfied, should be put an end to because it is a scandal to persons some thousands of miles distant, who have no part or concern in it. Let them send missionaries, if they please, to preach against it; and let
5 them, by any fair means (of which silencing the teachers is not one,) oppose the progress of similar doctrines among their own people. If civilization has got the better of barbarism when barbarism had the world to itself, it is too much to profess to be afraid lest barbarism, after having been fairly got under, should revive and conquer civilization. A civilization that can thus succumb to its
10 vanquished enemy must first have become so degenerate, that neither its appointed priests and teachers, nor anybody else, has the capacity, or will take the trouble, to stand up for it. If this be so, the sooner such a cizilization receives notice to quit, the better. It can only go on from bad to worse, until destroyed and regenerated (like the Western Empire) by energetic barbarians.

CHAPTER V.
Applications.

15 The principles asserted in these pages must be more generally admitted as the basis for discussion of details, before a consistent application of them to all the various departments of government and morals can be attempted with any prospect of advantage. The few observations I propose to make on questions of detail, are designed to illustrate the principles, rather than to follow them out to
20 their consequences. I offer, not so much applications, as specimens of application; which may serve to bring into greater clearness the meaning and limits of the two maxims which together form the entire doctrine of this Essay, and to assist the judgment in holding the balance between them, in the cases where it appears doubtful which of them is applicable to the case.
25 The maxims are, first, that the individual is not accountable to society for his actions, in so far as these concern the interests of no person but himself. Advice, instruction, persuasion, and avoidance by other people, if thought necessary by them for their own good, are the only measures by which society can justifiably express its dislike or disapprobation of his conduct. Secondly,
30 that for such actions as are prejudicial to the interests of others, the individual is accountable, and may be subjected either to social or to legal punishments, if society is of opinion that the one or the other is requisite for its protection.
In the first place, it must by no means be supposed, because damage, or probability of damage, to the interests of others, can alone justify the
35 interference of society, that therefore it always does justify such interference. In many cases, an individual, in pursuing a legitimate object, necessarily and

therefore legitimately causes pain or loss to others, or intercepts a good which they had a reasonable hope of obtaining. Such oppositions of interest between individuals often arise from bad social institutions, but are unavoidable while those institutions last; and some would be unavoidable under any institutions.

5   Whoever succeeds in an overcrowded profession, or in a competitive examination; whoever is preferred to another in any contest for an object which both desire, reaps benefit from the loss of others, from their wasted exertion and their disappointment. But it is, by common admission, better for the general interest of mankind, that persons should pursue their objects undeterred by this

10   sort of consequences. In other words, society admits no right, either legal or moral, in the disappointed competitors, to immunity from this kind of suffering; and feels called on to interfere, only when means of success have been employed which it is contrary to the general interest to permit — namely, fraud or treachery, and force.

15   Again, trade is a social act. Whoever undertakes to sell any description of goods to the public, does what affects the interest of other persons, and of society in general; and thus his conduct, in principle, comes within the jurisdiction of society: accordingly, it was once held to be the duty of governments, in all cases which were considered of importance, to fix prices,

20   and regulate the processes of manufacture. But it is now recognized, though not till after a long struggle, that both the cheapness and the good quality of commodities are most effectually provided for by leaving the producers and sellers perfectly free, under the sole check of equal freedom to the buyers for supplying themselves elsewhere. This is the so-called doctrine of Free Trade,

25   which rests on grounds different from, though equally solid with, the principle of individual liberty asserted in this Essay. Restrictions on trade, or on production for purposes of trade, are indeed restraints; and all restraint, *quâ* restraint, is an evil: but the restraints in question affect only that part of conduct which society is competent to restrain, and are wrong solely because they do not

30   really produce the results which it is desired to produce by them. As the principle of individual liberty is not involved in the doctrine of Free Trade, so neither is it in most of the questions which arise respecting the limits of that doctrine: as for example, what amount of public control is admissible for the prevention of fraud by adulteration; how far sanitary precautions, or

35   arrangements to protect workpeople employed in dangerous occupations, should be enforced on employers. Such questions involve considerations of liberty, only in so far as leaving people to themselves is always better, *cæteris paribus,* than controlling them: but that they may be legitimately controlled for these ends, is in principle undeniable. On the other hand, there are questions relating to

40   interference with trade, which are essentially questions of liberty; such as the

Maine Law, already touched upon; the prohibition of the importation of opium into China; the restriction of the sale of poisons; all cases, in short, where the object of the interference is to make it impossible or difficult to obtain a particular commodity. These interferences are objectionable, not as

5   infringements on the liberty of the producer or seller, but on that of the buyer.
     One of these examples, that of the sale of poisons, opens a new question; the proper limits of what may be called the functions of police; how far liberty may legitimately be invaded for the prevention of crime, or of accident. It is one of the undisputed functions of government to take precautions against crime

10   before it has been committed, as well as to detect and punish it afterwards. The preventive function of government, however, is far more liable to be abused, to the prejudice of liberty, than the punitory function; for there is hardly any part of the legitimate freedom of action of a human being which would not admit of being represented, and fairly too, as increasing the facilities for some form or

15   other of delinquency. Nevertheless, if a public authority, or even a private person, sees any one evidently preparing to commit a crime, they are not bound to look on inactive until the crime is committed, but may interfere to prevent it. If poisons were never bought or used for any purpose except the commission of murder, it would be right to prohibit their manufacture and sale They may,

20   however, be wanted not only for innocent but for useful purposes, and restrictions cannot be imposed in the one case without operating in the other. Again, it is a proper office of public authority to guard against accidents. If either a public officer or any one else saw a person attempting to cross a bridge which had been ascertained to be unsafe, and there were no time to warn him of

25   his danger, they might seize him and turn him back, without any real infringement of his liberty; for liberty consists in doing what one desires, and he does not desire to fall into the river. Nevertheless, when there is not a certainty, but only a danger of mischief, no one but the person himself can judge of the sufficiency of the motive which may prompt him to incur the risk: in this case,

30   therefore, (unless he is a child, or delirious, or in some state of excitement or absorption incompatible with the full use of the reflecting faculty), he ought, I conceive, to be only warned of the danger; not forcibly prevented from exposing himself to it Similar considerations, applied to such a question as the sale of poisons, may enable us to decide which among the possible modes of regulation

35   are or are not contrary to principle. Such a precaution, for example, as that of labeling the drug with some word expressive of its dangerous character, may be enforced without violation of liberty: the buyer cannot wish not to know that the thing he possesses has poisonous qualities. But to require in all cases the certificate of a medical practitioner, would make it sometimes impossible,

40   always expensive, to obtain the article for legitimate uses. The only mode

apparent to me, in which difficulties may be thrown in the way of crime committed through this means, without any infringement, worth taking into account, upon the liberty of those who desire the poisonous substance for other purposes, consists in providing what, in the apt language of Bentham, is called "preappointed evidence." This provision is familiar to every one in the case of contracts. It is usual and right that the law, when a contract is entered into, should require as the condition of its enforcing performance, that certain formalities should be observed, such as signatures, attestation of witnesses, and the like, in order that in case of subsequent dispute, there may be evidence to prove that the contract was really entered into, and that there was nothing in the circumstances to render it legally invalid: the effect being, to throw great obstacles in the way of fictitious contracts, or contracts made in circumstances which, if known, would destroy their validity. Precautions of a similar nature might be enforced in the sale of articles adapted to be instruments of crime. The seller, for example, might be required to enter in a register the exact time of the transaction, the name and address of the buyer, the precise quality and quantity sold; to ask the purpose for which it was wanted, and record the answer he received. When there was no medical prescription, the presence of some third person might be required, to bring home the fact to the purchaser, in case there should afterwards be reason to believe that the article had been applied to criminal purposes. Such regulations would in general be no material impediment to obtaining the article, but a very considerable one to making an improper use of it without detection.

The right inherent in society, to ward off crimes against itself by antecedent precautions, suggests the obvious limitations to the maxim, that purely self-regarding misconduct cannot properly be meddled with in the way of prevention or punishment. Drunkenness, for example, in ordinary cases, is not a fit subject for legislative interference; but I should deem it perfectly legitimate that a person, who had once been convicted of any act of violence to others under the influence of drink, should be placed under a special legal restriction, personal to himself; that if he were afterwards found drunk, he should be liable to a penalty, and that if when in that state he committed another offence, the punishment to which he would be liable for that other offence should be increased in severity. The making himself drunk, in a person whom drunkenness excites to do harm to others, is a crime against others. So, again, idleness, except in a person receiving support from the public, or except when it constitutes a breach of contract, cannot without tyranny be made a subject of legal punishment; but if either from idleness or from any other avoidable cause, a man fails to perform his legal duties to others, as for instance to support his children, it is no tyranny to force him to fulfill that obligation, by compulsory labor, if no other means are available.

    Again, there are many acts which, being directly injurious only to the agents themselves, ought not to be legally interdicted, but which, if done publicly, are a
5   violation of good manners, and coming thus within the category of offences against others, may rightfully be prohibited. Of this kind are offences against decency; on which it is unnecessary to dwell, the rather as they are only connected indirectly with our subject, the objection to publicity being equally strong in the case of many actions not in themselves condemnable, nor supposed
10   to be so.

    There is another question to which an answer must be found, consistent with the principles which have been laid down. In cases of personal conduct supposed to be blameable, but which respect for liberty precludes society from preventing or punishing, because the evil directly resulting falls wholly on the
15   agent; what the agent is free to do, ought other persons to be equally free to counsel or instigate? This question is not free from difficulty. The case of a person who solicits another to do an act, is not strictly a case of self-regarding conduct. To give advice or offer inducements to any one, is a social act, and may therefore, like actions in general which affect others, be supposed amenable to
20   social control. But a little reflection corrects the first impression, by showing that if the case is not strictly within the definition of individual liberty, yet the reasons on which the principle of individual liberty is grounded, are applicable to it. If people must be allowed, in whatever concerns only themselves, to act as seems best to themselves at their own peril, they must equally be free to consult
25   with one another about what is fit to be so done; to exchange opinions, and give and receive suggestions. Whatever it is permitted to do, it must be permitted to advise to do. The question is doubtful, only when the instigator derives a personal benefit from his advice; when he makes it his occupation, for subsistence or pecuniary gain, to promote what society and the State consider to
30   be an evil. Then, indeed, a new element of complication is introduced; namely, the existence of classes of persons with an interest opposed to what is considered as the public weal, and whose mode of living is grounded on the counteraction of it. Ought this to be interfered with, or not? Fornication, for example, must be tolerated, and so must gambling; but should a person be free
35   to be a pimp, or to keep a gambling-house? The case is one of those which lie on the exact boundary line between two principles, and it is not at once apparent to which of the two it properly belongs. There are arguments on both sides. On the side of toleration it may be said, that the fact of following anything as an occupation, and living or profiting by the practice of it, cannot make that
40   criminal which would otherwise be admissible; that the act should either be

consistently permitted or consistently prohibited; that if the principles which we have hitherto defended are true, society has no business, *as* society, to decide anything to be wrong which concerns only the individual; that it cannot go beyond dissuasion, and that one person should be as free to persuade, as another to dissuade. In opposition to this it may be contended, that although the public, or the State, are not warranted in authoritatively deciding, for purposes of repression or punishment, that such or such conduct affecting only the interests of the individual is good or bad, they are fully justified in assuming, if they regard it as bad, that its being so or not is at least a disputable question: That, this being supposed, they cannot be acting wrongly in endeavoring to exclude the influence of solicitations which are not disinterested, of instigators who cannot possibly be impartial — who have a direct personal interest on one side, and that side the one which the State believes to be wrong, and who confessedly promote it for personal objects only. There can surely, it may be urged, be nothing lost, no sacrifice of good, by so ordering matters that persons shall make their election, either wisely or foolishly, on their own prompting, as free as possible from the arts of persons who stimulate their inclinations for interested purposes of their own. Thus (it may be said) though the statutes respecting unlawful games are utterly indefensible — though all persons should be free to gamble in their own or each other's houses, or in any place of meeting established by their own subscriptions, and open only to the members and their visitors — yet public gambling-houses should not be permitted. It is true that the prohibition is never effectual, and that whatever amount of tyrannical power is given to the police, gambling-houses can always be maintained under other pretences but they may be compelled to conduct their operations with a certain degree of secrecy and mystery, so that nobody knows anything about them but those who seek them; and more than this, society ought not to aim at. There is considerable force in these arguments. I will not venture to decide whether they are sufficient to justify the moral anomaly of punishing the accessary, when the principal is (and must be) allowed to go free; of fining or imprisoning the procurer, but not the fornicator, the gambling-house keeper, but not the gambler. Still less ought the common operations of buying and selling to be interfered with on analogous grounds. Almost every article which is bought and sold may used in excess, and the sellers have a pecuniary interest in encouraging that excess; but no argument can be founded on this, in favor, for instance, of the Maine Law; because the class of dealers in strong drinks, though interested in their abuse, are indispensably required for the sake of their legitimate use. The interest however, of these dealers in promoting intemperance is a real evil, and justifies the State in imposing restrictions and requiring guarantees which but for that justification would be infringements of legitimate liberty.

A further question is, whether the State, while it permits, should nevertheless indirectly discourage conduct which it deems contrary to the best interests of the agent; whether, for example, it should take measures to render the means of drunkenness more costly, or add to the difficulty of procuring
5　them, by limiting the number of the places of sale. On this as on most other practical questions, many distinctions require to be made. To tax stimulants for the sole purpose of making them more difficult to be obtained, is a measure differing only in degree from their entire prohibition; and would be justifiable only if that were justifiable. Every increase of cost is a prohibition, to those
10　whose means do not come up to the augmented price; and to those who do, it is a penalty laid on them for gratifying a particular taste. Their choice of pleasures, and their mode of expending their income, after satisfying their legal and moral obligations to the State and to individuals, are their own concern, and must rest with their own judgment. These considerations may seem at first sight to
15　condemn the selection of stimulants as special subjects of taxation for purposes of revenue. But it must be remembered that taxation for fiscal purposes is absolutely inevitable; that in most countries it is necessary that a considerable part of that taxation should be indirect; that the State, therefore, cannot help imposing penalties, which to some persons may be prohibitory, on the use of
20　some articles of consumption. It is hence the duty of the State to consider, in the imposition of taxes, what commodities the consumers can best spare; and *à fortiori,* to select in preference those of which it deems the use, beyond a very moderate quantity, to be positively injurious. Taxation, therefore, of stimulants, up to the point which produces the largest amount of revenue (supposing that the
25　State needs all the revenue which it yields) is not only admissible, but to be approved of.

The question of making the sale of these commodities a more or less exclusive privilege, must be answered differently, according to the purposes to which the restriction is intended to be subservient. All places of public resort
30　require the restraint of a police, and places of this kind peculiarly, because offences against society are especially apt to originate there. It is, therefore, fit to confine the power of selling these commodities (at least for consumption on the spot) to persons of known or vouched-for respectability of conduct; to make such regulations respecting hours of opening and closing as may be requisite for
35　public surveillance, and to withdraw the license if breaches of the peace repeatedly take place through the connivance or incapacity of the keeper of the house, or if it becomes a rendezvous for concocting and preparing offences against the law Any further restriction I do not conceive to be, in principle, justifiable. The limitation in number, for instance, of beer and spirit-houses, for
40　the express purpose of rendering them more difficult of access, and diminishing

the occasions of temptation, not only exposes all to an inconvenience because there are some by whom the facility would be abused, but is suited only to a state of society in which the laboring classes are avowedly treated as children or savages, and placed under an education of restraint, to fit them for future admission to the privileges of freedom. This is not the principle on which the laboring classes are professedly governed in any free country; and no person who sets due value on freedom will give his adhesion to their being so governed, unless after all efforts have been exhausted to educate them for freedom and govern them as freemen, and it has been definitively proved that they can only be governed as children. The bare statement of the alternative shows the absurdity of supposing that such efforts have been made in any case which needs be considered here. It is only because the institutions of this country are a mass of inconsistencies, that things find admittance into our practice which belong to the system of despotic, or what is called paternal, government, while the general freedom of our institutions precludes the exercise of the amount of control necessary to render the restraint of any real efficacy as a moral education.

It was pointed out in an early part of this Essay, that the liberty of the individual, in things wherein the individual is alone concerned, implies a corresponding liberty in any number of individuals to regulate by mutual agreement such things as regard them jointly, and regard no persons but themselves. This question presents no difficulty, so long as the will of all the persons implicated remains unaltered; but since that will may change, it is often necessary, even in things in which they alone are concerned, that they should enter into engagements with one another; and when they do, it is fit, as a general rule, that those engagements should be kept. Yet in the laws, probably, of every country, this general rule has some exceptions. Not only persons are not held to engagements which violate the rights of third parties, but it is sometimes considered a sufficient reason for releasing them from an engagement, that it is injurious to themselves. In this and most other civilized countries, for example, an engagement by which a person should sell himself, or allow himself to be sold, as a slave, would be null and void; neither enforced by law nor by opinion. The ground for thus limiting his power of voluntarily disposing of his own lot in life, is apparent, and is very clearly seen in this extreme case. The reason for not interfering, unless for the sake of others, with a person's voluntary acts, is consideration for his liberty. His voluntary choice is evidence that what he so chooses is desirable, or at the least endurable, to him, and his good is on the whole best provided for by allowing him to take his own means of pursuing it. But by selling himself for a slave, he abdicates his liberty; he foregoes any future use of it, beyond that single act. He therefore defeats, in his own case, the

very purpose which is the justification of allowing him to dispose of himself. He is no longer free; but is thenceforth in a position which has no longer the presumption in its favor, that would be afforded by his voluntarily remaining in it. The principle of freedom cannot require that he should be free not to be free.
5   It is not freedom, to be allowed to alienate his freedom. These reasons, the force of which is so conspicuous in this peculiar case, are evidently of far wider application; yet a limit is everywhere set to them by the necessities of life, which continually require, not indeed that we should resign our freedom, but that we should consent to this and the other limitation of it. The principle, however,
10 which demands uncontrolled freedom of action in all that concerns only the agents themselves, requires that those who have become bound to one another, in things which concern no third party, should be able to release one another from the engagement; and even without such voluntary release, there are perhaps no contracts or engagements, except those that relate to money or
15 money's worth, of which one can venture to say that there ought to be no liberty whatever of retractation. Baron Wilhelm von Humboldt, in the excellent Essay from which I have already quoted, states it as his conviction, that engagements which involve personal relations or services, should never be legally binding beyond a limited duration of time; and that the most important of these
20 engagements, marriage, having the peculiarity that its objects are frustrated unless the feelings of both the parties are in harmony with it, should require nothing more than the declared will of either party to dissolve it. This subject is too important, and too complicated, to be discussed in a parenthesis, and I touch on it only so far as is necessary for purposes of illustration. If the conciseness
25 and generality of Baron Humboldt's dissertation had not obliged him in this instance to content himself with enunciating his conclusion without discussing the premises, he would doubtless have recognized that the question cannot be decided on grounds so simple as those to which he confines himself. When a person, either by express promise or by conduct, has encouraged another to rely
30 upon his continuing to act in a certain way — to build expectations and calculations, and stake any part of his plan of life upon that supposition, a new series of moral obligations arises on his part towards that person, which may possibly be overruled, but cannot be ignored. And again, if the relation between two contracting parties has been followed by consequences to others; if it has
35 placed third parties in any peculiar position, or, as in the case of marriage, has even called third parties into existence, obligations arise on the part of both the contracting parties towards those third persons, the fulfillment of which, or at all events the mode of fulfillment, must be greatly affected by the continuance or disruption of the relation between the original parties to the contract. It does not
40 follow, nor can I admit, that these obligations extend to requiring the fulfillment

of the contract at all costs to the happiness of the reluctant party; but they are a necessary element in the question; and even if, as Von Humboldt maintains, they ought to make no difference in the *legal* freedom of the parties to release themselves from the engagement (and I also hold that they ought not to make *much* difference), they necessarily make a great difference in the *moral* freedom. A person is bound to take all these circumstances into account, before resolving on a step which may affect such important interests of others; and if he does not allow proper weight to those interests, he is morally responsible for the wrong. I have made these obvious remarks for the better illustration of the general principle of liberty, and not because they are at all needed on the particular question, which, on the contrary, is usually discussed as if the interest of children was everything, and that of grown persons nothing.

I have already observed that, owing to the absence of any recognized general principles, liberty is often granted where it should be withheld, as well as withheld where it should be granted; and one of the cases in which, in the modern European world, the sentiment of liberty is the strongest, is a case where, in my view, it is altogether misplaced. A person should be free to do as he likes in his own concerns; but he ought not to be free to do as he likes in acting for another under the pretext that the affairs of another are his own affairs. The State, while it respects the liberty of each in what specially regards himself, is bound to maintain a vigilant control over his exercise of any power which it allows him to possess over others. This obligation is almost entirely disregarded in the case of the family relations, a case, in its direct influence on human happiness, more important than all others taken together. The almost despotic power of husbands over wives needs not be enlarged upon here, because nothing more is needed for the complete removal of the evil, than that wives should have the same rights, and should receive the protection of law in the same manner, as all other persons; and because, on this subject, the defenders of established injustice do not avail themselves of the plea of liberty, but stand forth openly as the champions of power. It is in the case of children, that misapplied notions of liberty are a real obstacle to the fulfillment by the State of its duties. One would almost think that a man's children were supposed to be literally, and not metaphorically, a part of himself, so jealous is opinion of the smallest interference of law with his absolute and exclusive control over them; more jealous than of almost any interference with his own freedom of action: so much less do the generality of mankind value liberty than power. Consider, for example, the case of education. Is it not almost a self-evident axiom, that the State should require and compel the education, up to a certain standard, of every human being who is born its citizen? Yet who is there that is not afraid to recognize and assert this truth? Hardly any one indeed will deny that it is one of the most sacred duties of the parents (or, as law and usage now stand, the father), after summoning a human being into the world, to give to that being an education fitting him to perform his part well in life towards others and towards himself. But while this is unanimously declared to be the father's duty,

5   scarcely anybody, in this country, will bear to hear of obliging him to perform it. Instead of his being required to make any exertion or sacrifice for securing education to the child, it is left to his choice to accept it or not when it is provided gratis! It still remains unrecognized, that to bring a child into existence without a fair prospect of being able, not only to provide food for its body, but

10 instruction and training for its mind, is a moral crime, both against the unfortunate offspring and against society; and that if the parent does not fulfill this obligation, the State ought to see it fulfilled at the charge, as far as possible, of the parent.

Were the duty of enforcing universal education once admitted, there would

15 be an end to the difficulties about what the State should teach, and how it should teach, which now convert the subject into a mere battle-field for sects and parties, causing the time and labor which should have been spent in educating, to be wasted in quarrelling about education. If the government would make up its mind to *require* for every child a good education, it might save itself the

20 trouble of *providing* one. It might leave to parents to obtain the education where and how they pleased, and content itself with helping to pay the school fees of the poorer classes of children, and defraying the entire school expenses of those who have no one else to pay for them. The objections which are urged with reason against State education, do not apply to the enforcement of education by

25 the State, but to the State's taking upon itself to direct that education: which is a totally different thing. That the whole or any large part of the education of the people should be in State hands, I go as far as any one in deprecating. All that has been said of the importance of individuality of character, and diversity in opinions and modes of conduct, involves, as of the same unspeakable

30 importance, diversity of education. A general State education is a mere contrivance for moulding people to be exactly like one another: and as the mould in which it casts them is that which pleases the predominant power in the government, whether this be a monarch, a priesthood, an aristocracy, or the majority of the existing generation, in proportion as it is efficient and successful,

35 it establishes a despotism over the mind, leading by natural tendency to one over the body. An education established and controlled by the State, should only exist, if it exist at all, as one among many competing experiments, carried on for the purpose of example and stimulus, to keep the others up to a certain standard of excellence. Unless, indeed, when society in general is in so backward a state

40 that it could not or would not provide for itself any proper institutions of

education, unless the government undertook the task; then, indeed, the government may, as the less of two great evils, take upon itself the business of schools and universities, as it may that of joint-stock companies, when private enterprise, in a shape fitted for undertaking great works of industry does not exist in the country. But in general, if the country contains a sufficient number of persons qualified to provide education under government auspices, the same persons would be able and willing to give an equally good education on the voluntary principle, under the assurance of remuneration afforded by a law rendering education compulsory, combined with State aid to those unable to defray the expense.

The instrument for enforcing the law could be no other than public examinations, extending to all children, and beginning at an early age. An age might be fixed at which every child must be examined, to ascertain if he (or she) is able to read. If a child proves unable, the father, unless he has some sufficient ground of excuse, might be subjected to a moderate fine, to be worked out, if necessary, by his labor, and the child might be put to school at his expense. Once in every year the examination should be renewed, with a gradually extending range of subjects, so as to make the universal acquisition, and what is more, retention, of a certain minimum of general knowledge, virtually compulsory. Beyond that minimum, there should be voluntary examinations on all subjects, at which all who come up to a certain standard of proficiency might claim a certificate. To prevent the State from exercising through these arrangements, an improper influence over opinion, the knowledge required for passing an examination (beyond the merely instrumental parts of knowledge, such as languages and their use) should, even in the higher class of examinations, be confined to facts and positive science exclusively. The examinations on religion, politics, or other disputed topics, should not turn on the truth or falsehood of opinions, but on the matter of fact that such and such an opinion is held, on such grounds, by such authors, or schools, or churches. Under this system, the rising generation would be no worse off in regard to all disputed truths, than they are at present; they would be brought up either churchmen or dissenters as they now are, the State merely taking care that they should be instructed churchmen, or instructed dissenters. There would be nothing to hinder them from being taught religion, if their parents chose, at the same schools where they were taught other things. All attempts by the State to bias the conclusions of its citizens on disputed subjects, are evil; but it may very properly offer to ascertain and certify that a person possesses the knowledge, requisite to make his conclusions, on any given subject, worth attending to. A student of philosophy would be the better for being able to stand an examination both in Locke and in Kant, whichever of the two he takes up with, or even if

with neither: and there is no reasonable objection to examining an atheist in the evidences of Christianity, provided he is not required to profess a belief in them. The examinations, however, in the higher branches of knowledge should, I conceive, be entirely voluntary. It would be giving too dangerous a power to
5 governments, were they allowed to exclude any one from professions, even from the profession of teacher, for alleged deficiency of qualifications: and I think, with Wilhelm von Humboldt, that degrees, or other public certificates of scientific or professional acquirements, should be given to all who present themselves for examination, and stand the test; but that such certificates should
10 confer no advantage over competitors, other than the weight which may be attached to their testimony by public opinion.

    It is not in the matter of education only, that misplaced notions of liberty prevent moral obligations on the part of parents from being recognized, and legal obligations from being imposed, where there are the strongest grounds for
15 the former always, and in many cases for the latter also. The fact itself, of causing the existence of a human being, is one of the most responsible actions in the range of human life. To undertake this responsibility — to bestow a life which may be either a curse or a blessing — unless the being on whom it is to be bestowed will have at east the ordinary chances of a desirable existence, is a
20 crime against that being. And in a country either over-peopled, or threatened with being so, to produce children, beyond a very small number, with the effect of reducing the reward of labor by their competition, is a serious offence against all who live by the remuneration of their labor. The laws which, in many countries on the Continent, forbid marriage unless the parties can show that they
25 have the means of supporting a family, do not exceed the legitimate powers of the State: and whether such laws be expedient or not (a question mainly dependent on local circumstances and feelings), they are not objectionable as violations of liberty. Such laws are interferences of the State to prohibit a mischievous act — an act injurious to others, which ought to be a subject of
30 reprobation, and social stigma, even when it is not deemed expedient to superadd legal punishment. Yet the current ideas of liberty, which bend so easily to real infringements of the freedom of the individual, in things which concern only himself, would repel the attempt to put any restraint upon his inclinations when the consequence of their indulgence is a life, or lives, of wretchedness and
35 depravity to the offspring, with manifold evils to those sufficiently within reach to be in any way affected by their actions. When we compare the strange respect of mankind for liberty, with their strange want of respect for it, we might imagine that a man had an indispensable right to do harm to others, and no right at all to please himself without giving pain to any one.

I have reserved for the last place a large class of questions respecting the limits of government interference, which, though closely connected with the subject of this Essay, do not, in strictness, belong to it. These are cases in which the reasons against interference do not turn upon the principle of liberty: the
5   question is not about restraining the actions of individuals, but about helping them: it is asked whether the government should do, or cause to be done, something for their benefit, instead of leaving it to be done by themselves, individually, or in voluntary combination.

    The objections to government interference, when it is not such as to involve
10 infringement of liberty, may be of three kinds.

    The first is, when the thing to be done is likely to be better done by individuals than by the government. Speaking generally, there is no one so fit to conduct any business, or to determine how or by whom it shall be conducted, as those who are personally interested in it. This principle condemns the
15 interferences, once so common, of the legislature, or the officers of government, with the ordinary processes of industry. But this part of the subject has been sufficiently enlarged upon by political economists, and is not particularly related to the principles of this Essay.

    The second objection is more nearly allied to our subject. In many cases,
20 though individuals may not do the particular thing so well, on the average, as the officers of government, it is nevertheless desirable that it should be done by them, rather than by the government, as a means to their own mental education — a mode of strengthening their active faculties, exercising their judgment, and giving them a familiar knowledge of the subjects with which they are thus left to
25 deal. This is a principal, though not the sole, recommendation of jury trial (incases not political); of free and popular local and municipal institutions; of the conduct of industrial and philanthropic enterprises by voluntary associations. These are not questions of liberty, and are connected with that subject only by remote tendencies; but they are questions of development. It belongs to a
30 different occasion from the present to dwell on these things as parts of national education; as being, in truth, the peculiar training of a citizen, the practical part of the political education of a free people, taking them out of the narrow circle of personal and family selfishness, and accustoming them to the comprehension of joint interests, the management of joint concerns — habituating them to act
35 from public or semi-public motives, and guide their conduct by aims which unite instead of isolating them from one another. Without these habits and powers, a free constitution can neither be worked nor preserved, as is exemplified by the too-often transitory nature of political freedom in countries where it does not rest upon a sufficient basis of local liberties. The management
40 of purely local business by the localities, and of the great enterprises of industry

by the union of those who voluntarily supply the pecuniary means, is further recommended by all the advantages which have been set forth in this Essay as belonging to individuality of development, and diversity of modes of action. Government operations tend to be everywhere alike. With individuals and
5   voluntary associations, on the contrary, there are varied experiments, and endless diversity of experience. What the State can usefully do, is to make itself a central depository, and active circulator and diffuser, of the experience resulting from many trials. Its business is to enable each experimentalist to benefit by the experiments of others, instead of tolerating no experiments but its
10 own.

The third, and most cogent reason for restricting the interference of government, is the great evil of adding unnecessarily to its power. Every function superadded to those already exercised by the government, causes its influence over hopes and fears to be more widely diffused, and converts, more
15 and more, the active and ambitious part of the public into hangers-on of the government, or of some party which aims at becoming the government. If the roads, the railways, the banks, the insurance offices, the great joint-stock companies, the universities, and the public charities, were all of them branches of the government; if, in addition, the municipal corporations and local boards,
20 with all that now devolves on them, became departments of the central administration; if the employees of all these different enterprises were appointed and paid by the government, and looked to the government for every rise in life; not all the freedom of the press and popular constitution of the legislature would make this or any other country free otherwise than in name. And the evil would
25 be greater, the more efficiently and scientifically the administrative machinery was constructed — the more skilful the arrangements for obtaining the best qualified hands and heads with which to work it. In England it has of late been proposed that all the members of the civil service of government should be selected by competitive examination, to obtain for those employments the most
30 intelligent and instructed persons procurable; and much has been said and written for and against this proposal. One of the arguments most insisted on by its opponents, is that the occupation of a permanent official servant of the State does not hold out sufficient prospects of emolument and importance to attract the highest talents, which will always be able to find a more inviting career in
35 the professions, or in the service of companies and other public bodies. One would not have been surprised if this argument had been used by the friends of the proposition, as an answer to its principal difficulty. Coming from the opponents it is strange enough. What is urged as an objection is the safety-valve of the proposed system. If indeed all the high talent of the country *could* be
40 drawn into the service of the government, a proposal tending to bring about that

result might well inspire uneasiness. If every part of the business of society which required organized concert, or large and comprehensive views, were in the hands of the government, and if government offices were universally filled by the ablest men, all the enlarged culture and practised intelligence in the
5   country, except the purely speculative, would be concentrated in a numerous bureaucracy, to whom alone the rest of the community would look for all things: the multitude for direction and dictation in all they had to do; the able and aspiring for personal advancement. To be admitted into the ranks of this bureaucracy, and when admitted, to rise therein, would be the sole objects of
10 ambition. Under this régime, not only is the outside public ill-qualified, for want of practical experience, to criticize or check the mode of operation of the bureaucracy, but even if the accidents of despotic or the natural working of popular institutions occasionally raise to the summit a ruler or rulers of reforming inclinations, no reform can be effected which is contrary to the
15 interest of the bureaucracy. Such is the melancholy condition of the Russian empire, as is shown in the accounts of those who have had sufficient opportunity of observation. The Czar himself is powerless against the bureaucratic body; he can send any one of them to Siberia, but he cannot govern without them, or against their will. On every decree of his they have a tacit veto, by merely
20 refraining from carrying it into effect. In countries of more advanced civilization and of a more insurrectionary spirit, the public, accustomed to expect everything to be done for them by the State, or at least to do nothing for themselves without asking from the State not only leave to do it, but even how it is to be done, naturally hold the State responsible for all evil which befalls them, and when the
25 evil exceeds their amount of patience, they rise against the government and make what is called a revolution; whereupon somebody else, with or without legitimate authority from the nation, vaults into the seat, issues his orders to the bureaucracy, and everything goes on much as it did before; the bureaucracy being unchanged, and nobody else being capable of taking their place.
30   A very different spectacle is exhibited among a people accustomed to transact their own business. In France, a large part of the people having been engaged in military service, many of whom have held at least the rank of non-commissioned officers, there are in every popular insurrection several persons competent to take the lead, and improvise some tolerable plan of action. What
35 the French are in military affairs, the Americans are in every kind of civil business; let them be left without a government, every body of Americans is able to improvise one, and to carry on that or any other public business with a sufficient amount of intelligence, order, and decision. This is what every free people ought to be: and a people capable of this is certain to be free; it will never
40 let itself be enslaved by any man or body of men because these are able to seize

and pull the reins of the central administration. No bureaucracy can hope to make such a people as this do or undergo anything that they do not like. But where everything is done through the bureaucracy, nothing to which the bureaucracy is really adverse can be done at all. The constitution of such
5   countries is an organization of the experience and practical ability of the nation, into a disciplined body for the purpose of governing the rest; and the more perfect that organization is in itself, the more successful in drawing to itself and educating for itself the persons of greatest capacity from all ranks of the community, the more complete is the bondage of all, the members of the
10 bureaucracy included. For the governors are as much the slaves of their organization and discipline, as the governed are of the governors. A Chinese mandarin is as much the tool and creature of a despotism as the humblest cultivator. An individual Jesuit is to the utmost degree of abasement the slave of his order though the order itself exists for the collective power and importance
15 of its members.

It is not, also, to be forgotten, that the absorption of all the principal ability of the country into the governing body is fatal, sooner or later, to the mental activity and progressiveness of the body itself. Banded together as they are — working a system which, like all systems, necessarily proceeds in a great
20 measure by fixed rules — the official body are under the constant temptation of sinking into indolent routine, or, if they now and then desert that mill-horse round, of rushing into some half-examined crudity which has struck the fancy of some leading member of the corps: and the sole check to these closely allied, though seemingly opposite, tendencies, the only stimulus which can keep the
25 ability of the body itself up to a high standard, is liability to the watchful criticism of equal ability outside the body. It is indispensable, therefore, that the means should exist, independently of the government, of forming such ability, and furnishing it with the opportunities and experience necessary for a correct judgment of great practical affairs. If we would possess permanently a skilful
30 and efficient body of functionaries — above all, a body able to originate and willing to adopt improvements; if we would not have our bureaucracy degenerate into a pedantocracy, this body must not engross all the occupations which form and cultivate the faculties required for the government of mankind.

To determine the point at which evils, so formidable to human freedom and
35 advancement, begin, or rather at which they begin to predominate over the benefits attending the collective application of the force of society, under its recognized chiefs, for the removal of the obstacles which stand in the way of its well-being, to secure as much of the advantages of centralized power and intelligence, as can be had without turning into governmental channels too great
40 a proportion of the general activity, is one of the most difficult and complicated

questions in the art of government. It is, in a great measure, a question of detail, in which many and various considerations must be kept in view, and no absolute rule can be laid down. But I believe that the practical principle in which safety resides, the ideal to be kept in view, the standard by which to test all

5   arrangements intended for overcoming the difficulty, may be conveyed in these words: the greatest dissemination of power consistent with efficiency; but the greatest possible centralization of information, and diffusion of it from the centre. Thus, in municipal administration, there would be, as in the New England States, a very minute division among separate officers, chosen by the

10 localities, of all business which is not better left to the persons directly interested; but besides this, there would be, in each department of local affairs, a central superintendence, forming a branch of the general government. The organ of this superintendence would concentrate, as in a focus, the variety of information and experience derived from the conduct of that branch of public

15 business in all the localities, from everything analogous which is done in foreign countries, and from the general principles of political science. This central organ should have a right to know all that is done, and its special duty should be that of making the knowledge acquired in one place available for others. Emancipated from the petty prejudices and narrow views of a locality by its elevated position

20 and comprehensive sphere of observation, its advice would naturally carry much authority; but its actual power, as a permanent institution, should, I conceive, be limited to compelling the local officers to obey the laws laid down for their guidance. In all things not provided for by general rules, those officers should be left to their own judgment, under responsibility to their constituents. For the

25 violation of rules, they should be responsible to law, and the rules themselves should be laid down by the legislature; the central administrative authority only watching over their execution, and if they were not properly carried into effect, appealing, according to the nature of the case, to the tribunal to enforce the law, or to the constituencies to dismiss the functionaries who had not executed it

30 according to its spirit. Such, in its general conception, is the central superintendence which the Poor Law Board is intended to exercise over the administrators of the Poor Rate throughout the country. Whatever powers the Board exercises beyond this limit, were right and necessary in that peculiar case, for the cure of rooted habits of mal-administration in matters deeply affecting

35 not the localities merely, but the whole community; since no locality has a moral right to make itself by mismanagement a nest of pauperism, necessarily overflowing into other localities, and impairing the moral and physical condition of the whole laboring community. The powers of administrative coercion and subordinate legislation possessed by the Poor Law Board (but which, owing to

40 the state of opinion on the subject, are very scantily exercised by them), though

perfectly justifiable in a case of a first-rate national interest, would be wholly out of place in the superintendence of interests purely local. But a central organ of information and instruction for all the localities, would be equally valuable in all departments of administration. A government cannot have too much of the kind
5 of activity which does not impede, but aids and stimulates, individual exertion and development. The mischief begins when, instead of calling forth the activity and powers of individuals and bodies, it substitutes its own activity for theirs; when, instead of informing, advising, and, upon occasion, denouncing, it makes them work in fetters or bids them stand aside and does their work instead of
10 them. The worth of a State, in the long run, is the worth of the individuals composing it; and a State which postpones the interests of *their* mental expansion and elevation, to a little more of administrative skill, or that semblance of it which practice gives, it the details of business; a State which dwarfs its men, in order that they may be more docile instruments in its hands
15 even for beneficial purposes, will find that with small men no great thing can really be accomplished; and that the perfection of machinery to which it has sacrificed everything, will in the end avail it nothing, for want of the vital power which, in order that the machine might work more smoothly, it has preferred to banish.

---

[1] These words had scarcely been written, when, as if to give them an emphatic contradiction, occurred the Government Press Prosecutions of 1858. That ill-judged interference with the liberty of public discussion has not, however, induced me to alter a single word in the text, nor has it at all weakened my conviction that, moments of panic excepted, the era of pains and penalties for political discussion has, in our own country, passed away. For, in the first place, the prosecutions were not persisted in; and, in the second, they were never, properly speaking, political prosecutions. The offence charged was not that of criticizing institutions, or the acts or persons of rulers, but of circulating what was deemed an immoral doctrine, the lawfulness of Tyrannicide.
If the arguments of the present chapter are of any validity, there ought to exist the fullest liberty of professing and discussing, as a matter of ethical conviction, any doctrine, however immoral it may be considered. It would, therefore, be irrelevant and out of place to examine here, whether the doctrine of Tyrannicide deserves that title. I shall content myself with saying, that the subject has been at all times one of the open questions of morals; that the act of a private citizen in striking down a criminal, who, by raising himself above the law, has placed himself beyond the reach of legal punishment or control, has been accounted by whole nations, and by some of the best and wisest of men, not a crime, but an act of exalted virtue; and that, right or wrong, it is not of the nature of assassination, but of civil war. As such, I hold that the instigation to it, in a specific case, may be a proper subject of punishment, but only if an overt act has followed, and at least a probable connection can be established between the act and the instigation. Even then, it is not a foreign government, but the very government assailed, which alone, in the exercise of self-defence, can legitimately punish attacks directed against its own existence.

[2] Thomas Pooley, Bodmin Assizes, July 31, 1857. In December following, he received a free pardon from the Crown.

[3] George Jacob Holyoake, August 17, 1857; Edward Truelove, July, 1857.

[4] Baron de Gleichen, Marlborough Street Police Court, August 4, 1857.

[5] Ample warning may be drawn from the large infusion of the passions of a persecutor, which mingled with the general display of the worst parts of our national character on the occasion of the Sepoy insurrection. The ravings of fanatics or charlatans from the pulpit may be unworthy of notice; but the heads of the Evangelical party have announced as their principle, for the government of Hindoos and Mahomedans, that no schools be supported by public money in which the Bible is not taught, and by necessary consequence that no public employment be given to any but real or pretended Christians. An Under-Secretary of State, in a speech delivered to his constituents on the 12th of November, 1857, is reported to have said: "Toleration of their faith" (the faith of a hundred millions of British subjects), "the superstition which they called religion, by the British Government, had had the effect of retarding the ascendency of the British name, and preventing the salutary growth of Christianity.... Toleration was the great corner-stone of the religious liberties of this country; but do not let them abuse that precious word toleration. As he understood it, it meant the complete liberty to all, freedom of worship, *among Christians, who worshipped upon the same foundation.* It meant toleration of all sects and denominations of *Christians who believed in the one mediation.*" I desire to call attention to the fact, that a man who has been deemed fit to fill a high office in the government of this country, under a liberal Ministry, maintains the doctrine that all who do not believe in the divinity of Christ are beyond the pale of toleration. Who, after this imbecile display can indulge the illusion that religious persecution has passed away never to return?

[6] *The Sphere and Duties of Government,* from the German of Baron Wilhelm von Humboldt, pp. 11-13.

[7] Sterling's *Essays.*

[8] There is something both contemptible and frightful in the sort of evidence on which, of late years, any person can be judicially declared unfit for the management of his affairs; and after his death, his disposal of his property can be set aside, if there is enough of it to pay the expenses of litigation — which are charged on the property itself. All the minute details of his daily life are pried into, and whatever is found which, seen through the medium of the perceiving and describing faculties of the lowest of the low, bears an appearance unlike absolute commonplace, is laid before the jury as evidence of insanity, and often with success; the jurors being little, if at all, less vulgar and ignorant than the witnesses; while the judges, with that extraordinary want of knowledge of human nature and life which continually astonishes us in English lawyers, often help to mislead them. These trials speak volumes as to the state of feeling and opinion among the vulgar with regard to human liberty. So far from setting any value on individuality — so far from respecting the rights of each individual to act, in things indifferent, as seems good to his own judgment and inclinations, judges and juries cannot even conceive that a person in a state of sanity can desire such freedom. In former days, when it was proposed to burn atheists, charitable people used to suggest putting them in a madhouse instead: it would be nothing surprising now-a-days were we to see this done, and the doers applauding themselves, because, instead of persecuting for religion, they had adopted so humane and Christian a mode of treating these unfortunates, not without a silent satisfaction at their having thereby obtained their deserts.

[9] The case of the Bombay Parsees is a curious instance in point. When this industrious and enterprising tribe, the descendants of the Persian fire-worshippers, flying from their native country before the Caliphs, arrived in Western India, they were admitted to toleration by the Hindoo sovereigns, on condition of not eating beef. When those regions afterwards fell under the dominion of Mahomedan conquerors, the Parsees obtained from them a continuance of indulgence, on condition of refraining from pork. What was at first obedience to authority became a second nature, and the Parsees to this day abstain both from beef and pork. Though not required by their religion, the double abstinence has had time to grow into a custom of their tribe; and custom, in the East, is a religion.